MW01118550

American Indian Tribes

American Indian Tribes

Volume 1

Culture Areas

Tribes and Traditions
Abenaki—Missouri

edited by
The Editors of Salem Press

project editor
R. Kent Rasmussen

Salem Press, Inc.
Pasadena, California   Hackensack, New Jersey

Essays originally appeared in *Ready Reference, American Indians*, 1995; new material has been added.

∞ The paper used in these volumes conforms to the American National Standard for Permanence of Paper for Printed Library Materials, Z39.48-1992 (R1997).

Library of Congress Cataloging-in-Publication Data
American indian tribes / edited by the editors of Salem Press ; project editor, R. Kent Rasmussen.
    p. cm. — (Magill's choice)
    Includes bibliographical references and index.
    ISBN 0-89356-063-4 (set : alk. paper) — ISBN 0-89356-064-2 (v. 1 : alk. paper) — ISBN 0-89356-065-0 (v. 2 : alk. paper)
    1. Indians of North America. I. Rasmussen, R. Kent. II. Series.
E77.A53 2000
970'.00497—dc21

                 00-044659

First Printing

Publisher's Note

American Indian tribes have captured the imagination of Europeans, their American descendants, and other immigrant peoples since contact between the Old and New Worlds began in the late fifteenth century. Nevertheless, few peoples have been the subject of as many cultural misconceptions and stereotypes as American Indians. The first Europeans to arrive in North America mistakenly believed they had reached Asia—which they called the "Indies"—and immediately mislabeled the people they encountered as "Indians." Although the inaccuracy of that name was realized after it was discovered that the Americas were not connected to Asia, ethnocentrism continued to blind Europeans to the reality that the people they were meeting in the New World belonged to thousands of distinct cultures (which Europeans dubbed "tribes") speaking hundreds of different languages. Far from being relatively undifferentiated bands of primitive "savages," the Native peoples of the New World actually made up one of the most diverse and rich culture regions of the world.

Meanwhile, the first three centuries of contact between the Old and New Worlds were devastating to the latter. American Indians were cut down by Old World diseases, massacred by ruthless European armies with superior weapons, driven from their homelands by land-hungry whites, manipulated and betrayed by national governments, and characterized as bloodthirsty savages. At the other extreme, many Indian societies were also romanticized as "noble savages"—an equally unrealistic stereotype.

When the social movements of the 1960's gave birth to modern Indian activism and Indian studies programs, long-overdue redefinitions of Indian history and culture began to occur. Indian voices were heard as never before, both in the political arena and in the university. Scholars in Indian studies programs fought against the Eurocentric views that had long permeated such academic disciplines as anthropology and history. Members of different Indian societies—which are typically officially known as tribes—increasingly worked together to address such issues as Indian sovereignty and historic land claims. Indians used the media to educate the non-Indian public about the realities of Native American life in the twentieth century. Today, therefore, any work that attempts to survey American Indian culture and history must encompass ancient cultural traditions, historical Indian-white relations, and contemporary concerns. *American Indian Tribes* is part of the effort to educate non-Indians about Indian peoples. By focusing on culture regions and individual tribes and cultural traditions, these volumes serve to point up the startling diversity of Indian cultures. It might be mentioned here that while these articles emphasize indigenous traditions and early history, modern Indian societies have been anything but static.

Articles in *American Indian Tribes* are taken from Salem Press's award-winning three-volume set, *Ready Reference: American Indians* (1995). The goal of that earlier set's Editors was to assemble articles on a wide range of topics—including personages, tribes, organizations, historical events, cultural features and traditions, and contemporary issues—and to present them in an alphabetical format for ease of access. *American Indian Tribes* itself is modeled on one of the most popular Magill's Choice titles, *American Indian Biographies* (1999). That one-volume book collected all the biographical essays from *Ready Reference: American Indians* and added material from other Salem reference publications, as well as some completely new material. *American Indian Tribes* collects all the *Ready Reference: American Indians* articles on culture areas, tribes, and cultural traditions, as well as the appendixes. Both the appendixes and individual article bibliographies are updated here.

Articles in this set are grouped under two broad headings: Culture Areas and Tribes and Traditions. The first section opens with a general introduction to the subject of culture areas, followed by ten alphabetically arranged essays on North American culture areas: Arctic, California, Great Basin, Northeast, Northwest Coast, Plains, Plateau, Southeast, Southwest, and Subarctic. Individual articles follow the ready-reference formatting of the original reference set. For example, articles on culture areas open with lists of the area's main language groups and tribes.

The second section contains 307 alphabetically arranged articles on individual tribes and prehistoric culture traditions.

In this reference set, as in its predecessor volumes, American Indians are considered to be the original inhabitants of the areas now included within the United States and Canada. Although care was taken to include articles on as many tribal groups as possible, some very small North American tribes do not have their own articles. On the other hand, major Mesoamerican and Caribbean groups such as the Aztecs, Caribs, and Mayas, are included.

Individual articles, which range in length from 200 to 3,000 words each, also begin with clearly marked lines of ready-reference information. For example, articles on tribes identify the culture areas and language groups to which they belong, along with their primary geographical regions.

Articles on prehistoric traditions—such as Clovis, Folsom, and Mississippian—are included in this set because these traditions are typically the historical bridges that link together the tribes within larger culture areas. Moreover, the names of some traditions—such as Anasazi, Hohokam, and Oneonta—are occasionally confused with tribal names, and covering them together should help to clear up confusion. Indeed, information given at the tops of articles on traditions identifies where the traditions developed and which other traditions and tribes each tradition affected.

All articles with 1,000 or more words contain bibliographies; bibliographies of articles 2,000 or more words include annotations. All bibliographies have been updated for *American Indian Tribes*. Appendixes provide information on subjects such as festivals and pow-wows; reservations; museums, archives, and libraries; and organizations. The back matter also includes a time line, mediagraphy, and bibliography.

A few comments must be made on certain editorial decisions. Terms ranging from "American Indian" to "Native American" to "tribe" are accepted by some and disapproved of by others. The Editors of Salem Press have incorporated the phrase "American Indians" into the titles of *Ready Reference: American Indians* and the two Magill's Choice sets because it is the most widely accepted collective name for the first inhabitants of North America and their descendants. At the same time, however, the Editors have allowed authors to use either "American Indian" or "Native American" in their articles as they see fit. Similarly, while the Editors used the term "Inuit" for the title article on that Arctic people, the term "Eskimo" also appears in the set, as it has a long tradition of scientific usage and encompasses a variety of Arctic peoples to whom "Inuit" does not adequately apply.

Contributors were also allowed to use singular or plural designations for tribal names, but the tribal names themselves been standardized throughout the set. The Editors have tried to use names and spellings that are both accepted by members of the tribes themselves and widely recognized. Readers who cannot find tribal names in their expected alphabetical positions should consult the index for assistance. There, for example, they will find that the "Chippewa" people are listed under "Ojibwa."

All articles in this set are written and signed by scholars, most of whom are academicians in fields relating to American Indian studies. A list of the their names, along with their affiliations, follows this note. Once again, we gratefully acknowledge their participation and thank them for making their expert knowledge accessible to general readers. We would also like, once again, to thank the consulting editor of the original *Ready Reference: American Indians*, Harvey Markowitz, formerly of the D'Arcy McNickle Center for the History of the American Indian at Chicago's Newberry Library.

Contributor List

James A. Baer
*Northern Virginia Community
    College*

Carole A. Barrett
University of Mary

Byron D. Cannon
University of Utah

Richard G. Condon
University of Arkansas

LouAnn Faris Culley
Kansas State University

Michael G. Davis
Northeast Missouri State University

S. Matthew Despain
University of Oklahoma

Linda B. Eaton
State University

Robert E. Fleming
Brigham Young University

Raymond Frey
Centenary College

C. George Fry
*Lutheran College of Health
    Professions*

Marc Goldstein
University of Rochester

Gretchen L. Green
University of Missouri at Kansas City

Carl W. Hoagstrom
Ohio Northern University

John Hoopes
University of Kansas

Philip E. Lampe
Incarnate Word College

William C. Lowe
Mount St. Clare College

Paul Madden
Hardin-Simmons University

Kimberly Manning
*California State University at Santa
    Barbara*

Patricia Masserman
Independent Scholar

Howard Meredith
*University of Science and Arts of
    Oklahoma*

Laurence Miller
Western Washington State University

Sean O'Neill
Grand Valley State University

Harald E. L. Prins
Kansas State University

John Alan Ross
Eastern Washington University

Glenn J. Schiffman
Independent Scholar

Burl Self
Southwest Missouri State University

Michael W. Simpson
Eastern Washington University

Contents – Volume 1

Culture Areas of North America

Introduction 3
Arctic 11
California 19
Great Basin 26
Northeast 30
Northwest Coast 36
Plains 43
Plateau 50
Southeast 57
Southwest 67
Subarctic 74

Tribes and Traditions

Abenaki 81
Achumawi 84
Adena 85
Ahtna 88
Ais 89
Alabama 90
Aleut 91
Algonquin 94
Alsea 96
Anadarko 97
Anasazi 97
Apache 101
Apache Tribe of Oklahoma . . . 108
Apalachee 111
Apalachicola 112
Arapaho 112
Archaic 118
Arikara 119
Assiniboine 121
Atakapa 123
Atsina 124
Atsugewi 125
Aztec 126
Bannock 131
Bayogoula 132
Basketmaker 132
Beaver 135
Bella Bella 136
Bella Coola 137
Beothuk 138
Biloxi 139
Blackfoot and Blackfeet
    Confederacy 140
Caddo tribal group 146
Cahuilla 153
Calusa 155
Cape Fear 156
Carib 156
Carrier 158
Catawba 159

Cayuga	160	Duwamish	235
Cayuse	161	Erie	236
Chasta Costa	163	Esselen	236
Chehalis	164	Fernandeño	238
Chemakum	165	Flathead	239
Cheraw	165	Folsom	242
Cherokee	166	Fox	243
Cheyenne	175	Fremont	251
Chiaha	180	Gabrielino	252
Chichimec	181	Gitksan	253
Chickasaw	182	Gosiute	254
Chilcotin	185	Guale	255
Chinook	186	Haisla	256
Chipewyan	187	Han	256
Chitimacha	188	Hare	257
Choctaw	190	Havasupai	258
Chumash	193	Hidatsa	259
Clallam	194	Hitchiti	261
Clatskanie	195	Hohokam	262
Clovis	195	Hopewell	263
Coast Yuki	196	Huchnom	265
Cocopa	197	Hupa	266
Coeur d'Alene	198	Huron	267
Columbia	200	Illinois	268
Colville	201	Ingalik	269
Comanche	201	Inuit	270
Comox	206	Iowa	275
Coos	206	Iroquois Confederacy	276
Copalis	208	Juaneño	282
Costanoan	208	Kalapuya	282
Coushatta	209	Kalispel	283
Cowichan	210	Kamia	285
Cowlitz	211	Kansa	286
Cree	212	Karankawa	288
Creek	216	Karok	290
Crow	222	Kaska	291
Cupeño	230	Kawaiisu	292
Desert culture	230	Kichai	292
Diegueño	231	Kickapoo	293
Dogrib	233	Kiowa	295
Dorset	234	Klamath	297

Contents

Klikitat	299	Maliseet	319
Koyukon	300	Manahoac	320
Kutchin	301	Mandan	320
Kutenai	302	Massachusett	322
Kwakiutl	303	Mattaponi	323
Lake	305	Mattole	324
Lenni Lenape	305	Maya	325
Lillooet	310	Menominee	331
Luiseño	311	Methow	335
Lumbee	312	Miami	336
Lummi	313	Micmac	338
Mahican	314	Mimbres	339
Maidu	316	Mississippian	340
Makah	317	Missouri	342

Contents – Volume 2

Miwok	343	Neutral	374
Mixtec	344	Nez Perce	374
Mobile	345	Niantic	378
Modoc	346	Nipissing	379
Mogollon	348	Nipmuck	380
Mohawk	349	Nisqually	380
Mohegan	351	Nooksack	381
Mojave	352	Nootka	381
Molala	354	Nottaway	383
Moneton	354	Ocaneechi	384
Montagnais	355	Ofo	384
Montauk Confederacy	356	Ojibwa	385
Mountain	357	Okanagan	388
Muckleshoot	358	Old Copper culture	389
Multnomah	359	Olmec	391
Nabedache	359	Omaha	392
Nanticoke	360	Oneida	394
Narragansett	361	Oneota	396
Naskapi	363	Onondaga	397
Natchez	363	Osage	398
Nauset	364	Oto	402
Navajo	365	Ottawa	403

Paiute, Northern	406	Shinnecock	477
Paiute, Southern	408	Shoshone	478
Paleo-Indian	412	Shuswap	480
Palouse	413	Siletz	481
Pamlico	415	Sinagua	482
Passamaquoddy	415	Sioux tribal group	484
Patayan	416	Siuslaw	492
Patwin	418	Skagit	493
Pawnee	419	Slave	494
Pennacook	421	Snohomish	495
Penobscot	422	Snoqualmie	496
Pequot	423	Sooke	497
Petun	425	Spokane	497
Pima	426	Squamish	499
Plano	427	Suquamish	500
Pomo	429	Susquehannock	500
Ponca	431	Swallah	502
Poospatuck	433	Tahltan	503
Potawatomi	433	Tanaina	504
Powhatan Confederacy	435	Tanana	505
Pueblo tribes, Eastern	438	Tenino	506
Pueblo tribes, Western	446	Thompson	507
Puyallup	453	Thule	508
Quapaw	454	Tillamook	509
Quechan	455	Timucua	510
Quileute	456	Tiou	511
Quinault	457	Tlingit	512
Salinan	459	Tohome	514
Salish	460	Tohono O'odham	515
Samish	462	Tolowa	516
Sanpoil-Nespelem tribes	462	Toltec	517
Sarsi	464	Tonkawa	518
Sauk	465	Tsetsaut	519
Sekani	466	Tsimshian	519
Semiahmoo	467	Tubatulabal	521
Seminole	468	Tunica	522
Seneca	471	Tuscarora	522
Seri	473	Tuskegee	523
Serrano	473	Tutchone	524
Shasta	474	Tutelo	525
Shawnee	475	Tututni	526

Contents

Twana	526	Wintun	550
Tyigh	527	Wishram	551
Umatilla	527	Wiyot	552
Umpqua	529	Woodland	552
Ute	530	Yahi	554
Veracruz	533	Yakima	555
Waccamaw	535	Yamasee	557
Waco	535	Yana	558
Walapai	536	Yaqui	559
Walla Walla	537	Yaquina	560
Wampanoag	538	Yavapai	561
Wanapam	540	Yazoo	562
Wappinger	540	Yellowknife	563
Wappo	541	Yokuts	564
Wasco	542	Yuchi	565
Washoe	542	Yuki	566
Wenatchi	544	Yurok	566
Wichita tribal group	545	Zapotec	568
Winnebago	546		

Appendixes

Festivals and Pow-wows	573	Reservations: United States	601
Museums, Archives, and		Reserves and Bands:	
Libraries	577	Canada	607
Organizations, Agencies,		Time Line	615
and Societies	592	Mediagraphy	624
Populations of U.S.		Bibliography	647
Reservations	597	Index	675

Culture Areas of North America

Culture Areas of North America

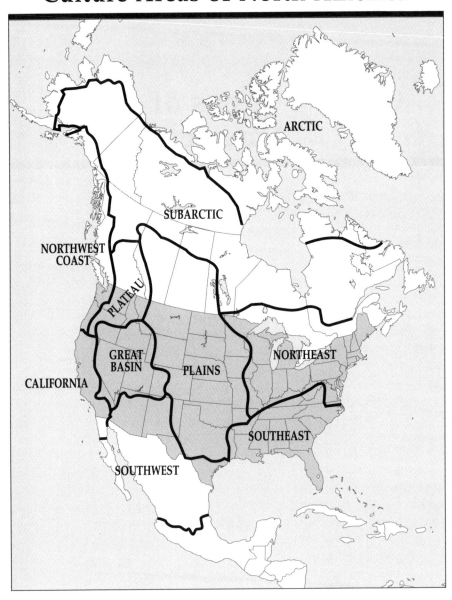

ARCTIC

SUBARCTIC

NORTHWEST
COAST

PLATEAU

GREAT
BASIN

PLAINS

NORTHEAST

CALIFORNIA

SOUTHEAST

SOUTHWEST

Introduction

No single method of assigning cultural boundaries between different groupings of Native Americans is fully adequate. Persuasive arguments exist for groupings that place primary emphasis, for example, on the most important language groupings (Algonquian, Athapaskan, Siouan, Tanoan, Muskogean, Caddoan, and Shoshonean). Because Native American groupings have undergone a series of displacements from region to region, however, their linguistic origins overlap, a situation which results in an equal amount of overlap in generalizations concerning original cultural traits.

Another mode of assigning culture areas draws on basic forms of technology—specifically on methods of producing household wares such as pottery and basketry. Here again one encounters a phenomenon of cultural overlap because of patterns of borrowing between tribal groupings.

To some degree, essential social indicators of culture can be transferred over time and space, making it difficult to draw boundaries between peoples of clearly distinct traditions. Such sociocultural factors include assignment of leadership, matriarchal versus patriarchal systems, degrees of formalization of kinship ties, and marriage patterns.

Considerations such as these make a division based on geographical/ ecological factors the most manageable and, indeed, the most commonly adopted one in the general literature. Such a comparison of Indian culture areas necessarily involves discussion of material and cultural questions shared by all human societies. Among these cultural differences are food subsistence, lodging construction, common artifacts, group organization, and spiritual expression. Each of these elements of Indian life was influenced by the environmental conditions that existed in relatively distinct geographical zones.

Arctic and Subarctic. The northern continental zone running from the Arctic north to British Columbia and eastward to Hudson Bay, while not one culture area, was characterized by a common practice: Natives survived primarily by hunting and fishing. Because the northern Arctic zone is frozen most of the year, Eskimo (Inuit) populations that specialized in sea mammal hunting (especially the Aleuts) stayed isolated in areas where access to prey was assured. Central Inuit hunters in the interior of Alaska and the Mac-Kenzie Territory, where kayak transportation was limited to a short summer season, reached their prey (usually caribou and moose) on toboggans or snowshoes.

Both Central Inuit and Athapaskan-speaking Dene peoples inhabited the less bountiful Subarctic zone that forms the interior land mass of northern Canada. Because of the limited density of animal populations, Subarctic hunters relied extensively on trapping devices spread over a vast network, according to the season. Limited food sources limited human population patterns as well, especially deep in the interior. Frequent displacement for subsistence meant that Subarctic tribes maintained semipermanent camps rather than substantial villages.

Like their Eskimo neighbors farther north, Subarctic Indians maintained a network of customs in common that, in good times, helped celebrate nature's bounty. One tribal meeting was the "potlatch," when food-gathering tasks were temporarily suspended and groups from afar could share shelter, gifts, and storytelling, either with distant kin or "friendly" neighbors.

Religious traditions in these northern areas were usually based on a belief in spiritual forces coming both from the sky and the earth, including living spirits in the form of animals or one's deceased kin.

Northwest Coast and Plateau. Indians in these areas lived more easily off nature's bounty, partially because the climate was less harsh, facilitating seasonal hunting of deer and bears. Abundant sealife near the coast of Washington and Oregon and easy hunting grounds inland made Northwest Indians such as the Wakashan and Chinook relatively "wealthy," in terms of both subsistence and displays of their "good fortune."

The Kwakiutl of the Wakashan showed their wealth through large houses of split logs. Their clothing and bodies were decorated with copper and ornate shell jewelry. Frequent public potlatches to commemorate social advancement (such as passage rites for youths and marriages) were paid for by the wealthiest families to attain recognition.

Farther inland was the Plateau, inhabited by tribes of two main linguistic groups: the Sahaptin (including Walla Walla and Nez Perce) and the Salish (Flathead and Wenatchi). In this region, freshwater salmon fishing could be combined with hunting. Plateau river communication networks were less extensive than those of the Northwest, limiting the scope of interaction, even between clans of similar tribal origin. When horses were introduced from the Great Basin Shoshones, some tribes moved seasonally over the mountains into Idaho to hunt buffalo. Such groups abandoned their traditional pit house structures for portable hide-covered tipis.

California. The Western coast and inland area farther south were more diversified in language groupings, which broke down into the main Penutian and Hokan families (the former including Klamath-Modoc, Miwok, and Central Valley Yokut and Maidu; the latter including Washoe and Yana in the north and in the central eastern zone near Nevada).

Three cultural zones corresponded primarily to ecological subregions. In the northwest corner, dense forests, rugged topography, and the absence of a coastal plain set off isolated (both linguistically and culturally) inhabitants from the fertile core of Penutian-Hokan groups around San Francisco Bay and in the much milder ecological zone of the Central Valley. In this core zone, economic patterns, based on hunting, fishing, and the gathering of available vegetal food sources (including a universal staple, acorn meal), tended to lend similarities to tribal social and cultural patterns. One similarity was the relative lack of formal institutional structures defining tribal organization and authority. Chiefs tended to be heads of the most numerous family among a multitude of generally equal family subdivisions of each clan. One of two main forms of lodging predominated: either the "house pit" scraped out of rolling knolls, or the wickiup, a bark-thatched covering stretched around portable poles. Central California tribes were highly skilled in basketweaving, some (mainly Pomos and Patwins) producing wares sufficiently tightly woven to serve as water containers.

South of the Central Valley, increasing aridity affected not only food-gathering conditions; basic technology (reflected in lodgings and artisanal production, including modes of dress) never attained levels that could be compared with tribes in the central region. Notable degrees of west-east interaction occurred, particularly between the Luiseños of present-day San Diego and Riverside counties (themselves of Shoshone stock) and Nevadan tribes. These contacts were reflected not only in trade of goods, but also in some shared cultural values that set the inland (less than the coastal) southern zone off from the relatively more developed Central Valley region.

Southwest. Beyond California was the inland culture area of the Southwest. Despite the ecological austerity of these vast expanses, nearly all Southwest Indians practiced some form of agriculture, supplemented by seasonally available wild plant foods. Most also developed technologically advanced cultures, as judged from the remains of their lodging and ceremonial sites (particularly the pueblos) and various artifacts, especially pottery and weaving.

A modern manifestation of pantribal solidarity was the Longest Walk—a protest march that began in San Francisco in 1978 and ended in Washington, D.C., where Indian leaders lobbied the federal government to recognize its existing treaty obligations.
(Library of Congress)

Among the several Indian subgroupings in the Southwest are the Hopi, Navajo, and Zuni. Their life patterns, although not identical, exemplify the main lines of Southwest Indian culture. Characteristically, Indian villages in the Southwest were constructed in the compact stone and adobe pueblo form, usually located on higher ground or on mesas for purposes of defense. The limited circumstances of dry farming often meant that plantations were located some distance from the pueblo.

In addition to being a dwelling and defense unit, the pueblo was a microcosm for both political and religious life. Particularly among the Eastern Pueblos, different responsibilities, from practical work tasks to ceremonial leadership, were traditionally divided between two fully cooperative factions. Living in different sections of the village, each faction maintained a kiva, or religiously designated meeting place for its elders, and ceremonial dance (kachina) groups, or medicine men, organized in societies. When a particular "season" for representation of the pueblo's ceremonial, political, or administrative needs was recognized, all loyalty was due to the kiva of the designated faction, while others rested from their responsibilities.

Southwest Indian religion and ceremonies were frequently tied to the concept of an "earth mother navel" shrine located in a sacred place within each pueblo. Around this ultimate source of bounty for the members of each tight-knit pueblo community were arranged the symbols of life (seeds and their products). Such symbols, plus other symbols of nature (especially rain) were incorporated into each pueblo's ceremonial dances, according to the season.

Great Basin. In the area wedged between California and the Plateau to the west, and the Southwest and Great Plains to the east, Indian cultures tended to be rather dispersed. Areas of habitation remained highly dependent on the availability of water and vegetation to sustain limited village life. Although broad tribal groupings existed (including Ute, Paiute, and Shoshone), the main activities of Indian life, from food gathering through marital, social, and political alliances, tended to be conducted in smaller bands. Contacts between subtribal bands (the Ute, on both the Colorado and Utah sides of the Rockies, counted some dozen territorial bands) could be only periodic. This rather lower level of tribal cohesiveness relative to Plateau and Southwest Indians, for example, allowed quarreling families from one band to "transfer" over to a band to which they were not tied by kinship; even lines between the tribes (Ute and Paiute, for example) were not that definitely drawn.

Some shared features of cultural existence within and between Great Basin tribes countered this general trend. Although religious consciousness among Great Basin Indians never attained a high degree of ceremonial sophistication, certain symbolic rites, among them the Sun Dance, provided a common cultural symbol in most regions.

Plains. It was among the Plains Indians that the most dramatic subsistence struggle was played out, by tribes such as the Sioux, Cheyenne, Pawnee, and Comanche. Acquisition of the horse from the Spanish after about 1600 transformed the subsistence potential of the Plains, which became the buffalo-hunting domains of competing Indian tribes. Pursuit of the great native herds of buffalo on horseback, beginning in the 1600's, created a situation of Indian nomadism on the Plains. Buffalo hunting affected not only food supply, but also provided raw material for the organization of Plains tribes' movable lodgings and the production of multiple lightweight artifacts. The high degree of mobility of Plains Indians also contributed to another key cultural trait: their tendency to war with rivals over hunting access.

Among the Sioux, the Lakota were drawn into the Plains from the Eastern Prairie region after becoming expert horsemen, well before the French entered the upper Mississippi Valley. Soon their nomadic way of life on the Plains allowed them to subjugate sedentary groupings such as the Arikara and Mandan, who were forced to trade their agricultural goods with the Lakota. The characteristic warring urge of such Plains nomads resulted in serious intertribal disputes, the best known resulting in the reduction and forced relocation of the Pawnee people after multiple encounters with representatives of the Sioux Nation.

The simplicity of the material culture of the Plains Indians was to some degree offset by the complexity of some of their social and cultural patterns. A number of honorary societies, ranging from warrior groups through "headmen" societies (elders who had distinguished themselves earlier as warriors or leaders), provided means for identifying individuals of importance emerging from each family or clan within the tribe. Recognition was also given, among the women, to highly skillful beadworkers, who defined qualification for entry into their "guild" and excluded inferior workmanship from being used in ritual ceremonies.

Another specialized subgrouping, particularly among the Dakota peoples, was the Heyoka, consisting of people who were recognized as possessing some form of supernatural or visionary power. Although not specifically connected to Plains religious beliefs (frequently associated with Sun Dance ceremonies and related celebrations of thanks for bounty, physical endurance, and interclan alliances), Heyoka status implied the ability to communicate with spirits, either good or evil. In some Siouan tribes, such as the Omaha, Heyoka societies were evenly divided into specialized branches, the most notable being one reserved specifically for individuals presumed to have the power to cure diseases.

Northeast and Southeast. In the eastern third of the continent, a higher degree of sedentariness among various tribes prevailed, although this did not necessarily mean that agriculture was more developed. Plantations for food tended to be scattered in the heavily wooded Northeast, with hunting and trapping at least as important in most tribal economies. Another product of the forest, the paperlike bark of the birch tree, served multiple purposes, ranging from tipi-building material to the famous birchbark canoes used to fish or to travel through the extensive river and stream systems of the region.

In general, social organization among the tribes of the Northeast bore two major characteristics. Groups that were known as hunters (such as the Micmacs of New Brunswick and Maine) lived as nuclear families, paramount status being reserved for the hunter-head of closely related kin. Lodgings might be limited to a single family (typically a tipi) or a grouping of families under the single roof of an extended longhouse. In most cases, ascription of chieftainship was determined by a hierarchy that also depended on hunting skills.

A second characteristic of Northeast Woodlands Indian life revolved around political confederations involving several tribes. The best known of these was the Iroquois "Five Nations," but other groups, including the Algonquins and Hurons, formed federations for mutual security against common enemies.

Although the Southeast region of the United States can, like the Northeast, be described as heavily wooded, offering a combination of possibilities for hunting and agriculture, the Indian cultures of this area were substantially different. Some experts argue that there was less communality in cultural development in the Southeast, making distinctions, for example, between peoples who were clearly reliant on the ecology of the first "layer" of the broad coastal plain (called the "Flatwoods," blanketed by conifers and scrub oaks); those inhabiting the so-called Piedmont (further inland, with higher elevations and differing vegetation patterns); and those living in the Appalachian woodlands, with their extensive hardwood forests.

Some experts, noting communality in traits (such as a horticultural maize economy, nucleated villages, and matrilineal clan organization) between key Southeastern tribes such as the Creek, Choctaw, Cherokee, Natchez, and the Iroquois, found farther north, assign a southeastern origin to the Iroquois. A substantial number of differences marked by cultural specialists, however, suggest closer ties between coastal and inland dwellers in the Southeast (especially in linguistic links) than between Southeast Indians as a whole and any of their Northeast neighbors. A series of lesser, but culturally significant, traits justify treating Southeast Indians as a largely homogeneous entity, including modes of processing staple nuts, especially acorns; rectangular, gabled houses with mud wattle covering; an absence of leather footwear; characteristic nested twilled baskets; and varied use of tobacco.

Even among key Southeast tribes, however, parallel traditions (such as matrilineal kinship descent) could be offset by striking differences. The Natchez tribe alone, for example, had a class system dividing tribal nobles (deemed descendants of the Sun), from whom the chief, or "Great Sun" was chosen, and commoners, who could not even enter the presence of tribal aristocrats.

Byron D. Cannon

Bibliography

Bancroft-Hunt, Norman. *Native American Tribes*. Edison, N.J.: Chartwell Books, 1997.

Birchfield, D. L., ed. *Encyclopedia of North American Indians*. 11 vols. New York: Marshall Cavendish, 1997.

Catlin, George. *Letters and Notes on the Manners, Customs, and Conditions of North American Indians*. New York: 1841. A recognized classic, including personal observations of Indian ceremonial practices and daily life. Some editions include extremely valuable illustrations, which have gained international fame.

Champagne, Duane, ed. *The Native North American Almanac: A Reference Work on Native North Americans in the United States and Canada*. Detroit: Gale Research, 1994.

Davis, Mary B. *Native America in the Twentieth Century: An Encyclopedia*. New York: Garland, 1994.

Driver, Harold E. *Indians of North America*. 2d ed. Chicago: University of Chicago Press, 1969. A widely cited textbook organized by subject area (for example, "Rank and Social Class," "Exchange and Trade") rather than geographical location.

Haas, Marilyn L. *Indians of North America: Sources for Library Research*. Hamden, Conn.: Library Professional Publications, 1983.

Hoxie, Frederick E., ed. *Encyclopedia of North American Indians*. Boston: Houghton Mifflin, 1996.

Kehoe, Alice B. *North American Indians: A Comprehensive Account*. 2d ed. Englewood Cliffs, N.J.: Prentice-Hall, 1992. Like the Spencer and Jennings book (below), this textbook is divided by geographical region. Less detailed on local conditions of life, it contains useful summary texts within each chapter and a number of translations of original Indian texts.

Klein, Barry T., ed. *Reference Encyclopedia of the American Indian*. 2 vols. 8th ed. New York: Todd, 1998.

Ross, Thomas E., and Tyrel Moore, eds. *A Cultural Geography of North American Indians*. Boulder, Colo.: Westview Press, 1987. Contains contributions by specialists dealing with several different geographical themes relating to culture, including "Spatial Awareness," "Land Ownership," and "Migration."

Spencer, Robert, Jesse D. Jennings, et al. *The Native Americans*. 2d ed. New York: Harper & Row, 1977. A very detailed text. Attention is given to diverse patterns of local division of labor, kinship, rites of passage, and so on.

Sturtevant, William, gen. ed. *Handbook of North American Indians*. Washington, D.C.: Smithsonian Institution Press, 1978-   . The Smithsonian series is a projected twenty-volume set, with a volume either published or planned for each of the culture areas. The scholarship and coverage are both first-rate. The set was initiated in 1978 with the volume on the Northeast, edited by Bruce Trigger, and nine volumes had been published by 1994.

Arctic

LANGUAGE GROUPS: Eskimo-Aleut (Aleut, Inuit-Iñupiaq, Yupik)
TRIBES: Aleut, Inuit, Yupik

The Arctic culture area encompasses a vast region of treeless, windswept tundra stretching across the northern coast of North America. It includes most of the Alaskan coastline from Prince William Sound in the southeast to the Arctic coast in the north, continues across the Canadian Arctic archipelago and mainland coast down into Labrador, and includes all of Greenland. While some parts of this culture area are more appropriately labeled Subarctic in terms of climate and vegetation (most specifically the Aleutian Islands, South Alaska, Southern Labrador, and South Greenland), the linguistic, cultural, and physical similarities among the native inhabitants are such that this region can be considered a highly integrated cultural unit.

Terminology. The term "Aleut" is of uncertain origin and appears to have been used first by the Russians to describe the inhabitants of the Near Islands. It was later extended to all Aleuts and even to the Pacific Eskimos (Koniag and Chugach). The result has led to some confusion, since the modern Koniag Eskimos refer to themselves as "Alutiiq" (an "Eskimoization" of Aleut in the current orthography) even though they are culturally and linguistically distinct from the Aleut. The term "Eskimo" is most often cited as originating from the Subarctic Montagnais (speakers of an Algonquian language) and has been purported to mean "eaters of raw meat." Two major cultural-linguistic groups of Eskimos are recognized: the Yupik of southwestern and southern Alaska and the Inuit of North Alaska, Arctic Canada, and Greenland. It should be noted that the term "Eskimo" has engendered some controversy (with many Canadian Arctic natives, for example, preferring "Inuit"), but it is used here because it incorporates a large number of groups that cannot easily be united under any other term and because it has a long scientific tradition of usage.

Environment. The Arctic culture area includes a wide range of environments both above and below the Arctic Circle and the tree line. In the

11

Arctic Culture Area

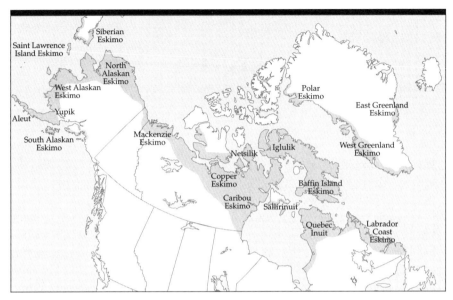

northern regions of Alaska, Canada, and Greenland, treeless Arctic tundra and a severe climate dominate. The combination of permafrost, extreme cold, and prolonged periods of midwinter darkness result in low levels of biological productivity, making adaptation to this region a great challenge to both humans and animals. The climate is less severe farther south. The coastlines of the Aleutian Islands, southern Alaska, southern Labrador, and western Greenland have a milder climate and less pronounced seasonal variation in temperature and photoperiod. These areas usually have access to open water all year round, with the result that their climates are heavily maritime influenced. In southern Alaska, for example, Koniag and Chugach Eskimos are reported to have gone much of the year in bare feet. In the High Arctic and interior regions of Canada and Alaska, a cold continental climate prevails.

Language. On the basis of sound and grammar, Eskimo and Aleut are recognized as being related. Although regarded as a unified language family, they are mutually unintelligible. Linguists generally agree that Eskimo and Aleut diverged at least four thousand years ago.

Within Aleut there is a high degree of uniformity. It has become a single language with only two dialects: a western dialect and an eastern dialect. Much greater variation exists within Eskimo, which is divided into two main languages: Yupik and Inuit-Iñupiaq. The distance between the two is very similar to the distance between German and English. Lexicostatistical studies suggest a divergence dating to between eight hundred and eighteen hundred years ago. The dividing line between these two languages is located around the Norton Sound region of western Alaska. Yupik displays much more variability than Inuit-Iñupiaq and is composed of five fairly distinct languages. The Inuit-Iñupiaq branch of Eskimo is characterized by a higher degree of uniformity, representing more a series of interconnecting dialects. The mutual intelligibility of these dialects is the result of the spread of Thule culture across Arctic Canada and Greenland.

Population. The Arctic culture area was not uniformly populated. At contact, the region was inhabited by about twelve thousand to fifteen thousand Aleut on the Aleutian Islands, twenty to twenty-five thousand Yupik in southern and southwestern Alaska (including St. Lawrence Island), twelve thousand Iñupiat in northwestern and northern Alaska, nine to twelve thousand Canadian Inuit, and nine to twelve thousand Greenlandic Inuit divided among 140 to 200 fairly distinct societies (or tribal groupings). The most densely populated regions were those with a relative abundance of food resources, more often than not with access to a combination of marine and riverine products. Prior to contact, the greatest populations could be found on the Aleutian Islands, southern and southwestern Alaska, and the southwest coast of Greenland.

The areas with the lowest population densities included the Central Canadian Arctic (associated with the Copper and Netsilik groups), the Barren Lands west of Hudson Bay (Caribou Eskimos), and North Greenland (Polar Eskimos). These groups lived in extremely marginal areas and were therefore forced to a high degree of nomadism. Starvation was probably relatively common, and the practice of infanticide has been well documented in these areas. Many of those Aleut and Eskimo in more abundant environments were able to live much of the year in relatively permanent houses (either aboveground wood-plank houses or semi-subterranean sod houses) within sedentary villages.

Economy and Subsistence. The stereotype of highly nomadic, snow-house-building, dogsledding Eskimos actually applies to only a small number of Inuit groups in the Central Canadian Arctic. Many Eskimo groups, most notably in southern and southwestern Alaska, never built a snowhouse, never traveled with dogs, and never even saw a polar bear. Despite a common cultural template, hundreds of years of adaptation to markedly different environments and contacts with different neighboring groups gave rise to distinct cultural forms, expressed in material culture, housing styles, and subsistence strategies.

While the primary economic focus in this culture area was (and continues to be) a maritime one oriented toward hunting of whales, seals, walruses, narwhales, and so on, a number of groups subsisted primarily from riverine or terrestrial resources. Yupik groups in the middle Yukon-Kuskokwim River region and Iñupiat groups on the Noatak and Kobuk rivers were heavily dependent upon fish resources at the expense of marine mammals. In the Barren Lands west of Hudson Bay, the Caribou Eskimo maintained a

Inuit (Eskimo) family living near Alaska's Kuskokwim River during the 1880's.
(Library of Congress)

heavy reliance upon seasonally migrating caribou herds. The typing of Eskimo groups as either maritime, riverine, or terrestrially focused can, however, be misleading, since many groups maintained a seasonal round in which all of these items were exploited. Longer exploitation cycles were also maintained, since certain resources that were abundant for one generation could easily disappear a generation or two later. Since marine and terrestrial ecosystems in the Arctic are extremely fragile, population crashes of certain important animal species could and did occur.

The Aleut appear to have had the most developed maritime adaptation, a fact reinforced by their mastery of kayak (*baidarka*) construction and their reputation for long-distance ocean travel. Their skill in adapting to a high-risk/high-yield maritime ecosystem ensured high population densities and a relatively high quality of life compared with those of most Eskimo groups. Other Arctic groups with a maritime adaptation included West Greenlandic and North Alaskan whaling communities which were oriented toward spring and fall hunting of large bowhead whales from open, skin-covered umiaks.

The seasonality of Eskimo subsistence is most vividly seen with Central Canadian Arctic groups such as the Netsilik and Copper Eskimo. Since these groups lived in an extremely marginal environment, they were forced to a high degree of nomadism. Winters were generally spent in large snow-house communities on the ocean ice, where hunters engaged in breathing-hole sealing. Summers, however, were usually spent inland dispersed in small family groups in search of fish, fowl, and caribou. Although these groups do not display the maritime skills of the Aleut or North Alaskans, they nevertheless had a clear maritime focus at certain seasons.

Material Culture and Trade. The material culture of all these groups was technologically sophisticated and highly functional. The toggle-headed harpoon, kayak, tailored clothing, semilunar woman's knife (*ulu*), and soapstone lamp are typical of much of the area. Throughout the region, there was heavy reliance upon animal products such as bone, horn, antler, and skin for the manufacture of clothing, hunting tools, and household goods. In the High Arctic, wood was an extremely valuable commodity and could be obtained only through trading networks or long trips to the tree line. For this reason, among groups such as the Polar Eskimo, Copper Eskimo, and Baffin Island Eskimo, wood was heavily curated. Prior to European contact, meteoric iron found in the Cape York region of North Greenland was cold hammered into hunting implements, while the Copper Inuit were known for surface mining deposits of copper, which was used for knives, scrapers, and harpoon points.

Despite the isolated nature of the Arctic culture area, intergroup trade was quite extensive. Elaborate trade networks and regional fairs facilitated the distribution of raw materials and manufactured goods. Iron from Siberia was traded across the Bering Strait into Alaska, while high-quality soapstone lamps from Coronation Gulf in the Central Canadian Arctic were traded into Alaska, where such materials were scarce. Even before the arrival of Russian, European, and American traders, the Seshalik fair in Northwest Alaska attracted two thousand or more individuals each summer in what has been described as the largest regular trade gathering anywhere in the Arctic culture area. Formalized trading partnerships were typical throughout the region. In the absence of trading fairs, individuals would initiate their own trading expeditions for desired resources.

Political Organization and Leadership. Forms of political organization and leadership varied greatly throughout the region. Egalitarianism defined the social relations of most Central and Eastern Arctic groups. An *isumataq* ("one who thinks") would often assume an informal leadership position over a number of related families. The degree of authority that the isumataq held varied from region to region, being relatively low among the Copper Inuit and high among the Iglulik and Baffin Island Eskimos. As one travels into Alaska, more formalized leadership structures appear. In North Alaska, the successful whaling captain (*umialik*) was an influential leader over both his family and the community as a whole. Some researchers have even suggested that the North Alaskan Eskimo, far from being an egalitarian society, were actually a highly ranked society. In South Alaska and the Aleutian Islands, leadership forms were even more formalized and appear to have been heavily influenced by the ranked societies of the Northwest Coast. In all regions, leaders were expected to be generous to the point of sharing their resources with all community members. Such sharing is most dramatically seen in North Alaska with the distribution of whale meat and muktuk from the successful whaling captain to the entire community.

Post-contact. The first contacts between Eskimos and Europeans probably occurred soon after the establishment of the Norse colonies in South Greenland in 985. From the sixteenth century onward, numerous expeditions ventured into the Canadian Archipelago seeking the Northwest Passage. These expeditions resulted in contacts between Europeans and Canadian Inuit, but most of these meetings had minimal long-term impact upon the Inuit.

A more significant influence was the establishment of a mission in West Greenland by the Danish missionary Hans Egede in 1721. Although he had hoped to minister to the (by then long-extinct) Norse colonies, he ended up converting the Greenlandic Inuit to Christianity and initiated the Greenlanders into a period of intimate cultural, economic, and political involvement with Denmark that continues to the present day.

In Alaska, the arrival of Russian fur traders soon after Vitus Bering's discovery of Alaska in 1741 had a devastating impact upon the Aleut, who were once quite numerous throughout the island chain. It is generally agreed that 80 to 90 percent of the Aleut population was wiped out from a combination of disease, warfare, and forced labor. Similar processes resulted in deaths among the Pacific Yupik, who were in the direct path of the Russian traders' advance. A smallpox epidemic in the 1830's wiped out a large portion of the Aleut and Yupik populations over a wide area of southern and southwestern Alaska, including many areas well outside the Russian sphere of influence.

Farther north, Inuit people were heavily impacted by the intensification of whaling in the late nineteenth century. Scottish and American whalers were active in Baffin Bay and Davis Strait from the 1830's on, while American whalers had established themselves in North Alaska by the 1880's and 1890's. These contacts had a significant impact on the Eskimos. Not only did infectious diseases take a heavy toll in many areas, but also the whalers introduced the Inuit to highly desirable material goods. Population losses were profound in some areas, such as Southampton Island, the Mackenzie Delta, and North Alaska.

Many Inuit were hired by whalers either as meat and fish providers or as laborers. With the collapse of whaling at the turn of the century, most whalers left the Arctic permanently, while others turned to trading activities. This marked the period when many Eskimo groups made the transition to trapping, as furs became a highly desirable commodity on the international fashion market. The 1940's and 1950's continued to be a difficult time for many Inuit and Yupik, who were plagued by poverty, high infant mortality, and high rates of tuberculosis. In Canada, increased government involvement in the late 1950's and early 1960's brought wage employment, social assistance, schools, medical facilities, and government-subsidized housing, all of which were designed to encourage the Inuit to move from their isolated hunting camps into centralized communities. Since the 1960's, the populations and infrastructure of these communities have grown at a rapid rate.

Richard G. Condon and Pamela R. Stern

Bibliography

Balikci, Asen. *The Netsilik Eskimos.* Garden City, N.Y.: Natural History Press, 1970. This ethnographic classic provides a detailed analysis of the material culture, social organization, and religious beliefs of a stereotypically classic Inuit group adapted to one of the harshest environments of the Arctic region.

Burch, Ernest S., and Werner Forman. *The Eskimos.* Norman: University of Oklahoma Press, 1988. Written for a nonprofessional audience, this work is a highly readable and informative introduction to the Eskimo culture area. The text is accompanied by 120 striking photographs by Werner Forman.

Damas, David, ed. *Arctic.* Vol. 3 in *Handbook of North American Indians.* Washington, D.C.: Smithsonian Institution Press, 1984. This work is undoubtedly the definitive resource on the Arctic culture area and contains detailed articles on prehistory, language, and contemporary issues as well as ethnographic chapters on each of the Eskimo groups. An extensive bibliography, which covers all relevant material published up to the early 1980's, is extremely useful.

Fienup-Riordan, Ann. *Boundaries and Passages: Rule and Ritual in Yup'ik Eskimo Oral Tradition*. Norman: University of Oklahoma Press, 1994.

Fitzhugh, William W., and Aron Crowell, eds. *Crossroads of Continents: Cultures of Siberia and Alaska*. Washington, D.C.: Smithsonian Institution Press, 1988. Designed to accompany the Smithsonian exhibition "Crossroads of Continents," this edited volume includes chapters written by international experts on the cultures of Alaska and Siberia and on the ancient contacts which have been maintained by the natives of the two continents. It is a highly informative work that contains a large number of useful maps, figures, and photographs.

Laughlin, William S. *Aleuts: Survivors of the Bering Land Bridge*. New York: Holt, Rinehart and Winston, 1980. This work, written by one of the world's leading authorities on Aleut culture, describes the archaeology, linguistics, physical anthropology, and culture of the Aleuts.

Mitchell, Donald. *Sold American: The Story of Alaska Natives and Their Land, 1867-1959: The Army to Statehood*. Hanover, N.H.: University Press of New England, 1997.

Skinner, Ramona E. *Alaska Native Policy in the Twentieth Century*. New York: Garland, 1997.

California

LANGUAGE GROUPS: Athapaskan, Chimariko, Chumashan, Esselen, Karok, Maiduan, Palaihnihan, Pomoan, Salinan, Shastan, Uto-Aztecan, Wintun, Wiyot, Yanan, Yokutsan, Yukian, Yuman, Yurok
TRIBES: Achumawi, Atsugewi, Cahuilla, Chemehuevi, Chumash, Costanoan, Cupeño, Diegueño, Esselen, Fernandeño, Gabrielino, Hupa, Juaneño, Kamia, Karok, Kato, Luiseño, Maidu, Mattole, Miwok, Patwin, Pomo, Quechan, Salinan, Serrano, Shasta, Tolowa, Tubatulabal, Wailaki, Wappo, Wintun, Wiyot, Yahi, Yana, Yokuts, Yuki, Yurok

The California culture area corresponds closely to the modern boundaries of that state. Approximately 300,000 people lived there when the Spaniards arrived in 1769, making it the most densely populated area within the present boundaries of the forty-eight contiguous United States.

Material Culture. The technology of the native people of California may have been among the least sophisticated in North America. The wheel, pottery, and metallurgy were rare or unknown. Furthermore, the people had not yet achieved any form of systematic agriculture, but relied on hunting (of almost all animal life in the area), fishing (in ocean, lake, and river), and gathering (primarily of acorns, but also of pinecones and other plants) for their basic sustenance.

Nevertheless, many artifacts of pre-contact years have survived into the modern era and provide insight into the lives of California's original people. Archaeologists have uncovered a large number of arrow points made of chipped stone; a wide variety of hooks and other fishing implements; mortars and pestles (although in many cases the grinding was done on a fixed mortar of bedrock with a grinding stone); bowls and eating implements made of such materials as wood, bark, steatite, and shells; combs or brushes of soap plant root; wedges of deer horn; and awls of bone.

Probably the most common surviving artifacts are the many baskets now on display in museums and other collections. Curiously, native Californians

California Culture Area

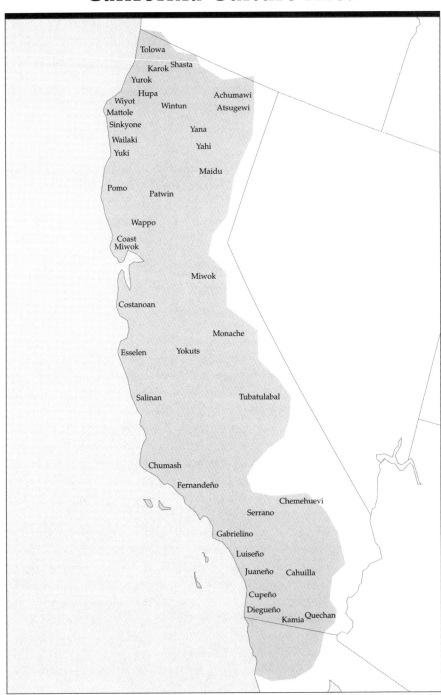

seem not to have utilized the simplest and easiest method of basketmaking: a basic in-and-out weave. Instead, more complex coiling or twining techniques prevailed. The materials were as diverse as the native vegetation of the region, with tule reeds, grass stems, and various barks serving as the ingredients for the baskets. Lacking pottery and metallurgy, native Californians utilized baskets for almost every conceivable purpose. In the richness and elaborateness of their basket decorations, Californians exceeded all other native people of North America.

Art and Architecture. Aside from the decorations on baskets, most California material culture is of a practical, rather than purely decorative and artistic, nature. One of the few art forms was rock painting and carving. Petroglyphs, or peckings in rock outcroppings, have been recorded at more than one thousand sites throughout the state, and many others were destroyed by urbanization before archaeologists could record and study them. The distribution of such rock art is somewhat uneven, with heavy concentrations in some areas (north coast, southwest coast, and central Sierra) but total absence in others. Pictographs, or painted rocks, are also scattered unevenly, with the heaviest concentrations in the extreme northeast, the southwest coast, the southern Sierra, and most spectacularly in the caves of the Chumash tribe on the central coast. Although some naturalistic or animalistic representations appear in both the pecked and painted art, most of the work appears in abstract styles, possibly with religious significance.

Artistic expression also manifested itself in body painting, beads, and clothing. Because the mild climate permitted men to go naked and women to wear a simple apron, clothing was limited. In colder weather, animal skins and furs provided the raw material for woven blankets or robes and provided some opportunity for creative artistry, usually with decorative uses of feathers.

The housing of California also provided little opportunity for creative expression because of its modest form. The structures varied, from quadrangular in some instances to circular and domed in others. Building materials were usually limited to available vegetation, with bundles of tule thatching serving as the most common fabric. Most houses were only about ten feet square, intended only for sleeping quarters for a single family. When houses became uncomfortable because of dirt or pests, they were simply burned and rebuilt. Few other structures were part of native villages.

Social and Political Organization. The typical form of social organization was the tribelet or village, usually of one hundred to five hundred residents. Although people were not nomadic, neither were they completely immobile. Entire villages were occasionally burned and rebuilt at another location; trading ventures required long trips within and outside of California; men often embarked on extensive expeditions in search of fish and game; even excursions to gather acorns and other plants occasionally required coverage of extensive areas.

Although men thus enjoyed mobility and movement over long distances, women were more typically confined to their home villages. Their lives revolved around the laborious and tedious processes of grinding acorns, leaching out the poisonous tannic acid, baking bread, and otherwise preparing food. Women also took on the chores of rearing children (usually in a communal fashion), weaving baskets, and obtaining wood and water.

Relations among the sexes were usually governed by marriage practices and rules that did not differ markedly from those of other Native Americans. People married soon after puberty, with families choosing the partners and the groom paying a bride price. Customary incest taboos prevailed, and marriages with partners of equivalent social class were encouraged. Monogamy was the norm, but exceptions did exist, especially for people of higher social rank. Divorce was readily available to either partner, although the necessity of refunding the bride price somewhat limited the freedom of women in such matters.

Several variables, especially wealth and inherited rank, determined social status. Wealth was measured by possession of a variety of tangible objects, including shells that acted as a form of money for the facilitation of trade. Although birth was normally the determinant of status, some social mobility was possible for people who worked hard and accumulated wealth or demonstrated special skills.

At the top of the social hierarchy in nearly every village were two officials: the chief and the shaman. The position of the chief, always a male, was normally inherited and usually correlated with wealth. Since warfare played a negligible or even nonexistent role for native Californians, the responsibility of the chief involved mostly the administration of the economic functions of the tribelet. He supervised food-gathering and hunting activities, directed trade with other peoples, and generally assumed responsibility for the economic survival of his people. His position carried with it several wives, the largest and most luxurious house, and possession of the largest store of wealth goods.

Religion. The other post of highest status was that of shaman. Although the position was essentially a religious one, its functions mostly involved healing, both physical and psychological. The shaman's knowledge of the healing properties of various herbs and other plants, along with sacred objects and chants, was essential to the performance of his duties.

As people close to nature, native Californians felt a part of it, and utilized animals for most of their myths. Typically, they believed that animals preceded men in occupation of the earth and were responsible for creation of both the earth and its human occupants. Natural phenomena all had explanations in mythology, although the accounts of the causes of earthquakes, thunder, phases of the moon, and similar events varied from tribe to tribe.

Religious ceremonies played a smaller part in the lives of the native people of California than for many other Native Americans, but they did exist. Puberty rites, funerals, marriages, and births were among the events that served as occasions for some type of ceremony. Because the allocation of functions between the sexes left men with more free time than women, they were able to engage in more frequent religious activity. Especially popular in much of the area was the use of the *temescal*, or sweathouse. A fire provided the heat and smoke (not steam) that caused the men to sweat and cleanse themselves, after which they took a dip in a nearby source of water. The function of the temescal is not entirely clear; it probably served both a social and ritualistic role.

History. White contact began in 1769 when Spanish missionaries, led by Father Junípero Serra, arrived to begin a process of Hispanizing the Indians.

Mono wickiup-style brush structure: both the dwelling and the baskets in front are representative of central California styles. (Library of Congress)

23

By 1823, the Spanish had established a chain of twenty-one missions, generally near the coast from San Diego to just north of San Francisco. The tribes within the Spanish area included the Chumash, Costanoan, Cupeño, Diegueño, Esselen, Fernandeño, Gabrielino, Juaneño, Luiseño, and Salinan. In 1821, Mexico became independent and sought to reduce the power of the Spanish missionaries, eventually by secularizing the missions around 1834. By that time, the population within the mission range had declined from about seventy-two thousand to approximately eighteen thousand. The causes of the decline are uncertain, but most likely disease, poor diet, psychological stress, and declining female fertility all played a part. Faced with disappearing converts, missionaries went on raids into the Central Valley to recruit Yokuts, whether by persuasion or force.

By the time of the U.S. invasion in 1846, the total native population of California had shrunk to less than 150,000, but that included people outside the coastal strip who were still living largely as they had for centuries. The discovery of gold shortly after the American conquest brought thousands of whites into the area, especially the Sierra foothills of the Miwok and Yokuts. Americans regarded the natives as "diggers," an inferior people suitable as targets for mass destruction. By 1900, the Indian population had reached its nadir at 15,500.

In the 1870's, the U.S. government began its policy of establishing reservations and, in at least a few instances, forcing people away from other land. Despite the harsh conditions on the reservations, the native population gradually rebounded in the twentieth century, reaching nearly twenty-two thousand on the first "Great Roll," conducted between 1928 and 1933, more than thirty-six thousand on the second roll, taken from 1950 to 1955, and more than ninety-one thousand in the census of 1970. The last figure reflects the influx into California of Native Americans from other culture areas, a process that continued throughout the 1970's and 1980's. The census of 1990 recorded the presence of approximately 236,000 American Indians within California; that figure is still less than the population in pre-contact times.

R. David Weber

Bibliography
Bahr, Diana M. *From Mission to Metropolis: Cupeno Indian Women in Los Angeles*. Norman: University of Oklahoma Press, 1993.
Cook, Sherburne F. *The Conflict Between the California Indian and White Civilization*. Berkeley: University of California Press, 1976. A collection of six articles, originally published in *Ibero-Americana* from 1940 to 1943 by the preeminent demographer of California's native peoples.

Harrington, John P. *Karuk Indian Myths*. Washington, D.C.: Bureau of American Ethnology, 1932. One of the few published works by one of the three great anthropologists of California natives. Harrington, working for the Smithsonian Institution, recorded vast amounts of linguistic and other data in California and other parts of the Southwest, but he infuriated his superiors by his general failure to write up his findings.

Heizer, Robert F., ed. *California*. Vol. 8 in *Handbook of North American Indians*. Washington, D.C.: Smithsonian Institution, 1978. The eighth volume in the comprehensive series by the Smithsonian, this encyclopedic work includes articles on each of the tribes as well as on such topics as environmental background, historical demography, trade and trails, and intergroup conflict. Complete with maps, photographs, tables, and bibliography.

Holmes, Marie S., and John R. Johnson. *The Chumash and Their Predecessors: An Annotated Bibliography*. Santa Barbara, Calif.: Santa Barbara Museum of Natural History, 1998.

Keeling, Richard. *Cry for Luck: Sacred Song and Speech Among the Yurok, Hupa, and Karok Indians of Northwestern California*. Berkeley: University of California Press, 1992.

Kroeber, Alfred Louis. *Handbook of the Indians of California*. Reprint. Berkeley: California Book Company, 1953. Originally published in 1925 as Bulletin 78 of the Bureau of American Ethnology, this remains a standard reference work. It includes fifty-three chapters on tribes as well as other general sections. The author, another of the three great figures in California anthropology, taught for many years at the University of California.

Lee, Gaylen D. *Walking Where We Lived: Memoirs of a Mono Indian Family*. Norman: University of Oklahoma Press, 1998.

McCawley, William. *The First Angelinos: The Gabrielino Indians of Los Angeles*. Novato, Calif.: Ballena Press, 1996.

Merriam, C. Hart. *Studies of California Indians*. Berkeley: University of California Press, 1955. Written by the third of the three giants in the field, this is a series of his papers published posthumously. Privately funded by a wealthy woman, Mary Harriman, Merriam often feuded with Kroeber.

White, Phillip M., and Stephen D. Fitt. *Bibliography of the Indians of San Diego County: The Kumeyaay, Diegueno, Luiseno, and Cupeno*. Lanham, Md.: Scarecrow Press, 1998.

Great Basin

LANGUAGE GROUPS: Hokan, Numic (Shoshonean)
TRIBES: Bannock, Gosiute, Kawaiisu, Mono (Monache), Numaga (Northern Paiute), Panamint, Paviotso (Northern Paiute), Shoshone, Ute, Washoe

The Great Basin, an area relatively high in altitude, includes all of Nevada and Utah, most of western Colorado, and portions of Idaho, Wyoming, southern Oregon, southeastern California, northern Arizona, and New Mexico. It is a "basin" between two large mountain ranges. Much of the region is steppe or semidesert, but true desert exists in southern Nevada and western Utah. The Great Basin covers an area of some 400,000 square miles, with internal river and stream drainage created by north-south mountain ranges that vary in elevation from 6,000 to 12,000 feet. Nomadic hunting and gathering people successfully inhabited the Great Basin for at least ten thousand years, and their ways of life remained relatively unchanged until European American incursion.

Language. All native speakers within the Great Basin, except the Hokan-speaking Washoe, are members of one of three Numic languages (western, central, or southern Numic), a division of the Uto-Aztecan language family of northern Mexico. The term "Shoshonean" is commonly used in referring to Numic-speaking groups of the Great Basin.

Technology and Subsistence. Depending on elevation and time of the year, vegetation types in the Great Basin vary greatly, with many plants of economic significance (such as creosote, various sagebrush, rice grass, and wheatgrass) found at lower elevations. In the higher elevations, the major seed tree is the piñon, which provided a so-called iron ration—its nuts and seeds are nutritious and store well.

The main food-obtaining activities of these highly mobile desert culture groups were hunting, gathering, and gleaning, strategies that required a relatively simple but effective multipurpose technology. Their annual subsistence round (annual migration pattern for exploiting various food

Great Basin Culture Area

sources) was based on obtaining the plant and animal resources that occurred at various elevations in different locations at regular times of the
year. The major source of calorie intake was plants, which made up 70 to 80
percent of the diet of Basin peoples. In early spring, lettuce, spinach, wild
potatoes, onions, rhubarb, and numerous rhizomes and shoots were collected. In late summer, a variety of seeds, berries, and medicines were

collected, often while deer hunting. Seeds from mustard, salt brush, rabbit-brush, sand grass, and other plants were stored for winter. After a killing frost, women gathered tules.

The men hunted deer, antelope, elk, mountain sheep, rabbits, hares, gophers, lizards, snakes, mice, sage hens, and rats. Even insects, such as crickets, locusts, ants, and grasshoppers, were collected. In some areas, larvae would accumulate in large mounds on beaches, and these were dried and stored in baskets or grass-lined pits for winter consumption.

Hunting was often done by individuals, rather than groups, using sinew-backed bows; in these instances the ability to stalk was more important than marksmanship. Rabbits and insects, however, were hunted in large collective drives that forced game into bush barriers, where they were killed. On occasion, secondary harvesting became necessary, as when seeds were taken from stores by rats or squirrels. Seeds could be collected from human feces and then roasted and ground into food.

Some areas of the Great Basin had lakes that were fished in late May and early June for large sucker and trout, using various technologies including torch-fishing, wide-mouth baskets, harpoons, and drag and dip nets. After removing the roe from some species, the fish were split and air-dried for future use.

Social Systems. In the absence of complex technology, the maintenance of a highly mobile and flexible social structure was critical as a "tool" in effectively exploiting the environment. The principal sociopolitical group in the Great Basin was the mobile and flexible extended family, or kin clique, which was self-sufficient and remained fairly isolated throughout the year. Families were nonlineal and bilateral-based. Similar in some ways to the Plateau Indians, groups were essentially egalitarian, and decisions were based on consensus of opinion. Leadership was frequently temporary, based on one's skill, though more sedentary groupings had a headman, a "talker," who kept his group informed of the condition and occurrence of food resources. This person encouraged cooperation and group tranquillity by resolving interpersonal conflicts.

Polygyny was not common, and it was usually sororal polygyny. The levirate and sororate were recognized, usually to intensify kin unions. There was some cross-cousin marriage. A significant division of labor by gender and age increased the group's efficiency and tended to reduce conflict.

Belief Systems. Not as complex as those of most other culture areas, Great Basin religion was basically individualistic, though at certain times of the year the people were concerned with collective rituals to ensure world renewal, availability and redistribution of resources, and sociopolitical tranquillity. The dominant religious practitioner was the shaman, either male or female, who had acquired a tutelary spirit and power for curing, hunting, gambling, and other concerns through dreaming or the vision quest. Curing shamans were concerned primarily with treating illness, which was considered the result of taboo violation, a ghost, or spirit or object intrusion by a sorcerer. Shamans were skilled in ventriloquism and legerdemain, possessed songs, and had an impressive array of sacred items. Usually people did not seek power, as power was feared; its possession was considered dangerous, since it could impose considerable strain on the individual and could bring on accusations of sorcery.

A primary individual religious concern was the avoidance and placation of ghosts and theriomorphic forms that inhabited an area if a person's burial was hastened or improperly conducted, or if any other number of moral transgressions were committed by the living. The afterlife was considered an enjoyable place, one of bountiful resources, dancing, games, and gambling.

John Alan Ross

Bibliography

Arkush, Brooke S. "The Great Basin Culture Area." In *Native North Americans: An Ethnographic Approach*, edited by Daniel L. Boxberger. Dubuque, Iowa: Kendall/Hunt, 1990.

Beck, Charlotte, ed. *Models for the Millennium: Great Basin Anthropology Today*. Salt Lake City: University of Utah Press, 1999.

Crum, Steven J. *The Road on Which We Came: Po'i Pentun Tammen Kimmappeh: A History of the Western Shoshone*. Salt Lake City: University of Utah Press, 1994.

D'Azevedo, Warren L., ed. *Great Basin*. Vol. 11 in *Handbook of North American Indians*. Washington, D.C.: Smithsonian Institution Press, 1990.

Fowler, Catherine S. "Subsistence." In *Great Basin*, edited by Warren L. D'Azevedo. Vol. 11 in *Handbook of North American Indians*. Washington, D.C.: Smithsonian Institution Press, 1986.

Grayson, Donald K. *The Desert's Past: A Natural Prehistory of the Great Basin*. Washington, D.C.: Smithsonian Institution Press, 1993.

Steward, Julian H. *Basin-Plateau Aboriginal Sociopolitical Groups*. Bureau of American Ethnology Bulletin 120. Reprint. Salt Lake City: University of Utah Press, 1970.

Stewart, Omer C. "The Basin." In *The Native Americans*, edited by Robert F. Spencer, Jesse D. Jennings, et al. New York: Harper & Row, 1965.

_____ . "Culture Element Distributions: XIV, Northern Paiute." *University of California Anthropological Records* 4, no. 3 (1941): 361-446.

_____. "Culture Element Distributions: XVII, Ute-Southern Paiute." *University of California Anthropological Records* 6, no. 4 (1942): 231-355.

Northeast

LANGUAGE GROUPS: Algonquian, Iroquoian, Siouan
TRIBES: Abenaki, Algonquin, Cayuga, Erie, Fox, Huron, Illinois, Kaskaskia, Kickapoo, Lenni Lenape, Mahican, Maliseet, Massachusett, Menominee, Miami, Micmac, Mohawk, Nanticoke, Narragansett, Neutral, Nottaway, Oneida, Onondaga, Ottawa, Pamlico, Passamaquoddy, Pennacook, Penobscot, Pequot, Petun, Piankashaw, Potawatomi, Sauk, Secotan, Seneca, Shawnee, Susquehannock, Tuscarora, Wampanoag, Wappinger, Winnebago

The northern boundary of the area known as the Northeast culture area is the southeastern margin of the boreal forest that stretches across Canada. The area includes the Great Lakes region and reaches (generally speaking) from the Atlantic Ocean in the east to the Mississippi River in the west. The boundary between the Northeast and Southeast culture areas is somewhat arbitrary, but the Northeast culture area is generally considered to extend to the Tidewater region of Virginia and inland through northern Tennessee. From prehistory, tribes and bands migrated throughout both Northeast and Southeast regions, and cultural influences of various groups upon one another were extensive.

The societies of the Southeast tended to have a greater dependence on agriculture and a denser population, and they were socially and politically more complex. The one natural feature that was common to the entire Northeast area was the forest. The region was blanketed by extensive coniferous and deciduous forests, and trees provided the materials for tools, shelter, and modes of transportation, such as the well-known birchbark canoe.

Often commented upon by anthropologists are the marked Mesoamerican influences on Northeast cultures, some of which seem to date back to antiquity and all of which apparently were filtered through Southeast cultures. The Northeast culture area seems to have evolved about three thousand years ago as a functionally integrated system interrelated with the

Northeast Culture Area

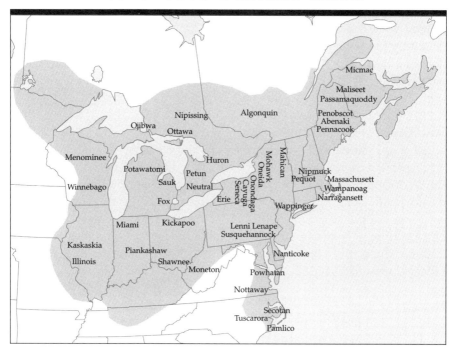

natural environment. Its tribes gleaned much from other cultures without being overrun by them until the arrival of the European invaders in the sixteenth century.

At the time of the arrival of the Europeans, the coastal regions of the Northeast were occupied by Algonquian-speaking people, and the inland waterways were occupied by Iroquian-speaking people. The entire area was crisscrossed by the trails of a vast trading network. The Hurons, who occupied the region between Lake Ontario and Georgian Bay and were in contact with the people of the Subarctic, were the preeminent traders of the region. Huron was the language of trade. Storable foods were traded for furs, nuts, obsidian, shells, flints, and other items.

Three Northeast Subregions. Many scholars consider the Northeast culture area to consist of three major subregions: the coastal region, the St. Lawrence lowlands region, and the Great Lakes-riverine region. The coastal region included the area from the Atlantic Provinces of Canada to as far south as North Carolina. It was inhabited primarily by Eastern Algonquian speakers in a continuum along the coast, with a few Iroquoian-speaking bands in what is now coastal Virginia and North Carolina. Among coastal

31

groups, the population grew denser, agriculture more important, and political organizations more complex as one went southward. These coastal Indians were the first to encounter the Europeans and the first to be decimated by the ravages of the diseases carried by whites. For the most part they had been wiped out or had been sent into forced migration by 1850, with the largest number surviving in Maine and the Maritime Provinces. Little of their culture was preserved or recorded by the religious refugees from England. In the years from 1615 to 1619, even before the Pilgrims arrived, disease carried by French and English adventurers and traders had killed an estimated two-thirds of the population of New England.

The St. Lawrence lowlands section included the St. Lawrence river area, southern Ontario, New York State, and the Susquehanna Valley. These were the homelands of Iroquoian-speaking peoples. ("Iroquoian" refers to speakers of the language group, whereas "Iroquois" refers to members of the League of the Iroquois—the Iroquois Confederacy—in most reference guides.) These tribes had similar patterns of horticulture, fishing, fortified villages, prisoner sacrifice, and spiritual rituals, and they had a highly codified matrilineal property system. Of the groups inhabiting the Eastern Woodlands (both Algonquian- and Iroquoian-speaking), those who were most agrarian were matrilineal, and those to the far north who subsisted as hunting bands were usually patrilineal.

The Great Lakes-riverine region was populated by Algonquian and Siouan-speaking groups who had limited contacts with whites until the late seventeenth century. Their politics were determined by pressure from the Iroquois League, whose warriors overran the lower Michigan peninsula in the 1600's and who established a hegemony over much of the region that lasted until after the American Revolution.

Cultural Similarities. There were many similarities between Iroquoian and Algonquian groups. Both were hunters and farmers, and both employed sachems to lead regional economic networks. Sachems came from elite families that collected and then distributed tribute in annual ceremonies of thanksgiving. The practice of living in seasonal camps took advantage of ripening food stocks in the north. Where a 160-day growing season existed, villages were stationary, and people grew corn as their staple. Where villages were stationary, more complex political systems evolved.

Most of the Indians south of the St. Lawrence River were village-dwelling people. Communal hunting of moose, deer, bear, and game birds supplemented agriculture based on corn, beans, and squash. Communal hunting techniques used fire, surrounds, and impounding techniques. Fish were also a significant food item; they were caught with traps, nets, hooks, spears, and poison. They could be taken through the ice in winter and, in

Somewhat fanciful depiction of a communal deer hunt. (Library of Congress)

the case of Atlantic salmon, caught on spawning runs. Wild plant foods, particularly berries, were so important that they were ceremonially gathered, as was maple sap. In the northern lake regions, wild rice was a staple.

The Algonquian tribes usually built oval-shaped or dome-shaped wigwams covered by mats or bark. Iroquoians, and Algonquians who had contact with the Iroquoians, lived in longhouses, usually about 20 feet wide and 50 to 100 feet long. As family units grew, the longhouses were extended.

Clothing consisted of animal skins, as did many parfleches, or carrying bags. Other containers were made from woven fiber or from clay. Necklaces, wristlets, earrings, and other items of ornamentation were made from hair, bone, native copper, shells, stones, and feathers.

Birchbark canoes were the primary mode of transportation of trade items. Wampum belts of shells and later beads described symbolically almost all dealings politically and ritually among and within tribes. The ritualized smoking of tobacco in ornately carved stone or clay pipes was common to all the tribes of the region.

Social organizations evolved from environmental necessity. Exploiting the environment in the north required small, autonomous, totemic, patrilineal bands. The other extreme was represented by the Iroquois tribes, who lived in fortified, stockaded villages, were matrilineal, and banded together into confederacies with very strong political and religious systems in which ultimate power was vested in the hands of the oldest "sensible" women of each clan. Some of the coastal Algonquians also organized into matrilineal clans.

Children were seldom physically punished. Iroquois men paid little attention to their own offspring; children were reared exclusively by women. At puberty, boys entered manhood through an initiation rite involving exile and fasting. Premarital and extramarital affairs were relatively common and carried no stigma. Marriages were arranged completely by clan mothers, and once marriage was consummated, divorce was very uncommon, because it would reflect poor judgment by the clan mothers. Murder within a clan was so uncommon that there were no rules governing its punishment.

Warfare between tribes was commonplace, but such activity resembled feuds more than organized wars. There was constant strife, even within language groups, until the fur trade and the economics of white society changed that forever. The Iroquois Confederacy, which may have been formed as a direct result of the fur trade, created the opportunity for the Five Nations of the Iroquois to establish a combined military force. In the mid-1600's, the Iroquois assembled an "army" of more than a thousand men and effectively eliminated the Huron, Erie, Petun (Tobacco), and Illinois from being factors in the overall scheme of the politics of the Northeast.

European Contact. Following European contact, life in the Northeast became very complicated. The existing fur trade intensified with the arrival of the French. The river systems that facilitated the fur trade created the basis of the relationship between whites and Indians. A growing European demand for furs transformed Indian political organizations. Most Northeast cultures were radically changed by the fur trade—in many cases even before any members of a tribe had even met a white person.

Geographical dislocations were common to every tribe and band. Tribal groups had three options: They could compromise with the invaders; they could adopt most of the outsiders' ways, including their religion; or they could violently reject the new cultures. As European encroachment advanced, some pantribal movements, such as those led by Tecumseh and Pontiac, evolved in an attempt to stop the whites. In other cases, refugees—for example, the Lenni Lenape—recombined to form new groups (in the case of the Lenni Lenape, the Delaware) and tried to make a stand while being pushed westward. Generally speaking, they were no match for the well-organized, commercially oriented, land-hungry Europeans.

Glenn J. Schiffman

Bibliography

Ballantine, Betty, and David Hurst Thomas, eds. *The Native Americans: An Illustrated History*. Atlanta: Turner Publishing, 1993.

Calloway, Colin G., ed. *After King Philip's War: Presence and Persistence in Indian New England*. Hanover, N.H.: University Press of New England, 1997.

_____. *Dawnland Encounters: Indians and Europeans in Northern New England*. Hanover, N.H.: University Press of New England, 1991.

Edmunds, R. David. *Kinsmen Through Time: An Annotated Bibliography of Potawatomi History*. Metuchen, N.J.: Scarecrow Press, 1987.

Grumet, Robert S. *Historic Contact: Indian People and Colonists in Today's Northeastern United States in the Sixteenth Through Eighteenth Centuries*. Norman: University of Oklahoma Press, 1995.

Hauptman, Laurence M., and James Wherry. *The Pequots in Southern New England: The Fall and Rise of an American Indian Nation*. Norman: University of Oklahoma Press, 1990.

Mandell, Daniel R. *Behind the Frontier: Indians in Eighteenth Century Eastern Massachusetts*. Lincoln: University of Nebraska Press, 1996.

Newcomb, William W., Jr. *North American Indians: An Anthropological Perspective*. Pacific Palisades, Calif.: Goodyear, 1974.

Strong, John A. *"We Are Still Here!": The Algonquian Peoples of Long Island Today*. 2d ed. Interlaken, N.Y.: Empire State Books, 1998.

Time-Life Books. *Algonquians of the East Coast*. Alexandria, Va.: Time-Life Books, 1995.

Trigger, Bruce, ed. *Northeast*. Vol. 15 in *Handbook of North American Indians*. Washington, D.C.: Smithsonian Institution Press, 1978.

Northwest Coast

LANGUAGE GROUPS: Athapaskan, Chinook, Penutian, Salish
TRIBES: Alsea, Bella Bella, Bella Coola, Chehalis, Chinook, Coast Salish, Coos, Eyak, Gitksan, Haida, Klamath, Klikitat, Kwakiutl, Nootka (Nuu-Chah-Nulth), Quileute, Quinault, Siuslaw, Takelma, Tillamook, Tlingit, Tsimshian, Umpqua

The Northwest Coast culture area extends from the modern regions of Yakutat Bay in southern Alaska south to Cape Mendocino in northern California. The temperate-zone rain-forest ecology and abundant resources contributed much to the diverse cultures which developed in the area.

Natural History. Until about thirteen thousand years ago, much of the Northwest Coast area was covered with the ice of the Pleistocene Ice Age. When the ice began to melt, new vistas opened for the spread of plant, animal, and human populations. The once-white land was covered with a blanket of verdure so lush that one can hardly imagine it in the twenty-first century.

There has been considerable debate regarding when humans first entered the area. Estimates range from about twelve thousand years ago to about fifty-five hundred years ago. Probably most arrived overland on foot, but quite possibly some came by boat as well. By the time of the first contact with Europeans there were more than 100,000 people populating the Northwest Coast area.

After the glaciers retreated but before human populations filled the environmental niches, the lushness of the land increased. Vegetation spread, and the animals followed; then came humans. Probably they came from Siberia over the so-called Bering Strait land bridge.

Cultural Geography. The diversity of physical types, languages, and cultures suggests multiple maritime origins. The coastal inhabitants appear unrelated to the Athapaskan stock said to have migrated overland from Eurasia, for example, and peoples north of the Columbia River are markedly different from those to the south. There is no consensus regarding the

Northwest Coast Culture Area

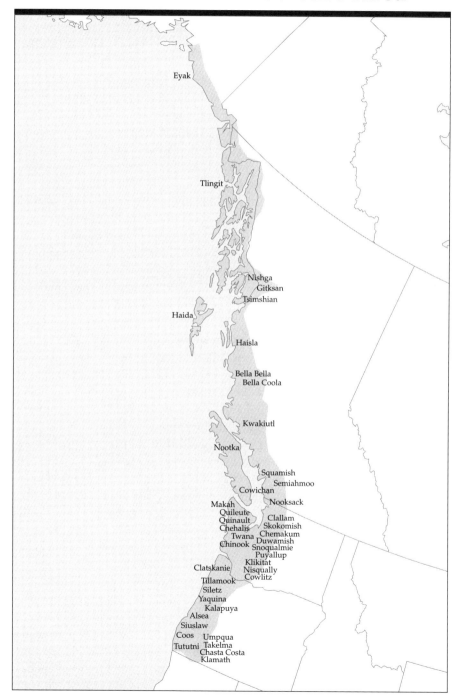

Eyak

Tlingit

Nishga
Gitksan
Tsimshian

Haida

Haisla

Bella Bella
Bella Coola

Kwakiutl

Nootka

Squamish
Semiahmoo
Cowichan
Nooksack
Makah
Quileute Clallam
Quinault Skokomish
Chehalis Chemakum
Twana Duwamish
Chinook Snoqualmie
Puyallup
Klikitat
Clatskanie Nisqually
Tillamook Cowlitz
Siletz
Yaquina
Kalapuya
Alsea
Siuslaw
Coos Umpqua
Tututni Takelma
Chasta Costa
Klamath

character of human penetration into the coastal ecosystem. Migratory groups appear to have settled gradually into their chosen coastal environments and developed into the cultures of the Northwest Coast culture area undisturbed over a period ranging from roughly twelve thousand to fifty-five hundred years ago.

Coastal cultures were originally river or river-mouth cultures, later beach cultures, and only finally (and only in part) seagoing cultures. They are said to have remained centered on the riverine and estuarine environments. Only some peoples took to sea. Among those who did not become maritime, such as the tribes south of the Columbia River, skills in canoe building were never as highly elaborated, nor was ceremonial life as complex, as among more northern groups.

Fishing and sea-mammal hunting were the most profitable activities. Harvesting maritime resources required tools that would allow hunters to use the available natural resources to the fullest extent, and most of the peoples of the coast developed such tools. Their lives moved with the rhythms of nature's cycles. Their needs were supplied by the forest and the sea. The materials needed for the construction of most of their material culture was readily available and at hand, yet they still engaged in widespread trade with other groups.

They used the moderate climate and wealth of resources well, creating bone fishhooks, harpoons, nets, and other hunting and gathering tools. They developed elaborate communities with ceremonial practices and intricate arts of a highly symbolic and abstract nature centuries before European peoples had laid the foundations of Western civilization. Their material culture was remarkable in its beauty, quality, and diversity.

Population density was influenced directly by the forest and the sea. Moreover, in richly provided areas, efficient food gathering and preservation created a large surplus of time that shaped community life and influenced the development of art and ceremonialism. The terrain was rough, a fact which discouraged farming and animal domestication. The fact that local stone was hard to work prevented the development of more advanced tools, and the absence of significant agricultural surpluses influenced trade patterns.

Village Life, Travel, and Trade. The Northwest Coast cultures lived peaceably for the most part, except for occasional slave raids or skirmishes over territorial boundaries. This condition led to the development of cultures with roomy, solid houses, seaworthy boats and canoes, elaborate art, intricate rituals and ceremonies, and a generally affluent and highly complex society. People lived in kinship groups, or clan units that were small and autonomous while being highly integrated into the overall cultural pattern of their area. Thus the village and the community it contained were of great significance in the social structure.

Peoples to the north were seagoing peoples and had an abundant surplus of resources. Peoples south of the Columbia River depended on the bays and the rivers for most of their livelihood; they had no need to look further. The sophistication of coastal peoples suggests that they had reached dynamic equilibrium with their environment and learned to maintain it long before Europeans came.

People of the Northwest Coast area probably arrived with their maritime adaptations intact and fully developed. Migration routes were coastal as well as interior. The Athapaskan-speaking peoples from Asia represent a later intrusion into a previously established cultural environment. There most likely were a number of basal cultures, or stable cultural traditions, in place by ten thousand years ago, and each culture was characterized by

This early twentieth century photograph of a Klamath chief standing by Oregon's Crater Lake reveals the influence of Plains culture on other culture areas. (Library of Congress)

slightly different sets of tools and slightly different ways of life. Early cultural traditions gradually became more consistent throughout the area because of the increasing similarity of the postglacial environment.

Adaptation to Nature. Natural events such as glacial retreat, opening of new land and migration routes, changes in sea levels, stabilization of the climate, the consistent spread of plants and animals into available niches, and ongoing episodic volcanism throughout the inland ranges of the Cascades (from Northern California northward into Canada) had a profound influence on the evolving cultural systems along the coast. When sea levels changed, for example, there was a corresponding change in the technology of coastal cultures that gave rise to cultures more easily recognizable as the ancestors of those later subjected to ethnographic study. These cultures' status systems were based on wealth and craft. The diffusion of technological innovations and new ideas, which led to even greater wealth among members of Northwest Coast culture area communities, was hastened by rapidly developing lines of trade; they were extensive and widespread, connecting distant groups.

Few generalizations regarding human origins are definitive. The Northwest Coast area has been habitable for more than forty to fifty thousand years and has probably been occupied continuously for the last seven thousand years at least. Stable cultural patterns probably have existed for more than five thousand years. The sources and processes of development of early culture on the coast are shrouded in mystery and myth. It is known that they had ceremonies, mythologies, rock art, and tooth pendants. Shamanic animism and the beliefs and practices associated with the power of guardian spirit entities were widespread. They smoked cultivated tobacco and used plants for healing rituals, in ceremonials associated with fertility, and in burials.

Status and Wealth. Wealth and status were interrelated in Northwest Coast cultures. Leaders had to be wealthy, a situation which led to ostentatious displays of rank and even to the ritualized destruction of wealth in the grand potlatches of the northern groups. Gift giving was a highly developed social practice. Some tribes, mostly to the south, appear to have practiced a less destructive form of potlatch in which wealth was displayed, then given away. In such cases the ceremony acted as a means of redistribution of wealth and an affirmation of status. Lineage granted hereditary family privileges and rights to those associated with certain family symbols, crests, or signs. The leadership system, then, was both a means of concentrating surpluses and of redistributing wealth among the general population.

Although the Northwest Coast is often regarded as a single culture area, this may or may not be the case. The great consistency among the material remains of early cultures in the forms of canoes, houses, clothing, basketry and weaving, carving in wood and stone, crafts, and technologies suggests a single areal culture. Yet it is clear that in spite of certain cultural consistencies (that may be attributed to the environment) coastal cultures were remarkably different from one another in important ways.

Some scholars therefore question the validity of the contention that this vast area is host to a single culture complex. The Salish-speaking peoples north of the Columbia River and the Penutian-speaking peoples to the south are not so alike as they might at first appear to be, and the ways of life of estuarine and riverine peoples are very different from those of seagoing maritime peoples.

Modern History. In the mid-1700's the Eurasian and European immigrants arrived: the Russians in 1741, the Spaniards in 1774, and the English in 1778. With these intrusions the prehistoric period came to an end and modern history began.

The fur trade emerged as a dominant influence, quickly drawing the indigenous communities into a growing world economy and giving them rapid access to luxury goods and metal-based technology. Yet social disintegration (as sources and concentrations of wealth changed), erosion of community identities in the face of decimating diseases, forced relocation to reservations, cultural decline because of the transformation of belief systems brought about by missionary activity, and loss of languages were widespread.

Colonization resulted in the loss of indigenous control over the environment and the eventual extinction of many smaller communities. Until European contact, Northwest Coast cultures were supported by a subsistence base distributed throughout a uniform, temperate, rain-forest environment. They were hunter-gatherers of the most advanced sort. In an environment of great abundance, diverse cultures developed that were highly civilized and comparable with civilizations elsewhere based upon agriculture and animal domestication. Their self-sufficient technologies were remarkably advanced.

This culture area contains the oldest and most variable evidence for flaked stone technological traditions in North America. It also contains the largest number of Native American languages and language families. Evidence suggests that many populations have lived at their present locations for long periods of time. Technological and linguistic diversity diffused rapidly as the historical period began, however, making it difficult to determine exactly how long cultures have been in residence.

Michael W. Simpson

Bibliography

Borden, Charles E. *Origins and Development of Early Northwest Coast Culture to About 3000 B.C.* Ottawa: National Museums of Canada, 1975. This is a complete archaeological survey of the data on the area.

Drucker, Phillip. *Indians of the Northwest Coast*. Garden City, N.Y.: Natural History Press, 1963. The author notes in this comprehensive survey that there is little physical data on where the first Northwest people originated and how they got to the Northwest.

Fladmark, Knut R. "The Feasibility of the Northwest as a Migration Route for Early Man." In *Early Man from a Circum-Pacific Perspective*, edited by Alan Bryan. University of Alberta Department of Anthropology Occasional Papers 1. Edmonton, Alberta: Archaeological Researchers International, 1978. Fladmark suggests there may be a variety of origins for the peoples who populated the area and suggests that the people of the Northwest are descendants of long-established Eskimo-Aleut culture area inhabitants.

Harkin, Michael E. *The Heiltsuks: Dialogues of Culture and History on the Northwest Coast*. Lincoln: University of Nebraska Press, 1997.

Miller, Jay. *Tsimshian Culture: A Light Through the Ages*. Lincoln: University of Nebraska Press, 1997.

Ruby, Robert H., and John A. Brown. *A Guide to the Indian Tribes of the Pacific Northwest*. Norman: University of Oklahoma Press, 1986. This book gives an excellent, updated listing of sources regarding the general history and current status of these tribes.

Smyth, Willie, and Esme Ryan, eds. *Spirit of the First People: Native American Music Traditions of Washington State*. Seattle: University of Washington Press, 1999.

Waldman, Carl. *Atlas of the North American Indian*. New York: Facts on File, 1985. An excellent summary description, with maps, of the Northwest Coast culture area.

Plains

Language groups: Algonquian, Athapaskan, Caddoan, Kiowa-Tanoan, Siouan, Uto-Aztecan

TRIBES: Apache of Oklahoma, Arapaho, Arikara, Assiniboine, Atsina, Blackfoot (Blood, Piegan, Siksika), Caddo, Cheyenne, Comanche, Crow, Hidatsa, Iowa, Kansa (Kaw), Kiowa, Mandan, Missouri, Omaha, Osage, Oto, Pawnee, Ponca, Quapaw, Sarsi, Sioux (Santee, Teton, Yankton), Tonkawa, Waco, Wichita

The Plains culture area extended from southern Canada to southern Texas and from the foothills of the Rocky Mountains to the Mississippi River. It included short-grass plains in the west, tall-grass prairie in the east, and mixed tall and short grasses in between. Many tribes from different regions and cultures moved into the area, but all adopted the basic Plains culture based on hunting buffalo. Aspects of the parent cultures were apparent in Plains Indian culture, but they were modified by the Plains environment and by cultural exchange with other tribes to produce the unique Plains culture.

Regional Prehistory. According to the most popular theory, the earliest Indians in the Plains area were descendants of Asiatic peoples who traveled from Siberia to Alaska over the Bering Strait land bridge some twelve thousand years ago. At the time, glaciers covered much of Eurasia and North America. The water in the great ice sheets was taken from the oceans, lowering sea level and exposing a 1,000-mile-wide land connection between parts of Siberia and Alaska that were not glaciated.

As the glaciers melted, a corridor of unglaciated land was opened to more southerly parts of North America. The prehistoric Indians (or Paleo-Indians) moved through that corridor, eventually reaching the tip of South America. The first North Americans hunted mammoths and other large mammals, but the populations that occupied the Plains area went through several cultural and economic transitions before the historic Indian tribes entered the Plains. The relationship between the Plains tribes occupying the

Plains Culture Area

Sarsi

Plains Cree

Blood
Blackfoot
Piegan

Atsina   Assiniboine

Crow   Hidatsa
              Mandan   Yankton
                              Sioux
                 Arikara
        Teton Sioux
                                Santee Sioux
    Cheyenne   Ponca
                      Yankton Sioux
                   Omaha
        Pawnee   Iowa

                    Oto
    Arapaho
              Kansa   Missouri

                         Osage
         Kiowa
                                Quapaw
                Apache of
    Comanche   Oklahoma   Caddo

                Wichita
                Kichai

                Tonkawa

    Lipan Apache

area at the time of European contact and the prehistoric Indians is obscure.

Most versions of the origins of modern tribes suggest that they moved into the grasslands from the Eastern Woodlands (the Sioux, Cheyenne, and Arapaho from the Northeast culture area and the Pawnee and Wichita from the Southeast) and the Southwest (Comanche and Kiowa). Subdivisions of tribes from other culture areas also used the Plains, and their cultures were molded to some extent by the Plains. The Ute and Shoshone of the Great Basin, Nez Perce of the plateau, and Cree from the Subarctic are examples.

Plains Indians hunting buffalo in the mid-nineteenth century. (Library of Congress)

Before Horses. Whatever their origins, the Plains Indians became nomadic buffalo hunters when they moved into the grasslands. Buffalo meat supplied food, some of which was smoked and dried for sustenance between hunts. Buffalo hides supplied robes, rawhide, and leather for other items of clothing and the cover for tipis. The Indians also hunted deer, pronghorn antelope, and other big game and used the meat and hides in similar ways. They gathered fruit, seeds, roots, and other vegetable foods as well. All these resources were important, but the buffalo was central to Plains Indian survival and culture.

The buffalo culture was firmly established before the Plains tribes obtained horses. Four main techniques were used to kill the buffalo: They were surrounded and killed with arrows and lances, driven over cliffs, driven into enclosures and killed there, and nearly surrounded by fire and killed as they fled the flames through the opening. These techniques were sometimes combined—for example, fire could be used to drive buffalo over a cliff.

The Indians followed the herds on foot using dogs, often pulling travois, to carry their possessions. The tipi, easily erected and taken down, lent itself to regular movement. The men hunted and waged war. The women cooked, preserved, sewed, collected plant foods, and put up and took down the tipi. Some tribes (Omaha and Ponca, for example) used tipis only during the buffalo hunts in early summer and in autumn. They lived in earthen lodges near the Missouri River during the rest of the year. There they planted gardens of corn, beans, and squash. The Pawnee, who lived south of the Platte River, practiced a similar schedule. The western Plains tribes (Arapaho, Cheyenne, and Teton Sioux) lived in tipis year round, came together in large groups for the hunting season and for ceremonies, and scattered in extended family groups to the protected valleys of the foothills of the Rocky Mountains for winter. In winter they continued to hunt but depended on food preserved from the summer buffalo hunts for much of their sustenance.

Religion, Status, and Art. The spiritual life of Plains Indians was closely integrated with secular life. They held elaborate ceremonies, such as the Sun Dance, when the tribe was together for the buffalo hunt. Most tribes had a sacred symbol, often a medicine pipe. The term "medicine" in this context is probably better translated "power," as the Indians believed the pipe to be a symbol of the power which assured their success in hunting, warfare, and other endeavors. Several such symbols were kept in a medicine bundle. The circle (wheel) was of great importance to the Plains Indians as a symbol of the unity and continuity of all aspects of nature.

Many individuals also kept a personal medicine bundle. The symbolic contents of these bundles were often obtained during a vision quest, in which a young man (occasionally a young woman) fasted alone in a wilderness area hoping to receive a vision from which he obtained his medicine (power), indicating his particular abilities and often giving direction to his life. His medicine bundle would then be made up, using symbols of his medicine.

Games, hunting, warfare, and choice of leaders were spiritual endeavors in Plains Indian culture. Games such as shinny (something like field hockey) were parts of certain religious ceremonies. Supernatural signs were sought to determine whether a raid or hunt should proceed. Daring deeds such as touching a live enemy ("counting coup") ranked above killing an enemy in determining the respect due a warrior. Leadership positions were obtained by performing such deeds, demonstrating skill in hunting, and practicing

Because of their economic reliance on buffalo herds, Plains Indian communities frequently moved. (Library of Congress)

generosity. Advancement through the male societies (lodges), which played important roles in tribal organization, depended on a man's bravery and his ability to provide for—and willingness to share with—the tribe. Most Plains tribes chose their chiefs based on these characteristics. Some tribes had hereditary chiefs, but to maintain a following the chief had to demonstrate these qualities.

Some Plains Indian art forms were spiritually symbolic and some were not. Pictographic art, usually produced by men, often depicted feats performed in hunting and warfare. The patterns used in much of the decorative art were based on straight lines, triangles, and diamonds, and their meaning was known only to the artist. Porcupine quills and later beads were extensively used for decoration. Any of these may have been produced simply for their beauty and symmetry, but it is likely that many such works also held spiritual meaning for their creator. Circles used in artworks probably were symbolic of the unity of nature.

Impact of Horses. The horse, introduced in historic times by the Spanish, fit beautifully into Plains Indian life. Buffalo hunting became easier and often involved a new technique in which individual buffalo were chased and brought down with bows and arrows. The travois was enlarged and fitted to the horse, so moves could be made more rapidly. Warfare could be carried out over greater distances, with greater speed and daring. Even when armed only with bows and arrows, Indians on horseback were skilled and fearless fighters, as the United States Army learned in the Plains Indian

47

wars. Rifles, obtained from European Americans to the east, made them even more formidable. Their conquerors ranked them among the greatest mounted warriors in history.

The wars were primarily fought as a result of repeated encroachment by European Americans on Indian land, and they came to a close so quickly primarily because of diseases (especially smallpox) and the near extinction of buffalo, not because of superior skill and strategy on the part of the invading armies. The most intense phase of the Plains wars began with the Sand Creek Massacre of Cheyenne and Arapaho (1864). This period included the Fetterman fight and Bozeman Trail war with the Sioux; the Red River war with the Comanches, Kiowa, and Cheyenne; and the battle with the Sioux and Cheyenne on the Little Bighorn River. It finally ended with the massacre of Sioux at Wounded Knee Creek in South Dakota (1890). The greater numbers and advanced technology of the whites left little doubt as to the outcome. Against these odds, the Plains Indians left an indelible mark on American history and the history of warfare.

Most elements of Plains Indian culture were not unique to those Indians but were shared with surrounding culture areas, especially the Woodland Indians to the east. The specific combination of characteristics, however, was found in no other group. With few exceptions, and with abundant variation, this combination was shared by all the tribes in the Plains. Symbolic of independent life lived in harmony with nature, Plains culture is the American Indian culture most familiar to the rest of the world.

Carl W. Hoagstrom

Bibliography

Ahler, Stanley A., Thomas D. Thiessen, and Michael K. Trimble. *People of the Willows: The Prehistory and Early History of the Hidatsa Indians*. Grand Forks: University of North Dakota Press, 1991.

Andrist, Ralph K. *The Long Death: The Last Days of the Plains Indians*. New York: Macmillan, 1964. An excellent outline of the Plains Indian wars. Evenhandedly puts Indian behavior and response to government initiatives into a cultural context. Maps, illustrations, index, and bibliography.

Bancroft-Hunt, Norman, and Werner Forman. *The Indians of the Great Plains*. Norman: University of Oklahoma Press, 1981. A well-written, extensively illustrated (with photographs) outline of Plains Indian culture. Index and brief bibliography.

Calloway, Colin G., ed. *Our Hearts Fell to the Ground: Plains Indian Views of How the West Was Lost*. Boston: Bedford Books of St. Martin's Press, 1996.

Carlson, Paul H. *The Plains Indians*. College Station: Texas A&M University Press, 1998.

Carter, Cecile E. *Caddo Indians: Where We Come From.* Norman: University of Oklahoma Press, 1995.

Ewers, John C. *Plains Indian History and Culture: Essays on Continuity and Change.* Norman: University of Oklahoma Press, 1997.

Fenelon, James V. *Culturicide, Resistance, and Survival of the Lakota "Sioux Nation."* New York: Garland, 1998.

Feraca, Stephen E. *Wakinyan: Lakota Religion in the Twentieth Century.* Lincoln: University of Nebraska Press, 1998.

Gonzalez, Mario, and Elizabeth Cook-Lynn. *The Politics of Hallowed Ground: Wounded Knee and the Struggle for Indian Sovereignty.* Urbana: University of Illinois Press, 1999.

Hoover, Herbert T. *The Yankton Sioux.* New York: Chelsea House, 1988. This is one volume in an excellent series of short books called *Indians of North America* (series editor, Frank W. Porter III). Other books in the series include *The Arapaho, The Cheyenne, The Comanche, The Crow, The Hidatsa, The Kiowa, The Osage,* and *The Quapaws.* Other topics, such as women, archaeology, and federal Indian policy, have their own books as well. All have illustrations, index, and brief bibliography.

Lowie, Robert H. *Indians of the Plains.* New York: McGraw-Hill, 1954. Reprint. Lincoln: University of Nebraska Press, 1982. Excellent introduction. Covers prehistory, history, and most aspects of culture. Maps, tables, illustrations, index, and a short bibliography. The preface (1982) gives additional information and references.

Meyer, Roy W. *History of the Santee Sioux: United States Indian Policy on Trial.* Rev. ed. Lincoln: University of Nebraska Press, 1993.

Sturtevant, William C., gen. ed. *Handbook of North American Indians.* 9 vols. in publication. Washington, D.C.: Smithsonian Institution Press, 1978-1990. This series is the best source on North American Indians available, with some volumes, including *Plains,* still to be published. Volumes on culture areas surrounding the Plains contain information of interest. Illustrations, extensive bibliographies, indexes.

Thomas, Davis, and Karin Ronnefeldt, eds. *People of the First Man.* New York: E. P. Dutton, 1976. An annotated abbreviation of the German aristocrat Maximilian's notes on Indians along the Missouri River in 1833-1834. Reprints of artwork by Karl Bodmer, the Swiss artist who accompanied him, are included. Maps; index.

Wolferman, Kristie C. *The Osage in Missouri.* Columbia: University of Missouri Press, 1997.

Plateau

LANGUAGE GROUPS: Penutian, Sahaptin, Salishan
TRIBES: Coeur d'Alene, Colville, Flathead, Kalispel, Kutenai, Lake, Lillooet, Methow, Mical, Modoc, Molala, Nez Perce, Okanagan, Palouse, Sanpoil, Shuswap, Spokane, Tenino, Thompson, Tyigh, Umatilla, Walla Walla, Wanapam, Wauyukma, Wenatchi, Yakima

The intermontane, semi-arid Plateau culture area consists of the low-elevation Columbia River basin of generally low, local relief, bounded on the west by the Cascade Mountains, on the east by the Rocky Mountains, to the north by the Fraser River, and somewhat to the south by the Blue Mountains. The most unique internal feature of the Plateau area is the numerous flood-scoured Scabland channels that are characterized by basalt cliffs, buttes, rock shelters, and thousands of small basins containing small lakes and seasonal wetlands. The Plateau was once viewed by anthropologists as a "transitional area" because of cultural influences from the Plains and the Northwest Coast. Archaeological evidence establishes an early and successful continuous inhabitation of eleven thousand years. The greatest influences on the Plateau cultures during the protohistorical period (1700-1805) were the adoption of the horse and prophetic religious revival.

The major shared cultural features of the Plateau were relatively simple political organization with leadership through consensus of opinion, riverine settlement patterns, reliance upon aquatic foods, a complex fishing technology, mutual cross-utilization of subsistence resources, extension of kin ties through systematic intermarriage, institutionalized trade, vision quest of a tutelary spirit, and an emphasis on democratic and peaceful relations. The introduction of the horse had a complex effect upon peoples of the eastern Plateau, particularly the Flathead and Nez Perce, who adopted many Plains traits in sociopolitical organization. The most devastating effects were created by numerous European American epidemics that greatly reduced aboriginal population.

Plateau Culture Area

Language. There were two major language families: In the southernmost Plateau was Sahaptin (Dalles, Klikitat, Nez Perce, Palouse, Umatilla, Walla Walla, Wanapam, and Warm Springs), and to the north was Salishan (Columbia, Kalispel, Lillooet, Okanagan-Colville, Thompson, and Shuswap). Other dialects were Wasco-Wishram, Carrier, Chilcotin, and Kutenai. Chinook (Kiksht) was a lingua franca (trade language) along the Columbia and Spokane rivers. There was no sign language except what was learned from the Plains. Many dialects were mutually intelligible, and most people were multilingual because of trade, intermarriage between different ethnic groups, and sustained polyadic relationships necessitated by differential resources.

Technology and Subsistence. Implements of hunting were often the same ones used for warfare, and men made their own implements and tools for hunting and fishing. Though various woods and cordate were gathered locally, lithic (stone) material for knives and projectile points often was traded. Men made mortars, pestles, pipes, beads, fishing weights, axes, and cutting tools. A woman's most important tools were a fire-hardened digging stick and those implements associated with tanning and sewing deer and elk hides. During the year women collected and stored great quantities of thinly split lengths of spruce, cedar, pine roots, and willow that were carefully stored for making baskets.

Though house types within the Plateau varied, the principal winter structure was, in the late prehistoric period, a tule mat-covered double apsidal pole-constructed lodge that housed one or more extended families who shared a cooking fire. The floor was covered with old tule mats, skins, bear grass, or white sage. Tules were important multipurpose plants for making mats, bundle boats, hats, and rain capes. Firewood and kindling were stored in an outside mat-roofed shed. Spring, summer, and fall structures were usually temporary and were built primarily for privacy and inclement weather.

As foragers, Plateau people lived for three to four months in permanent riverine winter villages in areas of low elevation, sometimes supplementing their stored animal and plant foods with occasional forays for land mammals and ice fishing. Winter villages had permanent semisubterranean storage pits, earth ovens, sweathouses, and family menstrual huts. Winter was a time of leisure when people repaired and manufactured predation technology, visited, and listened to elders telling often long accounts of creation and individual exploits. Acclaimed storytellers enjoyed high status. It was not unusual for shamans to conduct power duels in the winter.

Subsistence orientation was hunting, gathering, and fishing, regulated by season and a well-defined annual subsistence round. The southern Plateau diet consisted of approximately 40 percent plant food, 50 percent salmon, and 10 percent land mammals. The percentages varied according to a group's location, particularly in the northern Plateau. These activities commenced in early spring when groups would dismantle their winter houses and move to higher elevations to establish temporary camps to exploit traditional resource sites. Men would gather in great numbers in the spring to exploit fish stations mutually, using weirs, traps, harpoons, and spears, sometimes fishing until fall to harvest salmon and other fish. Food was preserved by drying and then cached in tree platforms and storage pits.

Women would visit traditional root fields in late spring to dig bitterroot, camus, numerous species of *Lomatium*, and other roots, which were dried and transported in great number to winter storage areas. In July and August, people would gather and pick numerous berry crops, particularly huckleberries. In late summer and early fall, groups would gain elevation—men to hunt deer and elk and women to gather medicines, hemp, and punk wood. After a killing frost the women cut and gathered tules.

Fishing was an important part of Plateau economies; this Kutenai fisherman was photographed in 1910. (Library of Congress)

Social Systems. The main feature of Plateau sociopolitical organization was village autonomy. There existed what may be called chiefs, however, men who influenced decisions of consensual opinion through judgment, knowledge, and example and who retained office through generosity, skillful decisions, oratory skills, and the possession of religious power. A chief's main responsibility was to maintain tranquillity by resolving differences of opinion and making final arbitration. This office, sometimes hereditary, was never based on the assumption of accrued wealth or material possessions. A composite band could have two or three petty chiefs. Salmon chiefs, shamans, and war leaders, all of whom had special religious powers, were apparent during specific occasions.

There was gender equality, and a bilateral kinship system existed. Marriage was commonly monogamous, but polygamy, particularly polygyny, occurred. A primary concern was to extend one's kinship ties through marriage. Social control was maintained by threats of sorcery, gossip, a high division of labor, myth, public opinion, public whipping, and resident rules.

Pregnant women observed strict dietary and behavioral taboos and were expected to work industriously during their confinement; violations were explanations for congenital defects or later aberrant behavior in the child. Women were delivered, if possible, in isolated delivery huts by their mothers, who would ritually dispose of the placentas and make the required prophylactic devices to protect the new child. A berdache or shaman could assist in a difficult delivery. Infanticide and abortions were considered moral transgressions. Naming usually occurred at birth, and an infant was often named for a deceased kinsperson.

Adolescent children were indulged by kinspeople, but prior to puberty rites children embarked upon rigorous physical training in preparation for adulthood. Grandparents spent inordinate time with grandchildren, and a child's first exposure to adult activities was frequently supervised by a concerned grandparent who also made prototype toys of adult activities. The most dramatic change in the individual's life was the puberty ceremony; for a girl it was her first confinement to the menstrual hut, and for a boy, his vision quest for a tutelary spirit.

Marriage, after a period of courtship, was usually arranged by both families with a feast. Though a man could later take a second wife, usually a widow who demonstrated certain skills, particularly hide processing, the cowives did not share the same dwelling. Divorce was with mutual consent, usually for reasons of laziness or adultery.

Upon death the individual was immediately removed from the structure, washed, and buried, usually with grave goods. Special rituals and taboos were followed to ensure the incorporation of the soul in an afterlife and to prevent the occurrence of lingering ghosts. The surviving widow or widower observed strict taboos for one year, at which time a feast was held to give away certain possessions of the deceased. A newborn was never named after a deceased sibling for fear of recurrence of death.

Belief Systems. Though there were group differences in the complex Plateau animistic mythical charter, the main concern was one's daily intimate relationship with the supernatural, which if violated could cause personal failure, illness, and even death. Complex notions of how order was brought from chaos during the origins of humankind were based essentially on the supernatural world, theriomorphic forces, and natural forces which controlled humans and animals. Shamans were religious practitioners (male or female) who had acquired their power in a variety of ways, particularly through dreaming, a vision quest, recurring events, special signs, and unique experiences.

Plateau peoples had various elaborate rites of intensification, usually during midwinter, when sacred communal efforts were strictly followed to ensure world renewal, personal well-being, return of migratory animals, and a renewal of one's power. Shamans were effective as curers, employing medicaments, legerdemain, ventriloquism, massage, sucking, and acupressure. They sought to rid a patient of sorcery-induced spirit or object illness or soul loss; they also heard confessions of moral transgressions. All of these, it was believed, could eventually kill a patient if not attended to. Shamans were capable of transformation, and they publicly demonstrated their power's flight from their body by enduring painful proofs of ordeal.

John Alan Ross

Bibliography

Hunn, Eugene S. "The Plateau Culture Area." In *Native North Americans: An Ethnohistorical Approach.* Edited by Daniel L. Boxberger. Dubuque, Iowa: Kendall/Hunt, 1990.

Kroeber, Alfred L. *Cultural and Natural Areas of Native North America.* Publications in American Archaeology and Ethnology 38. Berkeley: University of California Press, 1939.

Quinn, Arthur. *Hell with the Fire Out: A History of the Modoc War.* Boston: Faber & Faber, 1997.

Ray, Verne F. "Cultural Element Distributions: The Plateau." *Anthropological Records* 8 (1942): 99-257.

_____. *Cultural Relations in the Plateau of Northwestern America.* Los Angeles: Southwest Museum, 1939.

Ross, John A. "Aboriginal Peoples of the Plateau." In *Northern Columbia Plateau Landscapes,* edited by Michael Folsom. Cheney: Eastern Washington University Press, 1984.

Spencer, Robert F. "Plateau." In *The Native Americans,* edited by Robert F. Spencer, Jesse D. Jennings, et al. New York: Harper & Row, 1965.

Trafzer, Clifford E. *Yakima, Palouse, Cayuse, Umatilla, Walla Walla, and Wanapum Indians: An Historical Bibliography.* Metuchen, N.J.: Scarecrow Press, 1992.

_____, ed. *Northwestern Tribes in Exile: Modoc, Nez Perce, and Palouse Removal to the Indian Territory.* Sacramento, Calif.: Sierra Oaks, 1987.

Walker, Deward E. *Mutual Cross Utilization of Economic Resources in the Plateau: An Example from the Aboriginal Nez Perce Fishing Practices.* Laboratory of Anthropology Report of Investigations 41. Pullman: Washington State University, 1967.

_____, ed. *Plateau*. Washington, D.C.: Smithsonian Institution Press, 1998.

Wilkinson, Charles F. *Fire on the Plateau: Conflict and Endurance in the American Southwest*. Washington, D.C.: Island Press, 1999.

Southeast

LANGUAGE GROUPS: Algonquian, Atakapa, Caddoan, Chitimacha, Iroquoian, Muskogean, Natchez, Siouan, Timucuan, Tunica, Yuchi
TRIBES: Ais, Alabama, Anadarko (Hasinai Confederacy), Apalachee, Apalachicola, Atakapa, Bayogoula, Biloxi, Calusa, Cape Fear, Catawba, Cheraw, Cherokee, Chiaha, Chickasaw, Chitimacha, Choctaw, Coushatta, Creek, Guale, Guasco (Hasinai Confederacy), Hitchiti, Houma, Jeaga, Manahoac (Mahock), Mobile, Nabedache (Hasinai Confederacy), Natchez, Ocaneechi, Ofo, Pamlico, Pawokti, Powhatan Confederacy, Seminole, Texas (Hasinai Confederacy), Timucua, Tiou, Tohome, Tunica, Tuscarora, Tuskegee, Tutelo, Waccamaw, Yamasee, Yazoo, Yuchi

The Southeast culture area is located in the southeastern United States and is one of ten Native American culture areas found in the United States and Canada. The various Southeast Indian groups generally shared the following culture traits: a material culture that included dugout canoes, rafts, blowguns, shields, pipes, feather cloaks, basketry, mats, houses made of pole, thatch, or bark, and stockaded towns, and a nonmaterial culture based on hunting, gathering, and agriculture, dual leadership, socially powerful women, clans, social stratification with a sharply defined class system, sun symbolism, the Green Corn Ceremony, elaborate mortuary rituals, warfare, and war captive torture-sacrifice.

Culture Areas. The culture area concept was developed by Otis T. Mason (1838-1908), Clark Wissler (1870-1947), and Alfred L. Kroeber (1876-1960), among others. These scholars grouped North American aboriginal cultures into geographic regions, defined by cultures in each area which shared numerous similarities. These shared culture traits are considered to have regional significance, representing either common adaptations to the environment or diffusion among the aboriginal groups in the region. Culture areas provide synthetic overviews of human achievements within the different regions of North America. The areal typology organizes the cultural data into regional units which can then be further studied and analyzed. Culture areas allow anthropologists and geographers to move beyond the minutiae of local events to search for broad regional trends and to develop theories of culture contact, diffusion, and change. Taken to the extreme, however, the culture area concept can neglect the influences and histories of tribes and individuals within regions, since it emphasizes broad regional events rather than local occurrences. While the culture area typology was an important theoretical concern to early- to mid-twentieth-century anthropologists—and is still generally employed as a useful organizing principle for discussing Native American groups—anthropological theory has moved beyond the issues of innovation and diffusion that were so important in the early 1900's.

Southeast Geography. The Southeast culture area covers the southeastern United States and generally includes Louisiana, Mississippi, Alabama,

Southeast Culture Area

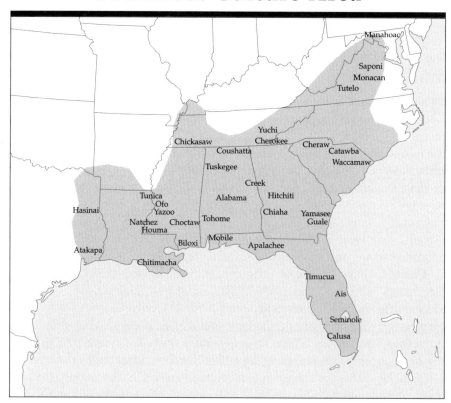

Florida, Georgia, southwestern South Carolina, western North Carolina, Tennessee, and southern Arkansas. The boundaries fluctuated, sometimes expanding to include portions of eastern Texas, eastern Arkansas, the Carolinas, Virginia, West Virginia, and Kentucky.

Generally, the Southeast climate is characterized by year-round warm temperatures and seasonally abundant precipitation, with local variation depending on the latitude or altitude. Physically, the Southeast consists of coastal plains and lowlands, interior fertile river valleys, including the lower reaches of the Mississippi River, and interior low plateaus, with occasional higher peaks, such as the Blue Ridge Mountains, the Appalachians, the Ozarks, and the Ouachita Mountains. The majority of the region is low-lying (elevations of less than 500 feet above sea level), and prehistoric and historic human settlement was concentrated in the coastal and riverine ecozones.

Language, Social Organization, and Subsistence. The Southeast was home to a large number of different Indian groups speaking diverse languages but sharing cultural traits. Speakers of the Muskogean languages dominated in terms of numbers, but there were also speakers of Algonquian, Caddoan, Iroquoian, and Siouan languages, as well as of Atakapa, Chitimacha, Natchez, Timucua, Tunica, and Yuchi.

Beginning in the late prehistoric or early historic period, some southeastern peoples also used a pidgin language for trading purposes, called Mobilian Jargon (also termed Mobilian Trade Jargon, or the Chickasaw-Choctaw Trade Language). The lexical sources are mostly from Muskogean languages, Chickasaw and Choctaw in particular.

Among the Indians of the Southeast, social complexity ranged from loosely structured small hunting and gathering groups to more complexly organized sedentary towns. Generally the settled agricultural peoples are emphasized in regional syntheses, since these groups, with their larger populations, had a greater impact on historical events in the Southeast. In addition, these cultures were featured in colonial documents and histories, since Europeans were better able to understand the lifeways of settled farming peoples than those of the less settled hunting and gathering groups.

Generally, regardless of the degree of social complexity, there was separation by gender in the daily activities of southeastern communities. Women often gathered or cultivated the plants, prepared the food, manufactured the pottery, made baskets, prepared animal skins, made clothing, and manufactured tools for these activities. Male tasks often included hunting, making tools, constructing buildings, clearing land, and waging warfare. The men's lives often revolved around the winter hunting season, whereas the women participated most actively in the planting cycle and household routines. The sexes were often physically separated in ceremonies, in the case of the women during menstruation or birth, and in the case of the men during raiding events.

Occasionally, men or women did not wish to participate in these culturally sanctioned gender roles. In these cases, among many of these groups, it was permissible for a male to behave as a woman or for a female to behave as a man. Transvestism might include a sexual relationship, although not necessarily, and generally such behavior was not censored. This gender-role switching was typically accepted in many North American Indian cultures.

Subsistence-related activities were aided by the manufacture of various tools. Fish were caught using the hook and line, spears, nets, traps, and weirs. Hunters used the bow and arrow and the blowgun, killing deer, turkeys, and buffalo, and often utilized fires or decoys to aid in capturing the animals.

Localized resources, such as salt or flint, were often traded among different groups. The Southeast was noted for the extensive trails and trading arrangements which connected communities to a vast regional system. With European contact, the newcomers contributed their goods and political power to this existing network, which resulted in further changes to a dynamic regional economy. For example, upon the adoption of European arms and trading strategies, aboriginal hunting was often conducted to obtain deer skins for trade rather than only for deer meat and hides for local use.

Farming groups grew domesticated corn, beans, and squash, plus many plants native to the Southeast, such as bottle gourds, sunflowers, sumpweed, chenopodium, pigweed, and knotweed. With the arrival of the Europeans, foreign crops and animals were rapidly adopted: figs, peaches, and watermelon, and chickens, pigs, horses, and cows. Corn served as the subsistence staple and appeared (either boiled, baked, or fried) at almost every meal. Food was preserved through drying, either over the fire or on the ground under the sun. Harvested crops were stored in the houses or sometimes in special granaries.

Farming groups generally lived in large established towns with a central plaza and meeting house. Villages in warmer locations often consisted of wall-less shelters. Some communities built summer and winter houses to cope with varying climatic conditions. Similar climatic adaptations determined the type of clothing, which ranged from minimalist skirts and breechcloths in summer to warmer garments in winter. People often tattooed their faces and bodies and wore various decorative adornments, such as armbands, bracelets, and other items made from copper, shell, or other raw materials.

Southeastern social organization was typically based upon matrilineal kinship—kin relationships traced through the female line of descent. Women could own land, houses, and other possessions and were often honored members of the community, as signified by the Creek and Cherokee "Beloved Women" titles.

Matrilineal kinship ties created a strong bond between the mother's brother and her children, since they were members of the same kinship unit. There was a different sort of bond between the father and his offspring, since they were members of different kinship groups. This fundamental difference in social relationships was not understood by the European colonists who were more accustomed to the father-son relationship typical of a patrilineal society (descent traced through the male ancestors). Europeans were accustomed to dealing with male power and authority, and they often insisted on conducting transactions with men. With colonialism, the traditional authority of women in some cultures was gradually eroded. In addition, colonial economics altered the marriage arrangements among many Southeast groups. The growth of the deerskin trade increased the value of women's work (hide preparation), for individual men could hunt vastly more animals than they could process. It seems likely that the economic incentives to increase deerskin production resulted in increased numbers of polygynous unions, since one man with several wives was a more viable economic unit.

Many of the groups in the Southeast had stratified social classes, often with some sort of dual organization. Many had two leaders, the peace chief and the war chief. In other cases, the villages might be divided into two types; among some Creek, for example, certain communities promoted peace and other communities were devoted to warfare.

Beliefs and Ceremonies. Many of the peoples of the Southeast had similar beliefs concerning the origins of the world and its structure. Often it was envisaged as possessing many levels, each with its own creatures, and special significance was generally attached to the four cardinal directions. For example, many cultures associated the west with the realm of the dead.

There were strong beliefs concerning purity and pollution. For many people, bathing in a stream was an appropriate way to begin the day, providing a sense of purity. Southeastern peoples consumed a ritual beverage, known as the Black Drink, prepared from the leaves of a species of holly (*Ilex vomitoria*), which served to purge their bodies both physically and spiritually.

Various individual rites of passage marked the significant steps from birth through puberty, marriage, and death. The mortuary ceremonies were much commented upon by the European colonists, since they were often spectacular, shocking, and public, in contrast to other more private rituals. For this reason, there is much information available concerning funerals and post-death treatment of the body. For example, the 1715 funeral of Tattooed Serpent, a Natchez war chief, is well documented. His death initiated a months-long chain of events which included public viewing of the body, the provision of food, human sacrifices, the burning of his house, and special treatment of the corpse. Such complex mortuary arrangements were typical for the southeastern elite.

Another ceremony which had importance among the southeastern farming groups was the Green Corn or Busk Ceremony. It was scheduled after the harvest, and therefore its exact occurrence varied from year to year and from south to north, ranging from May to September. This was an event celebrating the bounty of nature and often fertility in general. It typically involved fasting, sexual abstinence, and other forms of purification. The climax of the multiday ritual was the kindling of a new fire and the consumption of the new corn, accompanied by dancing, drumming, playing of the ball game, and other events.

Southeast History. European history of the Southeast commenced with the sixteenth century explorers. By midcentury, Spanish missions were established in Florida and Georgia, and by 1607, the English had founded Jamestown, Virginia. By the late seventeenth century, the English were heavily involved in Indian slavery and deer-hide trading in South Carolina, while the French were exploiting the Mississippi River territories. Southeast Native American life was forever altered by the impact of Europeans in the area, but it nevertheless continued.

Over the centuries, various wars, treaties, and legal maneuvers resulted in native peoples losing much territory; probably the most infamous of these events began with the 1830 Indian Removal Act signed by President Andrew Jackson. This act was designed to allow European settlers to establish farms on lands previously occupied by farming Native Americans. Ironically, it penalized those Indians who had assimilated most successfully into European American society, namely the "Five Civilized Tribes": the Cherokee, Chickasaw, Choctaw, Creek, and Seminole. From 1830-1839, these peoples were systematically marched from their southeastern homes to land in present-day Oklahoma. The routes they took became known as the "Trail of Tears," and they were marked by innumerable shallow graves and abandoned possessions. Despite these ordeals, once in Oklahoma, these refugee groups organized themselves as nations. In 1980, the Five Civilized Tribes in Oklahoma numbered approximately 60,000 Cherokee, 24,000 Choctaw, 15,500 Creek, 6,000 Chickasaw, and 5,000 Seminole.

Twentieth Century. As in Oklahoma, Native Americans in the Southeast have a variety of economic strategies for survival in the modern world. These range from individual money-making endeavors based on traditional crafts (such as basketmaking) or activities (fishing) to community financial undertakings such as bingo and other gambling and various industries. Modern Indian communities must decide on the balance that they wish to maintain between, on the one hand, a traditional Native American lifestyle and, on the other, the dominant American worldview. For many Indian groups, this decision-making process is marked by internal dissention and disagreement concerning the tribal future.

According to the 1980 census, the three largest Southeast Indian groups still in the Southeast are the Cherokee, the Choctaw, and the Seminole. The Eastern Band of Cherokee, located on the Qualla Reservation in North Carolina, had a census-reported population of 5,482; however, Eastern Band tribal rolls included approximately 9,000 members. These people maintain the Southeast's largest federal reservation, founded in 1889.

The Mississippi and Louisiana Choctaw number fewer then 5,000 (although there are 50,000 Choctaw in the United States). The Florida Seminole include approximately 10,000 people, of whom few live on reservations.

Current estimates of southeastern Native American numbers are imprecise measures, since there are many definitions of who is to be considered

Artist Robert Lindneux's 1942 painting Trail of Tears; *the painting is somewhat misleading in that most Indians made the arduous journey on foot.*
(Wollaroc Museum, Bartlesville, Oklahoma)

Indian; numbers vary depending on whether one is enumerating federally recognized Indians, state-recognized groups, or individuals who declare that they are "Indian." (Other ethnic groups in the United States and Canada generally are self-ascribed and do not have to demonstrate their ethnicity.)

In the United States, recognition by the federal government is based on Indian documentation and demonstration that the Native American community has possessed separate and distinct tribal government processes since European contact. The group must be able to prove descent from a historic tribe, and it must be identified in the available records as a distinct cultural entity. Because of these stringent federal criteria, most Native Americans in the Southeast are not federally recognized. Federally recognized groups in the Southeast include the Louisiana Chitimacha (520 members in 1985), the Louisiana Coushatta (350 members in 1985), the Louisiana Tunica-Biloxi (250 members in 1985), the Mississippi Band of Choctaw (8,080 enrolled members in 1990), the Alabama and Florida Poarch Band of Creeks (1,850 enrolled members in 1986), the Florida Seminole (approximately 1,600 enrolled members in 1990), the Florida Miccosukee (approximately 400 members in 1990), and the North Carolina Eastern Band of Cherokee (with a 1980 census population of 5,482 people, while tribal rolls list about 4,000 more members).

The Southeast also is home to a number of triracial groups, descendants of Native Americans, Europeans, and Africans. Generally, such groups have been cut off from federal benefits available to "Indians," although in some cases they have managed to obtain state recognition for their Indian ancestry. In the Southeast, the presence of these triracial groups and the racial divisions within twentieth century American society meant that many Native American peoples were denied educational opportunities. For example, the Houma Indians of southeastern Louisiana were classified as black and thus were not permitted to attend white schools. As a result, many southeastern Native Americans abandoned their Indian heritage in order that their children might have increased opportunities in a segregated society. The Civil Rights Act of 1964 worked to desegregate the schools, expanding the educational options of these Native Americans and permitting many Indian descendants to rediscover their heritage.

Susan J. Wurtzburg

Bibliography

Axtell, James. *The Indians' New South: Cultural Change in the Colonial Southeast*. Baton Rouge: Louisiana State University Press, 1997.

Barker, Alex W., and Timothy R. Pauketat, eds. *Lords of the Southeast: Social Inequality and the Native Elites of Southeastern North America.* Archaeological Papers 3. Washington, D.C.: American Anthropological Association, 1992. Anthology of articles concerning late prehistoric and early historic Native Americans. No comprehensive index.

Boxberger, Daniel L., ed. *Native North Americans: An Ethnohistorical Approach.* Dubuque, Iowa: Kendall/Hunt, 1990. Useful chapter on the Southeast. Charts, maps, illustrations, and photographs. No index.

DePratter, Chester B., ed. *The Late Prehistoric Southeast: A Source Book.* New York: Garland, 1986. An anthology of historically important articles dating from 1788 to 1974. Useful introduction and additional references, but no index.

Hann, John H. *A History of the Timucua Indians and Missions.* Gainesville: University Press of Florida, 1996.

Hann, John H., and Bonnie G. McEwan. *The Apalachee Indians and Mission San Luis.* Gainesville: University Press of Florida, 1998.

Hudson, Charles. *The Southeastern Indians.* Knoxville: University of Tennessee Press, 1976. Coverage of prehistory and history, beliefs, social organization, subsistence, ceremonies, arts, and games. Good index, illustrations, and maps.

Kehoe, Alice B. *North American Indians: A Comprehensive Account.* 2d ed. Englewood Cliffs, N.J.: Prentice Hall, 1992. Contains a useful chapter on the Southeast and recent Native American history. Index, charts, maps, illustrations, and photographs.

Milanich, Jerald T. *The Timucua.* Cambridge, Mass.: Blackwell Publishers, 1996.

Paredes, J. Anthony, ed. *Indians of the Southeastern United States in the Late Twentieth Century.* Tuscaloosa: University of Alabama Press, 1992. Anthology of articles concerning contemporary Native Americans. Comprehensive index, maps, and photographs.

Swanton, John R. *The Indians of the Southeastern United States.* 1946. Reprint. Washington, D.C.: Smithsonian Institution Press, 1979. Overview of Southeast Native American culture and a description of the individual groups. Index, charts, maps, drawings, and photographs.

Usner, Daniel H., Jr. *American Indians in the Lower Mississippi Valley: Social and Economic Histories.* Lincoln: University of Nebraska Press, 1998.

_____. *Indians, Settlers, and Slaves in a Frontier Exchange Economy: The Lower Mississippi Valley Before 1783.* Chapel Hill: University of North Carolina Press, 1992. Detailed reconstruction of the period 1699-1783. Index, charts, maps, and illustrations.

Williams, Walter L., ed. *Southeastern Indians Since the Removal Era*. Athens: University of Georgia Press, 1979. Anthology of articles concerning historic Native Americans. Comprehensive index, photographs.

Wood, Peter H., et al., eds. *Powhatan's Mantle: Indians in the Colonial Southeast*. Lincoln: University of Nebraska Press, 1989. Anthology of articles concerning historic Native Americans. Comprehensive index, maps.

Worth, John E. *The Timucuan Chiefdoms of Spanish Florida*. 2 vols. Gainesville: University Press of Florida, 1998.

Southwest

LANGUAGE GROUPS: Athapaskan, Keres, Kiowa-Tanoan, Uto-Aztecan, Yuman, Zuni

TRIBES: Acoma, Apache (including Chiricahua, Jicarilla, and Mescalero), Cochiti, Havasupai, Hopi, Isleta, Jemez, Karankawa, Laguna, Nambe, Navajo, Picuris, Pima, Pojoaque, San Felipe, San Ildefonso, San Juan, Sandia, Santa Ana, Santa Clara, Santo Domingo, Taos, Tesuque, Tohono O'odham, Walapai, Yaqui, Yavapai, Zia, Zuni

The United States Southwest includes Arizona, New Mexico, and southern Utah and Colorado. The area features rugged terrain and an arid landscape in which agriculture provided an unlikely but solid foothold for the growth of settled populations among the deep canyons and dun-colored mesas. It remains home to many of the most culturally conservative tribes, notably the Navajos and the Pueblo Indians. Southwestern archaeological remains—carefully planned masonry or adobe communities—are major tourist attractions in the region.

Paleo-Indian/Archaic Era. The earliest commonly accepted evidence for humans in the Southwest is from people archaeologists call Paleo-Indians. It dates from the last thirteen thousand years. Widespread habitation probably began about 9000 B.C.E., when highly mobile bands hunted large game animals, gathered wild plants, and killed smaller game as opportunities arose.

By 6000 B.C.E., many of the largest game animals were extinct, and early southwesterners shifted to more generalized hunting and gathering. Archaic period Indians probably operated from central base camps in defined territories by 1800 B.C.E. Archaic culture ended with the adoption of maize horticulture, probably around 1500-1000 B.C.E., but the people were cautious about depending on these new ways, continuing to hunt and gather along with caring for the crops.

Hohokam and Mogollon Cultures. The cultures of the Hohokam and Mogollon, known from their archaeological remains, had developed from

Southwest Culture Area

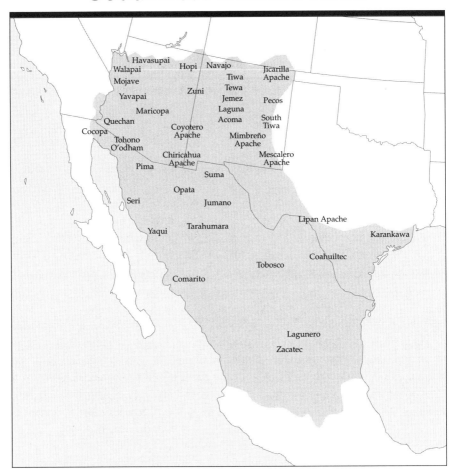

Archaic populations in southwestern New Mexico and southern Arizona by 200 B.C.E., the Hohokam in the valleys of the Gila and Salt rivers, the Mogollon in the uplands of those drainages. The Hohokam had irrigation technology by 700 C.E. There were 500 kilometers (slightly over 300 miles) of main canals in the Salt Valley alone, watering fields of corn, beans, squash, and cotton.

Raw or woven cotton was probably an important export in trade, as were elaborate shell ornaments, pottery, turquoise, jet, and obsidian. Copper bells, parrots, and macaws suggest trade ties to ancient Mexico, as do Hohokam ballcourts and platform mounds. Local exchange of goods and services, however, was probably the main cement that bound the culture together; they probably never shared a single government.

The Mogollon are known for making the earliest pottery yet found in the Southwest, about 300 B.C.E. They lived in small, egalitarian pit house villages with specialized ceremonial rooms, depending on a combination of agriculture and hunted and gathered resources. By 700 C.E. they were trading regularly with the Hohokam, and the cultures mixed at the Mogollon western edge. The Mogollon began irrigation and water run-off control about that time and, particularly in their eastern and northern areas, began to build aboveground architecture, sometimes with large ceremonial structures. The Mimbres Mogollon variant produced finely painted figurative pottery, ceremonially "killed" for interment with the dead.

Both Hohokam and Mogollon cultures disappeared around 1350-1400. The people of southern Arizona reduced the scale of their agriculture, probably because of depleted desert soils and climate change. The Mogollon population split, some withdrawing into northern Mexico while others faded into their Anasazi neighbors to the north.

Anasazi Culture. Most Pueblo Indians are descended from the Anasazi, a Navajo term meaning "ancient others." Anasazi territory included the Little Colorado, San Juan, and northern Rio Grande drainages in New Mexico, Arizona, Colorado, and Utah.

The Anasazi relied on horticulture, hunting, and gathering wild foods. The earliest Anasazi, the Basketmakers, began about 100 B.C.E. as a semi-nomadic population, ranging out from pit house villages. By 400-700 C.E. they were building separate, large ceremonial structures (kivas) and grew beans, cotton, and maize.

The Anasazi began building their characteristic masonry apartment-house-style pueblos about 700 C.E., along with irrigation and soil-control features. The bow and arrow replaced the spear, and the turkey was domesticated. Between 900 and 1100, the Anasazi built planned communities of up to eight hundred rooms throughout their territory. Probably the largest and best known are in Chaco Canyon, but outlying "great houses" of Chacoan style also dot the remainder of the San Juan basin. Another Anasazi variant of this period is represented at Mesa Verde National Park, Colorado. Both areas were largely abandoned by 1300, when prehistoric Puebloan peoples began concentrating in the areas where modern Pueblo tribes live.

The Pueblos. There are twenty different tribes of Pueblo Indians, representing four major language families and six languages. Three Tanoan languages (Tewa, Tiwa, and Towa) join Keresan, Hopi, and Zuni as language groups still actively spoken in their pueblos. A fifth language group, Piro, is now extinct in the Southwest.

The Tanoans and Keresans, called the Eastern Pueblos, live mainly along the northern Rio Grande and its tributaries in northern New Mexico. They include the Tanoan pueblos of Jemez, Taos, Picuris, Isleta, Sandia, San Juan, Santa Clara, San Ildefonso, Nambe, Pojoaque, and Tesuque, as well as the Keresan towns of Zia, Santa Ana, San Felipe, Santo Domingo, and Cochiti. Two other Keresan groups, Acoma and Laguna, are farther west. Zuni and Hopi are the Western Pueblos.

Despite linguistic diversity, the Pueblos share similar architecture and organization of their apartment-house-style villages; horticulture of corn, beans, squash, and sometimes cotton; finely made painted pottery; the beliefs of their ancestor-based kachina religion; and philosophy in which personal aggrandizement is discouraged and group harmony is of paramount importance.

Eastern Pueblo men, women, and children participate in kiva ceremonies. Societies are usually organized by division into moieties (halves), each associated with one kiva. Each moiety has a chief, and power is rotated between moieties semiannually. Moieties also organize community labor for such tasks as caring for the irrigation systems that bring Rio Grande water to the fields. Although many Eastern Pueblo people practice Christianity, indigenous religion also survives in belief and practice, closely guarded and distinct from introduced practices. Many Eastern Pueblo villages are famous for their fine pottery; Keresans are skilled workers in turquoise and shell beads.

The two largest Western Pueblo groups, Hopi and Zuni, are organized into matrilineal clans and into kiva societies in the kachina religion. Usually only men participate in kachina ceremonies, dancing for rain and fertility. Both Hopi and Zuni are noted for fine jewelry and pottery.

Navajos. The Navajos, or Diné, as they call themselves, are the largest traditional Indian tribe in the United States and have the largest land holdings.

Navajo oral and religious history accords with archaeological evidence that they came to their present area between six hundred and eight hundred years ago, probably from Canada. They and the Apaches, also Athapaskan speakers, were probably one group then. In 1598 early Spanish colonists in northern New Mexico encountered Apachean raiders and soon began to differentiate between corn-growing "Apaches de Navaju," probably ancestors of the modern Navajo, and those who were mainly hunters and gatherers, still called Apaches.

Differences between these two Athapaskan groups strengthened after the Pueblo Revolt of 1680, in which Pueblo Indians, aided by some Athpaskans, drove the Spanish colonists out of New Mexico for nearly twenty years. Fearing reprisal, many Rio Grande Puebloans fled to live with the

Navajos. Pueblo traits, such as masked dancers, painted pottery, masonry construction, and probably weaving, along with Spanish livestock, entered Navajo culture. In the mid-eighteenth century, after the Puebloans had returned home, most characteristics now considered a part of traditional Navajo life crystallized, including sheep and goat pastoralism, extended family household units based on the mother-child bond, and the Blessing Way (Chantways) ceremony.

The old raiding pattern remained also, and Navajos often came into conflict with their Pueblo, Spanish, and later American neighbors. This situation led eventually to the capture of more than nine thousand Navajos by Kit Carson in 1863; they were then marched 300 miles to internment at Fort Sumner, or Bosque Redondo, on the brutal "Long Walk." After five years of sickness and starvation, they were allowed to return to about 10 percent of their former range. Reservation lands have been increased many times since 1868. Navajos are known for their fine weaving and silversmithing.

In the arid climate of the Southwest, many societies depending on gathering food from such plants as the saguaro cactus.
(Library of Congress)

Apaches. For the other southern Athapaskans, the Apaches, raiding as an economic strategy became increasingly important in the eighteenth and nineteenth centuries. Although some Apache women planted corn, beans, and squash, the products of the hunt—whether wild or domestic animals—were far more integral to Apache life. Conflict between settlers and Apaches led to warfare, and then to the establishment of seven reservations, the Jicarilla and Mescalero in New Mexico and five Western Apache reservations in Arizona. Some of the Chiricahua and Lipan moved onto Mescalero lands; other Chiricahuas, those who had rebelled under Geronimo, were removed to Oklahoma. Most Apaches were settled by 1872.

O'odham. The modern descendants of the Hohokam people are the Akimel O'odham, or River Pima, and the Tohono O'odham, the Desert Pima or Papago, of southern Arizona. In the historic period, they have traditionally lived in rancherias (communities of family homesteads) near streams, irrigation canals, or wells. Homesteads usually consist of an elderly couple and the families of their married sons, who grow maize, beans, and pumpkins.

The O'odham had sporadic contact with the Spanish from 1540 on and adopted cattle, wheat, and fruit trees from them in the late seventeenth century. Contacts became increasingly negative, however, through the nineteenth century as ranchers and miners encroached on O'odham land, driving a few to become nomadic, living entirely on wild resources. Two main reservations were established in the late nineteenth and early twentieth centuries.

About four thousand Yaqui, a mainly northwestern Mexico tribe, also live in southern Arizona, having moved into the United States as a result of an early twentieth century sovereignty dispute with the Mexican government. Their traditional way of life was similar to that of the O'odham, though each rancheria belonged to one of eight towns. When Mexico wished to assert dominion over the eight towns in 1825, a rebellion began which has continued sporadically since.

Pai. The Yuman-speaking Pai, including modern groupings called the Walapai (or Hualapai) and the Havasupai, live along the most lowland drainage of the Colorado River and a tributary, the Gila. They are related to the Yuma, Mojave, and Maricopa and were once divided into numerous local groups of up to sixty persons who lived by hunting, gathering, and gardening. These small groups joined into larger units only at certain times of the year around particular resources—good gardening areas in summer or large stands of edible wild plants at ripening. At those times, marriages and friendship renewed connections between the groups. They were informally and flexibly organized, each local group coalescing around a respected leader who, though influential, was never in a position of command.

European and American contact with the Pai was sporadic and limited until the establishment of a gold field in their area in 1865 led to war from 1866 to 1869. They were ultimately placed on two reservations, the western and southern Pai together on the Walapai Reservation, and the northeastern band on designated Havasupai lands.

Linda B. Eaton

Bibliography

Anderson, Gary C. *The Indian Southwest, 1580-1830: Ethnogenesis and Reinvention.* Norman: University of Oklahoma Press, 1999.

Crown, Patricia L., and W. James Judge. *Chaco and Hohokam: Prehistoric Regional Systems in the American Southwest.* Santa Fe, N.Mex.: School of

American Research, 1991. A collection of articles on the complex archaeological societies of the Southwest.

Dilworth, Leah. *Imagining Indians in the Southwest: Persistent Visions of a Primitive Past*. Washington, D.C.: Smithsonian Institution Press, 1996.

Erickson, Winston P. *Sharing the Desert: The Tohono O'odham in History*. Tucson: University of Arizona Press, 1994.

Himmel, Kelly F. *The Conquest of the Karankawas and the Tonkawas, 1821-1859*. College Station: Texas A&M University Press, 1999.

John, Elizabeth A. H. *Storms Brewed in Other Men's Worlds: The Confrontation of the Indians, Spanish, and French in the Southwest, 1540-1795*. College Station: Texas A&M University Press, 1975. Outlines the early confrontations between Indians of the Southwest and the Spanish and French.

Kehoe, Alice B. *North American Indians: A Comprehensive Account*. 2d ed. Englewood Cliffs, N.J.: Prentice Hall, 1992. Kehoe includes an informative overview of Southwest cultures.

Ortiz, Alfonso, ed. *Southwest*. Vol. 9 in *Handbook of North American Indians*. Washington, D.C.: Smithsonian Institution Press, 1983. Articles by the currently recognized authorities on aspects of the Navajos, Apaches, Pimas and Papagos, Pais and other non-Puebloan peoples of the Southwest. Well illustrated, excellent bibliography.

Plog, Stephen. *Ancient Peoples of the American Southwest*. New York: Thames and Hudson, 1997.

Ricklis, Robert A. *The Karankawa Indians of Texas: An Ecological Study of Cultural Tradition and Change*. Austin: University of Texas Press, 1996.

Tiller, Veronica E. Velarde. *The Jicarilla Apache Tribe: A History*. Rev. ed. Albuquerque: BowArrow, 2000.

Trimble, Stephen. *The People: Indians of the American Southwest*. Santa Fe, N. Mex.: School of American Research, 1993.

Warren, Scott S. *Desert Dwellers: Native People of the American Southwest*. San Francisco: Chronicle Books, 1997.

Subarctic

LANGUAGE GROUPS: Algonquian, Athapaskan, Eskimo-Aleut
TRIBES: Ahtna, Beaver, Carrier, Chilcotin, Chipewyan, Cree, Dogrib, Haida, Han, Hare, Ingalik, Inland Tlingit, Koyukon, Kutchin, Montagnais, Mountain, Naskapi, Saulteaux, Slave, Tagish, Tanaina, Tanana, Tsetsaut, Yellowknife

The Subarctic culture area covers a huge region, spanning three continents and the coasts of three oceans. For the purposes of a study of North American native cultures, the area can be considered to cover Alaska, the Yukon, the Northwest Territories, Labrador, and the northern portions of British Columbia, Alberta, and Manitoba. There is, however, no clear break between the cultures of North America and those of Greenland, Siberia, and Northern Scandinavia, as these cultures spread long before current boundaries between nations were established, and the cultures remain very similar.

Generally, the native population of the area can be divided into three groupings: Eskimos and Aleuts, Athapaskan Indians (sometimes spelled Athabaskan—the actual sound is an aspirated *p*, which cannot be rendered in the English alphabet), and the Northwest Coast Indians. These are three distinct cultures and will be discussed separately below. It should be noted that the term "Eskimo" has engendered some controversy (with many Canadian Arctic and Subarctic natives, for example, preferring "Inuit"), but it is used here because it incorporates a large number of groups that cannot easily be united under any other term and because it has a long scientific tradition of usage.

Prehistory. The people of the Subarctic did not have a written language before the arrival of European explorers and missionaries, and physical evidence is in short supply owing to the harsh climate and sparse population. Most modern archaeologists, however, have agreed that the North American continent was first settled by immigrants from Asia during the last Ice Age, over a land bridge across the Bering Strait, which now separates Alaska from Siberia. During the Ice Age, sea level was considerably lower,

Subarctic Culture Area

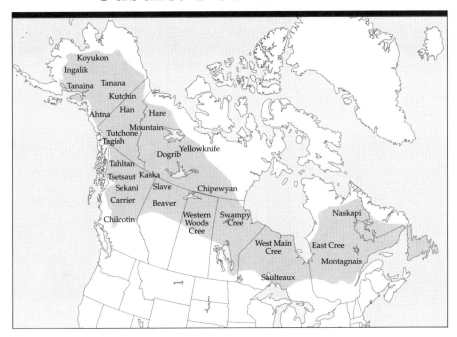

and the islands that now exist in the Bering Strait were once almost certainly mountain peaks on that land bridge.

At least two, and probably three, separate migrations occurred, according to linguistic evidence. It is impossible to date these migrations accurately, but the land bridge probably existed from about twenty-five thousand to ten thousand years ago, so the migrations must have taken place during those time spans. It is likely that the people we call Athapaskans were the first to arrive, because they later made much farther inroads south. Surprisingly, the Athapaskan languages of Alaska are closely related to the Apache and Navajo but are not apparently related to the language groups that exist in the huge area between Alaska and the Southwest United States. The area in between is populated by people who speak a completely different family of languages, including Tlingit, Haida, and Tsimshian in Alaska and a great number of languages in Washington, Oregon, and Northern California. The gap in cultures remains a mystery, but these groups may represent a second migration.

The third group involved were the Eskimos and Aleuts. Modern linguists generally believe that the two groups split about three thousand years ago. Between eight hundred and eighteen hundred years ago, the

Eskimo language split into a number of dialects, but the dialects are not nearly as different as one might expect, considering the huge distances involved. The language and culture of Eskimos in northern Alaska and in Greenland are similar enough so that the people can communicate more easily than can most people in bordering countries in Europe.

The Natural Environment. Before considering the conditions of modern-day Subarctic cultures, it is important to dispel some stereotypes that many people unfamiliar with the territory have formed. There is a stereotypical tendency to picture Eskimos in igloos, living in a frozen wasteland that is dark six months out of the year. While this environment certainly exists, it is limited to areas near the North Pole and at high elevations. Several other climatic situations exist in the Subarctic.

Along the west coast of Alaska, British Columbia, and Washington State, there is a warm ocean current (the Japanese Current), similar in nature to the Gulf Stream that warms the western coast of Europe, and the temperatures are warmer than one might expect. Temperatures in Anchorage, Alaska, are actually warmer, on the average, than in many parts of New York and New England. In the interior, temperatures can reach 70 degrees (Fahrenheit) below zero during the long winter nights, but summer days can be as warm as 80 above.

The Eskimos. The old Eskimo culture is a rapidly dying one. While there are still people living in igloos and wearing sealskins, and while Eskimo languages are still spoken, most modern Eskimos have taken advantage of Western civilization and removed themselves from the harsh life of their ancestors. By and large, it is only in the most remote places that Eskimo civilization as it once existed can still be found.

These areas are remote indeed. In Alaska, for example, only one road runs north of Fairbanks; beyond the Yukon River it is a private road built by the Alaskan Pipeline companies that is still inaccessible to the general public. The Alaskan Highway is built of gravel and is unsuitable for travel by car for approximately six months of each year. There are many villages that remain largely untouched by Western civilization. These villages can be reached only by plane or by dogsled, and they are hardly tourist attractions.

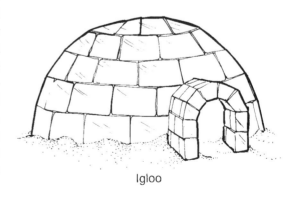

Igloo

According to archaeological evidence, Eskimos once occupied considerable inland territory that is now mostly inhabited by Athapaskans and people of European ancestry, but it is impossible to determine when they abandoned these lands to others. At present, Eskimos are largely confined to the coasts of the Arctic, Atlantic, and Pacific Oceans and probably number about thirty to forty thousand, an extremely sparse population considering the area involved.

The Aleuts. There are only a few thousand people in the present day who consider themselves Aleuts. They primarily inhabit the Aleutian Islands, an archipelago stretching southwest from the Alaskan mainland. They are apparently related closely to the Eskimos, at least linguistically, but they may also be related to the Athapaskans farther inland. They also may have a tie to the natives of Siberia, though this is much harder to determine.

The Athapaskans. The Athapaskans presently comprise a great number of tribes over a wide range of territory. For some undetermined reason, as mentioned above, they appear to be closely related to some of the tribes in the southwestern United States, but there is a large group of tribes in between. Currently, they inhabit most of interior Alaska as well as the Yukon and the Northwest Territories.

The Athapaskans encompass what is in some ways a strange mixture of cultures. They were among the last American Indians to be "discovered" by people of European descent and were largely unknown before the Alaskan gold rush of the late nineteenth century. When gold was discovered along the Yukon River, the Athapaskans were found to be already in control of the land; they were not especially upset by the arrival of whites. There was an attempt by Christian missionaries to convert the native people they found in Alaska and the Yukon. This effort was successful only on a superficial level. Until the 1970's, most of the territory the Athapaskans controlled in Alaska was still Indian Territory, never ceded to the United States by treaty. During that time, much of the land became national park or national monument land, but this has had little effect on the lives of the people who live there.

The largest numbers of Athapaskans in the Subarctic live along the Yukon and Tanana rivers in Alaska and the Yukon. Most speak English, although the native dialects are still used for religious ceremonies. Generally speaking, Christianity is common but has not replaced older customs. Like many American Indian groups, the Athapaskans believed in many gods and had no objection to accepting Jesus Christ into the pantheon. At important times such as births, deaths, and marriages, two ceremonies often take place: a Christian ceremony conducted in English and a native one conducted in the native language.

Marc Goldstein

Bibliography

Bancroft-Hunt, Norman. *People of the Totem*. New York: G. P. Putnam's Sons, 1979. A description of the Northwest American Indian culture, including a study of their history, ceremonies, and contemporary conditions.

Bandi, Hans Georg. *Eskimo Prehistory*. Translated by Ann E. Keep. College: University of Alaska Press, 1969. An archaeological study of early Eskimos, including illustrations, diagrams, and maps, and discussing their history from their arrival on the American continent until the 1960's.

Bone, Robert W. *Fielding's Guide to Alaska and the Yukon*. New York: Fielding Travel Books, 1990. A traveler's guide, mostly involving areas that can be reached by car. Includes some useful information about where to find artifacts and living examples of the native cultures of the area.

Catton, Theodore. *Inhabited Wilderness: Indians, Eskimos, and National Parks in Alaska*. Albuquerque: University of New Mexico Press, 1997.

Hamilton, Charles. *Cry of the Thunderbird: The American Indian's Own Story*. Norman: University of Oklahoma Press, 1972. A compilation of articles by American Indians about their culture, including memories of childhood, historical beginnings, and contemporary conditions.

Helm, June. *Prophecy and Power Among the Dogrib Indians*. Lincoln: University of Nebraska Press, 1994.

Hensel, Chase. *Telling Our Selves: Ethnicity and Discourse in Southwestern Alaska*. New York: Oxford University Press, 1996.

Lowry, Shannon. *Natives of the Far North: Alaska's Vanishing Culture in the Eye of Edward Sheriff Curtis*. Mechanicsburg, Pa.: Stackpole Books, 1994.

Spencer, Robert F., Jesse D. Jennings, et al. *The Native Americans*. 2d ed. New York: Harper & Row, 1977. An encyclopedic discussion of American Indian culture, from prehistory to contemporary times.

Tribes and Traditions

Abenaki

CULTURE AREA: Northeast
LANGUAGE GROUP: Algonquian
PRIMARY LOCATION: New England, Quebec
POPULATION SIZE: 1,469 Abenaki, 2,173 Penobscot in U.S. (1990 U.S. Census); 945 Abenaki in Canada (Statistics Canada, based on 1991 census)

The Abenaki form a cross-border ethnic group that is organized in several autonomous communities. There are three reservation-based Abenaki bands: Odanak (St. Francis) and Wolinak (Becancour) in southern Quebec, and Penobscot (Old Town) in Maine. The St. Francis/Sokoki band of Abenakis of Vermont is a landless group headquartered in Swanton. The total population of these groups has been estimated at fifty-five hundred. Their native tongue, spoken by few, belongs to the Eastern Algonquian language family. Calling their homeland *Wabanakik* ("Dawnland"), they draw their name from *Wabanaki* ("Dawnlanders"). Because of cultural similarities between the Abenaki and their neighbors, Wabanaki has become a collective term for western Abenaki (Odanak, Wolinak, and Swanton) and eastern Abenaki (Penobscot) as well as Passamaquoddy, Maliseet, and Micmac. Historically, it also embraced now-extinct communities at Moosehead Lake, Norridgewock (Kennebec River), Amesokanti (Sandy River), Amirkangan (Androscoggin River), Pequawket (Saco River), Pennacook (Merrimack River), Sokoki (Connecticut River), and Missisquois (Lake Champlain).

Prehistory. While tribal legends recall a culture hero, the mythic giant Gluskap (or Odzihozo, for western Abenaki), as creator of Dawnland humans, prehistoric evidence shows that Paleo-Indians migrated to this area eleven thousand years ago. It appears that Abenaki ancestors first arrived some three thousand years ago. The region features mixed spruce-fir and hardwood forests, interrupted by swamps, lakes, and rivers; it also has a long, indented coastline. Abounding with fowl, fish, and game, the region offered the migratory Abenaki a rich subsistence based on hunting (bear, deer, moose, beaver, and seals), fishing (eel, salmon, and sturgeon), collecting shellfish (lobsters, oysters, and clams), and gathering (roots, berries, and nuts). Moving about, they walked on snowshoes and pulled toboggans during winter, and they paddled birchbark canoes the rest of the year.

Periodically, Abenaki families banded together in groups of up to three hundred people, their birchbark wigwams clustered in temporary settle-

Mid-nineteenth century illustration of the Abenaki leader Samoset meeting the Pilgrims in 1621. (Library of Congress)

ments. Most of the year, however, they lived in smaller units of ten to fifty people, representing one or more extended families. They elected a band chief ("sakom") to whom they turned for leadership. With the exception of pottery, introduced approximately twenty-five hundred years ago, Abenaki culture remained largely unchanged until the introduction of horticulture between 1200 and 1600 C.E. In the fertile valleys from Lake Champlain to the Kennebec River, Abenaki women began to raise corn, squash, and beans in fields cleared by men. Becoming semipermanent sedentary communities of up to 1,500 people, some Abenaki groups began fortifying their villages against raiders. Because hunting, fishing, and gathering remained important, families shifted residence between these villages and temporary camps in their hunting territories.

Colonial Period. In the early 1600's, Abenakis began regular trade with European newcomers, bartering beaver and other pelts for commodities such as steel knives, axes, copper kettles, woolen blankets, and alcohol. Contact brought a series of epidemics (especially smallpox) and stunning mortality rates (90 percent), reducing Abenaki numbers from about 25,000 to 2,500 in a century. By the 1620's, English colonists had begun settling "widowed" coastal lands. Meanwhile, Abenaki survivors regrouped and armed themselves with muskets acquired from French and English merchants. Paying for trade goods with furs, Abenakis and neighboring groups soon faced shortages and competed for hunting grounds. This resulted in conflicts known as Beaver Wars, pitting Abenaki warriors against Iroquois and other enemies.

From the 1640's onward, French missionaries converted Abenakis to Christianity, and the baptismal ritual gave expression to their alliance with the French, which lasted throughout the colonial era. From 1675 onward,

Abenakis fought repeatedly against British aggressors: King Philip's War (1675-1676), King William's War (1688-1699), Queen Anne's War (1702-1714), Governor Dummer's War (1721-1726), King George's War (1744-1748), and the so-called French and Indian War (1754-1763). During these colonial wars, they were joined by Micmac, Maliseet, and Passamaquoddy, with whom they formed the Wabanaki Confederacy. Raids by English militia and scalp bounty hunters forced the Abenaki to flee most of their traditional settlements in New England. Their famous mission village at Norridgewock, where Jesuit missionary Sebastien Rasle had been active since the 1690's, was attacked and burned to the ground in 1724.

Modern Period. When France surrendered Canada to the British, thousands of white settlers invaded Abenaki lands. In New England, only Abenakis residing in the Penobscot Valley could secure a reservation (in 1796). Having found refuge in Roman Catholic mission villages in French Canada since the 1670's, Abenakis at Odanak and Wolinak also gained title to the small tracts where they had their settlements. In the nineteenth century, no longer able to subsist as hunters, some tried farming. Most turned to seasonal wage-labor (lumbering), guiding sport hunters, or making splint-ash basketry. Others drifted to cities such as Boston or Montreal for industrial employment.

Since the 1960's, Abenakis have embarked on a process of cultural revitalization. Fighting for native rights, they have booked numerous achievements. In 1980, the Penobscot settled an immense land claims case against the state of Maine, which gave them federal recognition and $40.3 million, mostly earmarked for land acquisition. By the mid-1990's they owned two hundred islands in their river and 55,000 acres of trust land in nearby Penobscot County. On a spiritual level, they have revived the sweat-lodge ritual and other ancient ceremonies. Similar efforts are made by their Abenaki relatives in Vermont and Quebec.

Harald E. L. Prins

Bibliography

Calloway, Colin G. *The Western Abenakis of Vermont, 1600-1800: War, Migration, and the Survival of an Indian People.* Norman: University of Oklahoma Press, 1990.

Day, Gordon M. "Western Abenaki." In *Northeast*, edited by Bruce G. Trigger. Vol. 15 in *Handbook of North American Indians*, edited by William Sturtevant. Washington, D.C.: Smithsonian Institution Press, 1978.

Haviland, William A., and Marjory W. Power. *The Original Vermonters: Native Inhabitants Past and Present.* Rev. ed. Hanover, N.H.: University Press of New England, 1994.

McBride, Bunny. *Women of the Dawn*. Lincoln: University of Nebraska Press, 1999.

Morrison, Kenneth M. *The Embattled Northeast: The Elusive Ideal of Alliance in Abenaki-Euramerican Relations*. Berkeley: University of California Press, 1984.

Prins, Harald E. L., and Bruce J. Bourque. "Norridgewock: Village Translocation on the New England-Acadian Frontier." *Man in the Northeast* 33 (1987): 263-278.

Snow, Dean. "Eastern Abenaki." In *Northeast*, edited by Bruce G. Trigger. Vol. 15 in *Handbook of North American Indians*, edited by William Sturtevant. Washington, D.C.: Smithsonian Institution Press, 1978.

Speck, Frank G. *Penobscot Man: The Life History of a Forest Tribe in Maine*. Philadelphia: University of Pennsylvania Press, 1940.

Achumawi

CULTURE AREA: California
LANGUAGE GROUP: Hokan
PRIMARY LOCATION: Northern California
POPULATION SIZE: 1,640 (1990 U.S. Census)

The Achumawi, also known as the Pit River Indians, live in the northeastern corner of California. They are not really one tribe, but eleven autonomous bands. "Achumawi," the name of one of these bands, serves as a kind of collective label. The other ten are the Aporige, Astarwawi, Atsuge, Atwamsini, Hammawi, Hewisedawi, Ilmawi, Itsatawi, Kosalextawi, and Madesi.

Like all California Indians, the Achumawi were well adapted to their environment. Summer houses were lashed-together poles covered by reed or tule mats; winter dwellings were semi-subterranean, with a wood frame covered by a layer of earth, tule, or bark.

The Achumawi fished, hunted, and gathered for their subsistence. Seeds, roots, and insects were collected, and game such as deer, beaver, and badger were hunted. The Achumawi dug pits to trap deer, a practice which led the first whites who came in contact with them to dub them the "Pit River people."

The Achumawi's clothing was made of deerskin and shredded juniper bark, and their basketry attained the level of fine art. Bows and arrows were used in hunting; the arrowheads were made of obsidian (a volcanic glass).

Among the Achumawi, shamans were highly respected for both religious leadership and their encyclopedic knowledge of medicine and healing. Boys would go out to the mountains to seek a *tinhowi*, or guardian spirit, when they reached adolescence. The *tinhowi* would impart supernatural powers to the young men.

The first whites to come to Achumawi lands were trappers in about 1828. There were about three thousand Achumawi at that time. Later, during the California gold rush, a great influx of white settlers threatened the Indians' way of life.

In spite of the problems of the past, the Achumawi are fortunate enough still to be living

Achumawi woman and her baby, in a traditional cradleboard, during the late nineteenth century. (Library of Congress)

on ancestral land. The X-L Ranch Reservation, founded in 1938, contains 8,700 acres in six parcels. Not all Achumawi live on the reservation. The tribe maintains a health-care center and tribal office at Burney, California. In the early 1990's, there were efforts by such companies as Pacific Gas and Electric to gain control of forested Achumawi reservation lands for development.

Adena

DATE: c. 1000 B.C.E.-200 C.E.
LOCATION: Southern Ohio, Indiana, Kentucky, West Virginia, western Pennsylvania
CULTURE AFFECTED: Hopewell

The Adena culture, which flourished between about 1000 B.C.E. and 200 C.E., was the first in a "spectacular series" of North American Early Woodland societies. With its classical heartland situated in a large area around Chillicothe, Ohio, the Adena culture was found in southern Ohio, eastern Indiana, northern Kentucky, West Virginia, and southwestern Pennsylvania. Its name is derived from Adena, the estate of an early Ohio governor that was situated near a mound on a hillside overlooking Ohio's first capital.

Mound Builders. The early American settlers of the trans-Appalachian West were astounded at the existence of thousands of earthen "mounds" in an area stretching from the Gulf of Mexico to the Great Lakes and from the Mississippi to the Saint Lawrence rivers. The tribes that were living in the region were as uninformed as to the origins of these earthworks as were the European American immigrants. Initially it was assumed that the prehistoric "mound builders" were one people. Only with the scientific exploration of these earthworks in the late nineteenth century did it become evident that there were a series of cultures represented in the construction of mounds, the earliest being the Adena. By about 500 B.C.E. they had produced the most complex and organized way of life found in the Americas north of Mexico.

Arriving in what is now the American Midwest by the start of the first millennium B.C.E., the Adenans avoided the malarial wetlands near the Great Lakes and the dense forestlands of Appalachia, preferring to settle in the open, rolling, well-drained valleys along the Ohio River and its tributaries. Here they practiced both food gathering (hunting, fishing, and harvesting fruits, berries, and herbs) and food producing (corn, squash, gourds, pumpkins, sunflowers, sumpweed, goosefoot, and, for use as a ceremonial substance, tobacco). Some mining (of gypsum) and trading (of copper, mica, and seashells) across the American heartland supplemented their economy, which was, perhaps, able to support a population density of one person per square mile.

Material Culture and Settlements. This rich and diverse economy enabled the Adenans to craft sophisticated tools and ornaments. Adenan sites have yielded such artifacts as stone and copper axes, adzes, celts, hoes, projectiles, crescents, gorgets, beads, bracelets, and carvings. Particularly remarkable are the stone tube pipes, such as one found at the Adena mound near Chillicothe, Ohio, which carries the effigy of a man wearing a set of large spool-shaped earrings and a breechcloth (decorated with the figure of a snake); he has bare feet (as if dancing), his hair is carefully braided, and his mouth is open (as if singing). Small stone blocks, deeply carved and engraved—for example with the picture of a hunting bird—have been found, perhaps having been used for printing designs on woven cloth. In addition to creating many types of woven materials, the Adenans were accomplished potters.

Adenan settlements were usually in the river valleys, near fields, gardens, and water. Both single-family units and structures capable of housing forty or more people have been found. Perhaps ten or more buildings characterize these permanent sites. The pattern of a typical Adenan house was circular in floor plan, conical in appearance. Perhaps 26 feet in diameter, the home would be sustained by six main uprights, drawing additional support from forty or fifty smaller staves around the circumference. The "roundhouse" had a hard-pounded dirt floor (with indentures for storage pits and the central hearth), with bark and thatch for a roof and walls of intertwined branches. There were also transient camps, used in hunting and trading, containing two to four dwellings.

Massive Earthworks. The Adenans are most remembered for their massive earthworks. Two major theories have been offered to explain the Adenan practice of building mounds. One, the diffusionist doctrine, suggests contact with Mexico and the dissemination of both corn cultivation and pyramid construction to the Ohio Valley at the same time. The other, the developmental theory, contends that the accumulation of surplus wealth through a successful economy enabled the Adenans to engage in gigantic public works projects. Perhaps the answer is found in a combination of both approaches. With better agricultural production, an increased population, improved social organization, and long-distance trade and communication, the Adenans had the means and the motive to engage in building monumental architecture.

Between three and five hundred Adenan mounds have been found; they vary greatly in size and purpose. Some are in ceremonial or symbolic shapes, such as the Great Serpent Mound near Peebles, Ohio. More than 1,330 feet long, 15 to 20 feet in width, and averaging a height of 4 feet, it represents an outstretched serpent (with coiled tail) with head and jaws closing on another mound, variously said to be an apple or an egg. Other Adenan mounds are circular or square, perhaps enclosing sacred sites where religious rites were conducted. Common are the tomb mounds. Some of these were burial plots for single funerals, and some were for multiple funerals. Both children and leaders (chiefs, priests, great hunters, warriors, and expedition leaders) had mound burials. Cremation and bodily burial were both practiced.

From archaeological excavation it has been determined that mound construction was a community project. Initially the ground was cleared—the scrub timber being burned and the site being leveled. If entombment was planned, either graves were dug in the base or corpses were placed in a log building erected on the site. Hundreds of laborers, carrying baskets and skin aprons full of dirt, would then complete a low, rectangular ridge of dirt and begin the "inner" or "first" mound. Sticks, shells, hoes, and animal bones were used to loosen soil. Over the core mound, the outer shell was raised, often being as much as 100 feet high and covering several acres.

The fate of these brilliant prehistoric builders is disputed. Since their influence is evident in subsequent cultures in the Ohio Valley, the best guess is that they were assimilated by their successors, especially the Hopewell people, after 200 C.E.

C. George Fry

Bibliography

Jennings, Jesse D., ed. *Ancient Native Americans*. San Francisco: W. H. Freeman, 1978.

Kehoe, Alice B. *North American Indians: A Comprehensive Account*. Englewood Cliffs, N.J.: Prentice Hall, 1981.

Korp, Maureen. *The Sacred Geography of the American Mound Builders*. Lewiston, N.Y.: Edward Mellen Press, 1990.

Scheele, William E. *The Mound Builders*. Cleveland, Ohio: World, 1960.

Silverberg, Robert. *The Mound Builders*. Athens: University of Ohio Press, 1986.

Waldman, Carl. *Encyclopedia of Native American Tribes*. New York: Facts on File, 1988.

Webb, William S., and Raymond S. Baby. *The Adena People, No. 2*. Columbus: Ohio State University Press, 1957.

Webb, William S., and Charles E. Snow. *The Adena People*. Lexington: University Press of Kentucky, 1945.

Ahtna

CULTURE AREA: Subarctic
LANGUAGE GROUP: Athapaskan
PRIMARY LOCATION: Copper River, Alaska
POPULATION SIZE: 101 (1990 U.S. Census)

The Ahtna were divided into Lower, Middle, and Upper autonomous bands, with a warlike stratified society of chiefs, nobles, commoners, and slaves organized into matrilineal clans and moieties. Their subsistence base was diversified with fishing, hunting, trapping, and gathering; their major food source was fish. They engaged in extensive trade with neighboring groups and distant Eskimo, and they utilized the potlatch to recognize status change, life crises, and for redistribution of traditional forms of wealth.

The first Ahtna-white contact was with Russian explorers in 1783, who established Copper Fort to protect fur-trading activities and who also introduced smallpox. The American fur trade began in 1876, and the 1898-1899 gold rush brought thousands of prospectors. Finally the military arrived in 1899 to explore the area and to protect the non-Indians, who had meanwhile introduced tuberculosis to the area.

The presence of the U.S. Army in Alaska during World War II intensified cultural change and the shift to a cash economy. Some employment is available through tourism, but most young people must leave to find employment in Anchorage. The number of college graduates among Ahtna youth is increasing.

Ais

CULTURE AREA: Southeast
LANGUAGE GROUP: Muskogean
PRIMARY LOCATION: Indian River, east coast of Florida

The Ais were a Muskogean-speaking tribe who occupied the area along the Indian River on the east coast of Florida. Their principal village was located near Indian River Inlet.

They were primarily fishers and gatherers who traveled the adjacent waterways in dugout canoes. In the seventeenth and eighteenth centuries the Ais apparently dominated neighboring tribes to the north and south, while they were dominated by the Calusa to the west.

A shipwrecked Basque sailor seems to have been the first Spaniard to live with them and learn their language. In 1565, the Spanish governor, Pedro Menéndez, visited and established relations with them. A peace treaty was signed in 1570. In the 1590's the Ais sought an alliance with the Spanish, but the overtures were fruitless, as were others in later years. In 1609 an Ais chief, joined by minor coastal chiefs, visited the city of St. Augustine, where the chiefs were baptized. Evangelization by the Spanish, however, was never successful. The remaining Ais, probably numbering a few hundred, along with neighboring Indians, were removed to Cuba after Florida was ceded to Great Britain in 1763.

Information on the Ais is derived primarily from Spanish sources. The spelling of their name varies: Aix, Aiz, Alis, and Jece.

Alabama

CULTURE AREA: Southeast
LANGUAGE GROUP: Muskogean
PRIMARY LOCATION: Alabama, Louisiana, Texas
POPULATION SIZE: 750 ("Alabama Coushatta," 1990 U.S. Census)

The Alabamas first came into contact with white explorers under Hernando de Soto in 1541, and by 1696 they were trading with Carolina traders. Later, they allied with the French. The tribe was part of the Creek Confederacy and lived on the Alabama River just below the junction of the Coosa and Tallapoosa rivers. They lived in permanent villages and were hunters, fishers, and farmers; they cultivated potatoes, corn, peas, and fruit trees.

In the mid-1700's many moved to Louisiana near the town of Opelousas, on the Opelousas River. The Alabamas who stayed took an active part in the Creek War of 1813-1814 and offered to help Andrew Jackson in the war against the Seminoles in 1828. This remnant was removed in 1836 to Indian Territory (Oklahoma).

After the Alabama migration, Louisiana was acquired by the United States in the Louisiana Purchase, and the Alabamas moved to the Spanish Territory of East Texas, near the town of Livingston. This settlement area was declared a reservation for the Alabama and Coushatta Indians in 1840. The state of Texas purchased the land in 1854 and vested the title in the Indians as a tribal unit.

The Alabamas prospered in Texas when game was plentiful but turned to farming as game decreased. The sandy soil produced poor crops, however, and poverty soon was widespread. By the late 1800's, the Alabamas were in great difficulty, surviving by finding work with logging companies. In 1928, citizens of Livingston as well as the Texas Federation of Women's Clubs succeeded in obtaining more than $100,000 from the U.S. government for the reservation, and Texas gave additional aid. When the Depression struck, the tribe suffered. Since that time, living conditions have improved. The reservation has a school and a hospital, and there are Indian-owned businesses.

The Alabamas have demonstrated remarkable patriotism. When the United States went to war in 1914, more than half the males of the tribe immediately volunteered. Many Alabamas served during World War II, and the members of the tribe bought more war bonds than the average citizen.

Aleut

CULTURE AREA: Arctic
LANGUAGE GROUP: Eskimo-Aleut
PRIMARY LOCATION: Alaska and the Aleutian Islands
POPULATION SIZE: 10,052 (1990 U.S. Census)

The Aleut, consisting of two main groups, the Atka and Unalaska Aleut, probably migrated from Siberia about 6000 B.C.E. into Alaska and moved into the Aleutian Islands around 2000 B.C.E. Their name comes from the Russian word meaning "barren rock." "Atka" is the Aleutian word for island, and "Alaska" comes from the Aleutian word for mainland. The Aleut people occupied about a dozen of the hundred or so islands (the Aleutians) that stretch from Alaska more than 1,200 miles into the Pacific. Their language resembles that of the Eskimos (Inuits). Aleuts and Eskimos moved to the New World significantly later than American Indians did. The Unalaskas live on islands close to the Alaska coast, while the Atkas live on remote islands in the Pacific.

Society and Subsistence. Aleut culture is similar to the Eskimo way of life. Both depend heavily on the sea for their existence. Seal hunting was the most important economic activity, and Aleuts became expert at this task. Most food came from the ocean, including whale meat, fish, oysters, and clams. Aleut hunters learned to navigate by following ocean currents, and they could travel on the water at night simply by feeling the direction of the wind. In times when hunting failed to bring home enough food, Aleuts ate seaweed and birds' eggs. The eggs were gathered by lowering a man on a rope over the side of a cliff to the nests, a very dangerous practice that led to many deaths and injuries.

Aleuts lived in small, isolated villages with populations of a hundred or less and no more than twelve houses. They built homes of logs, whale-bones, and skins sunk at least 3 feet into the ground. A ladder from the roof provided an entranceway, and people sat inside on mats in these window-less structures. Each house contained several families, and polygamy (a man having more than one wife) and polyandry (a woman having more than one husband) were both permitted. A chief (toyon) headed each community, and every village had its own leader; no central authority existed among the Aleuts. The chief, who inherited his office, settled quarrels, protected village hunting grounds, and led the villagers in time of war. In return he received a portion of all foodstuffs acquired by villag-ers during hunts. Chiefs usually became quite wealthy but could lose their positions if they exhibited cowardice during battle.

Because of the large number of villages, there were disputes and quarrels over hunting boundaries, and Aleuts frequently fought with one another. They usually attacked their enemies at dawn, killing the warriors and taking women and children as slaves. High-ranking enemies such as a chief and his sons could also be enslaved. Aleut society had three major classes: chiefs, warriors, and slaves.

Religion. Traditional Aleut religion revolved around worship of Agudar, the creator of the universe, the provider of good fortune, and the guardian of paradise. The men worshiped in a sacred place, usually in a cave or at a certain rock, and excluded women and children. Only adult males could make offerings of sealskins and feathers and learn the sacred language of the spirits. Aleuts believed that the human spirit lived on but became invisible after death and protected loved ones still in the earthly world from harm. Death led to cremation for slaves and commoners, but important leaders and young children were mummified by removing their internal organs through a hole in the chest. Family members then laid the body in a stream until it was clean, stuffed it with grass, oiled it, wrapped it in furs, and placed it in a dry cave. They suspended the body aboveground in a cradle and left. Shamans contacted the spirits of the dead and learned about hunting prospects and what the future held. Traditional religion disappeared after initial contact with Russian fur trappers and missionaries. Most Aleuts converted, sometimes forcibly, to the Eastern Orthodox faith, and it has remained the principal religion of survivors.

Material Culture. The severe climate and shortage of natural resources placed major limitations on Aleut material culture and art. They made clothes from fur, birdskin, and whale intestines. Generally, their parkas and dresses reached to their ankles. Aleuts did not wear shoes or foot covering. They made wooden hats, and hunters wore well-designed wooded eye shades to protect their eyes from the glare while at sea.

Artists produced masks and bowls from the bones and intestines of whales, sea otters, and other mammals. Pottery was nonexistent, and most food containers were skins. Aleut women made fine baskets of wild grasses, however, that became noted for their geometric designs and expert craftsmanship. Hunters built their own kayaks, an especially prized and important possession. They were light and fragile and built to individual body measurements. At sea they could travel at a relatively rapid 7 miles per hour. Hunters used spears thrown by hand from a sitting position in the kayak. Bows and arrows were used only in warfare. Aleuts killed whales with poison-pointed spears and let the bodies drift to shore, where they were butchered.

First contact with the Russians took place in the early 1700's, with devastating consequences for the native population. Between 1750 and 1780 almost 90 percent of Aleuts, who numbered about 25,000 before contact, died from smallpox, malnutrition, forced labor in Russian hunting parties, and even suicide. Aleuts proved such good hunters that Russian trappers forced them to pursue seals and otters almost constantly. The Russians forced all males to hunt seals and otters; refusal meant torture or death. Women and children left behind in isolated villages with little food during these forced hunts frequently starved to death. By the 1840's, after less than a century of Russian domination, fewer than 4,200 Aleuts remained alive. When the United States bought Alaska, which included the Aleutian Islands, in 1867, the Aleut population stood at fewer than 3,000. American control did not lead to better conditions. A tuberculosis epidemic in the 1890's and migration to the mainland reduced the number of islanders to 1,491.

Recent History. In 1911 the United States Department of the Interior prohibited the hunting of sea lions, a major resource of the Aleuts, because overhunting had led to a huge decline in their population. Two years later the Aleutian Islands became a National Wildlife Refuge, and the department banned most other hunting without a special permit. In the 1920's and 1930's a majority of Aleut males left their homes, heading for the Alaska coast to work in salmon canneries. During World War II the U.S. Navy removed all Aleuts from their island villages after the Japanese invaded Kiska and Attu in the far western Pacific and resettled them in southeastern Alaska. Only a few hundred returned to their homes when the war ended, and they found that many of their villages had been destroyed by American soldiers to prevent the Japanese from using them. Government officials gave the returnees rabbits to raise for food, but most of the animals died of disease or were eaten by rats. The experiment ended quickly. No crops could be raised in the rainy, cold (temperatures seldom get above 50 degrees), and windy climate.

Economic development was limited in the islands. The U.S. Navy built a large base on Adak Island but hired whites from the mainland for most available jobs. Work existed for only a few dozen native men, chiefly at the underground nuclear testing base on Amchitka Island. Those who remained in Alaska continued working in salmon and tuna canning factories. The death rate on the islands remained very high, especially among infants, into the 1970's, when the U.S. Public Health Service opened a facility on a remote island, the first hospital many Aleuts had ever seen. The Aleut League, formed in 1967, pressed for more economic assistance but had little success. The number of natives hovered around three thousand, far too few people to make any impression upon the federal government in Washington. Schools in the islands began bilingual education in 1972, and Aleut customs were taught, but extreme poverty remained the major problem. War on Poverty programs in the late 1960's provided some job training and literacy classes, but they created no new jobs, so out-migration continued. A majority of Aleuts now live on the mainland. Fewer than fifteen hundred live in the islands, where the only permanent jobs are found as support staff at government-owned facilities. The Department of Commerce, National Marine and Fisheries Service, controls seal hunting and pays hunters for their catches but in scrip, which can be spent only in local stores. For most Aleuts, life remains as hard and difficult as the climate in which they live.

Leslie V. Tischauser

Bibliography

Kohlhoff, Dean. *When the Wind Was a River: Aleut Evacuation in World War II.* Seattle: University of Washington Press, 1995.

Matthiessen, Peter. *Oomingmak: The Expedition to the Musk Ox Island in the Bering Sea.* New York: Hastings House, 1967.

Pallas, Peter S. *Bering's Successors, 1745-1780.* Edited by James R. Masterson and Helen Brower. Seattle: University of Washington Press, 1948.

Ray, Dorothy Jean. *Aleut and Eskimo Art: Tradition and Innovation.* Seattle: University of Washington Press, 1981.

_____. *The Eskimos of Bering Strait, 1650-1898.* Seattle: University of Washington Press, 1975.

Algonquin

CULTURE AREA: Northeastern
LANGUAGE GROUP: Algonquian
PRIMARY LOCATION: Ontario, Canada
POPULATION SIZE: 5,780 in Canada (Statistics Canada, based on 1991 census); 1,543 in U.S. ("Algonquian," 1990 U.S. Census)

The Algonquin people, originally from eastern Canada and what would become the northeastern United States, gave their name to the language group of Algonquian speakers. Central Algonquians, including the Ottawas, Potawatomis, and Illinois, were pushed westward to the Great Lakes region by their hereditary Iroquois enemies in the mid-seventeenth century. The Algonquins proper, also enemies of the Iroquois, stayed in areas colonized by both the French and the English. Their tendency to prefer trade and military alliances with the French worked to their advantage, since French colonial rivalry with Iroquois-supporting Britain meant periodic support from a European ally in inter-Indian warfare.

Until the British finally pushed the French out of Canada in the 1760's, this pattern enabled the Algonquins to hold considerable territory in the Ontario region, communicating with other related tribes in areas that would become the United States. Prominent examples of this included the Wabanaki (most notably the Passamaquoddies and Penobscots of Maine and the Micmacs of New Brunswick) and, farther south, the Wampanoag Federation. The latter had alliances with the famous seventeenth century tribe of Massachusetts (from the name of Massasoit, a dominant leader at the time of Pilgrim colonization).

The warring aggressiveness of the Iroquois, coupled with the already visible heavy hand of British colonialism on the Atlantic seaboard, caused the decline of the Algonquin tribal network by the end of the eighteenth century. Algonquins in Ontario, who became part of the Canadian reserve system, had a better chance of survival than those to the south in the United States.

Algonquin leader Massasoit (center), who gave his name to both a tribe and a state.
(Library of Congress)

95

By the nineteenth century, centuries of disruptions and dislocations had all but destroyed traditional Algonquin culture. Modern Algonquin population estimates vary according to what groups are considered "Algonquins." By the most inclusive definition, including the Abitibi, Kitcisagi, Nipissing, and other groups, there may be more than six thousand Algonquins in the U.S. and Canada.

Alsea

CULTURE AREA: Northwest Coast
LANGUAGE GROUP: Penutian
PRIMARY LOCATION: Oregon coast
POPULATION SIZE: 12 (1990 U.S. Census)

Alsea is the name given to the peoples of Yakonan stock occupying a small territory at (and near) the mouth of the Alsea River along the coast of western Oregon. The modern form of this name is a variant of the Alsean word *Alsi'*. Based upon linguistic classification, they are speakers of a language which is part of the Alsean family of the Penutian language phylum and appear to be most closely related to the Yaquina people.

Little is known of their early history. They remained on and around their traditional territory after they were assigned to the Siletz Reservation in the mid-1800's, because their territory was part of the original reservation. When the reservation was reduced in size in 1875, they were removed to the new Siletz Reservation.

Before the arrival of significant numbers of white settlers, the Alsea lived in small villages on both sides of the river and at the river mouth, engaged in a primarily riverine and woodland lifestyle based on fishing, hunting, and gathering. On the north side of the river were the villages of Kutauwa, Kyamaisu, Tachuwit, Kaukhwas, Yulehais, Kakhtshanwaish, Shiuwauk, Khlokhwaiyutslu, and Melcumtk. On the south side of the river were the villages of Yahach, Chiink, Kauhuk, Kwulisit, Kwamk, Skhakhwaiyutslu, Khlimkwaish, Kalbusht, Panit, Thielkushauk, and Thlekuhweyuk. At the mouth of the river was the village of Neahumtuk. The Alsea are affiliated with the larger political unit of the Confederated Tribes of Siletz Indians of Oregon. In the 1990 U.S. Census, twelve people identified themselves as Alsea.

Anadarko

CULTURE AREA: Southeast
LANGUAGE GROUP: Caddoan
PRIMARY LOCATION: North of Anadarko, Oklahoma; northwest of Nacogdoches, Texas

The Anadarko, or Nadako, were a tribe of the Hasinai Confederacy of the Caddo. They were first encountered by Europeans in northeastern Texas by members of Hernando de Soto's expedition in 1542. Later, in the late seventeenth century, they were living on the southern edge of what is now Rusk County, Texas.

The Anadarko and the other Hasinai formed a loose confederacy of settled farmers who lived in scattered ranchos in the bottomlands. They were primarily farmers and hunters and had elaborate religious and political systems. On a number of occasions the Spanish sought to establish missions among them, but to no avail. The French from Louisiana provided them with guns and trade goods, which allowed them to maintain their independence.

In the late eighteenth century, other Indian tribes and white Americans began to encroach on their lands. Protests to Spanish and, later, Mexican officials did little to restore their independence. Poor relations with the Republic of Texas drove the Anadarko and their Indian neighbors to central Texas. After Texas became a state, the Anadarko and other Indians were removed to Oklahoma in 1859.

After the Civil War they were finally able to obtain a reservation north of the Washita River and settled down to farming. In 1891 they ceded their lands to the government but had them restored in 1963. They are concentrated around their tribal center north of Anadarko, Oklahoma. The late twentieth century saw a cultural revival among Anadarko and other Hasinai.

Anasazi

DATE: c. 300 B.C.E.-1600 C.E.
LOCATION: Southwest
CULTURES AFFECTED: Navajo, Pueblo (Zuni, Hopi)

The term "Anasazi" is a corruption of a Navajo term meaning either "ancient ones" or "enemies of our ancient ones." The Navajo applied the term to ancient peoples responsible for extensive architectural ruins scattered throughout the modern states of New Mexico, Arizona, Utah, and Colorado. Throughout the nineteenth and early twentieth century, archaeologists believed these ruins to be a colonial or provincial extension of the Aztec or Toltec cultures of Mexico. During the 1920's, however, cultural anthropologists and archaeologists began to understand the Anasazi as an indigenous southwestern culture directly ancestral to the modern Pueblos.

Pre-contact History. Archaeologists have identified Anasazi sites throughout the southwestern United States, but the greatest concentration is in the Four Corners region of southern Utah and Colorado and northern New Mexico and Arizona. From these sites, archaeologists have reconstructed and named various stages of the evolution of Anasazi culture (some of the dates that follow are currently in dispute among archaeologists).

By 300 B.C.E., the agricultural/horticultural tradition that originated in central Mexico at least nine thousand years ago had spread to what is now the southwestern United States through cultural diffusion. Groups of Indians in the Southwest began cultivating maize, squash, and beans to augment the foodstuffs they acquired through hunting and gathering, often using primitive irrigation methods. Archaeologists call this formative period "Basketmaker I" and consider it to have begun around 300 B.C.E. (Some archaeologists consider Basketmaker I to be a part of the Archaic period.)

During the Basketmaker I period the Anasazi represented one group of agriculturalists among many in the southwestern area. Their art and architecture were virtually indistinguishable from those of other farmers scattered from present-day California to Texas: They constructed pit houses, wove textiles from wild plants, and left a few impressive paintings and carvings on rock walls.

Between 300 and 500 C.E., the Anasazi underwent a cultural revolution that made them clearly distinct from their neighbors. The Basketmaker II period among the Anasazi witnessed the introduction of large villages composed of pit houses (houses built largely underground). They began making distinctive pottery, beautiful baskets woven from native plants, and textiles woven from cotton.

During the ensuing Basketmaker III period (circa 500-750 C.E.), the Anasazi villages became larger and more numerous. Each village had a ritual room, which archaeologists call the kiva, used for religious ceremonies. The pit houses became larger and more complex, and each had an adjoining storage room for stockpiling food. Pottery making and textile weaving became more complex with the introduction of intricate designs and brilliant colors. Irrigation systems became more common and more elaborate as agriculture became the main form of subsistence, although hunting and gathering remained an important supplement to the Anasazi economy. The bow and arrow came into common use among the Anasazi during this period; they were probably imported from Mexico.

Archaeologists call the next stage of Anasazi cultural evolution the Developmental Pueblo period (circa 750-1100, called Pueblo I and Pueblo II in another common classification system). During this period, Anasazi communities greatly increased in number and size and spread as far west as Utah and northern Arizona. The pit houses gave way to multistoried houses constructed of dry masonry, adobe, or cut rocks joined to form massive structures somewhat resembling modern apartment complexes. These structures contained many kivas, some huge, some small, all increasingly elaborate, arguing for increasing religious diversity as the Anasazi absorbed neighboring tribal peoples. Famous Anasazi sites such as Chaco Canyon in New Mexico and Mesa Verde in Colorado originated during this period.Extensive trade began during the Developmental Pueblo period among the various Anasazi towns and between the Anasazi and cultures as distant as the Mississippi Valley, the Pacific coast, and Mexico. Pottery making and textile weaving became art forms as well as an integral part of the Anasazi economy.

Around 1100, Anasazi culture entered what archaeologists call the "Classic Pueblo" (Pueblo III) period, which lasted until around 1400. During this era,

The imaginatively named "Cliff Palace" in Mesa Verde National Park was built by the Anasazi, who suddenly abandoned it in the late thirteenth century. (PhotoDisc)

Anasazi architecture reached its zenith. The famous and impressive ruins at Chaco Canyon, Mesa Verde, and Kayenta assumed their modern proportions. Cut sandstone became the primary building material at many of the sites, which took on increasingly aesthetically pleasing contours, obviously planned by the builders. Some of the towns housed populations of ten thousand or more; the total Anasazi population increased to more than a hundred thousand. Pottery and textile weaving became more refined; trade and commerce became more important to the economies of the Anasazi communities, as evidenced by a well-planned road system connecting some of the towns.

The final stage of Anasazi civilization began in the fourteenth century and lasted until about 1610. Sometimes called the Regressive Pueblo Period (Pueblo IV), the era witnessed profound changes in Anasazi culture. Many classic towns were abandoned. Neighboring communities adopted Anasazi architectural and artistic styles. More primitive hunting and gathering peoples moved into Anasazi territory, some assimilating into Anasazi culture, others apparently waging war against the Anasazi towns. New styles of pottery making and coloring replaced classic Anasazi methods, and a religious revolution (apparently imported from Mexico) occurred with the introduction of worship of supernatural beings called kachinas.

European Contact. When the Spaniards under Francisco Vásquez de Coronado penetrated the Anasazi region in the mid-sixteenth century looking for the fabled seven cities of gold, the Anasazi entered the realm of history. The Spanish described ten Anasazi provinces whose people spoke at least six different languages. Older men and clan societies governed the individual towns, with warrior societies playing an important role. Inheritance was usually matrilineal, and the Spanish noted little social/economic stratification. Each town was politically independent, but during times of war it was not unusual for several towns to ally together against nomadic peoples or against other towns, or to ally with nomadic peoples against other towns. Only once, during the great Pueblo Revolt of 1680 against the Spanish, did all or most of the Anasazi cooperate together against a common foe. By the time of the Spanish penetration, the Anasazi had abandoned most of the stone towns and moved to locations in areas which had little stone suitable for architecture. They often built their new towns from adobe brick, which led archaeologists to characterize this era as "Degenerative Pueblo," a misleading label. The art and culture of the Anasazi people during this era were in no way inferior to those of the Classic period.

Conflict and animosity marked Spanish-Anasazi relations from the first contact between the two cultures. Most anthropologists date the end of the Anasazi period to 1610, by which time Spanish dominance in the former Anasazi area had become well established. Nevertheless, in a very real sense, the Anasazi are still with us in the form of several Pueblo towns that have survived to the present. Pueblo towns such as the one at Taos, New Mexico, retain many elements of Anasazi culture, relatively untouched by modern civilization.

Paul Madden

Bibliography
Ambler, J. Richard. *The Anasazi: Prehistoric People of the Four Corners Region.* Flagstaff: Museum of Northern Arizona, 1977.
Berry, Michael S. *Time, Space, and Transition in Anasazi Prehistory.* Salt Lake City: University of Utah Press, 1982.
Brody, J. J. *The Anasazi: Ancient Indian People of the American Southwest.* New York: Rizzoli International, 1990.
Cheek, Larry. *A.D. 1250: Ancient Peoples of the Southwest.* Phoenix, Ariz.: Arizona Highways, 1994.
Cook, Jeffrey, and William R. Current. *Anasazi Places: The Photographic Vision of William Current.* Austin: University of Texas Press, 1992.
Cordell, Linda S. *Prehistory of the Southwest.* Orlando, Fla.: Academic Press, 1984.
Ferguson, William M. *The Anasazi of Mesa Verde and the Four Corners.* Niwot: University Press of Colorado, 1996.
Morrow, Baker H., and Robert C. Heyder, eds. *Anasazi Architecture and American Design.* Albuquerque: University of New Mexico Press, 1997.
Muench, David, and Donald G. Pike. *Anasazi: Ancient People of the Rock.* New York: Crown, 1974.
Reid, J. Jefferson, and Stephanie M. Whittlesey. *The Archaeology of Ancient Arizona.* Tucson: University of Arizona Press, 1997.
Roberts, David. *In Search of the Old Ones: Exploring the Anasazi World of the Southwest.* New York: Simon & Schuster, 1996.
Sebastian, Lynne. *The Chaco Anasazi: Sociopolitical Evolution in the Prehistoric Southwest.* New York: Cambridge University Press, 1992.

Apache

CULTURE AREA: Southwest
LANGUAGE GROUP: Athapaskan
PRIMARY LOCATION: Arizona, New Mexico, Oklahoma
POPULATION SIZE: 50,051 (1990 U.S. Census)

The Apaches belong to the Athapaskan linguistic group, believed to be the last group to have crossed over to North America from the Asiatic continent. Most of the Athapaskan speakers spread out into northern Canada and down the Pacific coast, but ancestors of the Apaches pursued a more interior route, probably moving south along the eastern flank of the Rocky Mountains. At some point, the group that would become the Navajos split off, although retaining enough linguistic similarity to enable Navajo and Apache speakers to converse. The Apaches spread out in the Southwest, inhabiting primarily the areas now known as Arizona, New Mexico, Texas, and northern Mexico. They were driven west from the southern Plains in the eighteenth century by the Comanches.

Apache wickiup. Although this structure is commonly associated with the Apaches, the word "wickiup" itself is believed to come from the Algonquian languages of the Northeast. (National Archives)

Traditional Culture. They called themselves Tin-ne-áh, or "the people," as many American Indian groups did in their own languages. The origin of the name "Apache" is widely disputed but is agreed to have been given to them by their enemies. The Apaches separated into two broad groups,

Western and Eastern. The Eastern Apaches were the Plains groups, the Jicarilla and the Lipan, whose culture showed the influence of contact with other Plains tribes. To the west were three main divisions: the Mescaleros, the Chiricahuas, and the Western Apaches. Five major groups made up the Western Apaches. The White Mountain, which had a Western and an Eastern (often called Coyotero) band, held the largest territory. The remaining four Western groups were the San Carlos or Gileños, the Cibicues, and the Southern and Northern Tontos. These bands were further subdivided into smaller, extended family groups that supported their highly mobile existence, each designated by its own particular name, often associated with a favorite haunt. Defining early Apache bands is made difficult by the Spanish practice of naming a band for the location where they were encountered, or after a powerful chief.

Life in the deserts of the Southwest was harsh, and the Apache way of life prepared its members for survival with a rich and meaningful culture. Folktales involving Coyote and other animal spirits illustrated proper as well as improper behavior and its consequences. Spirituality was inherent in every aspect of life, and great care was taken to observe rituals and taboos. The number four was important, and the east was favored as the most holy direction.

Although bands were small and children were valued highly, a crying baby could betray the entire group to extinction by enemies. Thus, from early infancy, the Apache child was trained in self-control. The ability to remain motionless and to be quiet for long periods of time, a skill learned in the cradleboard, served the grown warrior well as he hunted or waited in ambush for an enemy.

The most important time in an Apache child's life occurred at puberty. For girls, this was marked by the onset of menses and celebrated by a puberty ceremony that lasted four days, involving blessings with sacred pollen and culminating in the girl's run to the east. During the four days, the girl assumed the identity of White Painted Woman, a supernatural figure of the Apache creation myth. An Apache boy was inducted into manhood by serving an apprenticeship to raiding warriors. The novice was required to observe certain taboos and carry special equipment on four raids, and was required to perform camp tasks such as gathering wood and cooking for the warriors.

Adult Apache men and women had clear, gender-defined tasks. Women were responsible for gathering and processing wild foods, cooking what they gathered as well as any meat brought in by the men and boys, and the manufacture of all necessary camp equipment, clothing, and personal effects—except weapons. Women also constructed the family dwelling. Although some of the Plains Apaches used the tipi, camps were usually composed of the brush-covered wickiups, easy to construct and then abandon. A man's primary task while in camp was to make weaponry, and arrow-making took up most of his time. His other responsibilities were hunting and raiding or war. A married man became an economic contributor to his wife's family.

Contact and Resistance. The earliest contact of Apaches with European explorers is believed to have occurred in the sixteenth century. The Spanish were pushing north from New Spain (Mexico), and several parties encountered bands whose description matched that of Apaches. Raiding for supplies was an important part of Apache life, leading inevitably to conflict with Europeans. The earliest known violence involved Gaspar Castano de Sosa, whose party set out for adventure and were raided by a band of Apaches, who captured some stock and killed an Indian with Castano's party. Men were sent to punish the raiders; they killed and captured several of the raiding party.

As colonization progressed, Spanish soldiers were accompanied by Roman Catholic priests eager to convert any subdued Indians. The converts were used as ready labor, often as slaves, to build missions and rancherias in the vast new country of the Southwest. In the seventeenth century, the Pueblo Revolt on the northeastern frontier sent the Spanish south, with Eastern Apaches attacking the Spaniards as they fled. The Spanish returned, however, and by 1697 once again occupied the region.

When the Mexicans won their freedom from Spain in 1824, peace agreements made with various Apache groups were abandoned. Raiding, which had never stopped, increased as the new government could not field any force to match the Apaches. Trouble on the Santa Fe Trail, which was established in 1822, led to a bounty being placed on Apache scalps. By the time the area passed into United States control after the Mexican-American War, Apaches had a reputation as fearsome enemies.

Apache and American relations were frustrating for both sides. The Apaches found that farming, which the United States government expected them to embrace as their new livelihood, did not always provide for their families—and they could not understand why the Americans opposed their continued raids into Mexico for supplies. Treaties made by the United States government were often broken for political expediency. Apache leaders were lured with promises of peace, then arrested and sometimes killed. Army officers would spend years establishing peaceful relations with key Apache leaders, only to see their efforts destroyed by a single party of drunken vigilantes bent on exterminating any Apaches they could find, these generally being helpless women and children.

Chiricahua Apache chief Geronimo in 1887, the year after his surrender to Nelson A. Miles. (National Archives)

The course of the Apache Wars is a tangled story of capitulation, betrayal, and outbreaks of tribes believed to have been "pacified." One by one the Apache bands were subdued as the U.S. military moved relentlessly west. Treaties settled the Jicarillas and Mescaleros on reservations, but occasional outbreaks occurred. After they made peace, some of the Lipans served as army scouts, as did Apaches from other groups.

There is some evidence that hostilities were prolonged by the machinations of a secret group known only as the "Tucson Ring" or "Indian Ring"; for a time, the only lucrative business for whites in Arizona was supplying the troops who were fighting the Apaches. To the west, the Mimbres band of the Chiricahuas led by Mangas Coloradas clashed openly with the Americans over matters of justice and harassment by settlers. Cochise, another Chiricahua leader, was provoked into war by the treachery of military authorities involving a white boy who had been captured by a different group of Apaches.

The peace sought by a band of Arivaipa Apaches led by Eskiminzin was broken by an attack on their farming settlement. One hundred twenty-five sleeping men, women, and children at Camp Grant were killed by a mob of civilians from Tucson, who had taken advantage of the absence of the fort's main garrison. Among the last Chiricahua holdouts were the famous Geronimo and Naiche, last hereditary chief of the Chiricahuas. More effective fighting on foot in the rugged hills of their familiar country in both Mexico and the United States, these Apaches managed to fight and elude army troops for years, surrendering only when they could no longer escape the Apache scouts used to hunt them.

Following their military defeat, various groups of Apaches were settled on reservations in Arizona, New Mexico, Texas, and Oklahoma. The Fort

Apache and San Carlos reservations in Arizona were established jointly in 1871 for Arivaipa, Chiricahua, Coyotero, Mimbreño, Mogollon, Puraleno, and Tsiltaden Apaches. This reservation was partitioned in 1897. Also in Arizona are the Fort McDowell, Tonto Apache, and Yavapai Apache reservations. The Jicarillas and Mescaleros each have reservations in New Mexico, with the Jicarilla reservation extending northward into Colorado as well. In Oklahoma, there is the Fort Sill Apache Reservation.

Modern Apaches. Far from being vanishing Americans, Apaches had grown in population to about fifty thousand by 1990. Weathering the extremes and changes of United States government policy, most Apaches have chosen to remain on their reservations. Some groups have been fortunate in the availability of natural resources; others have continued to struggle at subsistence-level poverty, assisted by government programs designed to help them with their specific needs.

The Jicarilla Apache tribe is a member of the Council of Energy Resource Tribes (CERT), founded in 1975; it obtains income from the exploitation of coal, natural gas, oil, and geothermal energy.

The San Carlos Apache Tribe is governed by a Tribal Council of elected officials serving four-year terms. Of a total reservation population of 10,000, enrolled tribal members equal 7,639; total enrolled tribal membership is 10,500. Located approximately 100 miles east of Phoenix, Arizona, the reservation has three distinct terrains: desert highlands, mountain ridges covered in grass and trees, and forested mountains abundant in wild game. The tribe has adopted an Integrated Resources Management Plan to exploit a stable economy. Timber, recreation and wildlife, agriculture, and ranching bring in additional revenue for the tribe and are being actively developed.

The White Mountain Apache Tribe, whose reservation is contiguous with the San Carlos, also govern by Tribal Council. They, too, benefit from the availability of exploitable natural resources, including an 800,000-acre ponderosa pine forest that supports the Fort Apache Timber Company. The tribe operates a ski resort which boasts the best ski runs in the southwestern United States and provides scenic campgrounds. Apache Enterprises operates businesses such as gas stations and restaurants throughout the reservation.

The Tonto Apaches have not been as fortunate. A small group numbering 106, with 88 members living on their reservation, they are also governed by Tribal Council. Economic development projects include a Tribal Market/ Smokeshop and an eighty-unit motel, but more space is needed for housing and other development. Irrigation of a 5-acre community fruit orchard is under way, and the tribe is attempting to acquire 1,500 acres of land.

Despite relocation efforts of the twentieth century, most Apaches desire to remain on their reservations in proximity to their families. Those who have left to seek employment off the reservation often return after a short while to their more familiar lifestyle and culture. Like so many Americans, Apaches are working hard to prosper while retaining their traditional cultural identity.

Patricia Masserman

Bibliography

Baldwin, Gordon C. *The Apache Indians: Raiders of the Southwest*. New York: Four Winds Press, 1978. Stated attempt is to be inclusive of Apache history and culture, rather than a rehash of the Apache Wars. Includes and treats the Navajo as an Apache tribe. Contains a map of "Apache Country," numerous photographs, and line drawings.

Boyer, Ruth M., and Narcissus D. Gayton. *Apache Mothers and Daughters: Four Generations of a Family*. Norman: University of Alabama Press, 1992.

Cuevas, Lou. *Apache Legends: Songs of the Wind Dancer*. Happy Camp, Calif.: Naturegraph Publishers, 1991.

Griffen, William B. *Apaches at War and Peace: The Janos Presidio, 1750-1858*. Norman: University of Oklahoma Press, 1998.

Haley, James L. *Apaches: A History and Culture Portrait*. New York: Doubleday, 1981. An excellent revisionist text that covers Apache history and culture in great detail. Intersperses narrative with brief tales gathered from Apache folklore. Draws upon a wide a variety of sources, including memoirs of U.S. military participants, to detail the painful course of Apache resistance and capitulation. Contains useful notes, secondary bibliography, and comprehensive index.

Hermann, Spring. *Geronimo: Apache Freedom Fighter*. Springfield, N.J.: Enslow, 1997.

Meadows, William C. *Kiowa, Apache, and Comanche Military Societies: Enduring Veterans, 1800 to the Present*. Austin: University of Texas Press, 1999.

Meed, Douglas V. *They Never Surrendered: Bronco Apaches of the Sierra Madres, 1890-1935*. Tucson, Ariz.: Westernlore Press, 1993.

Opler, Morris E. *Myths and Tales of the Chiricahua Apache Indians*. Lincoln: University of Nebraska Press, 1994.

Perry, Richard J. *Apache Reservation: Indigenous Peoples and the American State*. Austin: University of Texas Press, 1991.

Roberts, David. *Once They Moved Like the Wind: Cochise, Geronimo, and the Apache Wars*. New York: Simon & Schuster, 1993.

Stockel, H. Henrietta. *Survival of the Spirit: Chiricahua Apaches in Captivity*. Reno: University of Nevada Press, 1993.

_____ . *Women of the Apache Nation: Voices of Truth*. Reno: University of Nevada Press, 1991.

Sweeney, Edwin R. *Cochise: Chiricahua Apache Chief*. Norman: University of Oklahoma Press, 1999.

_____. *Mangas Coloradas, Chief of the Chiracahua Apaches*. Norman: University of Oklahoma Press, 1998.

Terrell, John Upton. *Apache Chronicle*. New York: World Publishing, 1972. A century-by-century account of the Apaches' contact with Europeans, beginning with the Spanish in the sixteenth century and ending with the final surrender of Geronimo in 1886. Contains notes, select bibliography, and index.

_____ . *The Plains Apache*. New York: Thomas Y. Crowell, 1975. Finding a dearth of works focusing solely on the Plains Apaches, Terrell sets out to fill in the gap with an extensive treatment of these groups who differed in aspects of culture and experience from their western cousins. Extensive notes, select bibliography, and index.

Worcester, Donald E. *The Apaches: Eagles of the Southwest*. Norman: University of Oklahoma Press, 1979. Focuses on hostilities between the Apaches and a succession of invaders: Spanish, Mexican, and United States troops. Notes, bibliography, and index.

Apache Tribe of Oklahoma

CULTURE AREA: Plains
LANGUAGE GROUP: Apachean (Southern Athapaskan)
PRIMARY LOCATION: Oklahoma
POPULATION SIZE: 1,400 (1993 tribal census)

The Apache Tribe of Oklahoma, or Na-i-shan Dené ("Our People"), sometimes misnamed Kiowa Apache, were a unique Apache-speaking tribe of Plains Indians distinct from the Apaches of the Southwest and politically independent of their Kiowa allies. There were a number of Apache groups on the Great Plains in the seventeenth and eighteenth centuries, but the small Na-i-shan Apache tribe was the only one to survive as Plains Indians until the reservation period. Their tribal traditions, which are supported by those of the Kiowas and other tribes, indicate northern origins for the Na-i-shan and long-term residence on the Great Plains.

History. It is difficult to identify the Na-i-shan in early documents because they were often known—both to other tribes and to Europeans—by names that also meant "Apaches" generally. They are identifiable on the northern Great Plains by 1805. At that time they were described as traders of horses to the farming tribes of the upper Missouri River. They are then recorded to have shifted their range gradually southward across the Plains until they were settled on the Kiowa, Comanche, and Apache (KCA) Reservation in present southwestern Oklahoma late in the nineteenth century. They seem to be the Apaches del Norte, whose arrival in New Mexico with a group of Kiowas was recorded early in the nineteenth century, as well as the Plains Lipans who reportedly arrived on the northern frontier of Texas at about the same time with Kiowa and Arapaho allies and were escorted farther south by Lipan emissaries.

The alliance and close association with the Kiowa tribe are said to be ancient; in the summer they joined in the Kiowa tribal Sun Dance encampment. The two tribes made an alliance with the Comanches about the year 1800 in the course of their movement southward. With the expansion of the frontier and the decimation of the buffalo, the Na-i-shan and their allies signed treaties with the United States. The last of these, the Treaty of Medicine Lodge in 1867, limited the apparently unsuspecting Kiowas, Comanches, and Na-i-shan Apaches to the reservation in present southwestern Oklahoma. That reservation was allotted in 160-acre tracts to individual members of the three tribes in 1901, over heated Indian protest. Most of the rest of the reservation was then opened to settlement by European Americans.

Traditional Culture. The nineteenth century Na-i-shan were a mounted buffalo-hunting people who lived in tipis and had Plains Indian medicine bundle, warrior, and medicine society complexes. The tribe has no traditions of a time before they lived on the northern Plains or of ever having practiced agriculture or making pottery or basketry. Their material culture was that of the Plains Indians; their economy depended upon the buffalo hunt and the trading of horses and mules taken in Mexico northward. They numbered about 350 and were unified by kinship, a common language and culture, reverence for their medicine bundles, and membership in their sodalities. Children of both sexes first joined the Rabbit Society, whose spirited dances were directed by a tribal elder. The Blackfeet Society was composed of warriors, and it acted as the tribal police. Senior warriors could belong to the *Klintidie*, whose vows required them never to retreat from the enemy. Elderly women might belong to the *Izouwe*, a secret society of grandmothers. Other societies existed as well, but little has been recorded of them. The societies generally owned certain songs, dance motifs, and regalia and met periodically, particularly when the tribe gathered for ceremonies and socializing and the summer buffalo hunt.

Recent History and Modern Life. The occupation of the former KCA Reservation by a flood of non-Indian homesteaders and speculators in 1901 took place when the Na-i-shan population had dwindled to its lowest point, about 150, primarily because of epidemic disease. Their recent history has been one of rapid population growth, gradual adjustment to the changed circumstances of increased involvement in the affairs of American society, and determined efforts to preserve their cultural heritage.

In the 1970's a tribal government was formed to administer federal programs and otherwise benefit the tribe's members. In the 1980's the tribe's official designation was changed from the misleading term "Kiowa Apache" to Apache Tribe of Oklahoma. The people generally refer to themselves as Plains Apaches or simply as Apaches. The tribe has an administrative complex, which it also uses for educational and social activities, in Anadarko, Oklahoma, as well as a nearby bingo facility and convenience store. Tribal pow-wows take place in June and August at their dance ground west of Fort Cobb, Oklahoma. In 1993 a formal committee of elders and a tribal research committee were organized to preserve their cultural heritage and facilitate relevant research. The Na-i-shan Apaches are notable for their rich repertory of traditional music and dance. They often excel in painting, silverwork, and beadwork, as well as in other arts and crafts.

Michael G. Davis

Bibliography

Beatty, John. "Kiowa-Apache Music and Dance." In *Occasional Publications in Anthropology*. Museum of Anthropology Ethnology Series Paper 31. Greeley: University of Northern Colorado, 1974.

Bittle, William E. "A Brief History of the Kiowa Apache." *University of Oklahoma Papers in Anthropology* 12, no. 1 (1971): 1-34.

Lassiter, Luke E. *The Power of Kiowa Song: A Collaborative Ethnography*. Tucson: University of Arizona Press, 1998.

McAllister, J. Gilbert. "Kiowa-Apache Social Organization." In *Social Anthropology of North American Tribes*, edited by Fred Eggan. Enlarged ed. Chicago: University of Chicago Press, 1955.

Meadows, William C. *Kiowa, Apache, and Comanche Military Societies: Enduring Veterans, 1800 to the Present*. Austin: University of Texas Press, 1999.

Merrill, William L., ed. *A Guide to the Kiowa Collections at the Smithsonian Institution*. Washington, D.C.: Smithsonian Institution Press, 1997.

Mooney, James. *Calendar History of the Kiowa Indians*. Bureau of American Ethnology Annual Report, 1895-1896. Vol. 2. Reprint. Washington, D.C.: Smithsonian Institution Press, 1979.

Apalachee

CULTURE AREA: Southeast
LANGUAGE GROUP: Muskogean
PRIMARY LOCATION: Northwestern Florida

The Apalachee, a branch of the Muskogean family, lived in northwest Florida along the Apalachee Bay. Their name comes from the Choctaw word *a'palachi* ("[people] on the other side"). The Apalachee were among a group of advanced tribes who migrated from west of the Mississippi River to the Southeast around 1300.

Their first recorded contact with whites was in 1528, with an expedition led by the Spanish explorer Pánfilo de Narváez. The encounter was marked by hostility and fighting on both sides. When another Spanish explorer, Hernando de Soto, came through in 1539, he and his men were also given a hostile welcome. De Soto noted in his journal that the Apalachee were skilled agriculturalists, growing corn, beans, pumpkins, and squash. His forces walked two days through one immense stretch of cornfields. By the early 1600's, the Apalachee had been visited by missionaries, and most had converted to Roman Catholicism. While many Apalachee eagerly accepted Christianity, and at least seven chiefs were baptized, there was still tension between the Indians and the Spanish. In 1647 a rebellion occurred; several missionaries were killed, and the churches were destroyed. The missionaries persevered. In 1655, there were approximately six thousand to eight thousand Apalachee living in eight towns, each built around a central Franciscan mission.

In 1703, the Apalachee were attacked by a company of a hundred whites and about one thousand Indians of various tribes. The force was sent by the English governor of Carolina, who wanted to disrupt Spanish influence in the area. Some two hundred Apalachee were killed, and another fourteen hundred were carried off into slavery and resettled near New Windsor, North Carolina. All the major Apalachee towns, missions, groves, and fields were destroyed. A year later, another raid killed several hundred more Apalachee. Small bands drifted away, joining other tribes or establishing independent villages. When the Yamasee War broke out, those who had been made slaves joined the Lower Creeks and were eventually absorbed. By the end of the nineteenth century, the tribe was no longer a distinct entity.

Apalachicola

CULTURE AREA: Southeast
LANGUAGE GROUP: Muskogean
PRIMARY LOCATION: Southwestern Georgia, southeastern Alabama

The matrilineal Apalachicola raised the "three sisters"—beans, corn, and squash—but were also river-oriented. They had individual and large communal hunts for deer, which supplemented their food bases and provided needed by-products. There were probably four large, permanent, and politically independent villages that maintained exchange of resources and alliances. According to oral history, when the Muskogee encroached upon Apalachicola territory a peace treaty resulted, which the Apalachicola negotiated and which led to the Creek Confederacy.

The Apalachicola were first contacted by the Spanish in the late sixteenth century, then by the French, and eventually by the British. After conflict with encroaching European Americans in 1706, the Apalachicola were resettled on the Savannah River. After the Yamasee War of 1716, they returned to their aboriginal area. During the years 1836-1840 they were forced onto the northern part of the Creek Reservation in Oklahoma, where they were gradually absorbed into other ethnic groups.

Arapaho

CULTURE AREA: Plains
LANGUAGE GROUP: Algonquian
PRIMARY LOCATION: West-central Wyoming, western Oklahoma
POPULATION SIZE: 6,350 (1990 U.S. Census)

The Arapaho were Plains Indians with a classical buffalo economy. They are closely related to the Atsina and were close associates of the Cheyenne. The Utes, Shoshones, and Pawnees were their constant enemies. Their relationship with the Sioux, Kiowa, and Comanche varied. The Arapaho were probably pushed west and south by the Sioux in their early days on the Plains, and in turn they pushed the Comanche and Kiowa south. At other times, they were allied with each tribe against other Indians and white Americans.

Early History and Traditional Lifestyle. Exactly when the Arapaho moved into the Plains is not clear, but at the end of the eighteenth century, when they first came to the attention of white Americans, they were established in eastern Colorado, southeastern Wyoming, and extreme western Nebraska and Kansas. They may have lived as farmers in western Minnesota until the sixteenth century and then moved west and south into the Plains, probably because of pressure from eastern tribes moving west under pressure from European immigrants. On the Plains, they established a nomadic lifestyle, almost entirely dependent on buffalo. Eventually, northern and southern subdivisions developed.

An 1870 photograph of an Arapaho camp near Fort Dodge, Kansas; note the buffalo meat drying on poles. (National Archives)

The Arapaho's early Plains lifeways are not well known either, but they probably followed buffalo herds, using travois pulled by dogs to move their belongings. They lived in lodges (tipis) made of buffalo hides stretched over a set of poles. Their hunting tactics included driving buffalo into enclosures and killing them with arrows and spears; they also drove groups of buffalo over cliffs.

Sometime before the middle of the eighteenth century, by raiding or trading, the Arapaho obtained horses from southwestern tribes. This acquisition changed their lives dramatically. The travois was adjusted to fit horses, so moves could be made rapidly. More important, the horses became their vehicle for hunting and fighting. The Arapaho were not the best-known horse Indians of the Plains; nevertheless, they were highly skilled at hunting and fighting from horseback.

Men hunted buffalo by separating the target individual from the herd and killing it with arrows and spears. Alternatively, if a large group of horsemen was available, the buffalo herd was surrounded and arrows were fired into the herd. Those wounded too seriously to keep up with the escaping herd were killed. Guns became available to the Arapaho shortly after they obtained horses, and buffalo hunting became even more efficient. The men butchered the buffalo at the site of the kill.

In camp, the women cooked some of the meat for immediate use and smoked or dried the rest. Women also scraped and treated the hides for use as tipi covers, clothing, or pouches for carrying various materials. They gathered and preserved berries, roots, and other plant foods. Tools, such as knives, scrapers, and arrowheads, were initially made of flint or buffalo bones. After trade was initiated with whites, metal was often used.

The Arapaho lived in groups of twenty to eighty families. Several such groups came together in spring and summer to hunt buffalo and for cere-monial events. The groups separated for winter, each moving to a stream in a protected valley in the foothills of the Rocky Mountains. The men, often on snowshoes, hunted deer, elk, and small game. The women cooked and made and decorated clothes and other articles.

Ceremonial and Religious Life. The Arapaho were deeply religious, holding ceremonies for each stage of life (the birth of a child, the child's first steps, selected stages of male maturity) and for every important event (the buffalo hunt, an individual's pledge of service to—or plea for help from—the Creator). Music and dance were important parts of all these ceremonies. The Flat Pipe, the most sacred symbol of the Arapaho Nation, is kept by an elder of the Northern Arapaho in a sacred bundle and is still used in a number of the nation's most sacred ceremonies. The Sacred Wheel is main-tained and used in the same way by the Southern Arapaho.

Arapaho men were almost all members of age-graded societies or lodges. These were of particular importance in the organization of the tribe and in assigning duties to the various tribal members. The first two were youth societies. Membership in the six adult male lodges was achieved with age and demonstration of responsible behavior, especially generosity. Regu-lar demonstration of generosity was essential for becoming an Arapaho leader. There were specific rituals associated with each lodge, and members of each had certain responsibilities in war and peace. The highest lodge comprised the seven Water Sprinkling Old Men and was attained by a few spiritual leaders. Each was responsible for a medicine bundle which contained items of spiritual importance to the tribe.

Arapaho women belonged to the buffalo lodge. There were also Seven Old Women, who, though they did not form a lodge, were the female counterparts to the Water Sprinkling Old Men. Their medicine bags contained the materials needed to teach the skills of making and decorating tipis, clothes, bags, and other tribal materials. The symbolic decorations were of great importance in tribal culture.

A vision quest was a personal religious undertaking. To gain insight into his particular role in life, a man would fast and pray alone in the plains until he received a vision. Often a small animal would be involved in the vision, and the man made his medicine bag from that animal's skin.

The best-known Arapaho ceremony was the Offerings Lodge, also called the Sun Dance. It was an elaborate, week-long ceremony initiated when an Arapaho, called the lodge builder, vowed to pay for the ceremony. This was done to petition the Creator for success in battle, recovery from sickness, or satsifaction of some other need or desire. Self-torture was the most infamous part of the Offerings Lodge. A man pushed skewers through his chest muscles, tied the skewers to the center pole, and hung suspended until the skewers tore through his flesh. According to one explanation, the man was asking the Creator to forgive and favor the tribe.

The Offerings Lodge was important in social as well as spiritual life, especially in maintaining the unity of the tribe. All Arapaho bands gathered for the ceremony. The other lodges were important in maintaining order and organization in Arapaho life. Tribal history, skills, and customs were passed from generation to generation by way of the age-graded societies and the Buffalo Lodge. Some authorities believe that the organization of the age-graded societies spared the Arapaho the conflicts between generations that other Plains tribes suffered during the transition from buffalo hunting to reservation life.

Transition and Modern Life. The Arapaho fought ably against other American Indian tribes and, as allies of the Sioux, Cheyenne, and Comanche, against white encroachment. Some raided settlements and wagon trains, stole livestock, and participated in battles with white Americans. They were less aggressive than some other tribes, however, and put more effort into trading than fighting. Friday, a Northern Arapaho, and Left Hand, a Southern Arapaho, spoke English and had many white friends. They counseled for peace throughout the white invasion. Northern Arapaho men were important scouts for the United States Army, and relationships between Arapahos and whites were often friendly.

The Arapaho's most important encounter with the U.S. Army was at Sand Creek, Colorado, on November 29, 1864. A group of Cheyenne and Arapaho, camped under the flag and protection of the U.S. government, were attacked by troops led by Colonel John Chivington. The chiefs in the camp, Left Hand and Black Kettle, a Cheyenne, were known advocates of peace, and the Indians present were primarily women and children. Chivington probably knew this before the attack. Most of the Indians killed were women and children, and soldiers mutilated the dead Indians. Left Hand died as a result of his wounds.

In response, many Arapaho joined the Cheyenne and Sioux in the Plains Indian wars, which finally ended in 1890, at Wounded Knee, South Dakota. Most Arapaho, however, followed chiefs Little Raven, of the southern group, and Medicine Man and Black Coal from the north and pursued peace. In 1869, the Southern Arapaho and Cheyenne were assigned to a reservation in Oklahoma; in 1878, the Northern Arapaho were placed on the Shoshone (Wind River) Reservation in western Wyoming. These areas were a minute fraction of the land that had been promised in the 1851 treaty of Horse Creek.

In response to settlers' demands for land from the new reservations and because of a determination to assimilate the Indians into white society, the General Allotment Act (Dawes Severalty Act) was passed in 1887. It gave a parcel of reservation land to each individual American Indian. Not coincidentally, there was reservation land left after all Indians had received allotments, and the law allowed whites to buy or lease the leftover land. Both Northern and Southern Arapaho were cheated by unfair loan, lease, and sale agreements, but the burden fell most heavily on the southern group.

The Northern Arapaho succeeded in retaining control of most reservation land through a long period of abject poverty. In the 1940's, a tribal business council of six elected representatives, working with the tribal elders and a similar Shoshone council, convinced the federal government to allow payments to individual families from reservation income. The income is derived from oil and gas production, land rental, and tribally owned businesses. In 1961, the Arapaho and Cheyenne won millions of dollars in compensation for broken treaties. As a result of these and other astute political maneuvers, Northern Arapaho economic conditions improved considerably. Many old problems continued, however, especially undereducation, unemployment, and attendant poverty.

The Southern Arapaho also received individual allotments, but for reasons unique to their situation, they were unable to maintain an intact reservation. Reservation land left after allotment was sold to white ranchers and farmers; in addition, many individual Arapaho sold their allotments.

Because of extensive fraud, sale prices were often well below market value. As part of the continuing attempt to assimilate American Indians into white society, the reservation was abolished in 1890. The Southern Arapaho subsequently scattered around western Oklahoma, and tribal unity, so important to the maintenance of Arapaho culture, was lost. An elected Cheyenne-Arapaho Business Committee now manages tribal resources. Many Arapaho live in the towns of Geary and Canton, Oklahoma, and the tribal offices are in Concho. Many tribal members are undereducated, unemployed, and living in poverty.

The two branches of the tribe maintain contact with each other. The Offerings Lodge is celebrated in Wyoming each year, and some southern members make the trip north to join in the celebration. The Arapaho language is on the verge of extinction, but members of both branches are striving to maintain their heritage while living in the modern world.

Carl W. Hoagstrom

Bibliography

Bass, Althea. *The Arapaho Way*. New York: Clarkson N. Potter, 1966. A description of Arapaho life based on the memory of a Southern Arapaho, Carl Sweezy. Illustrated with his paintings.

Coel, Margaret. *Chief Left Hand: Southern Arapaho*. Norman: University of Oklahoma Press, 1981. An outline of Southern Arapaho life and history, centered on the first Chief Left Hand and on the Sand Creek Massacre and its aftermath. Index, bibliography, maps, illustrations.

Fowler, Loretta. *The Arapaho*. New York: Chelsea House, 1989. A summary of everything Arapaho. Short index, bibliography, glossary, maps, and many illustrations.

_____. *Arapaho Politics, 1851-1978*. Lincoln: University of Nebraska Press, 1982. An excellent account of the Arapaho political system before and during reservation life. Index, bibliography, maps, illustrations.

Mann, Henrietta. *Cheyenne-Arapaho Education, 1871-1982*. Niwot: University Press of Colorado, 1997.

Shakespeare, Tom. *The Sky People*. New York: Vantage Press, 1971. A description of Arapaho life written by a Northern Arapaho.

Trenholm, Virginia Cole. *The Arapahoes: Our People*. Norman: University of Oklahoma Press, 1986. History of the Arapaho, including both northern and southern groups. Index, bibliography, and illustrations.

Zdenek, Salzmann. *The Arapaho Indians: A Research Guide and Bibliography*. New York: Greenwood Press, 1988. An invaluable source for nearly everything written on the Arapaho before 1988. Including U.S. government documents and archive and museum holdings.

Archaic

DATE: Beginning 8000 B.C.E.
LOCATION: North, Central, and South America
CULTURES AFFECTED: All

The term "Archaic" was designated by archaeologists Gordon Willey and Philip Phillips as nomenclature for the period between the end of the Paleo-Indian big-game hunting and gathering period and the beginnings of settled, agriculture-based village life. It has roughly the same meaning in the New World as the term "Mesolithic" does in the Old World. The Archaic tradition covers several millennia and is broadly construed. It includes societies that were highly nomadic, such as those of the Desert culture, as well as more sedentary groups, such as riverine and coastal shell-fishing peoples of the southeastern United States. Archaic cultures ranged from small, mobile bands that utilized sites such as Bat Cave to relatively large groups such as those who constructed Poverty Point.

A number of characteristics were shared by societies of the Archaic tradition. First and foremost of these was a reliance on wild plant and animal resources. Archaic peoples subsisted primarily by hunting (sometimes with domesticated dogs) and gathering. Strategies ranged from buffalo hunting on the central Plains and shellfishing on the Florida coast to intensive gathering of marsh elder in eastern Illinois.

The technology of the Archaic tradition included artifacts made of chipped and ground stone, bone, wood, shell, gourds, and a variety of fibers. Among these were ground-stone manos and metates, for grinding seeds and nuts, and polished axes. Over time, ground-stone techniques extended to the manufacture of elaborate stone bowls, axes, and adzes as well as objects such as birdstones and banner stones. Archaic peoples were adept at the use of leather, sinews, and plant fibers. Basketry was used for containers, sandals, and even shelters. Leatherwork, as well as twining and weaving, was used to make bags, hats, clothing, and sandals. Pottery was invented by Archaic peoples. In the lower Mississippi Valley, fired clay was used to make boiling "stones," while fiber-tempered vessels were manufactured in the Southeast. Simple metallurgy was also practiced in the Great Lakes region, where Archaic peoples made ornaments of hammered native copper.

Archaic peoples initiated the processes that resulted in the domestication of plant and animal species. In Mexico these included maize, beans, squash, chiles, avocados, amaranth, and goosefoot, as well as turkeys. In South

America they included gourds, cotton, potatoes, chiles, the guinea pig, llama, and muscovy duck, while in eastern North America they included squash, marsh elder, amaranth, goosefoot, and sunflowers. Other Archaic period innovations were the emergence of early social ranking, as evidenced by marked differences in the quality of burial goods found in cemeteries, and long-distance trade in rare minerals or craft items. It is likely that many of the religious traditions that became focal points of community activity in later times had their origins in Archaic times.

The Archaic tradition ends with the emergence of communities that relied more heavily on agricultural products than on wild resources. It is fair to say that it continued into the historic period among groups such as fishing societies of the Northwest Coast and can still be found in remote regions of South America.

Arikara

CULTURE AREA: Plains
LANGUAGE GROUP: Caddoan
PRIMARY LOCATION: North Dakota, South Dakota
POPULATION SIZE: 1,583 (1990 U.S. Census)

The Arikara, or Ricaree, lived along the lower Missouri River basin in what is presently North and South Dakota. This is prairie country, which was conducive to the Arikara hunting and agriculture practices. The tribe had originally been Pawnee but had at some point moved north up the Missouri to form their own tribe, maintaining much of the Pawnee language yet being influenced by the neighboring Sioux and various other tribes.

Hunting, farming, and fishing were all practiced by the Arikara. During the winter, the tribe spent its time on the hunt, ranging as far as forty miles in search of buffalo. During this time, the people lived in lodges constructed of animal hides. Yet these Indians were not renowned as great hunters, nor did they keep many horses in their own possession. Rather, they served as middlemen in the distribution of horses from the nomadic tribes south and west of the Missouri to other nomadic tribes north and east of the river.

When they were not engaged in hunting, the Arikara's housing was more permanent. Huts were constructed by driving four posts into the ground and laying timbers lengthwise between them. Smaller twigs were then filled in and overlaid with rushes, willows, and grass. The entire structure was plastered thickly with mud, with a hole left in the top for smoke and one in the side for a door. The finished home was round in shape. Each hut was excavated inside to a depth of 2 to 4 feet, making the interior tall enough for people to stand up and walk around in. Beds were located around the extremity of the interior circle. A covered passage about 10 feet in length was then constructed outward from the side opening, sloping gently from the exterior to the interior, with a wooden door helping to shut out the elements. Trenches were dug around the outside of the huts to guide rainfall away. Huts were placed randomly within the village, 15 to 20 feet apart, with no paths of any regularity among the dwellings. Cellars were dug within the houses for the storage of corn and other produce.

Corn was grown on family farms of about one acre each. Farming plots were separated by brush and rudely built pole fences. Women did the majority of the farming chores, using hoes and pickaxes made from shoulder blades of cows and deer, and rakes made from reeds. The corn, a variety of Indian corn with a small hard grain and stalks only 2.5 to 3 feet tall, was planted in April or May and then picked around the first part of August. The Arikara women picked the corn when it was still green, boiled it slightly, dried it, shelled it, and then stored it. Other popular crops were squashes, either boiled or eaten green, and pumpkins. Crops were subject both to occasional floods by the Missouri River and to drought. The Arikara held various rites and ceremonies related to the production of crops.

They also capitalized on their agricultural successes by trading crops with the American Fur Company for knives, hoes, combs, beads, paints, ammunition, and tobacco. In addition, they traded with the Sioux for buffalo robes, skins, and meats—and then, in turn, traded these items with whites for guns and horses.

The Arikara were known to be good swimmers and fishermen. The men would place willow pens in eddies of the river, and then throw the caught fish to shore. In the spring, the men would sometimes float out on melting ice cakes and gather rotting buffalo which had died in the winter, stack them on the shore, and then feast on the carcasses with fellow tribe members. Women were known to float out on ice floes in much the same manner to collect driftwood.

The Arikara were adept at making fired, unglazed pots; pans, porringers, and mortars for pounding corn; ornaments of melted beads; skin canoes of buffalo hide, and willows for hunting along the banks of the Missouri River. They made good use of the resources available to them and were generally considered to be a peaceful people.

Ruffin Stirling

Assiniboine

CULTURE AREA: Plains
LANGUAGE GROUP: Siouan
PRIMARY LOCATION: Alberta and Saskatchewan (Canada), Montana (U.S.)
POPULATION SIZE: 5,274 in U.S. (1990 U.S. Census); more than 3,000 in Canada

The Assiniboine (including groups sometimes called the Stoneys) lived in northeastern Montana, northwestern North Dakota, and adjacent Canada. They spoke a language of the Siouan language group, but their associations with the Sioux were generally antagonistic, as were their relations with the Blackfoot. They had a close and long-standing alliance with the Cree and became friendly with the Atsina after decades of fighting them. The Assiniboine were not important participants in the Plains Indian wars and were assigned to several reservations in Montana, Alberta, and Saskatchewan.

Early History and Traditional Lifestyle. The Assiniboine separated from the Sioux in the mid-seventeenth century while still living in the eastern woodlands. They moved into southern Ontario, where they became associated with the Cree. They trapped furs for Europeans and acted as intermediaries between western Indians and European traders until the establishment of trading posts on western rivers gave the traders direct access to those Indians.

With the westernmost members of the Cree, they moved into the northern Plains and took up buffalo hunting, at first on foot using dogs to bear their belongings on their treks across the Plains. Around the middle of the eighteenth century they obtained horses, and although they probably never had as many as other Plains Indians, the buffalo hunt and tribal movements in pursuit of the buffalo became easier and more efficient.

They followed the buffalo herds across the prairies and plains and obtained most of their food and material goods from them. They lived in tipis of buffalo hides sewn together and stretched across a group of poles. Readily put up and taken down, the tipi was ideal housing for a mobile society. Men hunted, butchered their prey, defended the tribe in war and made weapons and shields. Women cooked; gathered seeds, fruits, and vegetative parts of plants; preserved foods for future use; made clothing and tipi covers; struck camp; and put up camp with each move. They gathered in large groups to hunt buffalo, and broke up into smaller groups for the winter.

Nineteenth century engraving of Assiniboine men in traditional clothing. (Library of Congress)

The Assiniboine fought almost constantly with the Blackfoot, Crow, Sioux, and Atsina over buffalo ranges and horses. These wars, and diseases (especially smallpox and measles) introduced by Europeans, precipitated a decline in the Assiniboine population and in the tribe's ability to hold its territory. Around 1870, the Atsina-Blackfoot alliance disintegrated and the Assiniboine and Atsina became allies. This association may have been what enabled the two small tribes to resist constant Blackfoot and Sioux aggression.

Assiniboine ceremonial and spiritual life was typical of plains Indians. They held the Sun Dance, an elaborate spiritual ceremony lasting for days. Generally held when the tribe was gathered for the buffalo hunt, the Sun Dance was intended to assure a successful hunt; it was also used to invoke supernatural assistance in other undertakings, or to express gratitude for past assistance. Individuals went on vision quests, which involved days of fasting and praying in a secluded place, to obtain their personal "medicine" or source of power. The message, or inspiration, they received on the quest gave subsequent direction to their lives.

Men were organized into warrior societies, each with a particular responsibility in the life of the tribe. Men became eligible for membership as they accomplished feats of bravery, and practiced generosity. Chiefs were also chosen on the basis of these characteristics. While masks were not generally a part of Plains Indian ritual, members of the Assiniboine Fool Society (who mocked and acted contrary to societal standards to emphasize their importance) wore masks.

Transition and Modern Life. The Assiniboine contributed little resistance to the European American conquest of the Plains, in part because of the early interaction between Assiniboines and whites in the fur trade, as well as the reduced Assiniboine population because of disease and Indian warfare. They were placed on several reservations, representing a small fraction of the land over which they once hunted, in Montana, Alberta, and Saskatchewan.

Assiniboines face the poverty, unemployment, lack of education, and threats to their culture that other Indian groups face. Yet they have clung to their culture throughout government attempts at assimilation. One aspect of that culture in which they take particular pride, a willingness to assist one another in times of trouble or need, will be a great help in efforts to improve the tribe's condition and conserve Assiniboine culture.

Carl W. Hoagstrom

Atakapa

CULTURE AREA: Southeast
LANGUAGE GROUP: Atakapan
PRIMARY LOCATION: Southwestern Louisiana, southeastern Texas

The Atakapa lived in small groups scattered across southwest Louisiana and southeast Texas. Most of the Texas Atakapa were called Akokisa or Deadose by the Spanish.

According to Atakapa oral tradition, their ancestors were stranded in Texas after a great flood, and they later spread eastward. At the time of European contact, Atakapa subsistence depended on collecting wild plants and hunting (buffalo and deer) across the grasslands and swamps of southeast Texas and southwestern Louisiana. Unlike their neighbors to the east, such as the Chitimacha, the Atakapa did not depend on agriculture and had a less sedentary lifestyle. In common with other southeastern cultures, the Atakapa traded with neighboring peoples. Despite their contacts with the hierarchical societies of the Mississippi River, Atakapan sociopolitical organization was not stratified to the same degree. The seeming simplicity of their lifeways (hunting and gathering rather than farming and inhabiting permanent villages) meant that the European settlers recorded little information concerning them, and since their culture had vanished by the twentieth century, no other data were forthcoming.

The word *Atakapa* is Choctaw, meaning "people eater," and their cannibalistic reputation is upheld in the account of Simars de Belle-Isle, who was captured and enslaved by the Akokisa (the Atakapa on the Louisiana-Texas border) from 1719 to 1721.

The Louisiana Atakapa inhabited terrain deemed inappropriate for early European settlement, so they were initially spared the depredations suffered by other southeastern Native Americans. The Akokisa and Deadose of Texas were not so lucky. They were missionized in 1748-1749, from the San Ildefonso Mission in Texas. The combined influence of additional missions (begun during the middle to late eighteenth century) and an epidemic (1777-1778) resulted in the Akokisa and the Deadose no longer being mentioned in colonial records by the 1800's.

The Louisiana Atakapa were affected by European incursions dating from the mid-eighteenth century onward. The locations of several Louisiana Atakapa villages are recorded for the period 1760 to 1836, but afterward there are only scattered reports of Atakapa. In 1885, for example, two Atakapa speakers were living in the vicinity of Lake Charles, Louisiana. By the early twentieth century, the Atakapa had been absorbed into the European population or joined other Native American groups. Atakapa lifeways and history are described in John R. Swanton's *The Indians of the Southeastern United States* (1946).

Atsina

CULTURE AREA: Plains
LANGUAGE GROUP: Algonquian
PRIMARY LOCATION: Montana
POPULATION SIZE: 2,848 (1990 U.S. Census)

The ethnological origins of the Atsina, or White Clay People, are mysterious. The Atsina, also known as the Gros Ventre, once belonged to an Algonquian parent tribe that included the Arapaho. Until the seventeenth century, the Arapaho-Atsina hunted, gathered, and perhaps planted near the Red River of Minnesota. In the late seventeenth or early eighteenth century, the Atsina broke off from the Arapaho and moved northward and westward to the Eagle Hills in Saskatchewan. There the Atsina probably subsisted by gathering and pedestrian buffalo hunting, although they evidently also planted tobacco. In the middle of the eighteenth century, the Atsina acquired horses and became equestrian buffalo hunters. In the late eighteenth century, the Cree and Assiniboine pushed the Atsina from Saskatchewan southwest to the Upper Missouri River.

Like other Plains tribes, the Atsina alternately battled and allied with their neighbors. Atsina bands were often allied with the closely related Arapaho and the Algonquian-speaking tribes of the Blackfeet Confederacy. In 1861, however, the Atsina sought an alliance with their erstwhile enemies, the Crow. At some point in the mid-nineteenth century, the Atsina allied with their former enemies, the Assiniboine, to resist the encroachments of the Sioux into their hunting territory.

Atsina religion and social organization revolved around two medicine bundles containing the Flat Pipe and the Feathered Pipe. Stewardship of the bundles, which combined both religious and political authority, rotated among certain adult men every few years.

In the second half of the nineteenth century, the territory under the control of the Atsina steadily eroded. An executive order by President Ulysses S. Grant in 1873 established a large reservation for the Blackfoot, Assiniboine, and Atsina in northern Montana. In January, 1887, representatives of the federal government met with the Atsina and Assiniboine at the Fort Belknap Agency to negotiate the cession of most of the Indians' reserve. President Grover Cleveland signed the Fort Belknap agreement into law on May 1, 1888, reducing the Atsina and Assiniboine to a shared reservation of approximately 600,000 acres. Despite the diminution of their territory, the Atsina and Assiniboine of the Fort Belknap Reservation won an important United States Supreme Court decision in the early twentieth century that became a landmark in American Indian law. On January 6, 1908, the Supreme Court ruled in *Winters v. United States* that the Indians of Fort Belknap Reservation, rather than nearby white settlers, had first rights to the contested water of the Milk River.

In 1934, Fort Belknap became the first reservation in the Plains to establish a government under the auspices of the Indian Reorganization Act. For the Atsina, reorganization had the unanticipated consequence of merging their reservation government with that of the Assiniboine. Economic conditions at Fort Belknap languished until the mid-1960's, when many Atsina were able to take advantage of federal War on Poverty programs. By 1980, Fort Belknap had the highest percentage of college graduates of any reservation of the northern Plains.

Atsugewi

CULTURE AREA: California
LANGUAGE GROUP: Palaihnihan
PRIMARY LOCATION: Burney Valley and Mount Lassen, California

Prior to European contact, the Atsugewi were a socioeconomically stratified society, divided into two territorial groups: the Atsuge ("Pine Tree

People"), most of whose population was confined to five main villages, and the Apwaruge ("Juniper Tree People"), who occupied more extensive territory. People lived in either bark or earth lodges, with the village being the principal autonomous political unit. Traditional forms of wealth could be acquired and accumulated by anyone willing to be industrious. Fish and acorns, the staple foods, were acquired and stored by elaborate technologies, particularly the leaching of tannic acid from acorns and horse chestnuts.

First contact with European Americans was in 1827 with Peter Skene Ogden. By the 1830's, the Hudson's Bay Company was trapping in the area and had established a trail from Klamath to Hat Creek, which provided access to prospectors entering the area in 1851. Conflict erupted with settlers, some of whom were killed at Fall River, which led to a punitive war by white volunteers. Some Atsugewi were removed to the Round Valley Reservation, and many participated shortly after in the Ghost Dance revival of 1890.

Aztec

CULTURE AREA: Mesoamerica
LANGUAGE GROUP: Uto-Aztecan
PRIMARY LOCATION: Central Mexico

The Aztecs, or Mexica (Me-shee-ka) as they called themselves, became the most important tribe in Central Mexico and created a powerful empire that would last until the arrival of the Spanish in the early sixteenth century. The Aztec state disappeared, but the people and their culture left an important legacy; modern Mexicans refer to the founding of Tenochtitlán by the Aztecs in 1325—not the arrival of the Spanish—as the beginning of their nation. Moreover, more than a million people still speak Nahuatl, the Aztec language (a part of the Uto-Aztecan family).

Early History. Aztec origins are unclear. The people entered the Valley of Mexico in the thirteenth century from what is now northern Mexico, or perhaps Southwestern United States, from a land they called Aztalán, or Aztlán. They would later create an elaborate legend to describe how their principal god, Huitzilopochtli (the left-handed hummingbird), led them to a site where an eagle stood on a cactus with a serpent in its beak. This scene, pictured on the present-day flag of Mexico, marked the location of Tenochtitlán, capital city of the Aztecs and later the site of Mexico City.

Archaeologists tell a simpler story, suggesting that the Aztecs were a relatively unimportant Chichimec tribe from the north that entered the Valley of Mexico looking for more fertile land. Many important cities already existed around the great lake in the valley, and the Aztecs became tributaries of a more powerful tribe, serving them as mercenaries. The city of Tenochtitlán was originally a muddy mound in the middle of the lake, where the tribe could find protection after antagonizing important Indian leaders. They flourished in their new home, and their city expanded.

Society. The Aztecs were divided into clans, or capulli, each related by blood and engaging in a specific economic activity. The capulli were led by a council of elders, called the Tlatocan, who made the important decisions for the community. Though still under the domination of other tribes, the Aztecs chose Acamapichtli (who ruled from 1375 to 1395) as their leader. A new warrior class was created from these ruling families, known as the Pipiltin. When Acamapichtli died, his son became chief, beginning the Clan of the Eagle, a royal lineage that would last 125 years, until the defeat of the Aztecs by the Spanish.

Aztec nobles were priests, warriors, and judges. They were trained in a school called the Calmécac, where they learned discipline and special skills. Beneath the nobles in Aztec society were the merchants. Because they traded with distant lands, they were able to serve as spies for the expanding empire. Called Pochteca, these merchants amassed wealth but were denied the dress or status of nobility. Members of lesser groups could be put to death for wearing dress reserved for the nobility. Sandals, jewels, and feathered headdresses were the prerogative of the upper class.

Craftsmen formed a separate group in Aztec society. They worked with jade, gold, and feathers to make ceremonial costumes and jewelry. Commoners, the largest group, worked the fields, performed construction duties, and served the nobility. Their day began at dawn; rising from sleeping mats in small huts and wearing simple loincloths, they went out to work without any breakfast. At ten in the morning the first meal was taken, consisting of a simple bowl of porridge. The main meal was eaten at midday, during the hottest hours of the day. This meal consisted of maize cakes, beans, pimento, and tamales. Meat from turkeys or small game, routine fare for the upper classes, was rare among the commoners. Everyone would squat on a mat and eat quickly, drinking only water. This meal would often be the last of the day.

Nobles, by contrast, lived in larger homes and ate better meals. Their midday meal included meat and fruit as well as more common dishes made from corn. Nobles drank cocoa, at that time a bitter drink taken without sugar. Occasionally there were feasts that lasted most of the night at which

Painting depicting the Aztec foundation legend, according to which an eagle ate a snake to indicate where the capital city should be built. This motif also appears on the modern Mexican flag. (Institute of Texan Cultures, San Antonio, Texas)

pulque, a fermented alcoholic beverage, was consumed. The drug peyote was used, but only for religious ceremonies.

Religious Beliefs. The Aztecs believed that life was a struggle, and their religion was based on the need to appease the gods. They thought that the sun's journey across the sky would continue only if the gods were offered human sacrifice. The belief in human sacrifice was not unique to the Aztecs, but it became bound up with their expanding empire and came to dominate their society to a greater extent than in other tribes. In fact, much of Aztec culture, including their gods, was derived from earlier peoples of the Valley of Mexico. One aspect of this common culture was a calendar that combined the lunar and the solar years in fifty-two-year cycles. On the eve of the last year of the cycle, all the fires in the land were extinguished, symbolizing the people's fear that the world was about to end. Crowds gathered silently on the hillsides as priests climbed to the top of a mountain to await the hoped-for dawn. When the sun rose, and time did not end, a human sacrifice was conducted and a new fire kindled. The flame was used to relight fires throughout the land, and the people rejoiced. The Aztecs believed that only human sacrifice could save their society from destruction. They also believed that there had been four previous cycles of time, and that they were living in the fifth and final period.

Rise to Power. In the early 1400's the Aztecs, along with the people from the cities of Texcoco and Tlacopán, rebelled against the overlordship of Azapotzalco, the most powerful city in the Valley of Mexico. Once successful, the three cities formed a Triple Alliance to dominate the area around the great lake. The alliance was short-lived, however, and the Aztecs subdued the other tribes to emerge by 1440 as the greatest power in Central Mexico. At this time a shift occurred among the Aztecs that necessitated further expansion. In response to a number of natural disasters, Aztec priests claimed that additional sacrifices were needed to please the gods. Thus, the Aztecs began to combine wars of conquest with capture of warriors to be used as human sacrifices. Some estimates indicate that tens of thousands of sacrifices were conducted in major ceremonies such as those marking the dedication of temples. Even after the Aztecs had conquered most of the tribes in Central Mexico they conducted ceremonial "Flower Wars," whose purpose was to take prisoners for sacrifice. For more than half a century the Aztecs ruled this expanding empire, facing much discontent among their subject peoples who were seldom integrated into Aztec society.

Conquest and Legacy. When Hernán Cortés arrived in 1519 he heard about the wealthy city of Tenochtitlán and the great lord Montezuma. Cortés, with a small group of Spanish soldiers and a growing number of Indian allies hoping to be freed from Aztec rule, entered Tenochtitlán, which he described as one of the largest and most beautiful cities he had ever seen. Undaunted by the power of the Aztecs, and fully aware that Montezuma thought him to be the god Quetzalcóatl returning from the East, Cortés took the Aztec leader prisoner and attempted to control his empire. An Aztec assault forced him out of Tenochtitlán, but Cortés returned with more Indian allies and destroyed the city in 1521. The last of the Aztec leaders, Cuauhtémoc, was taken prisoner by the Spanish.

Cortés chose the site of Tenochtitlán for his new capital, Mexico City. Although many Aztecs died in the assault or later perished from disease, their language and many of their customs remained to influence the development of Mexican society.

James A. Baer

Bibliography

Boone, Elizabeth H. *The Aztec World*. Washington, D.C.: Smithsonian Institution Press, 1994.

Bray, Warwick. *Everyday Life of the Aztecs*. New York: Peter Bedrick Books, 1991.

Carrasco, David. *City of Sacrifice: Violence from the Aztec Capital to the Modern Americas*. Boston: Beacon Press, 1999.

Carrasco, David, Eduardo Matos Moctezuma, and Scott Sessions. *Moctezuma's Mexico: Visions of the Aztec World*. Niwot: University Press of Colorado, 1992.

Carrasco, David, and Scott Sessions. *Daily Life of the Aztecs: People of the Sun and Earth*. Westport, Conn.: Greenwood Press, 1998.

Caso, Alfonso. *The Aztecs: People of the Sun*. Translated by Lowell Dunham. Norman: University of Oklahoma Press, 1958. The focus is on Aztec religious beliefs. Recounts creation stories. Good color illustrations and plates. Lists gods of fire and gods of death.

Clendinnen, Inga. *Aztecs: An Interpretation*. New York: Cambridge University Press, 1991.

Florescano, Enrique. *The Myth of Quetzalcoatl*. Baltimore: Johns Hopkins University Press, 1999.

Knab, T. J. *A War of Witches: A Journey Into the Underworld of the Contemporary Aztecs*. San Francisco: HarperCollins, 1995.

Leon-Portilla, Miguel, ed. *The Broken Spears: The Aztec Account of the Conquest of Mexico*. Translated by Lysander Kemp. Expanded ed. Boston: Beacon Press, 1992. Offers an unusual account of the conquest by providing the background and events from an Aztec perspective.

McKeever-Furst, Jill L. *The Natural History of the Soul in Ancient Mexico*. New Haven, Conn.: Yale University Press, 1995.

Marrin, Albert. *Aztecs and Spaniards: Cortés and the Conquest of Mexico*. New York: Atheneum, 1986. A general history of the Spanish conquest that focuses on relations between Aztecs and Spaniards, especially Cortés and Montezuma.

Miller, Mary Ellen, and Karl A. Taube. *An Illustrated Dictionary of the Gods and Symbols of Ancient Mexico and the Maya*. New York: Thames and Hudson, 1997.

Read, Kay A. *Time and Sacrifice in the Aztec Cosmos*. Bloomington: Indiana University Press, 1998.

Roberts, Timothy R. *Gods of the Maya, Aztecs, and Incas*. New York: Metro Books, 1996.

Smith, Michael E. *The Aztecs*. Cambridge, Mass.: Blackwell, 1996.

Soustelle, Jacques. *Daily Life of the Aztecs on the Eve of the Spanish Conquest*. Translated by Patrick O'Brian. Stanford, Calif.: Stanford University Press, 1961. Presents much information on the society and beliefs of the Aztecs at their peak of power. Gives details about dress, food, housing, and commerce.

Taube, Karl A. *Aztec and Maya Myths*. 2d ed. Austin: University of Texas Press, 1995.

Townsend, Richard F. *The Aztecs*. London: Thames and Hudson, 1992. A general history of the Aztecs, with information on religious beliefs, families, and society. Good illustrations.

Weaver, Muriel P. *The Aztecs, Maya, and Their Predecessors: Archaeology of Mesoamerica*. 3d ed. San Diego, Calif.: Academic Press, 1993.

Bannock

CULTURE AREA: Great Basin
LANGUAGE GROUP: Uto-Aztecan
PRIMARY LOCATION: Fort Hall Reservation, southeastern Idaho
POPULATION SIZE: 218 (1990 U.S. Census)

The name "Bannock" derives from the tribe's Indian name, Banakwut. Originally a branch of the Northern Paiute tribe in southeast Oregon, they acquired horses in the eighteenth century and moved to Idaho.

The Bannock were closely allied with the Shoshone. They were primarily horsemen and ranged widely throughout Idaho, Montana, and Wyoming. Family units were organized into at least five larger bands. Each band was headed by a chief, who inherited his position through the male line subject to approval by band members. The Bannock traveled with the Shoshone to hunt buffalo, trade, or do battle against their common enemies, the Blackfoot—and sometimes the Crow and Nez Perce.

In the winter—and while traveling—the Bannock lived in buffalo-skin tipis, which they adorned with pictures of their personal exploits. In the summer they lived in dome-shaped grass-and-willow houses. The Bannock fished for salmon in the spring, gathered seed and roots in the summer, and communally hunted buffalo in the fall.

Their major ceremonies were four seasonal dances. The dead were buried with their heads pointed west, since souls were thought to journey west along the Milky Way to the land of the dead. Both men and women served as shamans responsible for healing illness, conducting ceremonies, and controlling the weather.

The California gold rush and opening of the Oregon Trail in the mid-nineteenth century brought hordes of whites through Bannock lands, with devastating results. Wagon trains destroyed their pastures and smallpox reduced their population from about 2,000 to 500. The Bannock and Shoshone fought in vain to protect their way of life. Finally, in 1868, they signed the Fort Bridger Treaty, agreeing to relocate to the Fort Hall Reservation. Adverse conditions there and bitterness over their losses led them to revolt in 1878 (the Bannock War). The revolt was suppressed by 1880, and the Bannock returned to their 500,000-acre Fort Hall Reservation, where most now live with the Shoshone.

Bayogoula

CULTURE AREA: Southeast
LANGUAGE GROUP: Muskogean
PRIMARY LOCATION: Alabama

The Bayogoula were largely dependent upon garden products, mainly maize, beans, squash, and different roots, berries, and nuts gathered by women. Men hunted, particularly for deer, and utilized various fishing technologies. The Bayogoula are known to have engaged in almost continual conflict with various neighboring tribes. In fact, oral history states that the Bayogoula nearly exterminated the Mugulasha people; later, the remaining Mugulasha deceived and massacred many of the Bayogoula.

The Bayogoula were probably first encountered by the explorer Pierre le Moyne Iberville in 1699. It is documented that the Houma inflicted considerable loss of life with a surprise attack upon the Bayogoula in 1700. The remaining Bayogoula were eventually removed to an area near New Orleans, but later they settled to the north between the Houma and Acolapissa tribes. There is debate as to the date, but probably by the early 1730's, the Bayogoula were decimated by a smallpox epidemic. The Bayogoula eventually merged with the Houma.

Basketmaker

DATE: 1-750
LOCATION: Arizona, New Mexico, Utah, Colorado
CULTURES AFFECTED: Anasazi, Pueblo

The term "Basketmaker" is used to refer to pre-Pueblo ancestors of the Anasazi culture in the Four Corners region of the American Southwest. The name is based on archaeological sites in the region that lacked pottery but had evidence of the production of basketry, nets, and sandals. It was introduced as part of a nomenclature for prehistoric peoples at the first Pecos Conference (1927), organized by archaeologist Alfred V. Kidder. Basketmaker I (Early Basketmaker), a designation that has since been dropped, was proposed for a preagricultural stage that is now recognized as the Archaic period. Basketmaker II (Basketmaker) refers to a pre-pottery agricultural stage during which time the atlatl, or spear thrower, was introduced. Basketmaker III (Post-Basketmaker) refers to the earliest pottery-making village farmers, who lived in characteristic pit house dwellings. The Basketmaker stages were followed by the Pueblo I through IV periods, corresponding to the appearance and growth of agricultural villages with contiguous, aboveground rooms.

Among the differences between Basketmaker and Pueblo peoples was their physical appearance. Basketmaker peoples had longer skulls, while skulls of the Pueblo period were flattened. This was originally thought to indicate genetic differences between the earlier and later populations. Actually, however, these differences are attributable instead to the adoption of hard cradleboards and their resultant modification of cranial shape. A continuity in population from the Basketmaker through the Pueblo periods is now widely accepted, and together these are referred to as part of the Anasazi tradition.

Basketmaker II: 1-450 C.E. The Basketmaker II period is transitional between the nomadic hunting and gathering patterns of the late Archaic period and later sedentary lifeways. Villages were small and widely spaced, with circular pit houses that were deeper in the west than in the east. Natural caves and rock shelters were favored locations for campsites and burials. Food was often stored in caves, using large, jar-shaped pits excavated into the floors and bins made of stone slabs and mud.

The most characteristic trait of Basketmaker II occupations is the absence of pottery at all but a few sites. The principal containers were coiled baskets, nets, and fiber bags. The former included a wide variety of useful containers, including large trays for winnowing grain, conical baskets for collecting seeds, and a range of serving bowls. As noted above, the atlatl, or throwing stick, was utilized during Basketmaker II times. This device improved the leverage of spears tipped with projectile points, increasing the speed, distance, and accuracy with which a spear could be thrown. Flaked projectile points of this period are typically side- or corner-notched, and they were attached to spears with hardwood foreshafts. Ground stone tools represent a continuity of Archaic technology and included a variety of milling stones, with large, basin-shaped grinding slabs and manos (handstones) made from large cobbles. At some sites, trough-shaped metates approach shapes typical of later periods.

The Basketmaker II people were the first people in the Anasazi tradition to utilize agriculture, but wild plant foods and hunting resources remained a significant part of the diet. Among the plant foods collected by Basketmaker II peoples were grass seeds, chenopodium, amaranth, and piñon nuts. There is some evidence for the cultivation of maize and squash, although beans are reportedly absent at this time. The transition to agriculture may have occurred as a response to pressures on wild resources that resulted from growing populations, periods of environmental deterioration, or a combination of the two. Experimentation with cultivated species, farming, and food storage would have provided an adaptive advantage in the face of diminished resources. As these strategies became more efficient, especially with changes in environmental conditions, agricultural populations grew in size and complexity.

Basketmaker III: 450-750. By 450, there was a noticeable preference for settlement near well-watered soils, probably because of an increased reliance on agriculture. Sites are found in both alluvial valleys and upland regions such as mesa tops. With greater utilization of cultivated foods as opposed to wild resources, there was less concern for access to a diversity of natural regions. Sedentism led to an increase in the size and density of settlements. Although some sites consist only of isolated pit houses and hamlet clusters, some villages had more than fifty structures for estimated populations of more than two hundred people. There is evidence for communal construction activities, such as an encircling stockade found at the Gilliland site in southwestern Colorado, and the building of ceremonial structures.

The typical dwellings of Basketmaker III people were pit houses with either circular or rectangular plans and antechambers or large ventilator shafts. These were often augmented with auxiliary storage units, built of jacal (poles and mud) on stone slabs. At Mesa Verde (Colorado), pit houses contained banquettes, clay-lined central hearths, wing walls, and four-post roof supports. In general, the plans of Basketmaker III villages do not indicate any type of organized arrangement. Exceptionally large pit houses, however, have been interpreted as the precursors to great kivas, used for councils and sacred rituals.

The subsistence patterns of this period differ from those of the preceding one in their emphasis on the cultivation of maize, squash, and beans. There is evidence for the keeping and possible domestication of turkeys, which would have replaced meat from hunting activities as the latter became less frequent. Bows and arrows, indicated by the use of basal-notched projectile points, replaced atlatls as the favored hunting weapon. The technology for food processing was modified by the introduction of two-handed manos and an increase in the use of trough-shaped over slab metates. The crafts of twined woven bags, nets, sandals, and coiled basketry continued, but Basketmaker III peoples also made and used pottery containers. The most common vessels were jars and bowls of a plain gray ware, although vessels decorated with simple black designs on a white base also appear during this period. In southeastern Utah, orange pottery with red designs appears toward the end of this period. The adoption of pottery use and changes in ground stone tools have been interpreted as signalling an intensification in household labor that accompanied village sedentism and an increased reliance on agricultural products.

John Hoopes

Bibliography
Blackburn, Fred. M. *Cowboys and Cave Dwellers: Basketmaker Archaeology in Utah's Grand Gulch*. Santa Fe, N.Mex.: School of American Research Press, 1997.
Glashow, Michael. "Changes in the Adaptations of Southwestern Basketmakers: A Systems Perspective." In *Contemporary Archaeology*, edited by Mark P. Leone. Carbondale: Southern Illinois University Press, 1972.
Guernsey, Samuel J., and Alfred V. Kidder. "Basket-maker Caves of Northeastern Arizona." In *Papers of the Peabody Museum in American Archaeology and Ethnology*. Vol. 8, No. 2. Cambridge, Mass.: The Museum, 1921.
Martin, Paul S. "The Hay Hollow Site, 200 B.C.-A.D. 200." *Field Museum of Natural History Bulletin* 38, no. 5 (1967): 6-10.
Matson, R. G. *The Origins of Southwestern Agriculture*. Tucson: University of Arizona Press, 1991.
Morris, Earl H., and Robert F. Burgh. *Basket Maker II Sites near Durango, Colorado*. Carnegie Institution of Washington Publication 604. Washington, D.C.: Carnegie Institution of Washington, 1954.
Rohn, Arthur H. "A Stockaded Basketmaker III Village at Yellow Jacket, Colorado." *The Kiva* 40, no. 3 (1963): 113-119.

Beaver

CULTURE AREA: Subarctic
LANGUAGE GROUP: Athapaskan
PRIMARY LOCATION: Northeastern Alberta and northeastern British Columbia, Canada
POPULATION SIZE: 1,405 (Statistics Canada, based on 1991 census)

The Beaver lived as three composite bands along the Peace River; their fundamental socioeconomic unit was the bilaterally extended family group, which was dependent upon buffalo, woodland caribou, moose, beaver, and hares. Their worldview, associated behaviors, and socioeconomic activities emerged from this dependence upon game. Social control, kinship, and traditions were maintained through stories, vision quests, food and behavioral taboos, dreaming, consensus of opinion, and threats of sorcery.

The Beaver, after being forced from their aboriginal area by the Cree in the mid-eighteenth century, displaced the Sekani on the eastern slopes of the Rocky Mountains. In the nineteenth century, the Beaver became increasingly involved in fur trading, and were influenced by Roman Catholic missionaries in 1845.

In 1900, treaties which established reserves were signed. By 1930, European American farmers had settled on most of the Beaver territory, and in 1942 construction of the Alaskan Highway further disrupted their lives. Most Beaver by the 1960's earned a living by guiding hunters and clearing brush for roads, pipelines, and powerlines. Although the number of Athapaskan-speaking Beaver has declined, some traditions remain viable.

Bella Bella

CULTURE AREA: Northwest Coast
LANGUAGE GROUP: Wakashan (Heiltzuk dialect of Kwakiutl language)
PRIMARY LOCATION: British Columbia, Canada
POPULATION SIZE: 1,580 ("Heiltsuk," Statistics Canada, based on 1991 census)

The Bella Bella originally lived on Milbank Sound in British Columbia. They were divided into three subtribes, the Kokatik, Oeltik, and Oealitk, and three matrilineal clans, the Haihaiktenok (Killer Whale), Koetenok (Raven), and Wikoktenok (Eagle).

The Bella Bella were a Kwakiutl tribe, and their cultural and social lives were similar to those of other Kwakiutl tribes. Central to their social life were secret societies, potlatches, and a highly developed mythology featuring a folk hero named Raven and a creator god. The Bella Bella lived in villages. Their houses were made of cedar planks and decorated with totem poles and the crests of their clan. They subsisted primarily on salmon and other wild animals and plants; their primary means of transportation was the dugout canoe, which they used for fishing, warfare, travel, and trade.

During their early history the Bella Bella were a warlike tribe. They were flanked on either side by the Tsimshian and Bella Coola, and they had to contend with Haida war parties. It is believed that this constant threat of war was responsible for the founding of the secret societies, the most important of which originated in war customs.

Europeans eventually moved into the area, attracted by Milbank Sound, which provided one of the few good openings into the inner passage to Alaska. The effects of this contact with Europeans were similar to the dismal effects visited on other tribes in the area: decline in population from war casualties, disease, and confinement to reservations. Additionally, the Bella Bella were largely Christianized by Protestant missionaries, such that most of their ancient culture, customs, and mythology have been largely forgotten.

Most modern Bella Bella live on a 1,622-acre reserve. The remaining Bella Bella live on numerous small reserves, totalling 1,759 acres, in British Columbia.

Bella Coola

CULTURE AREA: Northwest Coast
LANGUAGE GROUP: Coast Salish
PRIMARY LOCATION: Bella Coola Valley, British Columbia
POPULATION SIZE: 980 (Statistics Canada, based on 1991 census)

The Bella Coola occupied approximately sixty permanent villages built of split/hewn rectangular cedar houses along the major rivers and streams in the narrow Bella Coola Valley; they intermarried and traded with the Carrier, Chilcotin, and Bella Bella. A wide variety of fish was their major source of food, supplemented by various animals—particularly the mountain goat, which provided food, horn, and wool that was woven into blankets and capes. Both sexes wore fur robes and capes of woven cedar or rabbitskin.

Kinship was based on lineal ascent, and social organization centered on the extended household. Marriage was usually monogamous, though polygynous households existed. Though Bella Coola society was divided into nobility, commoners, and slaves, social mobility was possible. Potlatches acknowledged change of status; they also served to redistribute goods and wealth and commemorate rites of passage. Each stage of life—birth, puberty, marriage, and death—called for a specific ritual. Status was gained through family affiliation, hunting skills, shamanism, oratory, and wealth— the latter counted in pleated red woodpecker scalp capes, obsidian blades, copper, dentalium, and slaves.

Captain George Vancouver first met and traded with the Bella Coola in 1793 while surveying. Alexander Mackenzie came overland, establishing the Hudson's Bay Company post in 1869. The Bella Coola invited a Methodist minister, the Reverend William Pierce, a mixed-blood Tsimshian, to establish a mission in Bella Coola. The people experienced drastic change with depopulation and disease, and by the 1900's their traditional hunting, gathering, and fishing way of life had changed to one dominated by commercial fishing and logging.

Musical recordings, legends, and records of older art forms have become important in the revitalization of past woodworking and weaving skills, singing, Indian rights, and a renaissance of traditional medicine and beliefs during the 1970's. In 1980 the Bella Coola Band Council, in establishing their sovereignty, referred to their people as the Nuxalk Nation.

Beothuk

CULTURE AREA: Northeast/Subarctic
LANGUAGE GROUP: Algonquian
PRIMARY LOCATION: Newfoundland, Canada

The Beothuk lived in small villages in Newfoundland prior to the arrival of Europeans in the late 1500's. Each village consisted of three or four wigwams, cone-shaped houses made of sticks and birch bark, with a hole in the top to let out smoke. The Beothuk slept in trenches dug in the floor around a fireplace for cooking. They fished for salmon and hunted seal, birds, and caribou; they also gathered eggs, roots, and berries. The meat and fish were frozen or smoked for winter consumption. Little is known of where the Beothuk originated or of their history before contact with Europeans.

Their customs are known only through reports made by early missionaries. They had twenty-four-hour wedding ceremonies with much dancing and feasting. The men conducted purification ceremonies in dome-shaped sweat lodges. Inside the skin-covered huts were hot rocks and water to make steam. Individuals would enter for a while, then run out to jump in the snow, believing that this would cleanse their bodies of evil. Tribal members dressed in caribou-skin robes, with leggings, mittens, and fur hats for winter. They sewed together birch and spruce bark for dishes, buckets, and cooking pots.

The Beothuk buried their dead with their weapons and tools and small, carved wooden figures probably representing a god or goddess, but little is known about Beothuk religion. They placed the deceased in a wooden box and carried the body to a cave, setting it aboveground on a small scaffold.

English explorers made first European contact with the Beothuk and called them "red men" because they covered their bodies and hair with a reddish powder to repel insects. By the early 1700's, French fur-trappers from Labrador began trading with the Beothuk. Conflict with the Micmac who were also trapping furs for the Europeans, erupted into warfare and many deaths. By 1800, the Beothuk—who probably never numbered more than five hundred—were almost wiped out because of war, disease, and starvation. A few survivors migrated to Labrador, where they were absorbed into the Montagnais.

Biloxi

CULTURE AREA: Southeast
LANGUAGE GROUP: Siouan
PRIMARY LOCATION: Louisiana, Mississippi

French explorers first encountered a Biloxi village on the Pascagoula River about 1700. The Biloxi at that time were one of only two groups in the area that spoke a language from the Siouan linguistic family; the other was the Ofo. Both probably migrated from the Ohio River valley. The name Biloxi was a corruption of their own word for "first people"; others wrote it as "Moctobi."

The French observed that the Biloxi village contained thirty to forty cabins and was surrounded by a palisade that was 8 feet in height. Security was enhanced by the presence of three square watchtowers. During the French occupation, there were no more than five hundred Biloxi at any time, and they usually lived between the Pearl River on the west and the Pascagoula on the east, though there was an abortive attempt by the French to settle them closer to New Orleans.

The culture exhibited by the Biloxi fascinated the French. They were organized by clans with animal names, and kinship was traced through the mother. Chiefs were assumed to have religious as well as secular power, and after death their bodies were dried before a fire and stored in a temple with the remains of their predecessors. The Biloxi were adept at making pottery and weaving baskets, and their adornment included feather headdresses, tattoos, nose rings and earrings of bone, and necklaces of bone and bird beaks. One of their more enduring rituals proved to be stickball, which was abolished in the twentieth century because of the gambling associated with it.

After the French lost the area east of the Mississippi River in 1763, the Biloxi moved to Louisiana, together with other Indians from the Gulf Coast. Many Biloxi joined the Tunica and Choctaw Indians there, while some moved to Texas and the Indian Territory and blended with other groups. In 1975, the state of Louisiana officially recognized the Biloxi-Tunica tribe. At that time, there were about two dozen people who claimed Biloxi ancestry.

Blackfoot and Blackfeet Confederacy

TRIBES AFFECTED: Siksika (Blackfeet Proper), Kainah (Blood), Northern Piegan, and Southern Piegan
CULTURE AREA: Northern Plains
LANGUAGE GROUP: Algonquian
PRIMARY LOCATION: Montana (U.S.), Alberta (Canada)
POPULATION SIZE: 32,234 in U.S. (1990 U.S. Census); 11,670 in Canada (Statistics Canada, based on 1991 census)

The Blackfeet Confederacy consisted of four Algonquian tribes: the Siksika (Blackfeet Proper), Kainah (Blood), Northern Piegan, and Southern Piegan. Siksika is a Cree word meaning "people with black feet," which probably referred to moccasins dyed black or that turned black after contact with prairie fire ashes. "Piegan" means "poorly dressed robes" and referred to tribal members who lived in the foothills of the Rocky Mountains. The Blackfeet originally came from somewhere in the east and had a common language and similar religious beliefs; they frequently intermarried. Geography separated the tribes, particularly in the mountains where each branch of the Confederacy lived in a separate valley or along a different river. The Blackfeet came together to fight invaders, to hunt for food, and to celebrate weddings and successful hunts. The tribes moved about frequently in search of their primary source of food and clothing, the buffalo.

Customs and Culture. The four major tribes separated into smaller groups, the Northern and Southern Piegans having twenty-three bands, the Blood seven, and the Blackfoot or Siksika six. Each band had a headman, chosen because of bravery in battle. The headman took care of the poor and disabled and sponsored social and religious ceremonies. The headmen met together as a tribal council to decide on questions such as war and trade relations with neighboring tribes. Within each band, warriors were divided by age into military societies, dance groups, and religious clubs.

In traditional Blackfoot religion, the Sun Dance played a prominent role as it did in many Plains tribes. A woman—the "vow woman"—sponsored the event, usually after a great disaster such as a tornado or the loss of many lives in battle. In honor of the survivors she prepared a sacred dish of buffalo tongue and pledged to live a life of purity. A Sun Dance ceremony consisted of three days of preparation and four days of dancing. Male members of the tribe constructed a medicine lodge (okan) of a hundred newly cut willows and dedicated it to the sun, the source of all power and knowledge. They covered the okan with offerings of food and drink. Inside

Nineteenth century elk skin robe painted to depict horses, tipis, and Indians fighting. The robe belonged to a Piegan (Blackfoot). (National Museum of the American Indian, Smithsonian Institution)

they said prayers and conducted secret purification rites. The "vow woman" fasted while the lodge was built and presented herself to the assembled worshippers on the fourth day, wearing a sacred headdress, and led the people in prayers. If the prayer was not uttered precisely right or if too few presents, such as horses, blankets, and clothes, were given away by the woman and her family, more terrible disasters could strike the tribe. The Blackfoot Sun Dance did not include incidents of self-torture, such as among the Mandan. It remained the most important event in the yearly cycle of life, however, until ended by missionaries in the 1890's.

When a Blackfoot died, the body was placed in a tree and a horse was killed to accompany the deceased into the land of the dead. If the death took place in a tipi, the tipi was burned. Surviving relatives and friends mutilated themselves to show their grief—slashing their arms or legs, cutting their hair, or cutting off their fingers.

The Blackfeet lived in tipis made of skins. Women built the tipis; men painted them with sacred signs, including star constellations and animals. The men spent much of the summer hunting buffalo. In the fall and spring they gathered turnips, onions, cherries, plums, and berries. Women made clothing, cooked, sought out wood and water, and made pemmican, a favorite food made of dried meat pounded together with blueberries. Besides buffalo meat, the tribe also consumed deer, elk, and antelope. The buffalo, however, provided far more than food. Tribal members found more than sixty uses for various parts of the animal. The buffalo provided clothing and shelter (from the hides), tools (from the bones), and utensils, bags, and storage containers. Before horses were introduced, warriors hunted buffalo by chasing them on foot and stampeding them over cliffs. The Blackfeet learned how to use horses in the early 1700's from other tribes. Hunting strategies changed quickly; warriors now drove the buffalo into a box canyon where they shot them from horseback with bows and arrows. Their hunting territory now spread from central Montana to northern Saskatchewan.

Historical Period. The first contact with whites came in 1806 when Meriwether Lewis reported meeting people called Piegans. Not until the 1830's, however, did the tribe become involved in trade with white Americans. At this time John Jacob Astor's American Fur Company, headquartered in St. Louis, opened a series of trading posts in the northern Great Plains. The company sought buffalo robes and paid for them with guns, blankets, and ammunition. The Blackfeet gained control of a vast area of buffalo range through successful wars with the Flathead, Nez Perce, Crow, Cree, and other Plains tribes. Wealth and weapons acquired in the robe trade enabled the Blackfeet to keep their traditional customs, at least as long as the buffalo herds existed. The coming of the railroads and the increasing number of white farmers moving into the area greatly threatened those herds.

In 1855, the Blackfoot headman (chief) Lame Bull signed a treaty with United States government agents allowing construction of a railroad through tribal lands. American citizens would be able to travel through the territory unharmed. According to the terms of the treaty, the confederacy would receive $20,000 in useful goods and services immediately and $15,000 each year in the future "to promote civilization and Christianization." The United States promised the Blackfeet schools, agricultural training, and perpetual peace. The army established an office at Fort Benton in northern Montana Territory to distribute the goods and services. Beginning in 1856 about seven thousand Blackfeet a year received aid, though many crossed the border from Canada to get their annuities. The Indians, having never recognized such a border, ignored army agent complaints about giving aid to "Canadian" citizens.

In the years after the American Civil War (1861-1865), more and more whites moved into the region and demanded added protection from "savage Indians." Especially troublesome for the Blackfeet were the increasing numbers of cattle ranchers who fenced their lands with barbed wire to keep buffalo out. In 1870, war broke out in Montana after a massacre of 173 Blackfoot men, women, and children by a white volunteer militia. In addition to the dead, 140 women and children were driven from their village into the subzero weather, where they suffered horribly.

In 1874, President Ulysses S. Grant issued an executive order moving the reservation boundary much farther north than had been agreed upon by the Blackfeet. No payment was offered to the Indians. A smallpox epidemic in the new reservation reduced the tribe's population to three thousand, about one-fifth of what it had been a hundred years earlier. At this point, Chief White Calf ordered a halt to any more resistance; "further war would only result in our extermination," he explained.

The Blackfeet living in Canada managed much better than their American brothers. In 1877, the Canadian government signed a treaty creating a reserve on which Blackfeet could live, hunt, raise cattle, and receive government rations. Only at this point did the American-Canadian border achieve any significance in tribal history, as people north of the line improved the quality of their lives while those living south of it suffered a continuing population decline. By 1880, only twenty-two hundred Blackfeet lived on the United States reservation surrounded by a white population of over twelve thousand. The buffalo had practically disappeared, in all of North America only a few hundred having survived the hunters. With the annihilation of their main source of subsistence, the Blackfeet became impoverished; more than six hundred suffered horrible deaths in the "starvation winter" of 1883-1884. Rations provided by the army allowed 1.5 pounds of meat, 8 ounces of flour, and smaller amounts of beans, bacon, salt, and coffee for each individual. Another bitter winter hit the reservation in 1886-1887, but the rations still were not increased and hundreds more died.

The Roman Catholic church provided much of the education on the reservation in the early days. An elementary school had opened in 1859, but after thirteen years a new agent, the Methodist minister John Young, closed the school and opened one of his own. Catholics were forced to attend school off the reservation. Jesuit missionaries built a school a few miles away, but refused to allow parents the right to visit students during the school term. Isolating children from parents, it was hoped, would break down old loyalties and habits and encourage young Indians to adopt white ways. The reservation school taught English, Christianity, and "modern" ways. Whichever institution the students attended, any connection with their past customs and traditions was effectively torn away from them.

Reservation Life. In 1895, Blackfoot leaders leased thousands of acres of land back to the federal government, with Indians retaining the right to hunt, fish, and cut timber on the property. The leased land supposedly contained large deposits of gold, but prospectors actually found little of value in the territory. Much of this land became Glacier National Park a few years later.

After 1900, economic conditions on the reservation became even worse, largely because of a failed attempt by the Indian Office in Washington, D.C., to "civilize" the Blackfeet by teaching them how to farm. The leasing of land for grazing cattle had at least provided a meager income to the tribe, but now some experts in the Indian office believed that collecting grazing fees just made the Indians "lazy." Farming, it was decided, was a manlier, healthier, more appropriate way to make a living. Accordingly, the local agent contracted to have a huge irrigation system built. The reservation, however, had little water of its own. It was also windy and subject to extremes of temperature, and crops could not be grown. The irrigation project proved to be a costly waste of time and effort.

The agent in charge of the reservation then encouraged cattle ranching. In 1904, the Blackfeet paid to have their land fenced to keep out non-Indian cattle, but a drought that year, a tough winter the next, and an epidemic disease the next killed thousands of reservation cattle. The Blackfeet stayed poor. Other problems resulted from a rapid turnover in agents; from 1905 to 1921 ten different men filled the post. Some of the agents quit after being charged with corruption, while others were simply weak or incompetent. Weather continued to have a devastating impact on reservation life. The 1920's saw a long dry spell bringing fires and tremendous heat as well as grasshoppers, cutworms, and other plagues to the area. Grain and cattle prices fell, and many surrounding communities became ghost towns. The Blackfeet, of course, could not leave. Poverty, sickness, and hunger spread. Two out of three Blackfeet were living entirely on government rations.

A new agent in the late 1920's improved conditions somewhat by encouraging small gardens for each household and the raising of chickens and pigs. He also promoted adult education and literacy programs. Then the Great Depression hit, its impact on the reservations mirroring that on American society at large. The Indian Reorganization Act of 1934 promoted self-government and a return to cultural traditions. It also brought some money into the community for small construction projects. These helped many Blackfeet survive the worst ravages of the Depression years, but hunger and poverty persisted for many on the reservation.

The Great Northern Railroad provided some help by hiring Blackfeet to give performances at its lodge in Glacier National Park. The park had opened in 1910 and lay outside the territory the Blackfeet had actually lived in, but tourists enjoyed the Indian dances all the same. The Blackfeet still performed the Sun Dance but by the 1930's had moved the date of celebration to July 4. Missionaries who formerly had denounced the dance as heathen could hardly object when the dancers insisted that their only motive was to celebrate the birthday of their new homeland. Allowing Indians to practice their traditional religions, as provided for by the 1934 act, came too late to save many Blackfeet customs. Poverty, death, and disease had already taken their toll; meanwhile, white schools had ruined any opportunity for the Blackfeet to maintain their traditional language. Few young Blackfeet could speak the old tongue anymore, and with its passing went most of the traditions of Blackfoot life.

Conditions on the reservation improved somewhat after World War II, and only a few tribal members participated in the disastrous resettlement plan of the 1950's when the Bureau of Indian Affairs tried to force Indians from their reservations and place them in cities. In the 1960's, many Blackfeet got jobs through the War on Poverty as Head Start teachers, firefighters, and government welfare agents. Others obtained employment in the sugar-beet and hay fields of northern Montana. A few became teachers, doctors, lawyers, and engineers. Still, the per capita income on the reservation was well below the poverty level, and many Blackfeet in the late twentieth century found themselves trapped in joblessness and hopelessness.

Leslie V. Tischauser

Bibliography

Arima, Eugene Y. *Blackfeet and Palefaces: The Pikani and Rocky Mountain House: A Commemorative History from the Upper Saskatchewan and Missouri Fur Trade.* Ottawa, Ont.: Golden Dog Press, 1995.

Brandon, William. *The Indian in American Culture.* New York: Harper & Row, 1974. A massive volume covering the entire period of Indian-white relations, with a few pages devoted to the Blackfeet. Useful for placing the confederacy into the overall picture of Indian life in North America. Good index and bibliography.

Dempsey, Hugh A. *The Amazing Death of Calf Shirt and Other Blackfoot Stories: Three Hundred Years of Blackfoot History.* Saskatoon, Sask.: Fifth House Publishers, 1994.

_____. *Bibliography of the Blackfoot.* Saskatoon, Sask.: Fifth House Publishers, 1989.

Jenish, D'Arcy. *Indian Fall: The Last Great Days of the Plains Cree and the Blackfoot Confederacy.* Toronto: Viking Press, 1999.

Johnson, Bryan R. *The Blackfeet: An Annotated Bibliography.* New York: Garland, 1988.

McClintock, Walter, and William E. Farr. *The Old North Trail, or Life, Legends, and Religion of the Blackfeet Indians.* Lincoln: University of Nebraska Press, 1999.

McFee, Malcolm. *Modern Blackfeet.* New York: Holt, Rinehart and Winston, 1972. A scholarly, well-researched, and very readable volume on the problems of assimilation faced by the Blackfeet Confederacy. A look at life on the reservation, and a history of Bureau of Indian Affairs policies toward the Blackfeet. A detailed bibliography and useful index.

Washburn, Wilcomb E. *The Indian in America.* New York: Harper & Row, 1975. Essential reading for anyone interested in any tribe in North America. The best single-volume history of American Indians from their origins to the 1970's. Contains a comprehensive bibliography and detailed index.

Wissler, Clark. "Material Culture of the Blackfoot Indians." In *Anthropological Papers of the American Museum of Natural History, No. 5.* New York: American Museum of Natural History, 1910. Still-useful compilation of field notes and observations by an early student of American Indian ways of life. Good sections on the Sun Dance and Blackfoot customs and economics.

Caddo tribal group

CULTURE AREA: Plains
LANGUAGE GROUP: Caddoan
PRIMARY LOCATION: Oklahoma
POPULATION SIZE: 2,549 (1990 U.S. Census); 2,500 according to Caddo tribal roll

The Caddo Nation historically included the Hasinai, Kadohadacho, and Natchitoche alliances of peoples. It existed for centuries before the modern era in what is now the northwest portion of Louisiana, east Texas, southwest Arkansas, and southeastern Oklahoma. In this region of river valleys and upland forests, the Caddo hunted and cultivated the rich fauna and flora in a sustainable manner. They hunted deer, peccary, and bear as well as small game animals. Long expeditions were sent out on the Southern Plains to hunt buffalo and antelope in the spring and the fall. In early spring, migrations south to the Gulf Coast were made to feast on turtles, sea bird eggs, and early spring fruit. Vegetables, fruit, and berries were cultivated in riverine areas in great variety, including amaranth, blackberries, and potatoes.

With the introduction of bows and arrows, hunting became more efficient. Agricultural innovations made it possible to sustain larger populations. Especially important was the introduction of corn and pumpkin. The Caddo planted and harvested two varieties of corn, one smaller and early maturing, the other larger and more abundant. Intensive agricultural methods provided a reasonable harvest yet did not deplete the soil, especially when the corn was grown with beans. Corn and pumpkin were preserved through drying and roasting methods. Food surpluses strengthened the place of the Caddo Nation in relation to other peoples. Food was preserved and stored for future use or traded for items that further enriched the Caddo people. Agriculture continued as a principal means of supporting life for the Caddo well into the twentieth century. Agricultural patterns were based on observation. Each person was taught never to be false with the earth, for lack of respect only leads to destruction.

Classic Villages and Ceremonial Complexes. The classic Caddo villages and ceremonial centers dominated the river courses of the ancient landscape in the Arkansas, Red, Sabine, Neches, and Angelina valleys. Towns were surrounded by the fields given over to intensive forms of agricultural production of maize or corn, beans, pumpkins, squash, and other foodstuffs. Inside the circle of houses of extended families was the central plaza, the public meeting buildings, monuments, and community storage houses. Walkways connected the village's living areas with its community service areas, the fields, and the water courses.

Architectural and artistic evidence of the classical forms of Caddoan culture have been collected from villages and centers throughout the region of their existence. In the eastern and southern portions of the region, styles closely resemble those of the region of the Mississippi River populations, but in the core Caddo areas their own styles dominate, expressing genius in engraving and design. Elements of design unlike those originating elsewhere appear in important sites such as *Keewut'* (the Davis site near Alto, Texas, in the Neches River valley) and *Dit-teh* (the Spiro mound complex in the Arkansas River Valley in present-day Oklahoma).

The Davis site is on a high alluvial terrace above an old stream bed about a mile from the present course of the Neches River. The remains of this ceremonial complex extend over approximately 60 acres. The most prominent architectural features are three large mounds constructed of rammed earth, clay, and ash. Two of the mound structures are considered to be temple platforms. The third is defined as a burial mound. The outlines of houses and other material remains are concentrated around and between the mound structures. These include the remains of pottery and stone implements as well as marine shell, copper, high-quality flint, and galena, which were imported into the area.

The Spiro mound complex is dominated by two large monumental structures and a series of seven smaller mounds. The burial mound at the extreme eastern edge of the site is the largest in the ceremonial complex. It measures approximately 91 meters in length, 37 meters in width, and 10 meters in height at its highest point. Architectural features found within the burial mound structure are the primary mound, a clay basin area, a central chamber, and an earthen ramp extending northeast from the main structure. In the central chamber archaeologists found thousands of pearls, elaborate shell engravings, copper images, and carved cedar as well as shaped flint, stone celts, and axes. It is one of the most treasured collections of pre-Columbian art in North America.

Another way to look at the story of the Caddo Nation is through the facts and philosophies that are found within the framework of Caddo dance patterns and songs, notably the traditional Turkey Dance and Drum Dance. Some stories that form parts of the dances and songs relate specific events in the lives of the people, locating them in space and time. Others are historical only in that they communicate a sense of the meaning of history rather than present a record of events. Still others record natural events that have affected the lives of the people. The sequence of songs and dances is destroyed if the stories that speak to the meaning of the people's existence are ignored and only events themselves are expressed.

The Turkey Dance: Historical Insight. The Turkey Dance is always done in the afternoon. It relates the stream of events in relationship to the land through time that defines the Caddo peoples within the centering device of song and dance. The women dance the principal sequences expressing the active logic of the Caddo people.

For the dance, the drum is placed in the center of the dance ground. Male singers sit around the drum. They begin by calling the dancers through several songs. The first of these songs translates as "Come, you turkeys." As the women dancers begin to arrive in the dance plaza, they start to dance in a circle, dancing on the balls of their feet in a clockwise direction, in harmony with the earth.

The singers continue, describing the movement of the dancers. The next songs repeat the message of the first, but in the dialects of the various tribes within the Caddo Nation, including the Haish or Eyeish, Neche, Hainai, Yona, Ceni, and Keechi (Kichai). The Keechi are now affiliated with the Wichita Nation but are still remembered as part of the Caddo Nation. Only the Hasinai, Hainai, and Haish dialects are still spoken with any frequency, although each of the dialects is used in the song sequence.

By the end of the first sequence of songs, the dance ground is filled with the color and movement of the women in their traditional dresses. The Turkey Dancers wear clothing of every color—purples, reds, yellows, greens, and blues. The dresses are usually of one piece, with unmarried women having their clothing buttoned in the back and married ones having theirs buttoned in the front. Over the dresses are long aprons that are tied at the waist. The most distinctive feature of their clothing is the *dush-tooh*, a butterfly-shaped board tied to a silver crown worn in the hair. This is decorated with ribbon pendants and streamers with attached shell or small round mirrors.

The next cycle of songs is the longest. The women in single file follow the lead dancer, imitating the turkey's gait. They dart each foot forward in turn, then quickly draw it back before planting it on the ground. The feet then alternate in rapid succession. During this phase, the songs relate events and insights from the Caddo collective past. These are records of significant occurrences and understandings in the history of the people. These range from single military engagements to major natural phenomena. Songs carry the story of events that occurred both before and after the forced removal into Indian Territory that climaxed in 1859.

An example of the pre-removal record is that of an eyewitness account of the creation of Caddo Lake. The lake exists on the present Louisiana-Texas border northwest of Shreveport. Two brothers watched as the Caddo people danced through the night in the traditional sequence of dances that includes the Drum Dance, the Bear Dance, the Corn Dance, the Duck Dance, the Alligator Dance, the Women's Dance, the Stirrup Dance, the Quapaw Dance, the Vine Dance (sometimes known as the Cherokee Dance), the Bell Dance, and the Morning Dance. Several village populations were present at the dance. As it proceeded, the water near the dance ground began to rise. The brothers watched as the people continued to dance while the water rose around them. The older of the two brothers called out: "Let's go to higher ground—we might all drown." The people went on dancing despite his efforts. It was then that the brothers noticed movement to the east of the dance ground. They perceived something like a great serpent writhing across the stream bed. This undulating form was holding back the water. The dancers continued to dance, even as they disappeared beneath the surface of the water.

Finally, the younger brother went for help, but he did not return until after dawn. The lake was formed where the people had danced through the night. As the people surveyed the scene they found no serpent, but a natural ridge of land retaining the water, as it does to this day. Some say the people still dance beneath the surface of the water. Others say that the older brother was frozen in fright as he continued to watch the scene. His form is said to be found in stone on the high ground above the lake.

At times during the dance sequence, the women can go to the center of the dance plaza to give the singers some tobacco and tell a story involving an event or insight that further carried the Caddo sense of heritage. These stories are sometimes incorporated into the collected public history of the Caddo Nation in the form of a new song. (At other times, the woman may give tobacco to the singer and simply say, "I have no story.") In this way new materials are added to the history as the Caddo moved from their place of origin in southeastern North America up the valleys of the Red River, the Sabine River, and the Neches and Angelina rivers, out onto the southern Great Plains. The dance cycle continues until the end of the historical song sequences.

After an extended pause, the third sequence of songs begins. During this phase of the Turkey Dance, the singers relate a basic philosophical outlook. The dancers move to and from the center of the dance ground examining the singers at the center. As they continue, the dancers examine the center from a variety of perspectives around the dance plaza. The underlying thought is that the Caddo should examine every concern from a variety of perspectives, up close and far away, until they can bring about a decision that is appropriate for the community.

A final segment of the dance begins with a song that tells the women to select a male partner. They dance in a counter-clockwise fashion around the dance ground. Sometimes the women must choose the man and catch him for the dance. If he still refuses, he must offer her an article of clothing, which he must redeem at the end of the dance.

At the foundation of the Turkey Dance is the feeling that the Caddo people can find the center for the community in this analog. Throughout the centuries, all Caddo people have repeated these patterns in dance and song so that they know who they are. Without the Turkey Dance and the other dance sequences, the individuals are lost. The historiography of the dance and its songs provides a civilized frame of reference for lifeway concerns—for public and private decision making.

The Drum Dance: Governance and Development. The initial dance of the night-time dance sequence is the Drum Dance. It tells of the origins of the Caddo people as they emerged from the world of darkness into the world of light. It patterns the nature and structure of governance among the Caddo as well as the spiritual and economic underpinnings of traditional society. The patterns of the dance represent the self-organizing thought patterns that are critical to thought and feeling. The dance refers directly to the emergence of the sun in the universe, the place of emergence of the Caddo people, the ecology of sustainable development, and the village system of life. It also refers to cultural heroes such as Medicine Screech Owl, who introduced the bow and arrow and provided a code of behavior for the Caddo. It also refers to the importance of dreams and visions to appropriate behavior as well as to the symbolic loss and reintroduction of the drum in Caddo lifeways.

Tribal and International Relationships. The Caddo Nation maintained generally harmonious relations with the tribes in the region of the Mississippi Valley and the Southern Plains. They have had close associations with the Wichita Nation for centuries. They also worked with other tribes as they appeared on the Southern Plains, such as the Comanche, Kiowa, and Apache. The Caddo had more strained relations with the Chickasaw and the Osage as they were forced to hunt farther and farther west in the modern era.

Of the European nations, the Caddo Nation was recognized by both the Spanish and the French as the dominant force in the region between the Mississippi River and the Rio Grande. The Spanish named the province of Texas using a corruption of a Hasinai word for "friends," *ta'-sha*. While the Spanish attempted to introduce European feudal practices among the Caddo people, the French traded on a commercial scale which brought about more favorable relations. U.S. relations with the Caddo Nation primarily involved forceful removal from Louisiana to Texas and then to Indian Territory or Oklahoma, where the Caddo tribe is one of several federally recognized tribes in the area of Anadarko, Oklahoma.

In 1938, a measure of home rule was afforded the Caddo under the Oklahoma Indian Welfare Act of 1936 when it was accepted by the Caddo voters. A Caddo constitution was drawn up and accepted in 1938 along with an economic charter that provided for economic development. The Caddo constitution has been revised several times since the New Deal era to provide more effective governance. The constitution remains true to the federated style of government that has been Caddo tradition for centuries. The tribal council is chosen according to the district in which the member lives. The parliamentary style of governance is headed by the tribal chairperson, who is a member and chief officer of the council. The tribe supports a number of social and economic programs for the benefit of the Caddo people. It also enables cultural retention through the preservation of the Caddo languages, customs, music, dances, crafts, and values. In this way the Caddo maintain a bicultural perception of the world around them.

Howard Meredith

Bibliography

Carter, Cecile E. *Caddo Indians: Where We Come From*. Norman: University of Oklahoma Press, 1995.

Dorsey, George A., comp. *Traditions of the Caddo*. Washington, D.C.: Carnegie Institution of Washington, 1905. This material was collected by George Dorsey from Caddo informants in Indian Territory in the early twentieth century.

Early, Ann M., and Barbara Burnett. *Caddoan Saltmakers in the Ouachita Valley: The Hardman Site*. Fayetteville, Ark.: Arkansas Archeological Survey, 1993.

Gregory, H. F., ed. *The Southern Caddo: An Anthology*. New York: Garland, 1986. This is an excellent source of a variety of materials on ethnohistory, sociological tracts, linguistics, physical anthropology, archaeology, material culture, and arts.

John, Elizabeth A. *Storms Brewed in Other Men's Worlds: The Confrontation of the Indians, Spanish, and French in the Southwest, 1540-1795*. College Station: Texas A&M University Press, 1975. A narrative history of Indian-white relations that heavily involved the Caddo Nation.

La Vere, David. *The Caddo Chiefdoms: Caddo Economics and Politics, 700-1835*. Lincoln: University of Nebraska Press, 1998.

Meredith, Howard. *Southern Plains Alliances*. Lawrence: University Press of Kansas, 1994. This is an interdisciplinary study of the intertribal relationships of the Southern Plains tribes in which the Caddo Nation has participated from the early centuries of the modern era to the early 1990's.

Moss, William. *The Wisdom of Oat*. Austin, Tex.: Triangle Books, 1993. William Moss, a Caddo, is a direct descendant of Oat, a Caddo signer of the United States-Caddo Treaty of 1835. This is a reflection of the leadership tradition passed down through that family.

Newkumet, Vynola Beaver, and Howard L. Meredith. *Hasinai: A Traditional History of the Caddo Confederacy*. College Station: Texas A&M University

Press, 1988. This is the first academically published interpretation of the Caddo Nation and people by a Caddo author.

Perttula, Timothy K. *The Caddo Nation: Archaeological and Ethnohistoric Perspectives*. Austin: University of Texas Press, 1992. A sensitive overview of Caddoan cultural materialism that corresponds to tribal tradition. It contains useful maps and statistical information.

Smith, F. Todd. *The Caddos, the Wichitas, and the United States, 1846-1901*. College Station: Texas A&M University Press, 1996.

_____. *The Caddo Indians: Tribes at the Convergence of Empires, 1542-1854*. College Station: Texas A&M University Press, 1995.

Story, Dee Ann, ed. *Archeological Investigations at the George C. Davis Site*. Austin: University of Texas Press, 1981. This is a very readable study of a specific classical Caddoan site; it offers an excellent overview of Caddoan studies.

Swanton, John R., comp. *Source Material on the History and Ethnology of the Caddo Indians*. Washington, D.C.: Government Printing Office, 1942. Edited material collected from Caddo informants and foreign observers about the Caddo, which was deposited at the Smithsonian Institution, Bureau of American Ethnology.

Whitebead, Irving, and Howard Meredith. *"Nuh-Ka-Oashun*: Hasinai Turkey Dance Tradition."* In *Songs of Indian Territory: Native American Music Traditions of Oklahoma*, edited by Willie Smyth. Oklahoma City: Center of the American Indian, 1989. This is a study of the historical tradition of the Caddo by one of the most important lead singers of the Caddo tribe.

Cahuilla

CULTURE AREA: California
LANGUAGE GROUP: Uto-Aztecan
PRIMARY LOCATION: Southern California
POPULATION SIZE: 1,418 (1990 U.S. Census)

Cahuilla Indians lived at the southern tip of California. Men used the bow and arrow to hunt deer, rabbits, and mountain sheep; women roasted and dried surplus meat for winter use and gathered acorns, piñon nuts, seeds, beans, fruit, and berries. Many of the goods so gathered were ground into flour and stored in pots and baskets.

Cahuilla villages were situated near water, which became scarce in summer. The homes were constructed of brush gathered together and formed into dome-shaped structures; there were also some larger dwellings, rectangular in shape, that could be as long as twenty feet. Men wore deerskin loincloths; women wore skirts made from mesquite bark or deerskin. Rabbitskin blankets provided winter warmth.

Cleanliness was very important to Cahuilla. They regularly bathed and sweated in village sweathouses. It was a great disgrace for any foreign particles to be discovered on household utensils and baskets. They believed in supernatural spirits and a universal power which explained unusual or miraculous events. Elderly tribe members were greatly respected; they taught values and skills to the young and were regarded as repositories of knowledge.

In 1774, Spanish explorer Juan Bautista de Anza made the first documented contact with Cahuilla Indians. Because Cahuilla and other local tribes were hostile to Europeans, white settlers avoided the area for many years. Cahuilla Indians finally did become involved with Europeans through the Spanish missions. They adopted certain aspects of Spanish culture, including trade, Roman Catholicism, animal husbandry, and wage labor.

In 1863, a smallpox epidemic struck the Cahuilla, cutting their population in half. This left the tribe defenseless against the increasing number of

Early twentieth century Cahuilla woman, carrying nuts or berries in a decorated basket.
(Library of Congress)

Americans who began to settle in their region. After 1891, the U.S. government began overseeing Cahuillan life and activities. Schools and Protestant missions were opened, and several traditional practices—particularly Cahuilla religious activities— were discouraged.

During the 1960's, federal resources provided significant improvements in health, education, and general welfare. In the second half of the twentieth century, the Cahuillas raised cattle and worked in civil service, construction, social work, and blue collar jobs. Despite such modernization, a number of traditional foods were still favored and Cahuilla songs and dances were performed on holidays.

Calusa

CULTURE AREA: Southeast
LANGUAGE GROUP: Muskogean (probable)
PRIMARY LOCATION: Florida

The Calusa were a nomadic people who inhabited the south Florida peninsula from the Tampa Bay area to Lake Okeechobee, including the Florida Keys. They may have been related to the Muskogee family in North America. Stories of their cannibalism, human sacrifice, and piracy suggest a connection to the South American or Caribbean Indians.

Historians believe the Calusa numbered about three thousand at the time of their first contact with whites (around 1513), when the Spanish explorer Ponce de León attempted to enter Calusa land. The Calusa lived up to their name, which means "fierce people," and forced Ponce de León to retreat after a prolonged battle. Spanish missionaries made several forays into the area but abandoned the attempt to convert the Calusa around 1569.

The Calusas' success in repelling the European invaders also depended upon their reliance on hunting and fishing instead of agriculture. The tribe roamed freely throughout south Florida, harvesting the bounty of the sea and native plants that grew year round, rather than building more permanent villages and planting crops; sites of Calusa settlements along the Florida coast are marked by huge shell mounds. This nomadic life made them less vulnerable to the Spanish, who often subjugated the Indians by burning their storehouses, leaving the tribes without food for the winter.

Like most Southeastern Woodlands tribes, the Calusa probably followed a matrilineal clan structure: Familial relationships depended on the mother's connections. Calusa women prepared and preserved food, though they did not have to plant and cultivate like women of other tribes. The men, through their intimate knowledge of the sea, became excellent swimmers and divers, made strong, seaworthy canoes, and plundered sunken Spanish ships for gold and silver to make jewelry (as well as making captives of stranded crew members).

In spite of their independence, the Calusa population seems to have dwindled rapidly, probably from diseases introduced by the European invaders; by the time the Seminoles entered the area in the late 1700's, few members of the tribe remained. These few were probably assimilated into the Seminoles; some may have moved to Cuba.

Cape Fear

CULTURE AREA: Southeast
LANGUAGE GROUP: Siouan
PRIMARY LOCATION: Cape Fear River, North Carolina

The proper name of this tribe is unknown; they were designated "Cape Fear" by European Americans. The matrilineal Cape Fear group gained their subsistence primarily from different types of maize, squash, beans, and other plants tended by women, who also gathered numerous types of nuts, seeds, and roots. Hunting, trapping, and fishing supplemented their diet.

English settlers from New England may have been the first to contact the Cape Fear people in 1661, but they were driven away after the settlers kidnapped several Indian children, under the pretense of civilizing them. A small colony of settlers from Barbados arrived in 1663 but soon left. Numerous settlements were attempted by European Americans. In 1695 the Cape Fear asked Governor Archdale for protection, which was granted after the Cape Fear Indians rescued fifty-two passengers from a wrecked New England ship. After the 1716 Yamasee War they were moved inland from Charleston, South Carolina. Records indicate that by 1808 only twenty Cape Fear people remained.

Carib

CULTURE AREA: Mesoamerica
LANGUAGE GROUP: Cariban
PRIMARY LOCATION: Lesser Antilles

The Caribs, the third Indian group to migrate from the north coast of South America through the Lesser Antilles, began their move northward in the fifth century; by the end of the fourteenth century they had expelled or incorporated the Arawaks in the Lesser Antilles.

The Caribs, who were farmers and fishermen, located their villages high on the windward slopes of mountains near running water. Land was communally owned, but canoes and ornaments were personal property. Tobacco was used as money. The Caribs erected small, wood-framed, oval or rectangular houses with thatched roofs around a plaza with a communal fireplace.

The plaza served as the center of ceremonies and social life. Furnishings were few: small wooden tables, metates (grinding stones), griddles, stools, hammocks, gourds, and pottery. Their diet consisted of fish, lizards, crabs, agouti, corn, sweet potatoes, yams, beans, and peppers. Turtles and manatees were forbidden foods because of the fear that eating them would make a person slow. Men and women shared the tasks of making canoes, beer, baskets, and textiles. Both sexes shaped their skulls, wore amulets and charms, and decorated their bodies with flowers, coral or stone, gold dust, and red, white, and black paint. Persons of rank wore crescents of gold or copper.

The Caribs were closely related culturally to the Arawaks but were less organized socially. Their villages were small, usually populated by an extended family. The leader, often head of the family, supervised the activities of the village and settled village disputes. He also served as military chief and led raiding parties.

War was the main activity of the Caribs, who were fierce fighters. Their weapons included bows, poisoned arrows, javelins, and clubs embedded with sharpened flint. The Caribs were excellent sailors and could construct a war canoe from the trunk of a single tree that could carry more than a hundred men. They also lashed canoes together to form rafts for longer voyages. The Caribs raided Arawak settlements, reaching Puerto Rico by the 1490's. Captured Arawak men were killed and sometimes cooked and eaten. Captured women and children were taken away as slaves; the women were settled in breeding colonies which the Carib warriors visited periodically.

Carib religion had no elaborate rituals. Each individual Carib had a personal deity that could take many forms and to which the Carib sometimes offered cassava (a plant with a nutritious edible root). Good and evil spirits fought constantly, both within the body and everywhere in nature. Shamans attempted to ward off the evil spirits and to please the good ones.

The Spaniards did not settle the Lesser Antilles, but the Caribs' skill as fighters and their reputation as cannibals did not prevent other European nations from displacing them later. The Caribs were limited to the islands of St. Vincent and Dominica. On St. Vincent they mixed with shipwrecked slaves and became known as the "Black Caribs," who in 1795 were transferred by the English to Roatan Island off Honduras. They spread onto the mainland and northward into Guatemala. A small Carib population lives on a reservation on Dominica.

Carrier

CULTURE AREA: Subarctic
LANGUAGE GROUP: Northern Athapaskan
PRIMARY LOCATION: British Columbia, Canada
POPULATION SIZE: 6,910 (Statistics Canada, based on 1991 census)

The Carrier, members of the Northern Athapaskan language group, got their name because widows of the tribe carried the bones of their deceased husbands in a small bag on their backs during a one-year mourning period. The original location of the Carrier remains unknown, though they moved into the area of north-central British Columbia between the Rocky Mountains and the Coastal range several hundred years before first contact with whites. The Carrier lived in small subtribal groups in isolated villages. Ideas of individual ownership did not exist, and land belonged to the people using it. The Carrier fished for salmon; hunted caribou, mountain goats, and sheep; gathered berries and turnips; and—in the hard times of winter—survived by eating the bark of hemlock trees.

Carrier religion centered on a belief in a vast spirit world. Spirits could be talked to during dreams. A young man found a guardian spirit of his own after a two-week-long period of fasting, praying, and dreaming in the wilderness. This spirit was said to remain with a person for his entire life, offering protection and guidance. Potlatches were held every year by clan chiefs and wealthy tribe members, who gave away huge amounts of food and property to demonstrate their power and generosity. Individuals gained status by giving away goods rather than accumulating them as in European value systems.

Europeans first contacted the Carrier in 1793 along the Fraser River. The Carrier wanted guns and horses and gave furs to the whites in exchange. Until the 1850's, the Hudson's Bay Company provided the only contact with white civilization. Still, the trappers brought measles and smallpox with them which severely reduced the Indian population. A gold rush in 1858 brought thousands of prospectors, and then farmers and ranchers. The Carrier population continued to decline. The Canadian government established a reservation in 1876. Sawmills opened, and the lumber industry provided most of the employment for the Indians—though the greatest cash income for the tribe came from old-age assistance programs and welfare.

Catawba

CULTURE AREA: Southeast
LANGUAGE GROUP: Siouan
PRIMARY LOCATION: South Carolina
POPULATION SIZE: 1,078 (1990 U.S. Census)

The Catawba (or Katapu) tribe is the largest of the eastern Siouan tribes, the only one to have survived into the twentieth century under its original name. Like most Southern Woodlands tribes, the Catawba grew corn, beans, and squash, and were known for their skill in pottery making and basket weaving. The Catawba inhabited the area that would become the North/South Carolina border. The Catawba were sometimes known as Isswa, "the river people." The Catawba River and Catawba grape are both named for this group. First contact with whites probably occurred in the 1560's, when Spanish explorers occupied the region. The Catawba were generally friendly to the English, becoming their allies during skirmishes with the Tuscarora tribe in the early 1700's and later joining them against the French and northern Indians.

The Catawba, whose name means "strong" or "separated people," had a history of enmity with other tribes. A long-standing state of war existed between them and several other tribes, among them the Cherokee, the Iroquois, and the Shawnee. Battles were often prompted by white settlers' encroachment into Indian territory, forcing one tribe to move into another's domain. The Catawba took several smaller tribes (the Congeree, Sugaree, Wateree, Sewee, Santee, and others) under their protection and probably later assimilated the remnants of these groups. Between 1738 and 1776, the Catawba were ravaged by smallpox; the tribe never recovered their previous numbers or importance. In 1840, they were tricked into signing over their land in South Carolina in exchange for land in North Carolina. The North Carolinians refused to honor the treaty, however, and the Catawba were forced to retreat, homeless. They were eventually granted a reservation in York County, South Carolina, where some members of the tribe still remain. Others moved west, to Oklahoma, Arkansas, and Utah; many joined the Choctaw. In 1970, only seventy Catawba Indians lived on the South Carolina reservation (some records indicate that only mixed-blood descendants of the tribe existed); by the mid-1980's, they numbered more than a thousand and were engaged in a legal battle to regain some 140,000 acres of their homeland.

Cayuga

CULTURE AREA: Northeast
LANGUAGE GROUP: Iroquoian
PRIMARY LOCATION: New York State, Ontario
POPULATION SIZE: 1,048 in U.S. (1990 U.S. Census); estimated 1,000 in Canada

One of the original five tribes of the Iroquois Confederacy, the Cayugas occupied a homeland between the Senecas to their west and the Onondagas to their east in what is now west-central New York State. The Cayuga language is very closely related to those of the other Iroquois tribes and to other Iroquoian languages. The name Cayuga is thought to mean "where the boats were taken out," "where the locusts were taken out," or "mucky land." The Iroquois Confederacy Council name for the Cayugas refers to them as "those of the great pipe." Like their fellow Iroquois, the Cayugas were divided into matrilineal clans, with a spokesman for each clan in the political system appointed by the matron of each clan. The Cayugas were matrilocal—a marrying couple would live with the wife's family. Consequently, married men were guests in their wives' extended family households.

Men in Cayuga society traditionally spent much of their time away from the village hunting, fishing, trading, and engaging in warfare. Women were the primary breadwinners, raising the staple crops of corn, beans, and squash as well as tobacco and other agricultural products. Cayuga villages were composed of twenty to fifty longhouses, extended-family dwellings made of poles and bark coverings. Each longhouse housed between fifteen and thirty people. The Cayuga population was estimated at 1,500 in 1660, after the first epidemics of European diseases had taken their toll. For most of the eighteenth century, the Cayugas occupied only one village, and their population fell partly because of disease but also from extensive warfare. The Iroquois Confederacy was engaged in a series of wars with both other tribes and European powers, most notably the French. They initiated the "Beaver Wars" of the mid-1600's and were periodically involved in military expeditions until the American Revolution.

In the war of American independence, the Cayugas and most other Iroquois sided with the British, and they lost most of their homelands in what is now New York State. Most Cayugas moved to the Grand River in what is now Ontario, Canada, and settled on a large reserve set aside for the Six Nations of the Iroquois Confederacy. Many still reside there. A few remained in New York, and some moved to Sandusky, Ohio, in the early nineteenth century with some Senecas, eventually moving to Oklahoma. A few remain in Oklahoma. Some traveled with a group of New York Oneidas to Wisconsin in the 1830's, their descendants remaining there. The Cayugas still living in New York and Ontario retain much of their traditional culture: Their language is still spoken, and traditional ceremonies such as the Green Corn Ceremony and the Midwinter Festival are still held. Cayugas all live with other Iroquois people and must strive to maintain their distinctiveness in the face of larger numbers of Onondagas and Senecas.

Cayuga contact with the French, Dutch, and English in the colonial era was not as great as it was for the Onondagas and Mohawks. The Cayugas often were overshadowed by the larger Onondaga and Seneca tribes. Nevertheless, the Cayugas did deal with the French and succeeding English and American missionaries, who at times attempted to change their culture as well as their religious beliefs. Handsome Lake, a Seneca prophet who revitalized traditional Iroquois spiritual beliefs and blended them with Quaker Christian ideas in the early nineteenth century, had an impact on many Cayuga people; some still adhere to this Longhouse religion. Others are nominally Christian, a legacy of the various missionary attempts to proselytize the Iroquois.

Cayuse

CULTURE AREA: Plateau
LANGUAGE GROUP: Penutian, Sahaptian
PRIMARY LOCATION: Oregon and Washington
POPULATION SIZE: 126 (1990 U.S. Census)

The Cayuse tribe is generally considered a Plateau tribe, but some scholars consider the Cayuse a Great Basin group. The Cayuse were called "Cailloux," meaning "People of the Stones," by early French-Canadian fur traders. They were closely related to the Walla Wallas of southeastern Washington and to the Nez Perce, with whom they intermarried and whose more flexible language they eventually adopted. They lived primarily near the headwaters of the Walla Walla, Umatilla, and Grande Ronde rivers. The Cayuse acquired horses relatively early and became known as expert riders (the term "cayuse" was eventually adopted by whites to refer to Indian ponies generally).

Little is known of the pre-contact history of the Cayuse. Some of the earliest information about the tribe was recorded in the journals of the

Cayuse mother and child, photographed in 1910 by Edward S. Curtis, who recorded the traditional culture of North American Indians in thousands of photographs.
(Library of Congress)

Lewis and Clark expedition and in historical documents describing the activities of missionary Marcus Whitman in the Walla Walla, Washington, region.

By 1844, the number of European Americans arriving in Cayuse territory had escalated to the point that a dramatic increase in confrontations was occurring between the two groups. In the mid-nineteenth century, the Cayuse became regarded by whites as one of the more fierce and warlike tribes. Two sources of tension were the activities of missionaries and, later, the fact that whites repeatedly sought to move the Cayuse from their land. Among the missionaries in the area were Whitman, Samuel Parker, and Roman Catholic priests François Norbert Blanchet and Modeste Demers. In 1841, the two priests baptized several Cayuse chiefs and the baby of Chief Tauitau. In 1847, a group of Cayuse killed missionary Whitman along with thirteen others, beginning what is known as the Cayuse War (1847-1850). The Cayuse were angry and worried that he and other missionaries, in attempting to win converts, were beginning to destroy traditional Cayuse beliefs and lifeways. In return, a vigilante army launched a devastating attack on the Cayuse.

In 1856, about a year after the Walla Walla Treaty, a general war broke out among the Plateau tribes, who essentially wanted their lands back. The Cayuse were unable to keep their lands in the Walla Walla Valley, however, and they had to move to the Umatilla Reservation. In 1886, because whites wanted land that was part of the Umatilla Reservation, the reservation was reduced to about one-fourth of its original size.

The modern Cayuse population is small. Through the years, tribal members have intermarried with other groups, and their descendants tend to be scattered among the Colville, Nez Perce, Coeur d'Alene, and Umatilla reservations.

Chasta Costa

CULTURE AREA: Northwest Coast
LANGUAGE GROUP: Athapaskan
PRIMARY LOCATION: Rogue River and Chasta Costa Creek drainages, Oregon

Living in a mountainous area throughout their history, the socially stratified Chasta Costa were dependent upon trading with the Upper Coquille, the Galice to their southeast, and the coastal Tututni. These patrilineal groups were headed by polygamous chiefs whose position was maintained through consensus of opinion, oratorical skills, and leadership. The groups had complex ceremonies and engaged in warfare, primarily for status and for acquiring slaves. Subsistence was diversified through fishing, hunting land and sea mammals, and gathering of roots, tubers, berries, nuts, and acorns. Annual controlled burning improved resource areas; deer-hunting areas were burned over every five years. Permanent winter dwellings were of split cedar planks; the size of the structure was determined by one's status.

In April of 1792, Robert Gray began trade with people of this area, but little ethnographic information was recorded. These tribes were devastated by gold seekers, who introduced disease. The Rogue River War (1855-1856) was also destructive, as Chasta Costa were moved from their traditional territories. By 1871 the Ghost Dance was introduced, followed by the Warm House Dance in 1873.

Chehalis

CULTURE AREA: Northwest Coast
LANGUAGE GROUP: Coast Salish
PRIMARY LOCATION: Harrison River below mouth of Chehalis to Harrison Lake, Washington
POPULATION SIZE: 484 (1990 U.S. Census)

The marine-oriented Lower Chehalis lived, during the winter, in permanent gable-roofed dwellings of split cedar, each housing eight to twelve families. The inland Upper Chehalis were located on major streams and used similar structures. Marriage was outside the kin group and the village was the main socioeconomic and political group. Fish was the principal food, as reflected in fishing technology, ceremony, and various behavioral prohibitions and divisions of labor. Smelt, herring, lamprey, and shellfish were taken. Women collected roots, berries, and fruit.

Several other expeditions had made contact with the Chehalis before Meriwether Lewis and William Clark visited them in 1805. By 1811, Astoria was established, and fur traders began to exploit the area. The establishment of Fort Vancouver in 1825 by the Hudson's Bay Company encouraged further white settlement and use of the Cowlitz Trail, which traversed Lower Chehalis territory. The Chehalis Reservation was established in 1864, and in 1866 a smaller reservation was also established. Until Prohibition, most employment was in picking hops. By the late twentieth century, the Chehalis were earning their income in urban employment, logging, and fishing.

Chemakum

CULTURE AREA: Northwest Coast
LANGUAGE GROUP: Chemakum
PRIMARY LOCATION: Hadlock Bay and Port Townsend, south to Port Gamble, Washington

L ittle is known of the lifeways of the Chemakum before contact with European Americans. They were a marine-oriented society and lived in a stockaded village on Chimacum Creek. The area was sometimes subject to drought, placing an emphasis upon fish and sea mammals for food and various by-products. The Chemakum had linguistic and cultural connections with the Quileute.

European American disease and intertribal warfare reduced the Chemakum population. They were reported to be an aggressive people, having conflict with the Clallam, Duwamish, Makah, Snohomish, and Twana. By 1850, it was apparent that their decline was partially attributable to assimilation by other ethnic groups. In 1855, part of the Point No Point Treaty placed them on the Skokomish Reservation. By 1860, there were only seventy-three surviving Chemakum; that same year they dispersed north and relocated in eighteen lodges at Point Hudson, where they intermarried with the Clallam and Twana-Skokomish. Some Chemakuan people took up residence on the Skokomish Reservation.

Cheraw

CULTURE AREA: Southeast
LANGUAGE GROUP: Siouan
PRIMARY LOCATION: Head of Saluda River, South Carolina

T he matrilineal, horticultural Cheraw were socioeconomically stratified and had centralized authority. They lived in palisaded permanent riverside villages, with fields of maize, squash, beans, and other cultivated food plants. Men hunted and trapped large and small animals throughout the year to supplement stored foods. Principles of usufruct applied to acorn forests, deer-hunting areas, and berrying patches.

Hernando de Soto first mentioned the Cheraw in 1540, calling them Xuala. European American disease came in the late sixteenth century, reducing the Cheraw population. By 1700 they moved from their aboriginal territory to Dan River, and in 1710, after continual conflict with the Iroquois, they moved southeast and joined the Keyauwee. This close association of the tribes alarmed colonists of North Carolina, who declared war on the Cheraw. The Iroquois also maintained their attacks on the Cheraw, who between 1726 and 1739 became affiliated with the Catawba for protection. By 1768 only a few Cheraw remained.

Cherokee

CULTURE AREA: Southeast
LANGUAGE GROUP: Iroquoian
PRIMARY LOCATION: North Carolina, Oklahoma
POPULATION SIZE: 308,132 (1990 U.S. Census)

The largest and most powerful of the Eastern Woodland tribes in what is now the southeastern part of the United States was the Cherokee. Their population in the sixteenth century is estimated to have been about twenty-five thousand. Between their first major contact with Europeans in 1540 and their forced removal to the west in 1838-1839, the Cherokee adopted many aspects of European civilization. The Cherokee, Creek, Choctaw, Chickasaw, and Seminole, all southeastern tribes, became known as the Five Civilized Tribes.

Background and Tradition. The Cherokee language belongs to the Iroquoian language group, found primarily in the Northeast. Apparently a major war, perhaps against the Delaware (Lenni Lenape) along the East Coast, separated the Cherokee from the other Iroquoian tribes and led to their migration to the southern Appalachian highlands. Traditions of both the Delaware and the Cherokee support this theory.

The early Cherokee called themselves Ani-Yun-Wiya, which means "principal people." Neighboring tribes of the Muskogean language group called them Chilikee, or "people of a different speech." The chroniclers of Hernando de Soto in 1540 called the area Chalique. "Cherokee" is an Anglicized form of these last two names.

The Cherokee lived in approximately eighty towns, scattered over a large area of the southern Appalachians. There were three basic groups of towns, each speaking a distinct dialect. The lower towns were along the Tugaloo River in northeastern Georgia and the Keowee river in northwest South Carolina. The middle-valley towns were in western North Carolina, along the Nottely River, the upper Hiwassee River, and the Valley River. Across the mountains in eastern Tennessee was the third group, the upper or Overhill towns, which were located around the Little Tennessee River, the Tellico River, the lower Hiwassee River, and the headwaters of the Tennessee River. Although the Cumberland Plateau formed the western boundary of all Cherokee towns, their hunting grounds spread far beyond the plateau into middle Tennessee. The dialect of the middle-valley towns has been preserved by the Qualla Cherokee in North Carolina; the Cherokee Nation of Oklahoma has retained the Overhill dialect. The lower town dialect has disappeared.

Although the Cherokee had a loosely organized tribal government, most affairs were conducted at the town level. Both levels had a dual organization, one for peace and one for war. At the town level, the peace chief was an elder who also served as the chief priest. The war chief was a younger and highly successful warrior; he wielded great power in town affairs. Each town had a council, which met in a seven-sided town house, composed of seven clans: Deer, Wolf, Long Hair, Red Paint, Blue, Bird, and Wild Potatoes.

The customs of the Cherokee were similar to those of the other Eastern Woodland tribes. They lived in mud and thatch houses that were easy to build yet designed to be permanent. Marriage and family traditions were matriarchal and matrilineal. Women often rose to influential positions in town and tribal affairs, acquiring such titles as Ghighau (beloved or greatly honored woman). These women had an active role in town councils and could decide the fate of prisoners.

The major occupations of Cherokee men were hunting and warfare. Some historians classify them as the warlords of the southern Appalachians. Although most wars occurred on the town level, there were basic tribal rivalries, especially with the Creek, who lived south of the Cherokee, which led to major tribal wars. Honorary titles, such as Mankiller, Bloody Fellow, and The Raven were given to outstanding warriors.

Cherokee religion was polytheistic, but major emphasis was placed on Yowa, the creator god. Seven religious festivals, with elaborate ceremonies and artistic dancing, were held each year. One of the most beautiful of all Native American dances is the Cherokee Eagle Dance. Many elements of Cherokee religion, including Yowa, made it comparatively easy for many Cherokees later to convert to Christianity. In spite of this conversion, much religious tradition has been retained by modern-day Cherokees.

On the eve of their first contacts with Europeans, the Cherokee seemed to be at peace with their environment, contented with their lifestyles, and prosperous in their economic development. Beginning in 1540, these conditions began to change—first slowly, then very rapidly.

European Contact, 1540-1775. Although there are legends of white-skinned people visiting the southern Appalachians as far back as the twelfth century, the first documented contact was with the Spanish explorer and conqueror Hernando de Soto. De Soto landed at Tampa Bay in 1539, fought his way up the East Coast with an army of six hundred men, and entered Cherokee country in May, 1540. Along the way, several hundred other Native Americans had been enslaved as burden-bearers for de Soto's army. The goal of de Soto's expedition was gold, such as had already been discovered by other Spaniards in Central and South America. As he drew near to the Cherokee and heard accounts of their power, de Soto thought he had found what he was seeking.

The Cherokee were initially awestruck by the sight of de Soto's armor-clad warriors, thinking that the Spaniards had been sent by the gods to punish them for their sins. Later, realizing the true nature of the Spaniards, the Cherokee goal was to get their uninvited guests through and out of their territory as quickly as possible. This they accomplished by being hospitable but pressing de Soto to move on, which he did when he found no gold. De Soto moved west into Chickasaw territory, where, in 1542, he was buried in the Mississippi River. Twenty-five years after de Soto, another Spaniard, Juan Pardo, visited the Cherokee, also looking for gold (and also finding none). Following the exit of Pardo in 1567, the Cherokee enjoyed more than a century with no significant European contact.

That serenity ended in 1673, when Abraham Wood, a trader in the English colony of Virginia, sent two men to establish a commercial relationship with the Overhill Cherokee in eastern Tennessee. With the taste of the Spanish still lingering in their tribal memory, the Cherokee killed one of the men and made a temporary prisoner of the other. In spite of this rough beginning, commercial ties were soon established that endured until the American Revolution.

In 1730, six Cherokee warriors were taken on a visit to Great Britain, where they signed the Articles of Friendship and Commerce. This treaty, after being approved by the chiefs at home, meant that the Cherokee would trade only with—and fight only for—the British. For the next fifty years, the Cherokee tried to keep their word, even when the British were negligent in regard to theirs. This period included the French and Indian War (1754-1763), in which the Cherokee fought with the British against the French and their Indian allies. In the midst of that conflict, however, mistreatment by the British led to the brief Cherokee War (1759-1761) against the British. Following the end of the French and Indian War in 1763, peaceful cooperation between the Cherokee and the British was restored.

One of the warriors who visited Great Britain in 1730 was Attakullakulla, later called the Little Carpenter by the British because of his ability to build mutually beneficial relationships between his own people and the European settlers. Until his death in 1778, at about ninety-two years of age, Little Carpenter performed this task well.

The Cherokee were perplexed by the outbreak of the American Revolution in 1775, not understanding why British settlers were fighting Great Britain. When they did understand, true to the Articles of Friendship and Commerce, they gave support to the British. The desire of Little Carpenter and most other leaders was that the Cherokee would not become militarily involved. The British also, believing that the revolution would soon collapse, believed that it would be in the best interests of the Cherokee to remain neutral. One group of Cherokee warriors, however, had no desire for neutrality.

The Chickamauga, 1775-1794. On March 19, 1775, exactly one month before the first shots of the revolution were fired, the Treaty of Sycamore Shoals was signed in present-day Elizabethton, Tennessee. This treaty was between the Cherokee and their white neighbors, and it involved the sale of about twenty million acres of Cherokee hunting grounds to white leaders. The land, about half of the area originally claimed by the Cherokee, included much of Kentucky and middle Tennessee. Little Carpenter led the majority of the Cherokee in approving the sale. Dragging Canoe, the outspoken son of Little Carpenter, led the minority who opposed it. When he realized that his views were not going to prevail, Dragging Canoe left Sycamore Shoals, with a bitter warning of the violence to be expected when whites tried to settle the land being purchased.

In June, 1776, a delegation of northern tribes, led by a Shawnee chief named Cornstalk, visited the Cherokee capital of Chota, on the Little Tennessee River. Taking advantage of the American Revolution, Cornstalk was forming a coalition to drive the white settlers back across the Appalachian Mountains. Little Carpenter and other peaceful chiefs listened to Cornstalk's appeal, then watched in sad silence while Dragging Canoe accepted the war belt offered by the Shawnee chief.

Within a month of the meeting at Chota, Dragging Canoe was leading raids against the white settlements in east Tennessee. The settlements, however, were usually warned by friendly Cherokees such as Nancy Ward, a Ghighau (beloved woman). After being wounded in a raid that became an ambush, Dragging Canoe and his followers withdrew from Cherokee territory. Their new home was along Chickamauga Creek, a tributary of the Tennessee River. They occupied several abandoned Creek sites and began to call themselves the Chickamaugas, a name that means "river of death."

The raids against the settlements in east Tennessee continued until the original Chickamauga towns were destroyed by a retaliatory raid in April, 1779. After moving west to their Five Lower Towns, the Chickamauga launched new raids, this time against Fort Nashborough and the Cumberland River settlements on land bought at Sycamore Shoals. The raids, which continued for about ten years and covered a distance of about one hundred miles each way, could not prevent the settlement of that part of middle Tennessee.

In September, 1794, two years after the death of Dragging Canoe, the Five Lower Towns were destroyed by a surprise attack from Fort Nashborough. The surviving Chickamaugas were gradually assimilated back into the mainline Cherokee.

Cherokee Civilization, 1775-1830. The Long Island Treaty, signed in July, 1777, kept the majority of the Cherokee out of the American Revolution. By the terms of the Treaty of Hopewell, in 1785, the Cherokee recognized the supreme authority of the new government of the United States, which in turn promised to protect the rights of the Cherokee to the twenty million acres of land that they still possessed. In spite of this promise, by 1817 Cherokee lands had been reduced to about seven million acres in southwest North Carolina, southeast Tennessee, a large portion of north Georgia, and the northwest corner of Alabama.

The reduction in the size of Cherokee land led to major changes in their lifestyle. The basic means of support shifted from hunting to agriculture. Many Cherokee continued to supplement their income by trading with their white neighbors, who constantly moved closer and closer to the Cherokee towns.

Soon after the American Revolution, the Cherokee began adopting European standards of civilization. Their hope was that by so doing they would be able to remain in their homelands. The first step in civilization was the acceptance of Christianity. The evangelization of the Cherokee was begun by the Moravians in 1802. The most effective attempt was by the Brainerd Mission, beginning in 1817 in present-day Chattanooga; this was also the major source of education for young Cherokee men and women. Later Cherokee leaders such as Elias Boudinot and John Ridge began their formal education at Brainerd.

During the War of 1812, the Cherokee were given the chance to prove their loyalty to the United States. One of their traditional tribal enemies, the Creek, were fighting in Alabama. The Cherokee joined the volunteers of Andrew Jackson to defeat the Creek at Horseshoe Bend in 1814, a battle in which Yonaguska, a future Cherokee chief, saved the life of Jackson, a future American president.

Cherokee educational development took a major step forward in 1826, when Sequoyah, a part-blood Cherokee, invented a syllabary for the Cherokee language. With this creation, the first for any Native American tribe, the Cherokee soon began publishing their own newspaper: the *Cherokee Phoenix*, edited by Elias Boudinot.

The next significant step was the Cherokee adoption, on July 4, 1827, of a democratic constitution. This document was patterned after the U.S. Constitution. It established a national capital at New Echota, in north Georgia, and led to the election

Cherokee leader Sequoyah with the syllabary he developed to write the Cherokee language. (National Museum of the American Indian,

of John Ross as the first principal chief. Although only an eighth-blood Cherokee, Ross was pure Cherokee at heart, and he became the tribe's major protector and spokesman during the trying years that followed.

The Trail of Tears, 1830-1839. Beginning with the Georgia Compact in 1802, signed by President Thomas Jefferson, the United States government promised to aid in the eventual removal of the Cherokee from Georgia. The Jackson-McMinn Treaty in 1817 was the first step in that process; it provided for the voluntary relocation of Cherokee to the western territory, present-day Oklahoma. Between two and four thousand Cherokee accepted this offer; about sixteen thousand remained on their ancestral land.

The urgent demand to remove all Cherokee began in 1828, when gold was discovered on their land near Dahlonega, Georgia. In 1830, Congress passed the Indian Removal Act, authorizing President Andrew Jackson to pursue Cherokee removal vigorously. A representative of the president met with a pro-removal minority of Cherokee leaders at New Echota on December 29, 1835. The resulting treaty was ratified by the U.S. Senate; it gave the entire tribe until May, 1838, to move voluntarily to the west. The majority, led by John Ross, refused to move.

The forced removal began when the deadline expired. After a heartless roundup of unoffending Cherokee families, the deadly journey began. Under the guard of federal soldiers, the Cherokee were taken, first by water, then by land, to their new homes in the west. When the "trail where they cried" ended, in March, 1839, there were four thousand unmarked graves along the way. About one thousand Cherokee escaped the removal by fleeing into the mountains. They later became the nucleus of the Eastern Band of the Cherokee, on the Qualla Boundary in North Carolina.

A New Life. The tragedy of the Trail of Tears did not end with the arrival in the west. Those who had been forced to travel the trail harbored deep bitterness toward those who had signed the New Echota Treaty. The brutal assassinations of the leaders of the Treaty Party on June 22, 1839, did not end the bitterness. The murderers of Major Ridge, John Ridge, and Elias Boudinot were never identified or punished.

There was also friction between the Old Settlers, who had been in the west since 1817, and the more numerous arrivals of 1839. On July 12, 1839, the Act of Union, under the leadership of John Ross, helped create a unified direction for the uncertain future. On September 6, the first united council was held at Tahlequah, their new capital. Ross was elected as the first principal chief, and David Vann, an Old Settler, was chosen as assistant chief. The constitution for the tribal government was similar to the one adopted in 1827. A new treaty signed in 1846 helped to heal the rift with the Treaty Party.

A new Cherokee schism developed in connection with the U.S. Civil War. Both the Union and the Confederacy courted Cherokee support. John Ross, still the principal chief, led those who backed the Union. Stand Watie, the brother of Elias Boudinot, became a Confederate general.

Traditional tribal government for the western Cherokee Nation ended in 1907, when Oklahoma became a state. From that date until 1971, the principal chief was appointed by the president of the United States. In 1971, the Cherokee regained the right to elect their chief and a tribal council.

The last capital of the Cherokee before the Trail of Tears had been at Red Clay in east Tennessee. In 1984, an emotional meeting was held at the same location. It was the first full tribal council since 1838, with delegates from both Oklahoma and North Carolina attending. An eternal flame was lit to symbolize the new united spirit of all the Cherokee. In December, 1985, another history-making event occurred in Oklahoma, when Wilma Mankiller became the first female chief of any North American tribe. She was re-elected to four-year terms in 1987 and 1991.

A 1989 U.S. Census Bureau publication listed the population of the western Cherokee Nation at 87,059. According to the 1990 U.S. Census, the Qualla Boundary in North Carolina had a population of 5,388. The 1990 census figure for the total Cherokee population was much higher (308,132), because it included anyone who identified himself or herself as Cherokee.

Glenn L. Swygart

Bibliography

Anderson, William L. *Cherokee Removal: Before and After*. Athens: University of Georgia Press, 1991.

Andrews, John A. *From Revivals to Removal: Jeremiah Evarts, the Cherokee Nation, and the Search for the Soul of America*. Athens: University of Georgia Press, 1992.

Bays, Brad A. *Townsite Settlement and Dispossession in the Cherokee Nation, 1866-1907*. New York: Garland, 1998.

Camuto, Christopher. *Another Country: Journeying Toward the Cherokee Mountains*. New York: Henry Holt, 1997.

Cherokee Nation. *Cherokee Nation Code Annotated*. 2 vols. St. Paul, Minn.: West, 1993.

Corkran, David H. *The Cherokee Frontier: Conflict and Survival, 1740-62*. Norman: University of Oklahoma Press, 1962. Corkran's research emphasizes the effect of European contacts on the Cherokee. Special attention to their alliance with England and involvement in the French and Indian War.

Everett, Dianna. *The Texas Cherokees: A People Between Two Fires, 1819-1840*. Norman: University of Oklahoma Press, 1990.

Finger, John R. *Cherokee Americans: The Eastern Band of Cherokees in the Twentieth Century*. Lincoln: University of Nebraska Press, 1991.

_____. *The Eastern Band of the Cherokee, 1819-1900*. Knoxville: University of Tennessee Press, 1984. Covers the Cherokee in North Carolina, emphasizing problems after the Trail of Tears. Gives the reader a good picture of traditional Cherokee life.

French, Laurence. *The Qualla Cherokee Surviving in Two Worlds*. Lewiston, N.Y.: Edwin Mellen Press, 1998.

Gilbert, Joan. *The Trail of Tears Across Missouri*. Columbia: University of Missouri Press, 1996.

Hatley, M. Thomas. *The Dividing Paths: Cherokees and South Carolinians Through the Era of Revolution*. New York: Oxford University Press, 1993.

Hoig, Stan. *The Cherokees and Their Chiefs: In the Wake of Empire*. Fayetteville, Ark.: University of Arkansas Press, 1998.

Kilpatrick, Jack F., and Anna G. Kilpatrick. *Friends of Thunder: Folktales of the Oklahoma Cherokees*. Norman: University of Oklahoma Press, 1995.

Leeds, Georgia. *The United Keetoowah Band of Cherokee Indians in Oklahoma*. New York: Peter Lang, 1996.

McLoughlin, William G. *After the Trail of Tears: The Cherokees' Struggle for Sovereignty, 1839-1880*. Chapel Hill: University of North Carolina Press, 1993.

_____. *The Cherokee Ghost Dance*. Macon, Ga.: Mercer University Press, 1984. An interesting collection of essays covering Cherokee relations with other tribes, involvement in slavery, and contact with missionaries (1789-1861). Good tables.

_____. *Cherokees and Missionaries, 1789-1839*. Norman: University of Oklahoma Press, 1995.

_____, and Walter H. Conser. *The Cherokees and Christianity, 1794-1870: Essays on Acculturation and Cultural Persistence*. Athens: University of Georgia Press, 1994.

Mails, Thomas E. *The Cherokee People: The Story of the Cherokees from the Earliest Origins to Contemporary Times*. Tulsa, Okla.: Council Oak Books, 1992.

Malone, Henry. *Cherokees of the Old South*. Athens: University of Georgia Press, 1956. Presents a clear picture of the origin and pre-removal history of the Cherokee. Stresses tribal customs and civilization.

Mankiller, Wilma P., and Michael Wallis. *Mankiller, a Chief and Her People*. New York: St. Martin's Press, 1993.

May, Katja. *African Americans and Native Americans in the Creek and Cherokee Nations, 1830s to 1920s: Collision and Collusion*. New York: Garland, 1996.

Mooney, James. *Myths of the Cherokee, 1861-1921*. New York: Dover Publications, 1995.

Neely, Sharlotte. *Snowbird Cherokees: People of Persistence*. Athens: University of Georgia Press, 1991.

Norgren, Jill. *The Cherokee Cases: The Confrontation of Law and Politics*. New York: McGraw-Hill, 1996.

Perdue, Theda. *Cherokee Women: Gender and Culture Change, 1700-1835*. Lincoln: University of Nebraska Press, 1998.

_____, and Michael D. Green, eds. *Cherokee Removal: A Brief History With Documents*. Boston: Bedford Books of St. Martin's Press, 1995.

Phillips, Joyce B., and Paul G. Phillips, eds. *The Brainerd Journal: A Mission to the Cherokees, 1817-1823*. Lincoln: University of Nebraska Press, 1998.

Rice, Horace R. *The Buffalo Ridge Cherokee: A Remnant of a Great Nation Divided*. Bowie, Md.: Heritage Books, 1995.

Rozema, Vicki. *Footsteps of the Cherokees: A Guide to the Eastern Homelands of the Cherokee Nation*. Winston-Salem, N.C.: John F. Blair, 1995.

Thornton, Russell, Matthew C. Snipp, and Nancy Breen. *The Cherokees: A Population History*. Lincoln: University of Nebraska Press, 1990.

Wilkins, Thurman. *Cherokee Tragedy*. New York: Macmillan, 1970. Based on the Ridge family. A very emotional account of the Cherokee during the years preceding removal. Good photographs.

Woodward, Grace Steele. *The Cherokees*. Norman: University of Oklahoma Press, 1963. An excellent picture of Cherokee development up to Oklahoma statehood. Emphasizes internal problems. A help in understanding present-day Cherokee. Good bibliography.

Cheyenne

CULTURE AREA: Plains
LANGUAGE GROUP: Algonquian
PRIMARY LOCATION: Montana, Oklahoma
POPULATION SIZE: 11,456 (1990 U.S. Census)

The Cheyenne originally lived in woodland country in what is now southeastern Minnesota. The name "Cheyenne" comes from the Dakota Sioux, who called the Cheyenne *Shahiyena* or *Shahiela*, which means "people who talk differently," "people of alien speech," or, literally, "red speakers." They probably lived in permanent, small villages of two to three hundred and hunted, harvested, and gardened.

Early History. By the late 1600's the Cheyenne began to be displaced from their homeland by hostile neighboring tribes of Woodland Sioux, Cree, and Assiniboine. The Cheyenne sought escape by migrating westward to the prairie country in the southwestern corner of present-day Minnesota; however, they were forced by hostile Sioux to migrate northwest to the prairies of the Sheyenne River in the Dakotas. From 1725 to 1775 they established a number of fortified earthlodge villages along the river. They established cordial relations with, and learned horticultural techniques from, a number of tribes in the area, including the Oto, Iowa, Mandan, and Hidatsa. They also acquired horses and used them for hunting and war. Once again, however, they were forced to abandon their prosperous life, this time because of the depredations of the Chippewa and the European diseases of smallpox and measles.

Plains Phase. The Cheyenne left the prairie in the late 1700's and moved west across the Missouri River. A number of villages may have been established for a time on the Missouri River, but the Cheyenne had become a predominantly nomadic tribe. Upon crossing the Missouri into the Great Plains they encountered the Sutaio, who had been living on the plains for some time. The Sutaio also spoke an Algonquian dialect, and the two tribes became closely allied. By 1820 the two tribes had united, and the Sutaio became one of several distinctive bands within the Cheyenne.

The Black Hills, located in the northwest corner of South Dakota, became a spiritual and geographical center of the Cheyenne. The Cheyenne roamed over a vast area approximating a semicircle to the west, south, and east of the Black Hills. The half century from 1800 to 1850 represents the apex of Cheyenne culture. It was a period of stabilization, solidification, and prosperity. In 1840 the Cheyenne reached an accord with their traditional enemies the Kiowa and Comanche in order to fortify their southern flank against the Pawnee, Cherokee, and other tribes. They made peace with the Sioux to oppose their mutual enemies to the north, the Crow and Shoshone. By 1830 the Cheyenne had obtained sufficient numbers of horses to abandon village life completely and become nomadic hunters and traders. Sufficient firearms had been obtained that they were able to become a formidable warrior nation.

Culture in the Early Nineteenth Century. The Cheyenne lived in tipis made from animal skins by the women. The women were also responsible for dressing skins for clothing and for gathering various edible plants. The men hunted game, fought battles, and performed most of the tribal ceremonies. The Cheyenne fought in order to acquire access to new territory to hunt, to maintain their traditional territory, to obtain horses, and to revenge previous defeats and deaths. Military virtue and bravery were glorified. In a sense, warfare was a game or competitive activity in which the Cheyenne counted the number of "coups" a warrior accumulated. A coup could include killing or scalping an enemy but could also involve "show-off" accomplishments such as touching the enemy or being the first to find him.

The Cheyenne consisted of ten bands, including the Sutaio. The bands lived separately in the winter but came together in the summer for the communal buffalo hunt and to perform sacred ceremonies (the Great Ceremonies) of unity and renewal, such as the Sacred Arrow Renewal and the Sun Dance, which they learned from the Sutaio. A large circular camp was constructed, and each band had a particular position it occupied within the circle. The circle symbolized the family tipis and reinforced the belief that the tribe was one large family.

Bands were composed of closely related kindreds which customarily camped with one another. Kindreds were composed of individual conjugal and composite families. Each of the ten bands had a name, such as Eaters, Burnt Aorta, or Hair Rope Men. These were nicknames, often referring to a particular, unique characteristic of that band and emphasizing that each band had a distinctive identity and its own customs.

Each band was presided over by a chief, the man considered to be most outstanding in that band. A few members from each band were chosen as members of the Council of Forty-Four. This council had the responsibility for maintaining peace, harmony, and order among the Cheyenne bands and so was the supreme authority in the tribe. The Council of Forty-Four was composed of chiefs committed to peace. It was separate from the Society of War Chiefs, who were chosen from the seven military societies to which males belonged. All peace chiefs were warriors. Upon joining the council they could keep their membership in the war society but had to resign any position held. The Cheyenne recognized the virtues of separating civil and military powers. Each band contributed about four members to the council.

A council member served a ten-year term but could be reelected. A member had to be a man of highest virtue: even-tempered, good-natured, energetic, wise, kind, concerned for others' well being, courageous, generous, altruistic, and above reproach in public life. The council chose one of its members to be the head chief-priest of the entire tribe, the Sweet Medicine Chief. Four other chiefs chosen by the council served as the head's associates and were known, along with the Sweet Medicine Chief, as the five sacred chiefs. The tribal chief could not be deposed or impeached during his term, even if he committed a grievous crime such as murder.

The Council of Forty-Four symbolized the melding of spiritual, democratic, and moral values that characterized the Cheyenne. When the council was in session, the chief sat at the west side of the lodge, the center or zenith of the universe (*heum*). The five sacred chiefs were considered cosmic spiritual beings, and a number of other council members represented various spirits of the supernatural and mystical world. The council consisted of the wisest men and men in touch with the positive life forces from which emanated the good things which the Cheyenne desired. The high virtue of the council members symbolized the values the Cheyenne placed on dignity, chastity, courage, rationality, harmony with their environment, and a democratic tribal government.

1830's to 1870's. In the late 1830's, the Bent's Fort trading post was established in southern Colorado. Many Cheyenne moved south near the fort to establish a primary position of access to trade. This taxed the solidarity of the tribe because of the great distance separating those remaining in the north (who eventually became known as the Northern Cheyenne) from those who moved south (who eventually became known as the Southern Cheyenne). It became increasingly difficult for the whole tribe to assemble for the Great Ceremonies of early summer. Also, the tribal council met less frequently and thus lost much power in regulating tribal affairs. One of the last unified gatherings for the Great Ceremonies occurred in 1842. The Northern and Southern Cheyenne then separated from each other and went their own ways.

In the 1840's the westward movement of white settlers and gold seekers drastically upset traditional Cheyenne culture. Hunting areas were distributed, and a cholera epidemic in 1849 exterminated nearly half the tribe. The Santa Fe Trail ran through the heartland of Cheyenne territory. In 1851 the Cheyenne and eight other tribes signed the first Fort Laramie Treaty with the United States. The treaty formalized the separation of Northern and Southern Cheyenne, merged the Southern Cheyenne and Arapaho for treaty purposes, and assigned 122,500 square miles of territory (not a reservation) to them. It also permitted the United States to establish roads and forts on their territory (which had already been done).

The steady influx of settlers continued to disrupt tribal life, however, bringing the Southern Cheyenne and Arapaho to near starvation in 1853. The Indians retaliated, and wars broke out between 1856 and 1878. Notable events included the massacre at Sand Creek in 1864 and the death of Black Kettle in 1868 at the hands of Colonel George Armstrong Custer. The United States assigned the Southern Cheyenne and Arapaho to reservations in 1869, but they resisted until finally subdued in 1875. Some warriors were considered prisoners of war and sent to Florida.

On June 17, 1876—a week before the annihilation of George Armstrong Custer's Seventh Cavalry at Little Bighorn—Sioux and Cheyenne warriors combined to turn back General George Crook's forces at the Battle of Rosebud Creek. (Library of Congress)

The Northern Cheyenne joined with the Sioux in resisting the encroachment of gold seekers and settlers. Attempts by the army to confine them to reservations culminated in the Battle of the Little Bighorn, in which the Seventh Cavalry of George Armstrong Custer was annihilated in 1876. They were captured and confined to reservations by 1884.

Since the 1870's. Confinement to reservations effectively ended traditional Cheyenne culture. The Northern Cheyenne fared much better than did their southern brethren. They eventually settled in 1884 on the Tongue

River in Montana in an area they chose and which was isolated from whites. Most of their land remained unallotted. Unallotted lands were not made available to whites. The Northern Cheyenne own more than 275,000 acres of tribal land held in common and have been buying back parcels of the more than 150,000 acres of allotted land. Mineral resources, farming, and stock raising are the main sources of income.

The Southern Cheyenne and the Arapaho were confined to a reservation in the Indian Territory in 1875. Their traditional nomadic hunting society was stripped from them as the federal government tried to assimilate them into American society by molding them into educated Christian farmers. Religious ceremonies were banned. The Council of Chiefs had disappeared by 1892. The military societies were disbanded. Additionally, the government consistently failed to provide adequate support services so that hunger, disease, and hopelessness became daily miseries. The 1887 Dawes Severalty Act (General Allotment Act) ultimately resulted in the loss of 3,500,000 acres of unallotted reservation land that was bought by the government.

The Indian Reorganization Act of 1934 and the Indian Claims Act of 1947 redressed these injustices somewhat and encouraged increased self-government and the assumption of control over a number of services. This process was given further impetus by the 1975 Indian Self-Determination and Education Assistance Act. Economic development is a high priority, but success has been spotty and many Indians still live in poverty. Nevertheless, through all this the Cheyenne have retained their essential identity, character, and courage.

Laurence Miller

Bibliography

Becher, Ronald. *Massacre Along the Medicine Road: A Social History of the Indian War of 1864 in Nebraska Territory*. Caldwell, Idaho: Caxton, 1999.

Berthrong, Donald J. *The Cheyenne and Arapaho Ordeal*. Norman: University of Oklahoma Press, 1976. Describes in detail the life of these tribes on the reservation from 1875 to 1907 as they were subjected to government attempts to assimilate them into the population.

Boxberger, Daniel L., ed. *Native North Americans: An Ethnohistorical Approach*. Dubuque, Iowa: Kendall/Hunt, 1990. Contains an excellent chapter on Plains Indian history, culture, and contemporary life.

Boye, Alan. *Holding Stone Hands: On the Trail of the Cheyenne Exodus*. Lincoln: University of Nebraska Press, 1999.

Chalfant, William Y. *Cheyennes at Dark Water Creek: The Last Fight of the Red River War*. Norman: University of Oklahoma Press, 1997.

Greene, Jerome A. *Lakota and Cheyenne: Indian Views of the Great Sioux War, 1876-1877.* Norman: University of Oklahoma Press, 1994.

Hardhoff, Richard G. *Cheyenne Memories of the Custer Fight: A Source Book.* Spokane, Wash.: Arthur H. Clark, 1995.

Hoebel, E. Adamson. *The Cheyennes: Indians of the Great Plains.* New York: Holt, Rinehart and Winston, 1978. This second edition of a classic work adds chapters on contemporary life and issues through the mid-1970's, in addition to chapters on history and culture. Thorough, informative, and readable.

Josephy, Alvin M., Jr., ed. *The American Heritage Book of Indians.* New York: Simon & Schuster, 1961. Contains general information on the Cheyenne and other Plains Indians. Contains numerous excellent illustrations.

Mann, Henrietta. *Cheyenne-Arapaho Education, 1871-1982.* Niwot: University Press of Colorado, 1997.

Moore, John H. *The Cheyenne.* Cambridge, Mass.: Blackwell, 1996.

Powell, Peter J. *Sweet Medicine: The Continuing Role of the Sacred Arrows, the Sun Dance, and the Sacred Buffalo Hat in Northern Cheyenne History.* 2 vols. Norman: University of Oklahoma Press, 1998.

Svingen, Orlan J. *The Northern Cheyenne Indian Reservation, 1877-1900.* Niwot: University Press of Colorado, 1993.

Swanton, John R. *The Indian Tribes of North America.* Washington, D.C.: Government Printing Office, 1953. This standard reference contains brief but very informative accounts of the Cheyenne. Concentrates on a brief history, derivation of the name, location, and subdivisions and villages.

Viola, Herman J. *Ben Nighthorse Campbell, an American Warrior.* New York: Orion Books, 1993.

Viola, Herman J. et al. *Warrior Artists: Historic Cheyenne and Kiowa Indian Ledger Art Drawn by Making Medicine and Zotum.* Washington, D.C.: National Geographic Society, 1998.

Waldman, Carl. *Atlas of the North American Indian.* New York: Facts on File, 1985. Contains general information on Cheyenne life and their wars. Distinguished by excellent illustrations and maps.

Chiaha

CULTURE AREA: Southeast
LANGUAGE GROUP: Muskogean
PRIMARY LOCATION: Chattahoochee River, Georgia/Alabama border

The Chiaha (or Chehaw) were a horticultural people who lived in raised dwellings located in several large permanent villages within sight of their extensive fields of maize, beans, squash, and other plants (including tobacco). For men, hunting and trapping were favorite pastimes, and they encouraged relationships which were critical in trading and in political alliances. Chiaha society was somewhat stratified, but with central authority that was influenced by consensus of opinion. Men gained status through warfare, hunting, oration, and generosity. Women who were industrious and skillful were accorded status.

Hernando de Soto's narratives of 1540 provide the first description of these people, suggesting that the Chiaha were already members of the Creek Confederacy. The Spanish later established a fort in Chiaha territory in 1567, which the Chiaha destroyed. Because of ongoing conflict, numerous demographic changes affected the Chiaha, who eventually moved to Oklahoma and settled in the northeastern corner of the Creek Reservation. After the Civil War, many remaining Chiaha moved to Florida and settled among the Western Seminole.

Chichimec

CULTURE AREA: Mesoamerica
LANGUAGE GROUP: Nahuatl (Otomian)
PRIMARY LOCATION: Northern Mexico

The name Chichimec is used to describe several different tribes of northern Mexico, most of whom spoke the Nahuatl language. They were nomadic and were considered barbarians by the more developed tribes of the Valley of Mexico. Chichimec, in fact, means "people of dog lineage."

The city of Teotihuacán acted as a buffer between the Valley of Mexico and the Chichimecs. When it fell in 650 C.E., the way was opened to invasions by Chichimecs. An early group was the Tolteca-Chichimeca, or Toltecs. Beginning in the tenth century, they entered the Valley of Mexico under the leadership of Mixcóatl (Cloud Serpent), who has been called a "Mexican Genghis Khan." He established his capital at Culhuacán.

After Mixcóatl was assassinated by his brother, his pregnant wife fled into exile and bore a son, Ce Acatl Topilzin, who as a young man defeated his uncle and ascended the throne. He became a follower of the Feathered Serpent god Quetzalcóatl, assuming the name Topilzin-Quetzalcóatl. A dispute between the followers of two gods split the people. Topilzin-

Quetzalcóatl was tricked by opposing priests into committing the sins of drunkenness and incest. He voluntarily went into exile, promising to return from the east in the year Ce Acatl to resume his rightful place on the throne. In 1519, the year Ce Acatl, the Spaniards appeared from the east, raising the question of whether Hernán Cortés was Topilzin-Quetzalcóatl returned.

From the late eleventh century to 1156, droughts and famine weakened the Toltecs. Wars discouraged them until they abandoned their capital Tula, and the great Toltec diaspora began. The fall of Tula again opened the Valley of Mexico to invasions by primitive Chichimecs. By the first part of the thirteenth century, several Chichimec tribes had conquered the desirable areas; however, by the early fifteenth century, all the Chichimec cities had declined.

The most famous and successful of the Chichimec tribes was the Mexica, or Aztecs. The Aztecs were the last of the important nomadic Chichimecs to enter the Valley of Mexico. In 1111, the Aztecs migrated from Nayaret southward. From their capital, Tenochtitlán, on an island in Lake Texcoco, they conquered their neighbors, creating an empire that extended from the Pacific to the Gulf Coast and from the Valley of Mexico to the coast of Guatemala.

After their conquest of the Aztecs, the Spanish controlled the sedentary Indians, leaving the north-central plateau in the hands of the Chichimecs. After the silver strike at Zacatecas in 1545, Spain began to expand northward into the Gran Chichimeca. Between 1550 and 1590, the War of the Chichimeca occurred, the longest and most costly in money and lives of the frontier conflicts. Their military efforts were unsuccessful, so Spanish officials changed their policy in the decade of the 1590's to pacification by gifts of food and clothing and by conversion, using the mission system and sedentary Indians from the south. By 1600 the Chichimecs were incorporated into pacified Mexico.

Chickasaw

CULTURE AREA: Southeast
LANGUAGE GROUP: Muskogean
PRIMARY LOCATION: Oklahoma
POPULATION SIZE: 20,631 (1990 U.S. Census)

At the beginning of the historic period, the Chickasaws inhabited an area encompassing modern western Tennessee and Kentucky, northern Mississippi, and northwestern Alabama. They are closely related linguistically to the Choctaws, and the two tribes may once have been one. The Chickasaw way of life was similar to that of other southeastern tribes. They lived in towns and pursued an economy based on farming, especially corn, and hunting. Chickasaw social structure was based on a clan system. One's clan was derived from one's mother, and marriage between clan members was forbidden. While most affairs were handled locally, the High Minko, or principal chief of the tribe, was chosen by a council of clan elders. Though a relatively small tribe (around forty-five hundred at the time of European contact), the Chickasaws had a reputation among neighboring tribes as fierce warriors.

The Chickasaws were visited by Hernando de Soto's expedition in 1540, and they nearly annihilated the Spaniards the following year. In the seventeenth century, the Chickasaws became involved in a series of wars against the French and their Indian allies. Having established contact with English merchants, the Chickasaws became British allies in the eighteenth century and remained loyal to them through the American Revolution. By the late eighteenth century, a mixed-blood, acculturated minority was becoming increasingly influential in tribal affairs.

In 1786, the Chickasaws signed the Treaty of Hopewell with the new United States, acknowledging themselves to be under American protection and selling a small area at Muscle Shoals (modern Alabama) to the United States. The Chickasaws fought on the American side in the Creek War of 1813-1814; however, they soon came under pressure to part with more and more of their land. In 1818, General Andrew Jackson persuaded the tribe to sell all of its lands in Tennessee and Kentucky. After Jackson became president, the Chickasaws were pressured to sell the remainder of their lands east of the Mississippi. In 1832, the Chickasaws agreed to sell out and move to the Indian Territory (modern Oklahoma), where they would settle on land bought from the Choctaws. It took five years to work out mutually acceptable arrangements, but in the 1837 Treaty of Doaksville the Choctaws agreed to sell to the Chickasaws a large tract of land to the west of their Oklahoma settlements for $530,000 and to accept the Chickasaws as tribal citizens. A tribal census taken at the time of removal in 1838 counted approximately five thousand Chickasaws.

Though the Chickasaws had an easier "Trail of Tears" than other southern tribes did, they faced problems once in Indian Territory. They resisted absorption by the Choctaws and faced threats from the Plains tribes who were used to roaming the area. Only after army posts were established did full-scale resettlement take place. Friction with the Choctaws continued until, in 1855, the two tribes reached a relatively friendly divorce, and a separate Chickasaw Nation was constituted in what later became south-central Oklahoma.

The Chickasaws had brought about a thousand slaves with them on their trek west, and when the Civil War broke out in 1861, they allied with the Confederacy. The Chickasaw Nation was relatively unscathed by the fighting, but at the end of the war the tribe had to make peace with the United States. The tribe lost its claim to a large tract of southwestern Oklahoma, and accepted the end of slavery. Pressured to incorporate its former slaves (freedmen) into the tribe, the Chickasaw—alone among slaveholding tribes—avoided doing so.

In the later nineteenth century the tribe once again found itself in the path of expansionist policy. During the 1890's Congress moved to extend the policy of allotment (the division of tribal lands among individual Indians, with "surplus" land being sold off) to Indian Territory. Tribal powers were reduced, and the Dawes Commission was established to negotiate allotment terms. In 1906 a tribal roll was drawn up, counting 6,319 citizens of the Chickasaw Nation (1,538 of them full-bloods); the roll of Chickasaw freedmen numbered 4,670. On March 4, 1906, the tribal government came to an end. Each Chickasaw received 320 acres of land (each freedman got 40 acres). By 1934, 70 percent of the land had passed from Chickasaw ownership. Tribal government was eventually reorganized in the 1960's.

William C. Lowe

Bibliography

Aadland, Dan. *Women and Warriors of the Plains: The Pioneer Photography of Julia E. Tuell*. New York: Macmillan, 1996.

Cushman, H.B. *History of the Choctaw, Chickasaw, and Natchez Indians*. Norman: University of Oklahoma Press, 1999.

Foreman, Grant. *The Five Civilized Tribes*. Norman: University of Oklahoma Press, 1934.

_____. *Indian Removal: The Emigration of the Five Civilized Tribes of Indians*. Norman: University of Oklahoma Press, 1932.

Gibson, Arrell M. *The Chickasaws*. Norman: University of Oklahoma Press, 1971.

Hudson, Charles. *The Southeastern Indians*. Knoxville: University of Tennessee Press, 1976.

Perdue, Theda, ed. *Nations Remembered: An Oral History of the Cherokees, Chickasaws, Choctaws, Creeks, and Seminoles, 1865-1907*. 1980. Reprint. Norman: University of Oklahoma Press, 1993.

Chilcotin

CULTURE AREA: Subarctic
LANGUAGE GROUP: Northern Athapaskan
PRIMARY LOCATION: British Columbia, Canada
POPULATION SIZE: 1,705 (Statistics Canada, based on 1991 census)

The Chilcotin, named for a river flowing through their homeland, originally came from an area north of their present reservation in British Columbia. They fished for salmon, hunted caribou, elk, and deer, and gathered roots and berries. The Chilcotin had no group leaders. No one could force another tribal member to do anything. They lived in small isolated camps made up of brothers and sisters and their husbands, wives, and children. These camps grew larger in the winter when a number of family groups lived together in a cluster, but when spring came they moved to their separate hunting areas again. Parents usually arranged marriages. Sharing was a cultural the ideal; if people had things to spare, they gave them away.

The Chilcotin believed that ghosts and monsters filled the universe but had no direct influence in human affairs. No single, all-powerful supreme being was thought to exist. An individual could acquire a "guardian spirit" while a teenager—but only after fasting, meditating, and bathing during a vision quest lasting several weeks. This spirit protected an individual from harm and helped bring success in fishing, hunting, and gambling. Chilcotin art consisted of human heads carved in tree stumps, basketry, dancing, and drums for music.

White trappers first contacted Chilcotin along the Fraser River in the late 1700's. Until the 1850's, however, they had little contact with Europeans. Then, in 1857, a gold rush brought prospectors and railroad surveyors onto Chilcotin land. Within two years, a smallpox epidemic reduced the tribe's numbers from 1,500 to 550. The Chilcotin fought a brief war against white settlers in 1864, but after five Indians were hanged the war came to an end. In the 1870's, Roman Catholic missionaries established schools, and the Chilcotin moved onto a reservation in the 1880's. Ranching replaced hunting as the most important economic activity, and many of the natives became cowboys. In the 1960's, several resorts opened in the area and many Chilcotin found jobs as maids, cooks, and fishing guides.

Chinook

CULTURE AREA: Northwest Coast
LANGUAGE GROUP: Chinookan (perhaps Penutian)
PRIMARY LOCATION: Oregon/Washington coast
POPULATION SIZE: 798 (1990 U.S. Census)

The Chinook, a southern tribe of Northwest Coast Indians, controlled the Columbia River waterway from The Dalles (the location of a major waterfall) to the Pacific Ocean and lived on the coast in the area of the present states of Washington and Oregon. The Chinook charged a toll to other tribes who used the river for commerce and became principal traders in the area, partly because the falls at The Dalles made portaging necessary. The Chinooks' trade included slaves, canoes, and dentalia shells.

Engraving of a Chinook lodge in the Oregon Territory based on a sketch from the 1830's Northwest Coast. (Library of Congress)

The first documented contact that the Chinook had with European Americans was with explorer John Meares at Willapa Bay in 1788. The Chinook later met the overland Astor fur expedition as well as, in 1805, explorers Meriwether Lewis and William Clark. References in Chinook oral tradition imply earlier contact with Russian and perhaps even with Spanish ships.

The Chinook shared many characteristics with other tribes of the Northwest Coast—living in plank houses, building seaworthy canoes, telling Coyote stories, and participating in potlatch distributions of property. The Chinook, however, did not generally enjoy the wealth of coastal tribes to the north. While the Chinook produced twine basketry and sewed rush mats, they did not create the totemic art of the northern coastal tribes.

Salmon provided sustenance—spiritual and physical—to the Chinook. An important ceremony in the Chinook religion is the first salmon rite, which heralds the annual salmon run. The Chinook supplemented their diet with clams, crabs, oysters, seals, and small game hunting on land.

The Chinook language is unique in a number of respects and has been only tentatively affiliated with the widespread Penutian stock. "Chinook jargon," spoken from California to Alaska, bases its lexicon on the Chinook language but has characteristics of French, English, and other Indian (especially Nootka) languages.

Chipewyan

CULTURE AREA: Subarctic
LANGUAGE GROUP: Athapaskan
PRIMARY LOCATION: Saskatchewan, Manitoba
POPULATION SIZE: 9,350 (Statistics Canada, based on 1991 census)

The early Chipewyans occupied the edge of the northern subarctic forests and the tundra beyond, where the winters were long and severe and the summers moderate. By the late 1700's, some Chipewyans had moved into the forests. These people were nomadic hunters and fishermen. The most important animal was the caribou; it was the focus of their religious belief and oral literature, and it structured their life cycle and population distribution.

The Chipewyan tribe had no central organization but lived in regional bands, the size of which depended on the concentration of the caribou. Bands were larger during the caribou migrations and smaller when the caribou were dispersed. Hudson's Bay Company officials recognized two divisions: the Northern Indians (Chipewyans) and the Yellowknife. Chipewyan means "pointed skins," a term referring to the form of their dried beaver skins.

Early contact with Europeans came as a result of fur trading and brought both good and hardship. Furs were traded for basic necessities, but in 1781 smallpox, caught from the Europeans, destroyed a large number of the Chipewyans.

The Chipewyans had few ceremonies to mark life's events. If the band was traveling, a woman would give birth and continue traveling within a few hours. No ceremonies marked puberty or marriage. The husband hunted with the woman's family until the birth of the first child. Polygamy was permitted, and wives, especially the young and childless, were sometimes prizes in wrestling matches. The old and feeble had little value and could be abandoned if they could not keep up when traveling.

By the mid-1800's, the Chipewyans were divided into five regional bands, and their territories existed primarily within the forests. They were divided between living on the forest edge in order to hunt on the tundra and living deep within the forest close to trading posts and missions. In the 1960's there was an attempt to move some of the bands into towns. This was only partly successful; many families returned to their traditional areas and have remained hunters and fishermen. Some of the bands engage in commercial fishing.

Chitimacha

CULTURE AREA: Southeast
LANGUAGE GROUP: Chitimacha
PRIMARY LOCATION: Chitimacha Reservation, Charenton, Louisiana
POPULATION SIZE: 618 (1990 U.S. Census)

The Chitimacha are found on their reservation at Charenton, Louisiana. According to Chitimacha oral tradition, their homeland was in the Natchez, Mississippi, region. By the time of European contact (in the early 1700's), they occupied an extensive territory on the western side of the Mississippi River in southern Louisiana. Bayou Lafourche, a principal drainage flowing south from the Mississippi River, was known as the River of the Chitimacha.

The traditional lifeways and material culture are described in John R. Swanton's *The Indians of the Southeastern United States* (1946). Chitimacha subsistence involved agriculture, fishing, hunting, and gathering. They lived in palmetto hut villages, some with dance houses for religious celebrations. There is limited information concerning their complex social, political, and religious organization, although there are suggestions that in these matters they may have resembled the Natchez (a well-documented group at Natchez, Mississippi).

During the early years of colonialism, the European settlers were often short of food, and they relied upon the Indians initially to provide sustenance and later to exchange deerskins. As a result of this lucrative trade, Native Americans relocated to settlements more convenient to the foreigners, and farming groups, such as the Chitimacha, planted more extensive fields.

Despite initially peaceful interactions, the relationship between the Chitimacha and the Europeans became increasingly antagonistic. By 1706, a dispute between the Chitimacha and the Taensa had resulted in several French deaths. Chitimacha warriors attempted to retaliate against the Taensa (or Bayogoula) but were unable to locate them; instead, by chance, they encountered the French Jesuit Jean François Buisson de Saint-Cosme and his companions. As a result of this unfortunate meeting, Saint-Cosme and most of his party were killed. After this event, Jean Baptiste le Moyne, Sieur de Bienville, created a coalition of Mississippi tribes to revenge the French deaths. In 1707, they raided a Chitimacha village. From this time until 1718, the Chitimacha battled with the French.

In 1727, Father du Poisson made a trip up the Mississippi River and contacted the Chitimacha. His account mentions a chief named Framboise, who had been a French slave. The case of Framboise's enslavement was not an isolated incident, since many Chitimacha had been captured during the war with the French. In 1769, Governor Alejandro O'Reilly proclaimed that Indian slavery was forbidden, but as late as 1808, there were still Native American slaves.

Through the late eighteenth and nineteenth centuries, European settlement encroached further upon Chitimacha territory. In response, some Chitimachas retreated to more remote locations; others moved to New Orleans.

In 1925, the Chitimacha received federal recognition, and they later complied with the Indian Reorganization Act of 1934. Chitimacha property near Charenton consists of 262 acres and approximately three hundred people, although another few hundred may reside outside the reservation. The reservation possesses a school and a branch of the Jean Lafitte National Park. The Chitimacha are probably best known for their basketmaking skills.

Choctaw

CULTURE AREA: Southeast
LANGUAGE GROUP: Muskogean
PRIMARY LOCATION: Oklahoma, Mississippi, Louisiana, Alabama
POPULATION SIZE: 82,299 (1990 U.S. Census)

The Choctaw, a linguistic subgroup of the Muskogean people, first occupied portions of present-day Mississippi, Arkansas, and Alabama. By 1820 the Choctaw were considered part of the so-called Five Civilized Tribes because of their rapid adaptation to European culture. By 1830 the Choctaw were forced to cede all lands east of the Mississippi; their removal to Indian Territory (Oklahoma) took place between 1831 and 1833. Tribal lands and businesses of the Choctaw are textbook examples of progressive farming, ranching, and industrial development. The Choctaw have grown from a few thousand to more than 82,000 persons, making them the fifth largest tribe in the United States.

Prehistory and Traditional Life. The prehistory of the Choctaws centered on farming communities in the modern state of Mississippi. Their culture was an integral part of a large ethnolinguistic area stretching from the Atlantic Coast to the Mississippi Valley. A portion of this region was also occupied by other tribes of the Muskogean branch of the Gulf language stock, the Seminole, Chickasaw, and Chitimacha. Sixteenth century Spanish arrivals found the Choctaw in the last stages of mound building. They were preeminent agriculturalists and hunters, having an abundance of food, including sunflowers, corn, beans, and melons, as well as tobacco. Favored dietary items included bear ribs, turkey, venison, root jelly, hominy, corn cakes, and soup. In 1729 the Choctaw aided the French in a war against the Natchez Indians. Later they signed a treaty with the British, although they continued to support the French until the latter's defeat by Great Britain in 1763. During the American Revolution, Choctaw warriors served under the command of four American generals. (Choctaws continued to provide meritorious military service in World Wars I and II, Korea, Vietnam, Grenada, Panama, and the Persian Gulf.) The Naniaba (fish eaters) were a riverine Choctaw tribe; in the early 1700's they were located in close proximity to the Mobile and Tohome tribes in southern Alabama. Their earlier home was on a bluff (Nanna Hubba) near the confluence of the Alabama and Tombigbee rivers.

Removal. The Naniaba had provided fierce opposition to Hernando de Soto's advance in 1540, but by 1761 both the Naniaba and Mobile were lost to history as tribes. The Indian Removal Act of 1830, urged on Congress by President Andrew Jackson, provided for forcing southeastern natives to give up their ancestral homelands. The Treaty of Dancing Rabbit Creek, signed later that same year, officially legalized the deportation of the Choctaws. A small amount of land was reserved for Choctaw chiefs and other

Mid-nineteenth depiction of Choctaw men. (Library of Congress)

individuals; this land formed the basis of the present-day Mississippi Band of Choctaws. Although the Choctaw had never fought against the United States, they were forced to cede their lands in a series of treaties starting in 1801 and culminating in 1830. The forced deportation of the Choctaw, under army escort, to Indian Territory was cruel and involved bitter hardship and death from exposure and starvation. The road they and other tribes followed to Indian Territory has forever since been known as the Trail of Tears.

Modern Life. The Choctaw are divided into three areas: southeastern Oklahoma, with tribal headquarters located at Durant; Mississippi, with the band administrative center at Philadelphia; and the Apache, Jena, and Clifton bands of Louisiana and the Mowa band of Alabama. The Choctaw also reflect the geographic mobility of Americans in general. Most Choctaws live outside tribal enumerated census areas. Figures from the 1990 census include 82,299 persons total: Oklahoma, 28,411; Mississippi, 3,932;

Louisiana, 1,048; and Mowa Band of Alabama, fewer than 100 persons (total 33,400). Choctaws living outside enumerated areas totaled 48,899.

The Choctaw, rich in cultural heritage and spirit, are successful developers and managers of an array of cultural and business activities in Oklahoma, Mississippi, and Louisiana. Choctaw leaders have particularly focused their development efforts on a valuable commodity, the intellect and drive of the Choctaw people.

Burl Self

Bibliography

Carson, James T. *Searching for the Bright Path: The Mississippi Choctaws from Prehistory to Removal*. Lincoln: University of Nebraska Press, 1999.

Cushman, H.B. *History of the Choctaw, Chickasaw, and Natchez Indians*. Norman: University of Oklahoma Press, 1999.

Debo, Angie. *The Rise and Fall of the Choctaw Republic*. Norman: University of Oklahoma Press, 1934.

De Rosier, Arthur H., Jr. *The Removal of the Choctaw Indians*. Knoxville: University Press of Tennessee, 1970.

Faiman-Silva, Sandra. *Choctaws at the Crossroads: The Political Economy of Class and Culture in the Oklahoma Timber Region*. Lincoln: University of Nebraska Press, 1997.

Ferrara, Peter J. *The Choctaw Revolution: Lessons for Federal Indian Policy*. Washington, D.C.: Americans for Tax Reform Foundation, 1998.

Galloway, Patricia K. *Choctaw Genesis, 1500-1700*. Lincoln: University of Nebraska Press, 1995.

Kappler, Charles. *Indian Affairs, Laws, and Treaties*. 4 vols. Washington, D.C.: Government Printing Office, 1929.

Kidwell, Clara Sue. *Choctaws and Missionaries in Mississippi, 1818-1918*. Norman: University of Oklahoma Press, 1995.

Morrison, James D. *The Social History of the Choctaw Nation, 1865-1907*. Durant, Okla.: Creative Informatics, 1987.

Nelson, Will T., ed. *English Choctaw Dictionary*. 5th ed. Reprint of *A Dictionary of the Choctaw Language*, by Cyrus Byington. Oklahoma City: Council of Choctaws, 1975.

Spring, Joel H. *The Cultural Transformation of a Native American Family and Its Tribe, 1763-1995: A Basket of Apples*. Mahwah, N.J.: Lawrence Erlbaum Associates, 1996.

Chumash

CULTURE AREA: California
LANGUAGE GROUP: Chumashan
PRIMARY LOCATION: Ventura, Santa Barbara, and San Luis Obispo counties, California
POPULATION SIZE: 2,981 (1990 U.S. Census)

The Chumash were one of the largest (fifteen thousand is a likely estimate) and most sophisticated California Indian tribes at the time of European contact. Of the many unique features of their culture, two stand out as distinctive: their extensive rock art and their construction of boats. The Chumash area abounds in pictographs, mostly of abstract forms. By the time of the arrival of Europeans, no Indians were still living who could recall the origins or meaning of the paintings, and vandals have destroyed many of the sites. Many of the Chumash lived on islands in the Santa Barbara Channel, and trade and communication between those islands and the mainland was extensive. The Chumash became very proficient in making canoes of pine planks stitched together with deer sinews and sealed with thick asphaltum. Canoes varied in length from 8 to 25 feet, were usually painted red with shell decorations, and held two to twenty people.

While some scholars have attempted to identify and preserve native terms for regional subdivisions, others have simply borrowed the names of the five Spanish missions in the region: Tsoyińneahkoo or Obispeño for the San Luis Obispo mission (founded 1772); Ahmoo or Purisimeño for Purísima Concepción (1787); Kahshakompéah or Ynezeño for Santa Ynéz (1804); Kaśswah or Barbareño for Santa Barbara (1786); and Chumash or Ventureño for San Buenaventura (1782). Inland territorial districts have been named Hooíkookoo or Emigdiano and Kahshenahsmoo or Cuyama.

The Spanish expedition of 1769 reported the Chumash as friendly and peaceful, so missionaries were eager to enter the area. By the 1820's nearly all the Chumash, including those of the Channel Islands and the inland mountainous areas, had become part of the mission system. As happened elsewhere, however, the Chumash preserved many features of their own culture. Although they generally proved to be, as anticipated, a very peaceful people who quietly accepted Hispanization, the most serious uprising in the entire history of the California missions occurred in 1824 when a violent Chumash revolt at several missions resulted in the death of a number of Indians and whites. Historians are uncertain about the cause of that rebellion, but one explanation is that the Chumash were fighting to preserve some of their traditional social and marital patterns.

Despite their efforts to maintain their traditional lifestyle, the Chumash population experienced the familiar pattern of decline during and after the mission period. By 1832 they numbered only 2,471, by 1865 only 659, and by 1920 a mere 74. The federal roll of 1928 identified 31 Chumash, of whom only 8 were of unmixed ancestry. In May, 1941, Juan Justo, identified as the last surviving full-blood Chumash, died in Santa Barbara. The federal government had established the Santa Ynéz Reservation near the mission of that name on December 17, 1901. As of March 15, 1993, that reservation provided a home for 195 people of Chumash ancestry, with another 28 registered members living in adjacent areas. The 1990 U.S. Census reported a much larger population, with nearly three thousand people identifying themselves as Chumash.

Clallam

CULTURE AREA: Northwest Coast
LANGUAGE GROUP: Salishan
PRIMARY LOCATION: North side of Strait Juan de Fuca
POPULATION SIZE: 3,800 (1990 U.S. Census)

Prior to European American contact, the Clallam—including the Klallam, Skallam, and Tlallum—inhabited approximately a dozen permanent villages while intermarrying with other Central Coast tribes and thus encouraging trade and ritual exchange of wealth. They hunted inland to the Olympic Mountains and used dugout canoes to hunt seals, porpoise, sea lions, and sturgeon. They gathered numerous plant foods and by-products. Various complex ceremonies recognized status change and redistribution of food and goods.

By the 1820's, the Hudson's Bay Company had explored the area and established Fort Langley on the Fraser River in 1827. The Central Coast Salish territory was divided in 1846 by the Treaty of Washington. In 1855 the Clallam signed the Point No Point Treaty, consenting to cede their lands and live on the Skokomish Reservation. Most Clallam earned wages by picking hops and berries, working in canneries, and selling fish.

By the late twentieth century, issues of gaming and gill-netting confronted the modern Clallam, along with land claim settlements against the federal government.

Clatskanie

CULTURE AREA: Northwest Coast
LANGUAGE GROUP: Athapaskan
PRIMARY LOCATION: Chehalis River and mouth of Shockumchuck River, Washington

The Clatskanie (or Tlatskanai) were a riverine and maritime people, living in permanent frame, rectangular post and lintel dwellings. They depended largely on fish for subsistence, but also hunted. The women exploited the large root fields of their territory. Unfortunately, little ethnographic data was collected before their culture's demise. It is estimated that their population of approximately two thousand in 1780 had declined to 336 by 1904; by 1910, only three Clatskanie were living; this decline was primarily the result of disease introduced by European Americans and of conflict with other ethnic groups of the region. It is believed that the Clatskanie may have enforced a toll on people using the Columbia River for trading of goods.

Clovis

DATE: 10,000-9200 B.C.E.
LOCATION: Most of continental North America
CULTURES AFFECTED: Paleo-Indian

Archaeological evidence of Paleo-Indian peoples was unearthed near Clovis, New Mexico, in 1931, and subsequent discoveries of related artifacts at kill sites across the continental United States justified the designation of a Clovis cultural tradition. In the west the best-known Clovis sites are Blackwater Draw, New Mexico; Naco, Lehner, Murray Springs, and Escapule, Arizona; Union Pacific, Montana; Dent, Nebraska; and Domebo, Oklahoma. Of the many sites excavated in the east, rich Clovis finds have been unearthed at Plenge, Port Mobil, Dutchess Quarry, and West Athens, New York, as well as at Reagan, Vermont; Williamson and Flint Run, Virginia; Bull Brook, Massachusetts; Shawnee-Minisink, Delaware; Shoop, Pennsylvania; and Hardaway, Tennessee. Related discoveries have been found at a score of other locations.

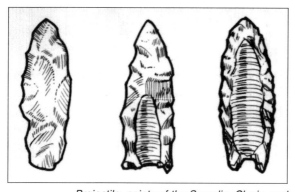

Projectile points of the Scandia, Clovis, and Folsom traditions.

The Clovis tradition apparently was short-lived, lasting from circa 10,500 B.C.E. to 9200 B.C.E., giving way to the somewhat different Folsom and then Plano traditions. Clovis peoples have been characterized chiefly as roving mammoth hunters, although they also stalked horse, buffalo, tapirs, caribou, giant armadillo, four-horned antelope, sloths, and dire wolves. Some kill sites continued in use for thousands of years, providing ample evidence of their distinctive Clovis fluted projectile points, prismatic and edge-chipped, flat-flaked knives, smooth or bone cylinders, burins, cleavers, picks, and uniface chipped scrapers. Quarries where the chert and jasper preferred for such toolmaking were obtained have likewise been found. The Clovis culture was well-acquainted with fire, and there are findings at the Thunderbird site at Flint Run, Virginia, as well as at locations in Massachusetts and Nova Scotia, which suggest that the Clovis tradition may have included construction of the earliest known houses in the Americas. Developed south of, though often close to, continental glaciation, the Clovis culture yielded to other adaptations as its chief prey, mammoths, disappeared.

Coast Yuki

CULTURE AREA: California
LANGUAGE GROUP: Yuki
PRIMARY LOCATION: Drainage of the Eel River, northwestern California

The coast Yuki, or Ukhotnom, were shell-mound dwellers. They comprised eleven groups who occupied approximately fifty miles of the Mendocino Coast. They lived in conical redwood bark-covered dwellings; in summer they utilized brush huts for privacy and windbreaks. Men hunted and fished, while women collected and gathered essential plant foods. Each group had its own elected headman and territory. Groups visited, traded, and had usury rights to resources of other villages. Though a marine-oriented people, they had no boats. Their diet consisted primarily of acorns, grass seeds, salmon, and mussels. Deer and elk were important for food and by-products.

In the early 1850's, the Coast Yuki were intruded upon by white lumbermen and ranchers, whose activities destroyed many natural resources. Many Indians were interned on the Mendocino Reservation in 1856, though some continued to work on white ranches. The Coast Yuki joined the Pomo Earth Lodge cult, a derivative of the Ghost Dance, and revitalized some traditional ways, but by the 1970's they were no longer considered a distinct group.

Cocopa

CULTURE AREA: Southwest
LANGUAGE GROUP: Yuman
PRIMARY LOCATION: Sonora, Mexico
POPULATION SIZE: 640 in United States (1990 U.S. Census); most live in Mexico

The Cocopas, sedentary dwellers of the Southwest, inhabited the region along the lower stretch of the Colorado River in what is presently Sonora, Mexico, bordered on the south by the Gulf of California. Along with the nearby Mojaves, Halchidhomas, Maricopas, and Yumas, the Cocopas were Yuman-speaking and were ancient inhabitants of this hot and dry region. Another neighboring tribe was the Chemehuevis of the Uto-Aztecan language family.

Because of their efficient use of the land and water resources available to them, the Cocopas were able to remain in one place, and didn't have to roam for hunting or gathering purposes. They utilized the annual flooding of the Colorado River, rather than irrigation, for the watering of their crops, which included corn, beans, pumpkins, gourds, and tobacco. Both men and women took part in tending the fields. Limited hunting of small game, including rabbits, supplemented the agricultural production for the tribe, as did the gathering of mesquite beans and other wild foods by the women. The Colorado River provided fish, which were caught by the men with seines, basketry scoops with long handles, weirs made from interlaced branches, and dip nets.

Because of the intense heat of the area, the men wore only narrow breechcloths, while the women wore front and back aprons. Sandals were worn while traveling. Men and women painted their faces and wore tattoos.

Hair was worn with bangs covering the forehead. The men twisted their hair in back into many thin strands, while the women wore their hair long.

The housing of the Cocopas also conformed to the hot, dry weather. Houses were little more than flat-roofed structures for shade, with open sides. In winter, rectangular structures with sloping sides and ends, all covered with earth, were utilized. Rabbitskin blankets provided warmth in winter.

The Cocopas lived with little formal government. They held a strong sense of tribal unity, with the family being the basic unit within the tribe. Chiefs held an advisory role, maintaining intratribal peace and conducting religious ceremonies. Shamans were held in high regard and accompanied chiefs on war parties. War raids were well organized, with the warriors using bows and arrows, clubs, heavy sticks, round hide shields, and feathered staves.

Most Cocopa people live in Sonora, Mexico; the 1990 U.S. census also reported 640 living in the southwestern United States.

Coeur d'Alene

CULTURE AREA: Plateau
LANGUAGE GROUP: Salishan
PRIMARY LOCATION: Northwestern Idaho
POPULATION SIZE: 1,048 (1990 U.S. Census)

The Coeur d'Alene, an Interior Salishan-speaking people, called themselves "Schitsu' Umsh." They occupied an area east of the Spokane River, around Coeur d'Alene Lake and all its tributaries, including the headwaters of the Spokane River, with eastern boundaries to the Bitterroot Mountains. Aboriginally they were composed of three distinct geographical bands with a population of approximately 3,500 until the smallpox epidemics of 1831, 1847, and 1850 reduced the population by half. After acquiring horses in the late 1700's, they, like the Flathead and Nez Perce, adopted a war ethos. At the time of European American contact, they had adopted many Plains traits, including the hide tipi, scalp taking, reed armor, and Plains-style clothing and ornaments. Their culture was further influenced when they ventured annually onto the western Plains for hunting buffalo and trading out roots, salmon pemmican, bows, and hemp.

They possessed bilateral descent, sexual equality, a strict division of labor, polygyny, rule by consensus of opinion, and elaborate ceremonialism that emphasized the Bluejay Ceremony, First-Fruit Ceremony, and Midwinter Ceremony. Other aspects of their culture included shamanism, the vision quest for skill-related tutelary spirits, an animistic belief system with a complex pantheon, the sweathouse complex, a trickster, and social control by public opinion and threats of sorcery.

First mention of the Coeur d'Alene was by Meriwether Lewis and William Clark in 1805, and their first contact with European Americans was with David Thompson, who surveyed the area in 1811. The first permanent white settler was Father Nicholas Point, who in 1842 established a Roman Catholic mission on the banks of the St. Joseph River. It was built by the Coeur d'Alene from 1843 to 1853 under the supervision of Father Anthony Ravalli and was later moved to the present Cataldo site; it is the oldest standing building in Idaho. The area was periodically exploited by encroaching settlers and miners, a situation which in 1877 caused the Sacred Heart Mission to be moved to its present location at De Smet, Idaho. An executive order of November 8, 1873, established the Coeur d'Alene Reservation, and the existing boundaries were ratified by Congress in 1894; it covers an area of 345,000 acres. In 1903 the Historic Sisters' Building was constructed by the Sisters of Providence and functioned as a boarding school for Indian girls until 1973.

The Coeur d'Alene, a sovereign nation created by executive order, are consolidated on the Coeur d'Alene Reservation on the southern portion of Coeur d'Alene Lake, Idaho. Tribal headquarters, containing the tribal archives, museum, and library, is southwest of Plummer, and the elected tribal council administers finance, planning, natural resources, a tribal farm, education, and social and health services. The Benewah Center features an Indian specialty store, post office, medical center, and supermarket. The two major employers are the Coeur d'Alene Tribe and Pacific Crown Timber Products, with additional monies gained from the successful management of agriculture, minerals, and water recreation facilities on adjacent Coeur d'Alene Lake.

Bibliography

Chalfant, Stuart A. "Ethnological Field Investigation and Analysis of Historical Material Relative to Coeur d'Alene Aboriginal Distribution." In *Interior Salish and Eastern Washington Indians,* edited by D. A. Horr. Vol. 4. New York: Garland, 1974.

Hale, Janet Campbell. *Bloodlines: Odyssey of a Native Daughter.* New York: Random House, 1993.

Peltier, Jerome. *A Brief History of the Coeur d'Alene Indians, 1805-1909.* Fairfield, Wash.: Ye Galleon Press, 1982.

_____. *Manners and Customs of the Coeur d'Alene Indians.* Spokane: Peltier Publications, 1975.

Ross, John Alan. "An Ethnographic and Ethnohistorical Survey of the Proposed Washington Centennial Trail Corridor." In *Archaeology of the Middle Spokane River Valley: Investigations Along the Spokane Centennial Trail*, edited by John A. Draper and William Andrefsky. Pullman: Center for Northwest Anthropology, Dept. of Anthropology, Washington State University, 1991.

Seltice, Joseph. *Saga of the Coeur d'Alene Indians: An Account of Chief Joseph Seltice.* Fairfield, Wash.: Ye Galleon Press, 1990.

Walker, Deward E., Jr. *American Indians of Idaho.* Anthropological Monographs of the University of Idaho, 2. Moscow: University of Idaho Press, 1971.

Columbia

CULTURE AREA: Plateau
LANGUAGE GROUP: Salishan
PRIMARY LOCATION: Northeastern Washington
POPULATION SIZE: 441 (1990 U.S. Census)

The so-called Columbia Indians were composed of seven bands who lived on the Columbia River and collectively called themselves Sinseloxw'i't ("big river people"). They numbered about twelve hundred at the time of contact with European Americans, and are generally considered to have included the Sinkiuse, Chelan, Methow, Sinkakaius, and Wenatchi. These hunters and gatherers had a definite annual subsistence round, regulated through marriage, trade, and availability of resources. Social control was achieved through threats of sorcery, gossip, consensus of opinion, behavioral and dietary taboos, high division of labor, and a complex mythical charter. Villages were autonomous, with chiefs, and descent was bilateral. The aboriginal population was drastically reduced by seven major epidemics; the first, in 1782-1783, was estimated to have reduced their population by one-half.

The first European Americans to spend time with the Columbia peoples were Alexander Ross of the Pacific Fur Company in 1810 and David Thompson in 1811. White incursion increased throughout the first half of the nineteenth century until it resulted in a series of wars involving Columbia peoples from 1855 to 1858. Eventually the militaristic, nontreaty Columbias were settled on the Colville Indian Reservation in 1884 under the leadership of Chief Moses after the July, 1884, "Moses Agreement." No full-blooded Columbias still exist; those people with Columbian ancestry live mostly on the Colville Reservation.

Colville

CULTURE AREA: Plateau
LANGUAGE GROUP: Salishan
PRIMARY LOCATION: Washington State
POPULATION SIZE: 7,140 (1990 U.S. Census)

The Colville, one of the largest branches of the Salishan family, lived between Kettle Falls and the Spokane River in eastern Washington. They spoke the same language as another Salishan tribe, the Okanagan. "Colville" is the name of the fort of the Hudson's Bay Company near which they lived, in villages of varying size. Because they relied on hunting and fishing—salmon was a chief staple of their diet—as well as on gathering roots and berries, they were forced to move throughout the year to find food in different seasons. This prevented the villages from growing and developing as political or social centers.

The Colville do not seem to have relied on agriculture. They were skilled with horses and used them in their travels seeking food. Generally, Salishan tribes enjoyed relatively peaceful lives. They were involved in no protracted struggles with their neighbors; there seems to have been enough food to go around, so no major disputes arose over hunting territory. The American explorers Meriwether Lewis and William Clark encountered the Colville in 1806. In 1872 the Colville Reservation was established in Washington, on 2.9 million acres. Some of that land was later allotted to white settlers, and the reservation had slightly more than 1 million acres in the late twentieth century. Toward the century's close, the Colville were making their living primarily by raising cattle, farming, and logging.

Comanche

CULTURE AREA: Southwestern Plains
LANGUAGE GROUP: Shoshonean
PRIMARY LOCATION: Oklahoma
POPULATION SIZE: 11,322 (1990 U.S. Census)

The Comanche tribe arose as an offshoot of the Shoshone tribe. They call themselves the Nemena, "the real people." The name Comanche has been said to come from the Ute word *komanticia* ("an enemy," or "one who fights all the time"). The Comanches ruled much of the southwestern Plains until the middle of the nineteenth century and did "fight all the time" to maintain their ascendancy. They were also called the Paducah (or Padouca, a Sioux name) by the French and the Americans, who mistakenly thought that they were an Apache tribe that had once inhabited the region. The Comanche lands once made up much of modern Texas, New Mexico, Oklahoma, Kansas, and Colorado. Most modern Comanches live on Oklahoma reservation lands.

Tribal History. Tribal legends suggest that the Comanches and the Shoshones split into separate tribes because of disagreements about the fair division of game or in the aftermath of a disastrous disease epidemic. The pre-1700 tribal split led the Comanches into the southwestern Plains and kept the Shoshones in the Wyoming and Montana mountains. The Comanches soon controlled 24,000 square miles and defeated all those who contested their control. This success was attributable to their being one of the first tribes who had horses and to their superb military horsemanship.

The Kiowas and the Comanches, at first bitter enemies, became military allies in the eighteenth century. The close alliance continued until the pacification of the Plains tribes placed them all on reservations. The main enemies of the Comanches were the Apaches, the Navajos, the Osages, the Pawnees, and the Utes. The Comanches ranged far into Texas and Mexico in raids seeking horses and other plunder.

Traditional Lifeways. The Comanche tribe was divided into thirteen autonomous bands that often cooperated in war but had no political consensus, no tribal chief, and no tribal council. Most numerous was the Penateka band (the Honey Eaters or Wasps). Other prominent Comanche bands were the Quahadi (the Antelopes), the Nokoni (the Wanderers), the Kutsueka (the Buffalo Eaters), and the Yamparika (the Yamp, or potato, Eaters). The Comanche tribal organization was so loose that any warrior could enter or leave a band at will. In battle, a war chief was in charge of all of a band's warriors. In time of peace, however, he had no power, and the tribespeople were autonomous, although they often listened to the advice of peace chiefs and of a council of elders.

Comanche men did not often marry until they were well-established warriors (usually at about age twenty-five). They were polygamous, especially as to marrying women who were the sisters or the widows of their brothers. Men could marry as many women as they were able to support, although most had only one wife. Each wife was given a separate dwelling, wherever polygamy occurred, but extended families shared most home-making activities. Divorce was simple and favored the Comanche man. Female adultery was punished by beatings or nose-clipping. Children were loved and doted upon by all Comanches.

The Comanche religion is not thoroughly documented. Their main deities were a Creator (the Great Spirit), the Sun, the Earth, and the Moon. Comanches revered the boisterous trickster spirit Coyote; hence, they did not eat coyotes or dogs. The young Comanche men, like those of most Plains tribes, went on vision quests to achieve their adult names and to obtain their medicine power. It was believed by the Comanches that all "the real people" who died went on to an afterlife unless they had been scalped, had died in the dark, or had been strangled.

Funerals included dressing the deceased in the finest clothing they owned, painting their faces, and interring them in caves or in shallow graves along with their finest possessions. Before 1850, a warrior's favorite wife was often killed to accompany him to the afterlife. During mourning, both family and friends gashed clothing and bodies, burned the dwellings of the deceased, and destroyed horses and other wealth in their honor. Afterward, the names of the deceased were never again mentioned by any tribe member.

Comanche bands had men's secret societies, many ritual dances, and many other medicine ceremonies. They were so secretive about these ceremonies, however, that very little is known about Comanche ritual, compared with that of many other tribes. The Sun Dance—very important to most other Plains Indian tribes—was not celebrated by the Comanches until the late nineteenth century.

Comanches lived in well-designed, finely decorated buffalo-hide tipis, made by women, and moved when new campgrounds were sought (sometimes because of the need for fresh forage for their horse herds). The buffalo provided many Comanche needs, including food. Comanches were nomad hunter-gatherers who neither farmed nor fished. Their plant foods, such as potatoes, nuts, and various fruits, were all gathered by women's foraging expeditions. In contrast, the Comanches were expert horse breeders, fine horse trainers, and excellent primitive veterinarians. Their horse herds were tremendous and contained exceptionally fine animals.

Comanche men's personal adornment included painting their faces and the heads and tails of their mounts before battle. Buffalo-hide shirts, leggings, and boots, as well as very elaborate headdresses, were also worn. Long hair was desired by all Comanche men, and they acquired it both via natural hair growth and interwoven horse hair. Prior to the use of firearms, Comanche weapons were buffalo-hide battle shields so strong that arrows and bullets did not easily pierce them, long war lances, heavy war clubs, and bows and arrows. The chief decorations of all Comanche weapons were feathers, bear teeth, and scalps of enemies. War was the main occupation of Comanche men, providing them with sport, horses, and other plunder. The Comanches were viewed as exceptionally fierce warriors.

Comanche chief Parker fought fiercely against confinement to reservations, but after 1875 he became an advocate of acceptance and assimilation. (Library of Congress)

Comanche cooking consisted mostly of the roasting of meat on sticks over open fires and of boiling it, with other foods, in skin pouches into which hot stones were dropped. Comanche eating utensils were very simple. Their weapons and shields, on the other hand, were very well-crafted and attractively adorned. Comanche bows, arrows, and lances were most often made of the very tough wood called bois d'arc (Osage orange) by the French explorers of North America.

Movement to Reservations. In the 1850's, the Penatekas were the first Comanche group to move to a reservation. After the Medicine Lodge Treaty and the Battle of the Washita, in the 1860's, most Comanche bands moved onto reservations. Comanche resistance ended in 1875, when Quanah Parker and his Quahadi band, the last Comanche warrior holdouts, surrendered. Slowly changing their ways but retaining their heritage, the Comanches have acclimatized themselves to mainstream American life. The 1930's passage of the Oklahoma Indian Welfare Act remedied some tribal grievances, and a Kiowa-Comanche-Apache Business Committee aimed at improving the lot of the three tribes was created. In the 1960's the Comanche Business Council began to seek to improve Comanche life. Modern Comanches have opened businesses, entered the general workforce and many professions, and are well represented in the American armed forces. At the same time they continue to fight to keep tribal traditions alive both in their homes and in the schools where their children are taught.

Sanford S. Singer

Bibliography

American Indian Publishers. *Dictionary of Indian Tribes of the Americas*. Newport Beach, Calif.: Author, 1980.

Fehrenbach, T.R. *Comanches: The Destruction of a People*. New York: Da Capo Press, 1994.

Foster, Morris W. *Being Comanche: A Social History of an American Indian Community*. Tucson: University of Arizona Press, 1991.

_____. *United States-Comanche Relations: The Reservation Years*. New Haven, Conn.: Yale University Press, 1976.

Hagan, William T. *Quanah Parker, Comanche Chief*. Norman: University of Oklahoma Press, 1993.

Kavanagh, Thomas W. *Comanche Political History: An Ethnohistorical Perspective, 1706-1875*. Lincoln: University of Nebraska Press, 1996.

Meadows, William C. *Kiowa, Apache, and Comanche Military Societies: Enduring Veterans, 1800 to the Present*. Austin: University of Texas Press, 1999.

Neeley, Bill. *The Last Comanche Chief: The Life and Times of Quanah Parker*. New York: John Wiley & Sons, 1995.

Noyes, Stanley. *Los Comanches: The Horse People, 1751-1845*. Albuquerque: University of New Mexico Press, 1993.

Noyes, Stanley, and Daniel J. Gelo. *Comanches in the New West, 1895-1908: Historic Photographs*. Austin: University of Texas Press, 1999.

Richardson, Rupert N. *The Comanche Barrier to South Plains Settlement*. Glendale, Calif.: Arthur H. Clark, 1933.

Wallace, Ernest, and E. Adamson Hoebel. *The Comanches: Lords of the South Plains*. Norman: University of Oklahoma Press, 1952.

Comox

CULTURE AREA: Northwest Coast
LANGUAGE GROUP: Central Salish
PRIMARY LOCATION: South of Johnstone Strait and west of Discovery Portage, British Columbia and Washington
POPULATION SIZE: 800 in Canada (Statistics Canada, based on 1991 census)

Prior to European American contact, the Comox were divided into the Island and Mainland groups, living in split-cedar gable-roofed houses, located for exploiting the Strait of Georgia and numerous streams of their territory. Their main source of food was fishing, supplemented by the hunting of deer, black and grizzly bear, mountain sheep, and goats. Smaller animals were caught with traps and snares. Most bird species were hunted, primarily for feathers and plumage. Women gathered seeds, berries, nuts, tubers, roots, and cambium.

By 1792, the British and Spanish had entered the Strait of Georgia, trading metal tools and beads for food. Maritime fur trade was active until the demise of the sea otter. Epidemics reduced native populations and brought some demographic shifting. Roman Catholics opened missions in the 1860's, denouncing the Winter Dance, potlatching, and other of the traditional ways, forcing people into a wage economy. Descendants of the Comox live primarily in British Columbia. There are three groups, the Homalco, Klahoose, and Sliammon.

Coos

CULTURE AREA: Northwest Coast
LANGUAGE GROUP: Coos
PRIMARY LOCATION: Coos Bay, Oregon
POPULATION SIZE: 216 (1990 U.S. Census)

The Coos tribe is a small estuarine community living in the Coos Bay area of southwestern Oregon. The words "Coos," "Coosan," and "Kusan" are of uncertain origin but might have originated with a word in their native tongue, Kusan, described as a dialect of the Macro-Penutian language spoken by several tribes of possible Yakonan stock in southern Oregon and northern California.

The Kusan culture, made up primarily of the Miluk and Hanis communities, lived exclusively around Coos Bay, Oregon, and upriver along its tributaries. They were part of a family of peoples composed of four related groups who shared territories covering parts of present-day Coos County. The name the modern people use for themselves is Miluk-Hanis. The Coos, Kusan, or Coosan peoples, as they are collectively known, were actually four communities who spoke related dialects of a source tongue and who shared an estuarine environment.

Western Coos County, from Ten Mile Lake to the north to the south bank of the Coquille River, and from two miles offshore inland to the crest of the Coast Range Mountains, was home to the Kusan peoples. The Melukitz lived on the far south and west sides of Coos Bay. The Naseemi lived on the banks of the Coquille River to the south. The Miluk occupied the north shore of the Coquille and ranged up the headlands of Cape Arago from Coos Head to the place on the bay now known as Tar Heel Point. The Hanis resided on the south side of the bay and up the estuary, from just south of the town of Empire to the downtown area of present-day North Bend.

These four branches of the Kusan family lived peaceably together in an unbelievably rich ecosystem. As a unit they are often grouped with several other cultural units to the north, usually categorized by language affiliation or genetic stock, such as their Yakonan-speaking ancestors, who remain as the Alsea, Kuitish, Siuslaw, Umpqua, and Yaquina. To the south are the distantly related language groups and cultures of the Klamath Basin Culture Area. The Kusan say they are not necessarily related to the riverine peoples to the north and south.

Indirect contacts with whites came in 1828. It is estimated that there were about two thousand people living around Coos Bay at that time. White settlement of the bay area commenced in the late 1840's. The Kusans did not fight; they tried to make treaties but were rapidly overwhelmed.

They joined with the Lower Umpqua and the Siuslaw to form the Confederated Tribes of the Coos, Lower Umpqua, and Siuslaw Indians in 1855. About that time they were forced to move to a reservation on the Siletz River. They did not return for many years to their homeland, which was taken over by American settlers during their absence. The confederation still exists and is recognized as an Indian nation by the U.S. government.

Copalis

CULTURE AREA: Northwest Coast
LANGUAGE GROUP: Salishan
PRIMARY LOCATION: Grays Harbor, Washington

Traditionally the Copalis, a relatively small group, lived in an area nearly surrounded by water. Division of labor was based on age, sex, status, and ability. The importance of fish and marine products was reflected in various rituals, technology, status, and the First Salmon Ceremony. Inland areas were hunted for bear, deer, and elk; smaller animals were taken by traps and snares for food, skin, and by-products. Rights of usufruct applied to whaling and clamming beaches, berry patches, barnacle stacks, and timber areas. Low tides provided a variety of foods. Numerous food plants were utilized, particularly camas.

Though earlier naval expeditions had probably visited the Copalis, first documentation was by Meriwether Lewis and William Clark in the years 1805-1806, who estimated the population to be two hundred, in a total of ten dwellings. By 1811, fur trappers and traders were in the area, but the opening of Fort Vancouver in 1825 by Hudson's Bay Company brought considerable socioeconomic change—including a major epidemic of malaria. Missionaries, loggers, and settlers in the Quinault and Lower Chalis area sustained deculturation.

Costanoan

CULTURE AREA: California
LANGUAGE GROUP: Costanoan
PRIMARY LOCATION: San Francisco Bay to Monterey Bay, California
POPULATION SIZE: 1,023 (1990 U.S. Census)

Historically, the Costanoan lived in approximately fifty politically autonomous tribelets or nations, each with a permanent village. Their culture was based on patrilineal clans that were divided into bear and deer moieties. Acorns were the most important plant food, but numerous seeds, berries, and tubers were collected by season, and animals were trapped and hunted. Waterfowl and numerous bird species were hunted for food and feathers. Gathered insects were an important source of protein.

First European American contact was in 1602 by the Sebastián Vizcaino expedition. Groups later explored Costanoan territory between 1769 and 1776. The mission period, 1770-1835, brought many devastating changes— particularly a population decline from disease and a diminishing birth rate. The missions discouraged traditional social and religious rituals. Later, secularization of the missions and the proliferation of settlers further disrupted the Costanoan culture, which by 1935 brought the language to extinction. By 1970, Costanoan descendants had united into a corporate unity, known as the Ohlone Indian Tribe. These people have never been compensated for the loss of their lands during the gold rush.

Coushatta

CULTURE AREA: Southeast
LANGUAGE GROUP: Muskogean
PRIMARY LOCATION: Texas, Louisiana
POPULATION SIZE: 1,269 (1990 U.S. Census)

The origin of the Coushatta tribe is unknown. Variants on the tribal name include Koasati, Coosawanda, and Shati. Differing folklore traditions place them coming from the north as well as Mexico. The first contact with Europeans occurred in 1540, when Hernando de Soto found the tribe living on Pine Island in the Tennessee River in Alabama. During the eighteenth century, Coushatta villages were connected with one another and with white settlements. The relationships between Indians were usually peaceful, and villages often engaged in athletic competition. The English settlers changed the Coushatta economy by trading cloth, munitions, and alcohol—all new to the Indians—for animal pelts.

The Coushatta lived side-by-side with other Creek peoples. They shared many cultural traditions, including a religion revering "Isakita immissi" or the "Master of Life/Holder of Breath." The deity was worshiped as "resident of the sky" and linked to sun worship. Many religious rituals and taboos regulated eating and drinking, as the Creeks believed that the consumer would acquire the qualities of the food he ate. Women gathered food and fuel; men hunted with blowgun and bow and arrow and fished with nets and spears.

The linking of the Creek people with one another fostered a flourishing trade of goods. Indian traders traveled, offering distant tribes items they could not obtain in their living area.

During the 1790's, the Coushattas retreated from white settlements into Spanish Louisiana. They flourished in Louisiana during the first half of the nineteenth century and pushed into Texas, where they suffered from disease and ultimately united with the Alabamas in one village. There they traded with the white communities and got along quite well. The land they settled had to be conducive to agriculture and on a navigable river. They built huts of wood with bark roofs. Their diet consisted of game, corn, and wild fruit.

Migration and white society had a negative effect on the social organization of the Coushatta. By the mid-1800's, the clan and town had little social meaning. Intermarriage between Coushattas and other tribes, whites, and African Americans was frowned upon but not uncommon. The family began to assume the traditional functions of the clan and town, including education and responsibility for children until they married.

In the twentieth century, the Coushatta are led by a chief chosen by a committee of medicine men and shamans. They also have a "war chief" who is the purveyor of justice in the community. The actual governance is carried on through an elected council. Many traditional religious rituals and practices have persisted to this day, though Christianity has now supplanted tribal religion. In 1990, approximately four hundred Coushattas lived in Louisiana and Texas on a 4,000-acre reservation; others lived in Alabama and Oklahoma. English is the primary language, although even as late as 1990 many of the older Coushattas spoke their native language. Most Coushattas in Texas and Oklahoma earn their living in either the timber or tourism industry.

Cowichan

CULTURE AREA: Northwest Coast
LANGUAGE GROUP: Salishan
PRIMARY LOCATION: Vancouver Island, British Columbia
POPULATION SIZE: 9,360 (Statistics Canada, based on 1991 census)

The Cowichan (the Cowichan included the Pilalt and Sumass) inhabited six villages on the lower course of the Cowichan River, on Malahat, and one village on Saanich Inlet. Permanent dwellings were large rectangular post-and-lintel constructions of split and hewn cedar. Households cooperated in numerous ceremonies and for mutual protection. The Cowichan were dependent upon a wide variety of marine products, some of which were stored for winter consumption and trade. The harpoon was used for

Cowichan masked dancer. (Library of Congress)

sea mammals. Hunting and trapping of land mammals were the responsibilities of the men; women gathered a wide variety of food and utilitarian plants.

In 1775, the Bruno de Hezeta-Juan Franscisco de la Bodega y Quadra expedition became the first European American group to have contact with the Cowichan, and they brought small-pox with them. Malaria, measles, influenza, dysentery, and typhoid followed. Fort Langley prevented attacks by the Cowichan upon the Upper Stalo Salish, but they continued to fight with the Clallam, Lummi, and Musqueam. In the 1860's, the Cowichan encroached upon Pentlatch territory to use the Qualicum fishery.

Cowlitz

CULTURE AREA: Northwest Coast
LANGUAGE GROUP: Salishan
PRIMARY LOCATION: Lower and middle course of Cowlitz River, Washington
POPULATION SIZE: 773 (1990 U.S. Census)

The socially stratified Cowlitz were dependent upon the local streams where they located their permanent villages for fishing. Eulachon, when dried, was a valuable trade fish. Inland game was also fully exploited for food and needed by-products. The Cowlitz harvested great amounts of camas, which stored well—as did numerous types of berries, tubers, and nuts. Canoes and rafts were utilized for water transport. Dwellings were of split hewn cedar and housed as many as ten families.

In 1812 the first fur traders, from Astoria, penetrated Cowlitz territory, and by 1833 the Hudson's Bay Company regularly used the Cowlitz Trail. The company established the Cowlitz Farm in 1839. The 1850 Treaty of

Washington and the Oregon Donation Act of 1850 permitted European Americans to enter and exploit the region. The estimated Cowlitz population of a thousand declined to 105 by 1910.

The Cowlitz were not compensated for the loss of their lands until the 1960 and 1969 Indian Claims Commission hearings. The Cowlitz award was held in trust until 1988.

Cree

CULTURE AREA: Subarctic
LANGUAGE GROUP: Algonquian
PRIMARY LOCATION: Surrounding and to the east of Hudson Bay
POPULATION SIZE: 119,810 in Canada (Statistics Canada, based on 1991 census); 8,290 in U.S. (1990 U.S. Census)

The first European contact with the Cree occurred in 1611, but it was fully a hundred years before extensive contacts between the Hudson's Bay Company and the Cree created one of the most lucrative settler-Indian partnerships for a colonial economy in North America. The arrangement initially had advantages for the Cree as well. When the Hudson's Bay Company first established contacts and trading posts on the shores of Hudson Bay, they planted themselves in the center of Cree territory. The Cree dominated all contact with the white traders by controlling the waterways from the lands west of the bay, allowing only their allies the Assiniboine to have equal contact with the Europeans. The fame of the Cree comes from their essential role as a "middleman" in relations with Indians far to the west of Hudson Bay itself. According to Leonard Mason, the history of Cree-settler contact can be divided roughly into three periods: the period of the Cree initiating contact with settlers (1610-1690), the period of settlers initiating contact with the Cree (1690-1820), and Indian rehabilitation (1820-1940).

Traditional Lifeways. The traditional lands of the Cree lay between Hudson Bay and Lake Winnipeg—to the southeast, south, and southwest of Hudson Bay itself. The Crees' geographic location did not allow an extensive agricultural base to develop for tribal subsistence, so the Cree were famed hunters, who also gathered berries from the harsh boreal landscape when they were available. The long winters in this region can be devastating, and failure to gather enough food during prime hunting seasons could lead to disaster during the snowy winter months. The Cree hunted caribou, moose, black bear, beaver, otter, mink, muskrat, fox, wolf, wolverine, geese, and duck.

The Cree people, related to the larger Algonquian cultural tradition, did not live in large settlements and often traveled in small bands, a situation that led to a separate identity for some of the Cree peoples. There are no strong clans or lineage traditions that unify a larger Cree identity. The Cree themselves recognize three large "divisions," corresponding roughly to the lands and ecological niches that they occupy: the "Swampy People" (*maskekowak*), inhabiting lands between Hudson Bay and Lake Winnipeg, the "Woods People" (*saka-wiyiniwak*), in the forested lands away from the shores, and the "Prairie People" (*paskwa-wiyiniwak*), who wandered farther east into the high Canadian prairie. Another division, known as the Tete de Boule Cree, who occupy lands in the lower St. Maurice River in Ottawa, were already separated from the others at the time of contact with white settlers. Some scholars simply differentiate between Woodlands and Prairie Cree, considering the "Swampy Cree" label to apply to the Woodlands group and implying that this is the major division between the two groups.

The Woodland/Swampy Cree are surrounded by the Beaver and Chipewyan tribes to the north and west, the Saulteaux to the south, and Hudson Bay itself to the east. The Cree social organization is rather simple, with no central authority or formal leadership patterns. They are reputed to remain a reserved people to this day, exercising social control through reputation (maintained through frequent gatherings to exchange information and rumor) and the threat of conjuring and witchcraft. The separation of the Prairie Cree, from about 1790, transformed the canoe-based Cree culture of eastern Canada along the tributaries of the bay into a Plains culture based on hunting, warring, and buffalo.

In the movement of the Woodlands Cree up the rivers of Canada, they came into contact with the Blackfoot, who would transform Cree life. It is difficult to date this meeting with precision, but scholars suggest that by 1690, the initial contacts had been made. The Cree were able to take great advantage not only of their connections with the trapping interests of the Hudson's Bay Company but also of their alliance with the Blackfoot, to whom they supplied European weapons in the Blackfoot wars against the Snake. A second major change in the culture of the Plains Cree came after securing horses; new alliances were formed in an attempt to secure a steady supply of horses from southern tribes in the United States area. The securing of horses can possibly be dated to just before 1770. The importance of horses to the Plains Cree greatly increased with the expansion of European trading posts farther and farther up the various tributaries. This expansion reduced dependence on the canoe and increased reliance on horses. These inland trading posts also demanded more supplies from their Cree contacts. They needed food as well as furs, and the Cree began to supply it from hunting the buffalo. It has been suggested that beaver populations were also declining, putting pressure on trapping as an economic resource for the Cree.

With all this adoption of the Plains lifestyle and dependence on the buffalo, the decimation of the buffalo herds had a devastating impact on the Cree, since the buffalo herds first disappeared from their lands in Canada. The response of the Plains Cree was to solidify their territorial claims in the mid-1870's and to make war on the Blackfoot, their former allies, who still had access to the remaining herds. The defeat of the Prairie Cree made them dependent on relations with the Blackfoot. The traditional partners, and occasional adversaries, of the Cree were the Blackfoot, the Hidatsa, and their perennial allies, the Assiniboine.

Religion and Social Organization. Cree religious life is dominated by the influence of Christian missionaries; however, some aspects of traditional belief remain. Religion does not consist of a dominant ideology in Cree life, except for important rituals that surround the killing of prey in hunting, widely reported in most discussions of Cree religion and ritual. There are varying forms of belief in a central "great spirit" (*kitci manitu*) as well as varying versions of a belief in a malevolent, evil spirit (*matci manitu*) who must occasionally be placated in order to prevent illness and other problems in social life. There are shamans who are practiced in various forms of witchcraft. One of the most prevalent features of Cree religious/social life is the "shaking tent." This is a tent reserved for ceremony and storytelling. The shaking tent is regularly a feature of larger Cree social gatherings.

The Cree traveled in small bands, and membership in these bands was fluid, changing with circumstances and environmental factors. Leadership was gained through prestige, particularly through success in warfare, for the Plains Cree. There were warrior societies among the Cree, led by a warrior chief. The highest office was "chief," selected from among the warrior chiefs. As was the case in other Plains societies, however, peacemaking was considered one of the most honorable virtues of a Cree leader. The second manner of acquiring status was through generosity. Food gathered by the band was distributed to all, and a form of "Plains communalism" maintained a balance with those possessions that were considered to belong to an individual.

The Cree experienced, as did other Native North Americans, a series of devastating plagues that considerably reduced their numbers. There were serious smallpox outbreaks in 1780 and 1782, and one of the more extreme estimates from historians is that only one in fifty survived. The native peoples could not believe that illness could transfer from one person to another. Estimates of the Cree population in 1809 ranged around 5,000 individuals, increasing to 13,000 in 1860. Flu epidemics of 1908, 1909, and 1917 had a devastating impact on the Cree population. In 1924, census figures indicated a population of roughly 20,000. Present estimates of the Cree population vary widely, with some sources putting the population at 100,000 or more.

When the fur trapping economy began to break down in the nineteenth century because of a decreasing interest in the European markets, the economic incentive for settler contact with the Cree also broke down. The Cree had become economically dependent on their settler contacts, and the reduction in the fur trade had a devastating effect on Cree independence. By 1940 there was a situation of serious dependence on the Canadian government for continued subsistence.

Daniel L. Smith-Christopher

Bibliography

Beardy, Flora, and Robert Coutts, eds. *Voices from Hudson Bay: Cree Stories from York Factory.* Buffalo, N.Y.: McGill-Queen's University Press, 1996.

Cummins, Bryan D. *"Only God Can Own the Land": The Attawapiskat Cree, the Land and the State in the 20th Century.* Cobalt, Ont.: Highway Book Shop, 1999.

Dusenberry, Verne. *The Montana Cree: A Study in Religious Persistence.* Norman: University of Oklahoma Press, 1998.

Gagne, Marie-Anik. *A Nation Within a Nation: Dependency and the Cree.* New York: Black Rose Books, 1994.

Goddard, John. *Last Stand of the Lubicon Cree.* Vancouver, B.C.: Douglas & McIntyre, 1991.

Grand Council of the Crees of Quebec. *Never Without Consent: James Bay Crees' Stand Against Forcible Inclusion Into an Independent Quebec.* Buffalo, N.Y.: ECW Press, 1998.

Jenness, Diamond. "Hunting Bands of Eastern and Western Canada." In *The North American Indians: A Sourcebook*, edited by Roger Owen, James Deetz, and Anthony Fisher. New York: Macmillan, 1967.

Jiles, Paulette. *North Spirit: Sojourns Among the Cree and Ojibway.* St. Paul, Minn.: Hungry Mind, 1996.

Kupferer, Harriet J. "The Cree Indians of the Subarctic." In *Ancient Drums, Other Moccasins: Native North American Cultural Adaptation.* Englewood Cliffs, N.J.: Prentice Hall, 1988.

Mason, Leonard. *The Swampy Cree: A Study in Acculturation.* Anthropology Papers of the National Museum of Canada, Ottawa, 13. Ottawa: National Museum, Ottawa, Dept. of the Secretary of State, 1967.

Milloy, John S. *The Plains Cree: Trade, Diplomacy, and War, 1790-1870.* Studies in Native History 4. Winnipeg: University of Manitoba Press, 1988.

Niezen, Ronald. *Defending the Land: Sovereignty and Forest Life in James Bay Cree Society.* Boston: Allyn & Bacon, 1998.

Rordam, Vita. *Winisk: A Cree Indian Settlement on Hudson Bay.* Nepean, Ont.: Borealis Press, 1998.

Creek

CULTURE AREA: Southeast
LANGUAGE GROUP: Muskogean
PRIMARY LOCATION: Alabama, Oklahoma
POPULATION SIZE: 43,550 (1990 U.S. Census)

While tribal tradition held that the Creeks, or Muskogees, originally came from west of the Mississippi, they occupied large areas of Georgia and Alabama by the seventeenth century. The name "Creek" is of English origin and derived from Ochesee Creek, a tributary of the Ocmulgee River. (Ochesee was the name given the Muskogees by neighboring Indians.) English traders originally referred to the Muskogees as Ochesee Creeks but soon shortened the name to Creeks. The Creeks were not originally a single tribe, and not all Creeks spoke Muskogee. They were instead a collection of groups that included, among others, Muskogees, Alabamas, Hitchitis, Coushattas, Natchez, Yuchis, and even some Shawnees. Those living along the Alabama, Coosa, and Tallapoosa Rivers came to be regarded as Upper Creeks, while those along the Chattahoochee and Flint Rivers came to be known as Lower Creeks. Over time, the English (and later American) habit of regarding the Creeks as a single nation and dealing with them as such encouraged more of a sense of overall Creek identity. Few tribes, however, could match the ethnic and linguistic diversity of the Creeks.

Traditional Culture. Despite their diversity, the Creeks did share something of a common culture. At the time of contact with the English, the Creeks were an agricultural people whose major crop was corn. The green corn ceremony, or busk, was held in July or August. It marked the beginning of the new year and remained the ritualistic focal point of Creek culture.

The Creeks generally lived in towns centered on a square ground. The major towns of the Upper Creeks included Abihka, Atasi, Fus-hatchee, Hilibi, Kan-hatki, Kealedje, Kolomi, Okchai, Pakana, Tali, Tukabachee, Wiwohka, and Wokakai; Coweta, Eufala, Kashita, and Osachi were important Lower Creek towns. Each town (or *talwa*) had its chief (or *micco*), as well as its military leader (*tastanagi*). There was no chief of all the Creeks, though a Creek National Council met annually to discuss matters of common concern. Loyalties to individual towns were strong, and individuals were more likely to think of themselves as Tukabachees or Cowetas than as Creeks.

The social structure in all the towns was based on clans. An individual was born into the clan of his or her mother, but marriage within the clan was strictly forbidden. Since clans transcended town boundaries, the clan system helped to keep the Creek towns united in a rather loose confederacy.

Warfare was an integral part of Creek society as it was through military exploits that males earned the reputations that brought status within the tribe. Traditional enemies included the Cherokees and the Choctaws. Warfare also played a symbolic role in Creek social organization: Towns (and clans) were considered to be either "red" or "white." White towns were considered to be more oriented toward peace, and red towns to war. Over time this distinction lost much of its meaning, but into the nineteenth century it was customary for civil matters to be discussed at councils in white towns, while military affairs were discussed in red towns.

European Impact. The Creeks first encountered English traders in the seventeenth century. Finding clothes, weapons, and other goods attractive, the Creeks became willing participants in trade, providing deerskins in return. Hunting parties ranged extensively, returning with the hides that allowed them to purchase the English goods that were increasingly deemed necessities. As long as English settlements did not threaten Creek hunting grounds, the trade appeared to benefit both sides.

The commerce in deerskins, however, changed Creek society. Not only did the Creeks become increasingly dependent on European manufactures, but white traders came to live among the Indians, often intermarrying with Creek women. This introduced a mixed-blood element into Creek society that often brought with it increasing acculturation to European ways. Traders also brought their slaves with them, introducing an African influence. Though there was some precedent for slavery in traditional Creek society, the institution took root more slowly among the Creeks than among some of the other southern tribes; Africans also intermarried with Creeks.

Creeks and European Americans. After the American Revolution, the Creeks felt increasing pressure from white settlers. In the first treaty made by the United States after ratification of the Constitution, Alexander McGillivray and other Creek chiefs ceded some of their lands in Georgia in 1790. As American influence became more intense, it became increasingly difficult to maintain the deerskin trade. Some Creeks looked to Britain for protection, while others believed it wiser to come to terms with the Americans. Increasingly, Creek society divided. Some of the more acculturated Creeks, often of mixed blood, sought a closer relationship with the United States and followed the advice of Indian agent Benjamin Hawkins, who encouraged the Creeks to take up American-style agriculture and to put away tribal traditions such as the communal ownership of property. The McIntoshes of Coweta prospered by following such advice and became increasingly powerful. Many such Creeks came from Muskogee backgrounds and wanted to see the Creek National Council become a centralized government.

Others, however, resisted and sought to retain the old ways. Many of these were of non-Muskogee backgrounds. They were reluctant to abandon the deer-hunting economy and to see the autonomy of the towns reduced. Traditionalist Creeks were much affected by a religious revival that swept the Indian country in the early 1800's, calling for a return to old tribal ways as a means of restoring order to a disordered world. The traditionalists were also influenced by the pan-Indianism of Tecumseh, and the Shawnee leader (whose mother was a Creek) won many supporters when he visited Creek country in 1811.

The Creek War. The increasing divisions in Creek society led to bloodshed in 1812 when the traditionalists retaliated against the National Council's attempt to punish Creeks involved in attacks against settlers. A Creek civil war erupted, with Red Sticks (as the traditionalists were called) launching attacks on the towns of Creeks friendly to white settlers. In 1813, the war expanded to include the United States, which was itself at war with Great Britain. Despite early successes, notably at Fort Mims, an aroused United States inflicted a crushing defeat on the Red Sticks. In the Treaty of Fort Jackson (1814), Creek chiefs were forced to agree to the cession of roughly one-half the tribe's remaining lands. Some Red Sticks escaped into Florida, where they joined their Seminole kinsmen. There they kept up resistance until defeated in the First Seminole War (1817-1818).

Removal. The influx of settlers into former Creek lands spelled the end of the deer-hunting economy and made it increasingly difficult for Creeks to live as Indians. As whites eyed remaining tribal lands, some of the more acculturated leaders were receptive to suggestions that the Creeks move west. In 1825, William McIntosh signed a treaty ceding all that was left of Creek lands in Georgia. His subsequent assassination was evidence that many Creeks disagreed. McIntosh's heirs and some others voluntarily departed for the Indian Territory (modern Oklahoma).

Though most Creeks remained in the South, President Andrew Jackson's removal policy proved inescapable. In 1832 a new treaty was signed that paved the way for removal. Though some traditionalists resisted, in the spring of 1836, the bulk of the tribe left peacefully for the Indian Territory under Opothleyaholo's leadership. The Creeks' Trail of Tears was less dramatic than that of the Cherokees, in part because most of the Lower Creeks moved by water, but at least 10 percent of the tribe perished en route, and as many died in the first year in their new homeland.

In August, 1813, the Creeks made a successful attack on Fort Mims that brought down heavy U.S. military reprisals. (Library of Congress)

Creeks in Indian Territory. Once in Oklahoma, the Creeks attempted to re-create the social order they had known in the South. New towns were founded, often bearing the names of ones left behind, and sacred fires kindled from ashes brought from Alabama burned in the square grounds. Settling largely along the Canadian and Arkansas Rivers, the Creeks adjusted to their new surroundings as one of the Five Civilized Tribes of transplanted southern Indians. The Creeks were slower than the other tribes to organize a tribal government, however; not until 1867 was a constitution drafted and a national government created with its capital at Okmulgee.

By this time, internal division had reappeared. During the Civil War the more acculturated Creeks, led by the sons of William McIntosh, committed the tribe to an alliance with the Confederacy. The traditionalists, led by Opothleyaholo, were pro-Union. Another Creek civil war resulted, in which the pro-South faction gained the upper hand. The eventual Union victory brought an imposed treaty that cost the tribe half of its Oklahoma lands and required that the Creeks incorporate their former slaves within the tribe.

The life of the Oklahoma Creeks continued to be marked by division— one reason, perhaps, for the organization of the country's first tribal police force (the Creek Lighthorse) in 1877. Though the more acculturated Creeks generally controlled the nation's government, traditionalists periodically attempted to oust them, sometimes by force. The most serious conflict arose in the Green Peach War (1882), when Isparhecher and his followers fought with the tribal government. Around the end of the nineteenth century, Chitto Harjo (Crazy Snake) led a religious revival among traditionalists that sought to stem the tide of acculturation.

Twentieth Century Changes. By 1900, the Creeks were again coming under pressure from the outside. The Five Civilized Tribes had been ex- empted from the General Allotment Act (1877). The desirability of their land, however, and the assimilationist thrust of government policy led to passage of the Curtis Act (1898), which provided legal authority to allot the lands of the Five Civilized Tribes and to dissolve their governments. In 1901 the Creeks agreed to allotment, with each individual receiving 160 acres. Though some traditionalists resisted by refusing to take up their allotments, they acted in vain. By 1936, fewer than 30 percent of Creeks still held their allotments. In preparation for Oklahoma statehood, the tribal governments of all Five Civilized Tribes were abolished on March 6, 1906.

Under the Oklahoma Indian Welfare Act (1936), Indians in the state were allowed to organize governments again and to hold land communally. Creeks initially responded to the act at the town level, and in 1939 three towns adopted constitutions. In 1970 Congress allowed the election of principal chiefs in the Five Civilized Tribes, and the Creeks adopted an updated constitution that restored tribal government with elected legisla- tive, executive, and judicial branches. Resurgent population growth made the Creeks the country's tenth largest tribe by 1990.

The twentieth century also saw a revival among the descendants of the small number of Creeks who evaded removal in the 1830's. Though largely acculturated, several hundred individuals maintained a Creek identity in southern Alabama. After several decades of struggle, they received federal recognition as the Poarch Band of Creeks in 1984.

William C. Lowe

Bibliography

Braund, Kathryn E. H. *Deerskins and Duffels: The Creek Indian Trade with Anglo-America, 1685-1815*. Lincoln: University of Nebraska Press, 1993.

Green, Michael D. *The Politics of Indian Removal: Creek Government and Society in Crisis*. Lincoln: University of Nebraska Press, 1982. The best account of the removal era, bringing out the internal divisions within Creek society. Index and bibliography.

Hudson, Charles. *The Southeastern Indians*. Knoxville: University of Tennessee Press, 1976. Best overall account of the traditional cultures of the Five Civilized Tribes. Contains much information on the Creeks and provides a useful context for comparing them with neighboring tribes. Illustrations, comprehensive index.

Littlefield, Daniel F., Jr. *Africans and Creeks: From the Colonial Period to the Civil War*. Westport, Conn.: Greenwood Press, 1979. An excellent account of the role of African Americans in Creek society.

Martin, Joel W. *Sacred Revolt: The Muskogees' Struggle for a New World*. Boston: Beacon Press, 1991. Account of the Creek War that stresses the religious motivations of the Red Sticks. An outstanding account of the worldview of Creek traditionalists.

Owsley, Frank L., Jr. *Struggle for the Gulf Borderlands: The Creek War and the Battle of New Orleans, 1812-1815*. Gainesville: University Presses of Florida, 1981. The best narrative account of the Creek War. Stresses the international context. Good bibliography.

Paredes, J. Anthony, ed. *Indians of the Southeastern United States in the Late Twentieth Century*. Tuscaloosa: University of Alabama Press, 1992. A collection of essays that includes an account of the Poarch Creeks' successful struggle for federal recognition. Photographs.

Saunt, Claudio. *A New Order of Things: Property, Power, and the Transformation of the Creek Indians, 1733-1816*. New York: Cambridge University Press, 1999.

Sims, Louise M. *The Last Chief of Kewahatchie*. Raleigh, N.C.: Pentland Press, 1997.

Swanton, John R. *Early History of the Creek Indians and Their Neighbors*. Gainesville: University Press of Florida, 1998.

Warde, Mary Jane. *George Washington Grayson and the Creek Nation, 1843-1920*. Norman: University of Oklahoma Press, 1999.

White, Christine S., and Benton R. White. *Now the Wolf Has Come: The Creek Nation in the Civil War*. College Station: Texas A&M University Press, 1996.

Wickman, Patricia R. *The Tree That Bends: Discourse, Power, and the Survival of the Maskoki People*. Tuscaloosa: University of Alabama Press, 1999.

Wright, James Leitch, Jr. *Creeks and Seminoles: The Destruction and Regeneration of the Muscogulge People*. Lincoln: University of Nebraska Press, 1986. Best overall history of these related tribes from European contact through removal. Emphasizes ethnic differences as the root of Creek divisiveness. Illustrations and a good bibliography.

Crow

CULTURE AREA: Plains
LANGUAGE GROUP: Siouan
PRIMARY LOCATION: Montana
POPULATION SIZE: 8,588 (1990 U.S. Census)

The Crow tribe, of Siouan ancestry, split off from the agriculturalist Hidatsa tribe. Crows, who called themselves Absaroka (bird people, or children of the long-beaked bird), were hunter-gatherers who inhabited parts of Montana and Wyoming. The tribe was divided into three groups by yearly migration patterns. They were one of the tribes which cooperated with European settlers and the U.S. government (as army scouts, for example). This policy, and the accomplishments of astute Crow chiefs, led to preservation of some Crow ancestral lands as a Crow reservation. Modern Crows have been fairly successful in accommodating to modern American ways while retaining tribal values. Among their many achievements are the election of a Crow to the Montana State Senate and a Crow Fair, which creates income from tourism.

Tribal History. The Crow or Absaroka are a Hokan-Siouan tribe. It has been said that the name "Crow" (or Kite) came from misconceptions of French explorers and that the tribe was actually named for the sparrow hawk. The Absaroka arose between the mid-sixteenth and early seventeenth centuries, after two groups broke away from the Hidatsa tribe. Hidatsas were Indian agriculturalists who lived along the Missouri River. There are several Crow legends about the basis for the split. It is believed that the first Crows were Awatixa Hidatsas who became disenchanted with the lifestyle associated with farming and sought the excitement to be found in a society of nomad hunter-gatherers. Certainly this is what they became, nomads whose economy was based mostly on the buffalo. Later, after obtaining horses—probably by trade with the Shoshone—the Crow evolved into a mobile and powerful fighting force and became wide-ranging hunters.

The Crow originally inhabited the eastern part of the Rocky Mountains at the head of the Yellowstone and Missouri rivers. They were subdivided into three distinct groups. Mountain Crows (Acaraho), originally the Awatixa Hidatsa, settled in the Big Horn and Absaroka mountains. They hunted there most of the year but wintered in warmer areas south of the modern Wyoming-Montana border. River Crows (Minisepere) were a second group of dissatisfied Hidatsas, whose migration pattern followed the Missouri River. The third group, an offshoot of the River Crows, "Kicked in the Belly" Crows (Erarapio), migrated through the Little Bighorn and Powder River valleys.

These three groups interacted peaceably and protected one another from encroachments of the Blackfoot, Shoshone, and Sioux to the north, south, and southeast, respectively. The Crow allied themselves with the Hidatsa and other nearby tribes, including the Mandan. These alliances were particularly important because the Crow tribe was not large (reportedly never exceeding sixteen thousand people) and their tribal land abounded with game, making it desirable to others.

In the 1820's, non-Indians began to arrive in Crow territory. Initially, most were traders, who introduced Crows to metal tools, enhanced their use of rifles for hunting and war, and provided glass beads as well as other materials useful in Crow handicrafts. Non-Indians also brought European disease that decimated the Crow population. According to several sources, smallpox was the main factor that dropped the Crow population from sixteen thousand to under three thousand.

By 1851 various trading posts and forts had been built in Crow territory, and the expanding westward flood of American settlers began to force other tribes (especially the Sioux and Blackfoot) off their own lands. This situation put them in serious competition for Crow lands. The U.S. government brought the Plains tribes together at Fort Laramie in 1851 to define "Indian homelands." This action, probably aimed mostly at protecting American settlers from the results of Indian wars, resulted in defining the Crow country as a 38-million-acre area bounded on the east, north, south, and west by the Powder River, the Missouri and Musselshell rivers, the Wind River Mountains, and the Yellowstone River, respectively.

The generation of fixed boundaries of a Crow homeland represented the first loss of territory by the tribe. It was followed, in rapid succession, by the disappearance of most of their territory and by huge disruptions of every facet of Crow tribal life. All this occurred despite the friendliness of the Crows to American settlers and their service as army couriers and scouts. First, in 1868, the Crows, under chief Middle of the Land, were stripped of nearly 30 million acres of the homeland granted to them in 1851. They retained 8 million acres bounded on the south by the Montana-Wyoming border, on the east by longitude 107 degrees, and on both the west and the north by the Yellowstone River.

The 1868 treaty involved subjugating the Crow tribe in order to "prepare them for civilized life." It did this by placing them under the control of Indian agents, who were to "help them to blend into American mainstream life." This blending—not desired by the Crow tribe—included establishment of schools to modernize them, churches to Christianize them, supplementation of their food supply, and an attempted precipitous conversion of hunter-gatherers into farmers.

Then, three successive steps—in 1882, 1891, and 1904—diminished the Crow reservation to its present 3 million acres, divided into individual

Crow Indians gathering to receive the annuities they are owed for agreeing to live on a reservation. (National Archives)

farms and ranches. As time went by, the Crows were forced more and more into mainstream American culture. They resisted in a variety of ways, such as the introduction into their religion of the Shoshone Sun Dance, a ritual which enabled young Crow men to prove their bravery by bearing great pain (it replaced the earlier Crow Sun Dance).

The retention of the rites of their Tobacco Society, an important part of traditional Crow life, was also very influential here, as was the development of the Native American Church, which utilizes peyote in its ceremonies. In addition, the strength and solidarity of Crow family life, the retention and routine use of the Crow language, and the annual Crow Fair have helped to maintain Crow tribal identity. Always essential, throughout Crow interaction with mainstream American society, have been the achievements of a continuum of insightful Crow leaders; these statesmen include Eelapuash (Sore Belly), Medicine Crow, Plenty Coups, and Robert Yellowtail.

Traditional Lifeways. The Crow were subdivided into thirteen clans, described in detail in Robert H. Lowie's *The Crow Indians* (1956). Each of these tribal subgroups (large groups of closely related families) was headed by a man with a distinguished record in intertribal war. Members of all clans were found in the Acaraho, Minisepere, and Erarapio encampments.

Each encampment was governed by a council of chiefs, shamans, and tribal elders. Chiefs were individuals who attained this title by performing four specific deeds: leading successful war parties, counting coup by touching an enemy and escaping, taking an enemy's weapon from him, and cutting loose a horse from an enemy camp. One member of the tribal council, usually a chief, was elected head of each encampment. At all levels, chiefs lost their power if they stopped living up to Crow ideals.

The Crow men were divided into men's military societies such as Foxes, Lumpwood, Crazy Dogs, Big Dogs, and Ravens. Membership in the societies was open to any proven warrior. The societies, each having its own rules and customs, competed to recruit the most promising young men. Every spring, one military society was appointed as the tribal police force to keep order in Crow encampments, enforce discipline during important tribal activities such as the buffalo hunt, and keep war parties from setting out at inappropriate times.

Crows almost always married outside their own clans, sometimes by interclan wife-capturing (in which the wives-to-be were willing candidates). More often, wives were purchased from their families for a bride price. Most women were married by the time they reached puberty. Marriage taboos forbade men and women to look at or talk to mothers-in-law or fathers-in-law, respectively. Other elaborate rules governed the behavior of other family members.

Fathers lavished attention on their sons, praising them for any good action. In addition, all adults lavished praise on youngsters for achievements in hunting, war, and general life (for example, boys returning from a first war party would be praised by all their relatives). Inappropriate actions, on the other hand, were handled by people called "joking relatives," who gently and jokingly ridiculed bad behavior. Such teasing discipline was much more effective than harsh treatment in a society in which cooperation was essential for tribal survival. Youngsters, in turn, treated all adults respectfully.

The most important tribal religious ceremonies were those of the Tobacco Society and the Sun Dance (later replaced by the Shoshone-Crow Sun Dance), which helped men to prove their bravery. The Tobacco Society ceremonies were held three times each year: at the spring planting of tobacco (the sole Crow crop), when the tobacco was harvested, and at initiations. The Sun Dance was held when needed; it was most often associated with acts of revenge or initiation into war. One religious hero of the Crow tribe was Old Man Coyote, the creator of the world, a smart, clever being who was the subject of many lively and educational Crow tales.

The Crow Indians lived in skin tipis. These skin houses were often 25 feet high and could accommodate forty people. They were made of as many as twenty buffalo skins, sewn together and supported by lodgepoles. The preparation of a new tipi was communal woman's work. It was carried out by a skilled woman, hired by the owner of the planned dwelling, and a group of her friends. Inside each tipi was a draft screen, painted with pictures that depicted important tribal events and the brave deeds of the tipi owners. At the rear of each tipi, directly opposite its door, was a place of honor for its owner or special guests.

When a Crow died, the body was taken out through a hole cut in one side of the tipi, rather than by the door; it was believed that if a body were taken out by the door, another tipi occupant would soon die. Dead bodies were placed on wooden scaffolds in their best clothing, where they remained until their decomposition was complete. At that time the remains were taken down and buried. Common Crow mourning practices included giving away property, cutting the hair, tearing clothing, and gashing the body. In some cases mourners cut off a finger joint.

The main food source of Crow Indians living on the plains was buffalo, which were hunted by driving them over cliffs, surrounding them on horseback and shooting them, or driving them into traps. Deer were another major meat source. Most meat was roasted over fires, cooked in the ashes of fires, or boiled in skin-lined pits. Some meat was mixed with berries and fat and dried to produce pemmican food reserves. Edible roots, berries, and fruit such as wild plums were harvested by women to supplement meat, which was the main Crow food.

Crows were exceptionally fine horsemen and possessed huge numbers of horses per capita. Many of these horses were obtained by theft from other tribes, and the Crows had the reputation of being exceptionally accomplished horse thieves. They were also, however, very successful horse breeders.

The tools and weapons of the Crow were of fine construction. Their bows were fabricated from hickory and/or ash and horn, when possible. Crow bow and arrow makers were very skilled, and all Crow artifacts, including buffalo horn cups and wooden bowls, were well made. Crow handicrafts such as clothing, arrow quivers, and various adornments were of very fine quality and were sought after. These adornments enhanced the appearance of a people who were usually relatively tall (many men were near 6 feet). Crow men rarely cut their hair, letting it grow very long and lavishing much attention on it. Hence, many traders called Crows "the long-haired Indians."

Clothing, blankets, and other items that modern society manufactures from cloth were made of animal skins. Preparation of the skins began by soaking them in water for several days. Then, loosened hair and scraps of flesh were scraped off, a paste of animal brains was added to soften the skins, and scraping continued. Finally, the skins were tanned and used to make garments that were soft and flexible in any weather. Prior to the advent of European traders, skin objects were decorated with dyed porcupine quills and feathers. Later, glass beads replaced quills.

Modern Life. Modern Crow life, to a large extent, has been that of the reservation. In the 1880's, buffalo had become nearly extinct because of hide hunting. At this time, a Crow named Wraps His Tail (Sword Bearer) excited some Crows into revolt, but his death at the hands of Crow reservation police ended the movement.

The next forty years saw strong efforts by the Bureau of Indian Affairs to force the Crow tribe to enter modern life completely. Their program included attempting to force the Crows to remain on the reservation, to become Christians, to follow mainstream marriage and social customs, and to farm or ranch. At this time Crow children were forced to attend boarding school, which was intended to turn them into mainstream Americans. Up to the end of World War II, Crows reacted by constructing a cultural base which preserved the core of their culture. In essence, Crows went their own way while acceding to many demands of the federal government. This action was complicated by a need to interact with the world outside the reservation, a world in which Crows were often treated with contempt.

Most Crows thus remained on the reservation whenever possible, where most social relationships were regulated by Crow tradition. For example, Crows often belonged to an Indian Christian church but married and interacted according to Crow custom. Ironically, the Crow tribe, which had generally interacted peacefully with the American government, was the least tractable Plains Indian tribe in parting with their traditions. Canny and pragmatic, they made the best of advantages of mainstream culture without losing sight of their Absaroka culture. This feat was not accomplished without mental anguish, and some Crows fell victim to depression and alcoholism.

By the 1940's the peyote religion of the Native American Church and the Crow-Shoshone Sun Dance were firmly in place in Crow life. The church provided an alternative to straight Christian worship. Combined with other shamanic rituals, the Sun Dance both provided Crow health care and enabled Crow young men to prove courage in a variant of the old way. In addition, the tribal customs of gift giving, respecting the family, and using "joking relatives" were applied to situations as disparate as winning an athletic event or having a young relative be graduated from high school or college.

In the political arena, Crows developed political and legal machinery to defend the reservation against further encroachment by whites. Primary among their leaders was Robert Yellowtail. In addition, in 1948 the Crow tribe adopted a reservation constitution based on their traditional tribal council but allowing every Crow adult to vote. The council elected officers, including a chairman, and established committees to solve tribal needs.

Abetted by a federal government policy more sensitive to American Indian needs, Crow leaders became ever more useful to the tribe. Successful legal action against the federal government, sale of the land used for Yellowtail Dam (named after Robert Yellowtail), and a recreation site on the Bighorn River, as well as royalties on coal discovered on the reservation, swelled the coffers of the tribe.

In the early 1990's a third of reservation residents were non-Indians, and 20 percent of Crows lived off the reservation. Many modern Crows work for the tribal government, which has improved health care, education, and housing for tribe members with funds from the tribal treasury. They also teach at nearby colleges and other schools, work at many levels in local industry, and successfully own and run ranches and farms. The annual Crow Fair is a valuable tourist attraction. Robert Yellowtail died in 1988; however, others, including his son (Bill Yellowtail), have followed him. Bill Yellowtail has been a Montana State senator.

Sanford S. Singer

Bibliography

Albright, Peggy. *Crow Indian Photographer: The Work of Richard Throssel.* Albuquerque: University of New Mexico Press, 1997.

Algier, Keith W. *The Crow and the Eagle: A Tribal History from Lewis and Clark to Custer.* Caldwell, Idaho: Caxton, 1993.

Hayne, Coe Smith. *Red Men on the Bighorn.* Philadelphia: Judson Press, 1929. These vignettes on the Crows describe aspects of Crow culture, the training of young men to embody Crow ideals, and aspects of the lives of some well-known Crows. This interesting reading expands understanding of the Crow and some of their problems between 1871 and the 1920's.

Hoxie, Frederick E. *The Crow.* In *Indians of North America*, edited by Frank W. Porter III. New York: Chelsea House, 1989. A brief but thorough book that describes many historical and cultural aspects of the Crows. Major topics are the creation legend, tribe origins, the arrival of white people and its consequences, the reservation era, and the modern Crows. Fine illustrations give a sense of the Crows and show how their tribal lands diminished.

_____. *Parading Through History: The Making of the Crow Nation, 1805-1935.* New York: Cambridge University Press, 1995.

Lowie, Robert H. *The Crow Indians.* New York: Holt, Rinehart and Winston, 1956. This thorough, definitive work covers in depth tribal organization, life, artifacts, burial custom, military societies, religion, clans, rites and festivals, and many other topics.

_____. *Myths and Traditions of the Crow Indians.* Lincoln: University of Nebraska Press, 1993.

Medicine Crow, Joseph. *From the Heart of the Crow Country: The Crow Indians' Own Stories.* New York: Orion Books, 1992.

Voget, Fred W. *The Shoshoni-Crow Sun Dance.* Norman: University of Oklahoma Press, 1984. Crow life, aspects of Crow history, and events (including reservation life and abandonment of the Crow Sun Dance) that led the Shoshone Sun Dance to become part of their lives are described. The book also identifies Crow efforts to retain their cultural identity.

Voget, Fred W., and Mary K. Mee. *They Call Me Agnes: A Crow Narrative Based on the Life of Agnes Yellowtail Deernose.* Norman: University of Oklahoma Press, 1995.

Yellowtail, Thomas, and Michael O. Fitzgerald. *Yellowtail: Crow Medicine Man and Sun Dance Chief: An Autobiography.* Norman: University of Oklahoma Press, 1991. Via description of the life of Thomas Yellowtail, Crow history, Crow efforts to conserve traditions in modern times, and the Crow religion are illuminated.

Cupeño

CULTURE AREA: California
LANGUAGE GROUP: Cupeño
PRIMARY LOCATION: San Jose de Valle valley, California
POPULATION SIZE: 371, including Agua Caliente (1990 U.S. Census)

The Cupeño were patrilocal and married outside their kin groups. With no direct access to the ocean, the Cupeño relied on acorns, seeds, berries, deer, quail, and small animals. They occupied two politically autonomous villages, united by trade, marriage, rituals, and language. Clans were headed by men through inheritance; they maintained the clan's ceremonial dance house and paraphernalia. Ceremonies were concerned with mortuary rituals, world-renewal rites, and an eagle-killing ritual.

The Cupeño were first contacted by the Spanish in 1795, but no sustained contact was established until 1820 when *asistencias* were built by the Spaniards to graze their cattle. With control of their lands gone, the Cupeño were forced to work as serfs until eventually the "owners" of Cupeño lands wanted them removed in the late 1890's. Years of litigation and national protest prevented this, until the California Supreme Court removed the Cupeño to the Pala Reservation in Luiseño territory.

Desert culture

DATE: Since 8000 B.C.E.
LOCATION: Southwest, Great Basin
CULTURES AFFECTED: Paiute, Shoshone

The term "Desert culture" is used to refer to a widespread pattern of small, mobile, hunting and gathering populations adapted to dry environments of western North America. The Desert culture tradition begins around 7000 B.C.E. and continues into the historic period with peoples such as the Paiute of the Great Basin. In general, this term—coined by Jesse Jennings in the 1950's—has been replaced by more specific cultural phases in different geographical regions that emphasize regional and temporal variations as revealed by increasingly detailed archaeological data. The majority of these occur during a time referred to by archaeologists as the Archaic period.

As originally conceived, Desert culture referred to a lifestyle characterized by small social groups or band-level societies composed of extended families numbering, at most, twenty-five to thirty individuals. These groups moved across the landscape in annual cycles, taking advantage of a wide variety of different resources that varied with altitude, rainfall, soil conditions, and seasonal availability. Material possessions were limited to portable objects that were easily manufactured as needed. Among these were baskets and milling stones, used in the transport and processing of plants and seeds, and chipped-stone projectile points. Vegetable foods were supplemented by hunting, primarily of small mammals, birds, and reptiles and mainly through the use of traps, snares, and simple weapons.

The earliest (and latest) manifestations of Desert culture occurred in the Great Basin region. Danger Cave, in western Utah, yielded traces of slab milling stones, twined basketry, bone awls, and various small projectile points dating to between 8000 and 7000 B.C.E. Coiled basketry was found in later levels, accompanied by wooden darts, skewers, and pins, a variety of bone implements, and cordage made from hides and vegetable fibers.

One of the regional variants of the Desert culture is the Cochise tradition of the southwestern United States. Its earliest phase, Sulphur Spring, dates to about 7000 B.C.E. and is characterized by percussion-flaked projectile points together with simple *manos* and *metates*. It is followed by several thousand years of successive phases, known mostly from open sites, that provide evidence of gradual changes in both chipped- and ground-stone technology. At the site of Bat Cave (New Mexico), evidence for the use of maize appears in the context of a late Cochise tradition occupation.

The Desert culture, in its broadest conception, is the oldest and most persistent indigenous tradition in North America. This is probably attributable both to its simplicity and to its versatility in the face of environmental change. Desert culture represents the most flexible adaptation to a landscape in which food resources were varied and widely dispersed. During difficult climatic conditions, the Desert culture way of life permitted the survival of small populations as populations of large game hunters declined.

Diegueño

CULTURE AREA: California
LANGUAGE GROUP: Hokan
PRIMARY LOCATION: Southern California
POPULATION SIZE: 2,276 (1990 U.S. Census)

Modern Diegueño woman pounding acorns the way her hunter-gatherer ancestors once had done. (National Museum of the American Indian, Smithsonian Institution)

The range of the Diegueño, a Southern California group, extended across deserts and mountain valleys. Actually, the term "Diegueño" is misleading, a throwback to Spanish colonial designations. The Tipai and Ipai together, peoples who were linguistically and culturally related, made up the Diegueño. Technically, the Diegueño were not a true tribe, but rather groups of autonomous bands or tribelets.

The Southern California climate was very warm in summer, but winters were mild. Dwellings varied according to the season: brush shelters in summer; frameworks of bent poles covered by thatch, bark, or pine slabs in winter. The tribelets usually were composed of a single clan; leadership was provided by a clan chief and his assistant. Shamans cured the sick, presided over ceremonies, and interpreted dreams.

To the Diegueño, as for many California native groups, the acorn was a major staff of life. Acorns were gathered, ground into meal, then baked or made into a kind of mush. Great care was taken to leach out the bitter tannic acid from the acorns.

The Tipai-Ipai/Diegueño were the first California Indians to experience repression under Spanish colonial rule, when Mission San Diego de Alcalá was founded in their territory in 1769. Early conversions to Christianity were probably genuine, but the Tipai-Ipai soon found that they had traded freedom for a kind of semiserfdom as the Spanish tried to suppress native culture and religion in the name of civilization.

After a few years of repression, however, the Tipai-Ipai, now called Diegueño after the mission, staged a revolt in November, 1775. Led by a mission Indian named Francisco, eight hundred warriors stormed Mission San Diego, burning the buildings and killing three Spaniards. Superior Spanish weaponry eventually restored control over the Diegueño, and the mission was restored. By the 1990's, the Diegueño were scattered on four-teen reservations of varying size, from six to fifteen acres. Modern Diegueño call themselves "Kumeyaay," since the former term is associated with the colonial past.

Dogrib

CULTURE AREA: Subarctic
LANGUAGE GROUP: Northeastern Athapaskan
PRIMARY LOCATION: Northwest Territories, Canada
POPULATION SIZE: 2,845 (Statistics Canada, based on 1991 census)

The Dogrib, a tribe of the Athapaskan language group, get their name from a traditional legend according to which the first tribesmen came from the mating of a woman and a dog. Dogrib people have lived since the 1500's in the Northwest Territories of Canada, between Great Slave and Great Bear lakes along the Mackenzie River. Their earliest contact with Europeans dates to 1771, when French trappers encountered tribal members and began trading for furs and caribou hides. Epidemics began to take their toll, however, and the population began a rapid decline. By the 1880's, caribou herds began to decline, and musk-ox robes became the main trade good. By this time, Roman Catholic missionaries had entered the area, built mission schools, and converted most of the Dogrib to Christianity. In 1900, when the population had dipped below 1,000, tribal leaders signed a reser-vation treaty with Canadian authorities retaining control of much of their traditional homeland. A gold rush in the 1930's brought an influx of whites, who built the town of Yellowknife.

Traditionally, the tribe had divided into six regional bands. Each band had a leader, who generally was the best hunter and the most generous gift-giver to the group. The Dogrib believed that human beings got their power from spirits inhabiting animals and trees—and that these spirits caused sickness, controlled the population of animals to be hunted, and dictated the weather. Illnesses could be cured by confession of sins and misbehavior in front of group leaders.

Many Dogrib practiced their traditional way of making a living until the 1960's. They hunted beaver and muskrat in the spring and caribou in the summer, and fished in the river until the October freeze-up. Winters were the hardest times because of the intense cold and dwindling supply of animals. Government assistance programs began in the 1960's, with health and medical services, a public housing program, schools, and a new highway. The population began to increase, although many Dogrib remained poor. Employment came mainly from these government programs, and after construction was completed the only jobs available were as fishing guides, or janitors and clerks in the assistance programs.

Dorset

DATE: 950 B.C.E.—1000 C.E.
LOCATION: Canada's eastern Arctic, southern Greenland
CULTURE AFFECTED: Inuit

The Dorset cultural tradition is said to have begun around 950 B.C.E. Pre-Dorset hunters were the earliest known occupants of the central and eastern Arctic, and they were living in the area by 3000 B.C.E. They established themselves there during a period of postglacial warming.

By 950 B.C.E., during another period of climatic warming, pre-Dorset culture had evolved into the distinctive Dorset tradition, centered at northern Foxe Basin and southern Baffin Island. Thereafter, from roughly 200 B.C.E. to 200 C.E.—the period of its maximal distribution—the Dorset tradition was marked by viable colonies scattered throughout the Arctic from Banks Island in the west, around Hudson Bay in the center, to Greenland, Labrador, and Newfoundland in the east. Dorset colonies in Newfoundland were planted farther south than Inuit have ever been discovered. By 1000 C.E., the Thule people, moving out of the western Arctic with superior technology, began occupying areas previously marked by the Dorset tradition. Anthropologists are unsure whether the Dorset were already in decline or whether the Thule merged with or simply displaced them.

Many Dorset cultural characteristics were continuations of pre-Dorset patterns; subsistence still rested heavily on hunting seal, walrus, and smaller whales along shorelines and ice floes, activities which were supplemented by organized drives to kill caribou as well as by fishing for salmon and trout. Accordingly, the Dorset tradition developed a wide range of distinctive hunting weapons: flaked chert harpoons, slotted bone and barbed harpoon heads, beveled slate lance points, fish spears, flaked chert snub-nosed scrapers, flaked chert bifaced knives, beveled slate flensing knives, burins, and snow knives for igloo building. Though lacking bows or floating drags for kayak hunting, the Dorset built hand-drawn sledges, used dogs for hunting or food, crafted blubber lamps, constructed several types of housing, were expert at grinding and polishing tools, and carved elaborate magico-religious art objects.

Duwamish

CULTURE AREA: Northwest Coast
LANGUAGE GROUP: Salishan (Nisqually)
PRIMARY LOCATION: Seattle
POPULATION SIZE: 201 (1990 U.S. Census)

The Duwamish were divided into five different territorial groups. Although they were a maritime people and fish was a staple, they also depended on vegetable foods and land animals. Numerous types of waterfowl were caught, and tidal foods were abundant, particularly shellfish. Traditional forms of wealth were dentalia, slaves, canoes, blankets of dog and mountain goat wool, fur robes, and clamshell disk beads.

The first European-American contact with the Duwamish was in 1792, when George Vancouver explored Puget Sound. John Work of the Hudson's Bay Company explored the region in 1824. In 1833, the company established Fort Nisqually as a trading post, which brought many changes through increased trade. In 1854 and 1855 the Treaties of Medicine Creek and Point No Point reserved land for some tribes. By the 1880's, the Indian Shaker Church had spread through the area.

The final Judge George Bolt decision in 1979 denied the nonreservation Duwamish their fishing rights. In 1988, a petition for recognition by the Duwamish and other landless tribes of western Washington was drawn up and was still in litigation in the early 1990's.

Erie

CULTURE AREA: Northeast
LANGUAGE GROUP: Iroquoian
PRIMARY LOCATION: South shore of Lake Erie

The Erie were a powerful sedentary tribe closely related to the Hurons, occupying lands south of Lake Erie down to the Ohio River in the early seventeenth century. With an economy based on horticulture, the women produced the crops of corn, beans, squash, and sunflowers, while men hunted and fished, thereby creating a varied and stable diet. Consequently, the Erie people numbered as many as fourteen thousand in the early seventeenth century, living in palisaded villages. They were matrilineal and matrilocal. Known as excellent warriors, they frequently clashed with the Iroquois tribes to their east, particularly the Senecas, over hunting grounds. The Erie had only limited contact with Europeans, mainly French missionaries who called them "the Cat (*chat*) Nation" because of their customary dress style of animal skin robes complete with tails. (The name "Erie" came from the Huron term for "it is long-tailed.")

In 1651, the Erie Nation was attacked and destroyed by the Iroquois, although the victors adopted more Erie people into their families than they killed. The Erie did not survive this attack as a distinct group, and their language became extinct as their descendants were forced to speak Iroquois languages. The Iroquois were successful at destroying the Erie Nation not because of superior numbers of warriors or greater skill in battle, but rather because of the firearms they had acquired from the Dutch. The Erie did not have access to such weapons. After having engulfed these people, the Iroquois claimed Erie territory as their ancestral hunting grounds.

Esselen

CULTURE AREA: California
LANGUAGE GROUP: Esselen
PRIMARY LOCATION: Monterey County, California

Not only were the Esselen one of the smallest of the California Indian tribes, they were also probably the first to disappear ethnographically. Because no identifiable Esselen could be located by anthropologists even in the nineteenth century, nobody knows what name they may have had for themselves. "Esselen" or variant spellings appeared in Spanish records referring to a village in the area that is now modern Monterey County, and scholars adopted it for the tribe in the absence of any other information.

The Spanish explorer Sebastián Vizcaíno entered Monterey Bay in 1602 and observed many Indians, some of whom may have been Esselen. Actual European contact, however, did not begin until 1769, when the Spanish expedition led by Gaspar de Portolá passed through Esselen territory. The population at that time has been the subject of widely divergent estimates, but 750 is a probable compromise figure. In 1770, Spanish missionaries established Mission San Carlos, originally on Monterey Bay but later moved to the mouth of the Carmel River. From that mission, which served as the headquarters of Junípero Serra and Fermín Francisco de Lasuén, the padres recruited Esselens for conversion to Christianity and Spanish culture. Mission Soledad, founded in 1791 on the Salinas River, also included some Esselen among its converts.

Mission life did not agree with the Esselen, and by the early nineteenth century their numbers had dropped precipitously. By the time of the secularization of the missions around 1834, both San Carlos and Soledad were nearly abandoned because of the near extinction of both Esselen and non-Esselen populations. No significant features of Esselen culture and very few Esselen people survived the mission experience. By 1928, when the federal government undertook to enroll all California Indians, only one person claimed Esselen ancestry, and that was a one-quarter link of questionable authenticity.

Since anthropologists and other scholars have had essentially no informants on which to base their research, the little knowledge of Esselen culture has been obtained from a few scattered records of the Spanish missionaries, members of other tribes who could recall a few Esselen words and cultural features, and the archaeological record. Although some Esselen lived along the Pacific coast and utilized fish and abalone for subsistence, most inhabited the mountainous regions of southwestern Monterey County and relied on acorns and other plants. Since they lacked bows and arrows, hunting was not possible, but the Esselen snared skunks, rabbits, lizards, and dogs. Some rock art, a few burial sites of cremated remains, some chipped-stone artifacts, and a large number of bedrock mortars have been found. The relative paucity of artifacts has led one archaeologist to suggest that the alleged Esselen sites were only visited periodically by Indians of other tribes and to question whether an actual Esselen tribe ever existed. The only evidence of distinct Esselen culture is linguistic and is mostly from indirect secondary sources.

Fernandeño

CULTURE AREA: Southern California
LANGUAGE GROUP: Hokan
PRIMARY LOCATION: Northern San Diego County, Southern Orange County

The Fernandeño are among the small California tribal groupings that once occupied the area of modern-day Los Angeles county, specifically the northern valley areas or present San Fernando Valley. The modern Fernandeño live slightly to the south. Their near neighbors, the Gabrielino, also had villages on the islands of Catalina, Santa Barbara, San Nicolas, and San Clemente. The name "Fernandeño," like the Gabrielino, derives from the people who surrounded the San Fernando Mission, one of the early Roman Catholic missionary stations founded in the Southern California region. Fernandeño speak a dialect, also called Fernandeño, of the Gabrielino language, which is part of the Shoshonean division of the Uto-Aztecan linguistic division.

Little is known of either Gabrielino or Fernandeño life because of the decimation of their traditional lifestyle and ideologies before trained recorders were available to record aspects of their life. It is known that their homes were domed, circular huts with thatched roofs, and reports indicate that some of these dwellings were large enough to hold fifty people.

The noted anthropologist of the California native groups, Alfred Kroeber, estimated that the Fernandeño and Gabrielino combined totaled approximately five thousand in 1770. California Indians generally are not to be understood as "tribes," but rather "tribal groups" of perhaps a hundred persons at most, usually not all of them permanent members, which surrounded a centrally recognized permanent village. The Fernandeño shared many common cultural traits with other village communities up and down the California coast, including a simple artistry in basket weaving, simple agriculture, and architecture. As with other Southern California native peoples in the region's near-tropical climate, the Fernandeño typically dressed very lightly.

Most Fernandeño live in the southern Orange County and northern San Diego County areas. There are no reservations. As with the Gabrielino, Fernandeño religious expressions were focused largely on the cult of the god Chingichngish, who was also recognized among related peoples such as the Luiseño and the Serrano. There was a fully developed shamanism, whose members were rain-makers, finders of lost objects, and healers (as well as instigators) of illness.

Bibliography
Bean, Lowell John, and Charles Smith. "The Gabrielino (and Fernandeño)." In *Southwest*, edited by Alfonso Ortiz. Vol. 9 in *Handbook of North American Indians*, edited by William Sturtevant. Washington, D.C.: Smithsonian Institution Press, 1978.
Kroeber, Alfred. "The Indians of California." In *The North American Indians: A Sourcebook*, edited by Roger Owen, James Deetz, and Anthony Fisher. New York: Macmillan, 1967.
Miller, Bruce W. *The Gabrielino*. Los Osos, Calif.: Sand River Press, 1991.

Flathead

CULTURE AREA: Plateau
LANGUAGE GROUP: Salishan
PRIMARY LOCATION: Montana, Northern Idaho
POPULATION SIZE: 4,455 ("Salish," 1990 U.S. Census)

The Flathead, or Inland Salish, are related to the Shuswap, Thompson, Wenatchi, Columbia, Okanagan, Sanpoil, Colville, Kalispel, Spokane, and Coeur d'Alene. They live in northern Idaho, eastern Washington State, and Montana. The modern Flathead share their reservation with the Kutenai, around Flathead Lake near Dixon, Montana. A Flathead Indian museum is maintained in St. Ignatius, Montana, and a traditional pow-wow of the Flathead/Kutenai tribes is held in early July every year. They are united by their common use of the "Inland Salish" dialect, as differentiated from the dialect of the Coastal Salish peoples.

The name "Flathead" is a misnomer, apparently deriving from European descriptions of people holding their hands on either side of their faces, a sign-language gesture that was misunderstood by the settlers. The name has nothing to do with a tradition of "flattening heads" of children which was practiced among other western coastal peoples. The people themselves prefer "Salish."

Around 2000 B.C.E., internal migrations of native peoples forced some Salish to the area of Bitterroot Valley, which is considered to be the tribal homeland. Around 1700 C.E., the Salish language dialects became a kind of *lingua franca* of the West Coast, since there were Native Americans who could be found as far away as present-day Montana who could understand them.

The Inland Salish are to be sharply differentiated in their culture development from their coastal cousins. The Inland Salish developed into a Plains people, hunting buffalo, and were largely nomadic in the summer as they engaged in hunting and fishing. While the Flathead remained in the Rocky Mountains, they fished the many tributaries of the Columbia River, but they shifted to buffalo hunting as they moved eastward. The women traditionally prepared food and made clothing while the men hunted, guarded camp, and made weapons. As with other Plains-dwelling native nations, the domestication and use of the horse revolutionized Inland Salish life, allowing far more wide-ranging travel for food. The Flathead got most of their horses, according to Flathead tradition, from trade with the Shoshone. For dwellings, the Flathead used the traditional Salish "longhouse" structures until they adopted a tipi-like structure later in their Plains development. Unlike other Plains tribes, they never used skins around the conical pole frame, but spread vegetation and bark around it and then partially buried the base.

Constant wars with the Blackfoot forced the Flathead/Inland Salish people to flee to various locales. Peace was established between the Blackfoot and the Flathead through an intermediary, Pierre Jean de Smet, a Jesuit missionary who lived with the Flathead between 1840 and 1846.

Flathead camp on the Jocko River during the late nineteenth century.
(Library of Congress)

Tribal ceremonies and religious life were generally simple among this group. The Flathead consider themselves to be the descendants of Coyote, whom they believe to be responsible for the creation of human beings. There was a belief in countless numbers of spirits, and supernatural powers were consulted to ward off the evil effects of others' power and the evil spirits of animals. There were dances and prayers directed to the sun and moon, largely for success in hunting and for general success in life. Power was demonstrated by wealth and luck, and men often carried a pouch containing symbols of their various powers. Shamanism was practiced as a healing and supernatural art. An interesting aspect of Flathead oral tradition was the arrival of "Shining Shirt," possibly an Iroquois, who acted as a prophetic figure announcing the coming of the "black robes" (the Jesuits). Other Iroquois followed, and it is possibly from their influence that Roman Catholic Christianity was established among the Flathead.

Historic estimates of the population of the Inland Salish people vary from four thousand to fifteen thousand; they were decimated by smallpox epidemics between 1760 and 1781. In 1805, the Flathead chief Three Eagles encountered Meriwether Lewis and William Clark, who immortalized the Flathead people in their journals. Although relations with the settlers were always friendly, by the 1850's both war with the Blackfoot and the settlers' diseases had reduced their numbers to fewer than five hundred. Estimates of the modern Flathead population vary from three thousand to five thousand, counting those who live away from the reservations.

The Flathead people first requested missionary educational support in 1841; the earliest respondents were the Jesuits, who formed mission schools that had wide-ranging and extensive influence on Native American life. In 1891, Chief Charlot sold the traditional Bitteroot land, and the Flathead people were moved to the reservation lands that they now share with the Kutenai.

Daniel L. Smith-Christopher

Bibliography
Bigart, Robert. "Patterns of Cultural Change in a Salish Flathead Community." *Human Organization* 30 (Fall, 1971): 229-237.
Bigart, Robert, and Clarence Woodcock. *In the Name of the Salish and Kootenai Nation: The 1855 Hell Gate Treaty and the Origin of the Flathead Indian Reservation*. Pablo, Mont.: Salish Kootenai College Press, 1996.
Fahey, John. *The Flathead Indians*. Norman: University of Oklahoma Press, 1974. "The Flathead." In *Northwest Coast*, edited by Wayne Suttles. Vol. 7 in *Handbook of North American Indians*, edited by William Sturtevant. Washington, D.C.: Smithsonian Institution Press, 1978.

Johnson, Olga Wedemeyer. *Flathead and Kootenay*. Glendale, Calif.: Arthur Clarke, 1969.
Ruby, Robert, and John Brown. *A Guide to the Indian Tribes of the Pacific Northwest*. Rev. ed. Norman: University of Oklahoma Press, 1992.
Waldman, Carl. "The Flathead." In *Encyclopedia of Native American Tribes*. New York: Facts on File, 1988.

Folsom

DATE: 9000-7500 B.C.E.
LOCATION: Folsom, New Mexico (site); North America (tradition)
CULTURE AFFECTED: Folsom

Folsom is the name of the prehistoric site near Folsom, New Mexico, where the antiquity of people in the Americas was finally accepted by the scientific community in 1926. Folsom also is the name of the Paleo-Indian tradition associated with the distinctive Folsom projectile point. The Folsom discovery marked a significant turning point or "paradigm shift" in American archaeology in 1926: The presence of people in the Americas at the same time as Ice-Age or Pleistocene animals that are now extinct was accepted with the discovery of a Folsom "fluted" point embedded in the ribs of an extinct species of bison, *Bison antiquus*. The site's investigators, Jess Figgins, director of the Colorado Museum of Natural History, and Harold Cook, a geologist, telegraphed leading scientists in North America asking them to view and validate the find in the ground, which effected immediate acceptance. Since 1926, the occurrence of Folsom fluted points across North and Middle America has been regarded as part of the Folsom Paleo-Indian tradition, dated between 9000 and 7500 B.C.E.

Folsom fluted points are distinctive stone tools manufactured by flaking two sides of a narrow blade struck from a stone tool, normally chert. The point has a channel or flute removed from each side at the base. In contrast to the earlier Clovis points, the Folsom points are smaller, but the flute extends virtually the entire length of the point.

The subsistence for Folsom Paleo-Indians was based on hunting the now extinct bison, as discovered at the Folsom site. Excavations at the Olsen-Chubbuck site in Colorado by Joe Ben Wheat uncovered a kill site where about 157 bison had been stampeded into a dry gulley and trampled to death. Seventy-five percent of the animals were butchered, which Wheat estimates provided meat for a hundred people for one month. Other bison-kill sites are located at Lindenmeier, Colorado, excavated by Frank Roberts in the 1930's; Casper, Wyoming, excavated by George Frison; and the Jones-Miller site in Colorado, excavated by Dennis Stanford.

Despite poor preservation of plant or animal remains from Paleo-Indian times, remains at other sites indicate that the diet included other animals. At Debert, Nova Scotia, George MacDonald suggested reliance on caribou (*Rangifer*), which has been substantiated by caribou bones at other sites in northeastern North America, notably at the Udora site by Peter Storck and Arthur Spiess and at the Sandy Ridge site by Lawrence Jackson and Heather McKillop in Ontario, Canada, and at the Holcombe site in Michigan by Charles Cleland. As the large Pleistocene animals became extinct, the Folsom Paleo-Indians adapted their hunting strategies to small animals and began to gather plants during what archaeologists refer to as the Archaic tradition in North America.

Fox

CULTURE AREA: Northeast
LANGUAGE GROUP: Algonquian
PRIMARY LOCATION: Iowa, Kansas, Nebraska, Oklahoma
POPULATION SIZE: 4,517 ("Sac and Fox," 1990 U.S. Census)

The Fox are generally thought to have originated in southern Michigan. They belong to the Algonquian family and are closely related to the Sauk (or Sac), Kickapoo, and perhaps the Mascouten. The designation "Fox" was given them by French explorers; the group's name for themselves was Mesquakie (in other transliterations, "Meshwakihug" or "Meshwakie"). Another name for the tribe is Outagami, which they were called by other tribal groups.

Mesquakie means "the people of the red earth" and may signify either the soil coloring of their primal homeland or a mythological belief that they were created from the "red earth." When the French called them the Reynards (Foxes), they were probably confusing a clan designation with the name of the entire people. Since the eighteenth century, the Fox have been closely identified with the Sauk people; the two groups are often regarded as a single entity by the U.S. government (as in census figures). The Fox have a long and tragic history, an economic life combining features of both the Eastern Woodlands and the Great Plains, a rich social and cultural heritage, and a modern existence characterized by survival and revival.

Prehistory and French Contact. William T. Hagan has described the history of the Fox as "a case study of the results of the clash of two civilizations." The Fox encounter with Western culture—as embodied successively in the French, the British, and the Americans—was inherently tragic. Near genocide was followed by their displacement from their ancestral homeland in the Midwest. By the dawn of the twentieth century the Fox had declined in numbers (from about twenty-five hundred in 1650 to only 264 in 1867) and were scattered among a tribal farm in Iowa and governmental reservations in Kansas, Nebraska, and Oklahoma.

Oral tradition suggests that prior to the arrival of Europeans the Fox had been eased westward from their lands in central Michigan because of pressure from the Chippewas. Resettled in southern Wisconsin and northern Illinois, the Fox were primarily located along the Wolf River, with a territory extending from Lake Superior to the Chicago River and from Lake Michigan to the Mississippi. A western Great Lakes nation, they were known as "People of the Calumet" because of the sacred pipes they employed in their tobacco ceremonies.

Initial contact with Europeans was made when French traders, explorers, and missionaries visited Fox country in the early seventeenth century. Confusion commenced immediately, the French misnaming the tribe "Renards." Conflict quickly ensued from major disagreements between the French and the Fox, resulting in an unusual chapter in American colonial history, the Fox being one of the few North American tribes to oppose the French actively. Several reasons for this anomaly have been offered. The Fox disapproved of the French policy of facilitating the fur trade by repressing even legitimate disputes between tribes. When the French extended the fur trade to their enemies, the Dakota, they protested. To the Fox, French trade goods and prices were inferior to those proferred by the British through their former enemies, the Iroquois, who now sought an alliance. Tribes hostile to the Fox fanned the fires of disagreement. Open warfare was almost inevitable.

The French-Fox War (1712-1737) was occasioned by the Fox demand that French traders pay a transit toll when plying the Fox River in Wisconsin. This the French refused to do, retaliating by arming the traditional enemies of the Fox, the Dakota and the Ojibwa. For a quarter of a century furious combat transpired. A brave and warlike people, the Fox were nevertheless vastly outnumbered. Many scholars believe they continued to wage war even though they realized that the French had adopted a deliberate policy of genocide. The French hoped to annihilate their adversaries through war and disease. Some French officials even suggested the total elimination of the Fox people through their deportation to the West Indies to work as slaves in the sugar colonies. Peace was restored only in 1737 when the French, weary of war, offered a general pardon to the Fox. A permanent legacy of distrust had been generated.

From 1750 to the Reservation Era. Fox survival had been facilitated through a close alliance with the Sauk. By the mid-eighteenth century the Fox and the Sauk were regarded by outsiders as a single people. The "Dual Tribes" moved westward and southward, inhabiting lands along the Mississippi River by the 1760's, modifying their Eastern Woodlands lifestyle with elements of the Siouan culture of the Great Plains. The disappearance of French rule with the signing of the Treaty of Paris (1763) and the advent of British hegemony did little to dissipate Fox distrust of Europeans.

The actions of the American government confirmed the Fox's fears. Not signatories to the Treaty of Fort Greenville (1795), the Fox and the Sauk resisted white settlement; they were active in Little Turtle's War (1790-1794) and in Tecumseh's Rebellion (1809-1811). Certain leaders, however, argued for "peace and accommodation," accepting, in 1804, an annual annuity from the United States government in return for the legal cession of Fox lands east of the Mississippi. Many Fox were angered and fearful after the British failure in the War of 1812. Chief Black Hawk, a Sauk warrior, argued for armed resistance. In the last Indian war in the Old Northwest Territory, Black Hawk War (1832-1833), the Sauk and their Fox allies were routed. Most of Black Hawk's army was killed, and Black Hawk himself was captured by the U.S. Army and exhibited as a "trophy" during a tour through the East. Removal of the Sauk and Fox to lands west of the Mississippi River was now a foregone conclusion.

As a consequence of the Treaty of Chicago (1833), the Fox and their allies were removed to Iowa. This arrangement was not satisfactory for a number of reasons. The steady press of American settlers was a threat. Illegal seizure of the Fox lead mines near Dubuque, which had provided a revenue in excess of $4,000 annually from sales to traders, provoked outrage. There was a steady erosion of the traditional Fox way of life.

By 1842 the Fox and the Sauk had migrated to Kansas. Reservation life led to serious disputes between the Fox and the Sauk. Disagreements centered on the distribution of annuity payments, fears of removal to Oklahoma, apparent government favoritism toward the Sauk, the inability to make a good living on the reservation (poor land, limited hunting opportunities), and the gradual loss of a separate Fox identity. The spread of epidemic disease was the "last straw." By the 1850's many of the Fox wanted to return to Iowa. In 1856 an act of the Iowa state legislature legalized the residence of the Fox within that jurisdiction. The following year five members of the tribal council purchased land in Tama County, the original 80 acres eventually becoming 3,000. As a nonreservation community, the Iowa Fox settlement avoided both assimilation and federal restrictions. The settlement survived through the twentieth century. By the 1990's the Fox people had been divided three ways: Some of them lived on the tribally owned lands in Iowa, some on reservations in Kansas and Nebraska, and the remainder in Oklahoma with the Sauk.

Economic Life. The Fox were unique among Algonquian peoples in that they were economically at home in both the Great Lakes and the Great Plains regions. In the course of their long history, the Fox adapted well to both areas.

Originally, the Fox inhabited the Great Lakes region, living in Michigan and later in southern Wisconsin and northern Illinois. The opportunities afforded by the Eastern Woodlands were fully exploited. Though the climate was harsh, the Fox prospered. Fishing was practiced; hunting was profitable. The marshlands provided a sky filled with waterfowl. On the eastern Plains were buffalo. In the primeval forests a wide variety of game flourished, including deer and moose, both of which were used for hides and meat. Trapping for furs began in earnest after contact with the Europeans. Food gathering supplied the Fox diet with nuts, berries, honey, tubers, herbs, fruits, and especially the "wild rice" (named "wild oats" by Americans) so common in the Midwest wetlands. Food producing occurred along rivers near Fox villages, the women raising corn, beans, squash, pumpkins, and melons. Tobacco was cultivated for ceremonial purposes. The forests of beech, birch, conifers, elms, oaks, and chestnuts offered materials for canoes, snowshoes, containers, writing materials, daily implements, and house construction. Maple sugar was harvested in winter. Surface metals (and copper) were mined for trading purposes.

Later in their history the Fox adjusted well to the economic opportunities of the Great Plains. This shift in lifestyle was stimulated by a variety of factors. Pressure from the Chippewas forced the Fox to flee Michigan for Wisconsin and Illinois. Contact with the Siouan peoples familiarized them with the possibilities of the prairie habitat. The arrival of Europeans supplied them with horses, firearms, and markets. Perhaps the most striking change was the adoption of the Great Buffalo Hunt. While the Fox continued their earlier seasonal economic cycle of food gathering and food producing, they significantly increased their dependance on the hunt.

A virtual exodus took place after the planting of crops in April and May, as Fox hunters went west of the Iowa-Missouri watershed seeking buffalo. During the long, dry summer they searched for bison herds. Prior to the extensive use of rifles, the hunters would surround the herd, start a grassfire, panic the buffalo, have a skilled bowman shoot the lead animal, and then start the "kill." Robert Cavalier Sieur de La Salle, the seventeenth century French explorer, reported that it was not unusual for two hundred buffalo to be taken in a single day. Women accompanying the hunters would strip, clean, pack, and dry the meat while tanning the hides. By August and the advent of harvest time, the hunters would return to their permanent villages with meat for the winter and hides to trade for ammunition. A smaller winter hunt was not unknown. By 1806 the Fox were reckoned the best hunters in the Mississippi and Missouri valleys, and American pioneer Meriwether Lewis estimated the value of their annual fur sales to be $10,000. By then the Fox had become part of the American economy, relying on traders for credit and a wide variety of consumer items (knives, blankets, arms, ammunition, tobacco, and various luxuries).

The end of the traditional Fox economy was evident by the start of the nineteenth century. In 1804 chiefs accepted an annual annuity of $400 from the United States government in exchange for surrender of the ancestral lands east of the Mississippi. Large numbers of whites were settling Fox territories. By 1820 the golden age of the Great Buffalo Hunt was over. Forced removal to Iowa in the 1830's doomed the traditional Fox way of life.

Social, Political, and Religious Life. The Fox have a rich and diverse heritage involving complex familial, tribal, and religious organizations. The fundamental social unit of Fox society was the family. Sometimes polygamous, often monogamous, the immediate family was composed of husband and wife (in plural marriages the additional wives were often sisters) and children. Courtship occurred around age twenty, with marriage resting on the consent of the bride (and her parents) to the suitor's proposal. Remarriage following death or divorce was permitted, although marital fidelity was strictly enforced. Initially the bride and groom would reside in the home of her parents, but following the birth of the first child (in the "birthing house") the new family would move to its own dwelling. Often there was a summer lodge (for farming and hunting) and a more permanent winter home (aligned along an east-west axis), conical in appearance, built around a central hearth. Families normally varied in size from five to more than thirty members.

Families, in turn, were organized into exogamous patrilineal clans. Anthropologists have identified eight (some claim fourteen) clans including Bear, Wolf, Swan, Partridge, Thunder, Elk, Black Bear, and Fox (from which the French apparently misnamed the tribe). The clan was a cohesive group, certain honors being hereditary within each extended family (as the office of peace chief). An institution called the moiety, also practiced among other Native American groups, helped lessen clan rivalries. Across kinship lines the Fox tribe was divided into two moieties (or societies), the White and the Black. Created by random division, these associations were utilized for games, ceremonies, and even warfare. This arrangement provided fellowship and friendship without distinction as to bloodline or office and was a solidifying force in tribal life.

The life of the individual Fox was regulated and supported by the family, the clan, the moiety, and the entire tribe. Children were prized highly and were reared with considerable affection and attention; corporal punishment was rare. By the age of six or seven, boys were imitating the hunting ways of the males and girls were assisting in farming and homemaking with the women. Puberty was a major event for both genders. Following her initial menstruation, a girl was sent to a separate lodge for ten days to reflect on her new status as a young woman. Boys at puberty were to experience the "vision," preceded by fasting and followed by a heroic deed. By the age of nineteen or twenty, both boys and girls were expected to be integrated fully into the adult life of the tribe.

The tribe had various types of leaders. One was the office of peace chief (often hereditary within the Bear clan), a male who was respected as an administrator, president at the tribal council, and person of wisdom, experience, and sound judgment. Another was the office of war chief (usually elected from warriors who had proved themselves repeatedly in combat), who, in times of danger, had near-dictatorial power and who was entrusted with leading the tribe to victory. A third office was ceremonial chief or shaman, a position depending on both heredity and demonstrated charismatic gifts. Though the shaman had no exclusive monopoly on spiritual functions, he was a major contact person with the supernatural. Temporary raiding chiefs were selected, men who, following fasting and a vision, would gather a band of warriors for a specific mission. Following the venture, the band dissolved. Lesser chiefs sat with the paramount chiefs in the tribal council, which decided matters of war and peace, the selection of hunting grounds, and diplomatic relations with other tribes and with Europeans.

The religious life of the Fox centered on a reverence for nature and its powers. The universe was divided into two portions: the Powers of the Sky (or the Upper Region, ruled by the Great Manitou) and the Powers of the Earth (the Lower Region, ruled by lesser spirits). The Lower Region was organized along the four points of the compass, the east (ruled by the sun), the north (ruled by the Creator), the west (the land of departed spirits), and the south (the region of the god of thunder). A powerful animism invested the earth, the sky, the waters, the forests, and all creatures with intelligent souls which could either help or hinder human activity. The Midewiwin, or Grand Medicine Society, was a secret group who believed themselves able to enlist the support of the spirit world for the tribe.

Religious rituals occurred in harmony with the change of seasons (as the Green Corn Feast at the onset of the harvest) and the various stages of life, as puberty and death. Funeral customs were intended to guarantee the happiness of the deceased person's spirit, burial being either in the earth (seated, or even seated on top of a dead foe, for a warrior) or on a scaffold. Gifts were buried; sometimes sacrificial animals (such as a dog) were also buried to serve as companions in the afterlife.

Modern Life. The United States Census of 1990 reported 4,517 Sauk and Fox Indians. Since the nineteenth century, the Fox have been divided into three groups: Some live in reservations in the Plains states (130 lived in Kansas and Nebraska in the 1970's), some live in Oklahoma (1,000 lived on the Oklahoma reservation in the 1970's), and the remainder live in Iowa. Since the 1820's there has been, for most Fox, little marked separation from the Sauk people. Those in Iowa have the most clear-cut identity.

The wisdom of Fox tribal elders was demonstrated in the 1850's when they purchased 80 (later 3,000) acres near Tama, Iowa. They won recognition by the state legislature as to the legitimacy of their residence, thus freeing themselves from the restrictions accompanying reservation life. They prospered in Iowa, and by the end of World War II there were 653 Fox living on the tribal farms. Some commuted to urban jobs, while others managed land rentals (to white farms). In Iowa, family, clan, and tribal life continues, with nearly all Fox speaking the ancestral language (one-third speak it exclusively, the rest being bilingual). While some have accepted Christianity, the majority belong to medicine societies and practice the ancestral faith (with some adhering to the Native American Church). Though only a remnant of the once proud Fox, or Mesquakie, Nation, the Iowa tribal community demonstrates the power of the people to survive and gives evidence of a revived hope for the twenty-first century.

C. George Fry

Bibliography
Callendar, Charles. "Fox." In *Northeast*, edited by Bruce G. Trigger. Vol. 15 in *Handbook of North American Indians*, edited by William Sturtevant. Washington, D.C.: Smithsonian Institution Press, 1978. A definitive eleven-page essay, complete with illustrations and notes, which surveys the history, beliefs, and social life of the Fox.
Edmunds, R. David, and Joseph L. Peyser. *The Fox Wars: The Mesquakie Challenge to New France*. Norman: University of Oklahoma Press, 1993.
Foley, Douglas E. *The Heartland Chronicles*. Philadelphia: University of Pennsylvania Press, 1995.

Gearing, Frederick O. *The Face of the Fox*. Chicago: Aldine, 1970. A concise (158-page) volume that combines a readable text with reliable information. A good first book on the Fox.

Hagan, William T. *The Sac and Fox Indians*. Norman: University of Oklahoma Press, 1958. This 290-page study is a meticulous survey of Fox history since 1804.

Josephy, Alvin M., Jr. *The Indian Heritage of America*. New York: Alfred A. Knopf, 1968. Provides information on the Fox and their allies and adversaries.

Lambert, Joseph I. "The Black Hawk War: A Military Analysis." *Journal of the Illinois Historical Society* 32 (December, 1939): 442-473. A stunning piece of original research reviewing tactics and strategy employed in the last Indian War east of the Mississippi River.

McTaggart, Fred. *Wolf That I Am: In Search of the Red Earth People*. Boston: Houghton Mifflin, 1976. In brief compass (195 pages), with an excellent bibliography, this sympathetic study of the Fox proves to be reliable and enjoyable reading.

Owen, Mary Alicia. *Folklore of the Musquakie Indians of North America*. London: D. Nutt, 1904. Though dated, this short survey (147 pages), with revealing illustrations, has value as a turn-of-the-century view of the Fox.

Stout, David Bond, Erminie Wheeler-Voegelin, and Emily J. Blasingham. *Indians of Eastern Missouri, Western Illinois, and Southern Wisconsin, from the Proto-Historic Period to 1804*. New York: Garland, 1974. A vintage study of the Fox and their neighbors from the Stone Age to the era of Lewis and Clark in 319 pages. Plates, maps.

Tax, Sol. "The Social Organization of the Fox Indians." In *Social Anthropology of North American Tribes*, edited by Fred Eggan. Chicago: University of Chicago Press, 1937. A Depression-era analysis of Fox life showing the conflict of traditional and modern ways. Though dated, it still has merit.

United States. Indian Claims Commission. *An Anthropological Report on the Sac, Fox, and Iowa Indians*. 3 vols. New York: Garland, 1974. A classic study in 381 pages (with maps) based on field observations of Fox folkways.

Young Bear, Ray A. *Black Eagle Child: The Facepaint Narratives*. Iowa City: University of Iowa Press, 1992.

Fremont

DATE: 650-1250
LOCATION: Western Colorado plateau, eastern Great Basin
CULTURE AFFECTED: Paleo-Indian

The Fremont culture, named for the Fremont River in south central Utah, was first defined in 1931 by Harvard University anthropologist Noel Morss. Geographically, Fremont remains extend from the eastern Great Basin to the western Colorado Plateau. Although material traces go back much further, archaeologists estimate the main Fremont period to have been between 650 and 1250 C.E.

Some theories have tied the visibly less-developed Fremont to the better-known Anasazi because the last stages of both cultures, which were roughly modern, seem to have involved spatial retreats—the Anasazi into the Pueblo area, and the Fremont into the Southern Paiute, Ute, and Shoshone areas of the eastern Great Basin. Similarities in geometric designs on pottery are noted among remains left by both groups in both regions. Other archaeological evidence, however, suggests such major differences (beyond the obviously more substantial buildings and ceremonial sites left by the Anasazi) that Morss's separate classification has remained largely unchallenged.

A main characteristic of Fremont sites is that, although some general cultural links show similarities between groups, local diversitites are notable. Similarities have been traced through a unique single-rod-and-bundle method of basketmaking. Another distinctly Fremont artifact is the moccasin made from a single piece of deer or mountain sheep hocks. Although local variations are found in construction methods associated with both these artifacts, one area of Fremont archaeology shows a nearly universal practice: the use of a characteristic gray clay to fashion coil pottery forms. Although objects made by Fremont groups, and the designs used to decorate them, are not essentially different from those found in neighboring cultures, the material used is unique. Within the extensive Fremont zone, distinctions are made on the basis of proportions of granular rock added to the gray clay, or degrees of temper in the final baking. Subgroups have been labeled "Snake Valley Gray," "Sevier Gray," "Emery Gray," "Uinta Gray," and "Great Salt Lake Gray."

In terms of decorative style, Fremont artists used a unique trapezoidal shape reproduced in large numbers in small clay figurines with characteristic hair "bobs" and ornate necklaces. The same stylized human shape appears in the famous canyon petroglyphs at various sites in the Fremont Zone, particularly in the Colorado Plateau region.

Because some important differences exist between remains left by groupings on the Colorado Plateau and those inhabiting the Great Basin, there has been a tendency to refer to two general zones of Fremont archaeology: the Fremont proper and the Sevier-Fremont. Two key examples help explain this division. Stone not being as available in the Great Basin zone, most building remains (although nearly identical in form and function) were made of mud bricks. Trapezoidal baked clay and small stone-etched objects are far more common in the Sevier-Fremont zone, whereas petroglyphs predominate in the eastern Fremont.

Gabrielino

CULTURE AREA: California
LANGUAGE GROUP: Shoshonean
PRIMARY LOCATION: Northern San Diego County, southern Orange County
POPULATION SIZE: 634 (1990 U.S. Census)

The Gabrielinos are among the small California tribal groupings that once occupied the land where modern-day Los Angeles is located. The name "Gabrielino" derives from the fact that the people once lived around the San Gabriel Mission, one of the early Roman Catholic missionary stations founded in the Southern California region. (This is also the case with the name "Fernandeño" for those peoples once surrounding the San Fernando Mission in the present San Fernando Valley, just northwest of urban Los Angeles.) The Gabrielinos are thus closely affiliated with the Fernandeños as part of the Shoshonean branch of the Uto-Aztecan linguistic division.

Anthropologist Alfred Kroeber's estimate for the Gabrielino population in 1770 was approximately five thousand, including the Fernandeños as well. California Indians generally are not to be understood as "tribes" but rather as small "tribal groups" of a hundred persons at most (groups were usually not permanent) that surrounded a centrally recognized permanent village. The Gabrielinos shared many common cultural traits with other village communities up and down the California coast, including a style of basket weaving, simple agriculture, and architecture. As with other Southern Californian natives in this near-tropical climate, the Gabrielinos typically dressed very lightly, if at all.

The Gabrielinos are among the few native peoples of the Los Angeles region. The Gabrielinos are divided in modern California along extended family lines. Unlike many other California groups, who have accepted the usefulness of the nontraditional office of "chief," the Gabrielinos recognize no central leader. Rival factions among the Gabrielinos have created problems in settling cultural questions and in being able to deal with issues of heritage, such as finding archaeological sites and approving construction projects. A representative of one family or faction may approve a project, thereby creating a great protest from those who do not recognize the authority of the Gabrielinos working on the project. There are even conflicts over the number of Gabrielinos because of the same factionalism and an inability to agree on who is and is not Gabrielino. Most modern Gabrielinos live in the southern Orange County and northern San Diego County areas. There is no Gabrielino reservation.

Bibliography
Kroeber, Alfred. "The Indians of California." In *The North American Indians: A Sourcebook*, edited by Roger Owen, James Deetz, and Anthony Fisher. New York: Macmillan, 1967.
McCawley, William. *The First Angelinos: The Gabrielino Indians of Los Angeles*. Novato, Calif.: Ballena Press, 1996.
Miller, Bruce W. *The Gabrielino*. Los Osos, Calif.: Sand River Press, 1991.

Gitksan

CULTURE AREA: Northwest coast
LANGUAGE GROUP: Tsimshian
PRIMARY LOCATION: British Columbia, Canada
POPULATION SIZE: 4,560 (Statistics Canada, based on 1991 census)

The Gitksan are a tribal group of western-central British Columbia, closely related in language and culture to the Tsimshian, their neighbors to the west. They originally occupied the Skeena River valley; since 1900, however, some have moved into parts of the adjacent Nass river system to the northwest, where they have intermarried with some members of the Nishga, another group closely related to the Tsimshian.

The Gitksan possess many of the same general cultural features of other Northwest Coast groups. They rely on predictable and abundant salmon runs, fish for ocean species such as halibut and cod, and collect shellfish, including several species of clams. The Gitksan also traditionally hunted elk, blacktail deer, beaver, fox, and several types of sea mammals.

In general, Gitksan social organization resembles that of other west-central coastal groups. Traditionally they traced descent through the female side (matrilineal descent), but married couples were obligated to reside in or near the house of the groom's parents (patrilocality). Cross-culturally, this is an unusual pattern. Some anthropologists have speculated that the Gitksan, along with other Northwest Coast groups, may have been exclusively matrilineal/matrilocal in the past, but because through time so much wealth and property was being accumulated by males, cultural evolution favored a shift to institutions sanctioning male control over residence and the eventual transference of property through the male line.

On October 23, 1984, the Gitksan, along with other native groups of central-western Canada, filed a land claim for a little more than 35,000 square miles of central British Columbia. In 1991, the Canadian Government decided against the Gitksan. These same groups, along with the Gitksan, subsequently filed an appeal. The Gitksan have also filed for what has been termed "community-based self government." This, in principle, is similar to the autonomy achieved by such groups as the Navajo (Diné) of the southwestern United States. If successful, the Gitksan would have more control over their local economic, political, and social circumstances.

Gosiute

CULTURE AREA: Great Basin
LANGUAGE GROUP: Shoshone
PRIMARY LOCATION: Near Deep Creek, the Great Salt Lake, and Skull Valley, Utah
POPULATION SIZE: 282 ("Goshute Shoshone," 1990 U.S. Census), 416 (1994 Gosiute tribal record)

Historically, the Gosiute (or "Goshute") were a mixed tribe of both Shoshone and Ute heritage; though they spoke Shoshone and were a splinter group of that tribe, Gosiutes often intermarried with Utes. Gosiutes roamed the vast area between Ruby Valley, Nevada, and the Utah Wasatch Mountain Range. Their date of arrival in the area has yet to be established.

Because they resided in a barren, desert region of Utah and Nevada, it is believed that the early Mormon settlers of Utah were the first whites to visit the Gosiutes. The ensuing years, however, witnessed many gold miners passing through Gosiute territory on the overland route to California. During the 1860's, the Pony Express route also crossed Gosiute lands, and overland mail stations were erected on that tribe's territory. After the White Pine War of 1875, many Nevada Gosiutes relocated permanently to Deep Creek Utah.

The Gosiute, or "desert people," had only a loose tribal association and two isolated settlements. An 1866 Indian agent described them as "peaceable and loyal." In the rare instances when they fought, it was usually to defend themselves. Gosiutes often roamed in small groups, scouring the desert for meager amounts of food. Men hunted small game, primarily jackrabbits, while women gathered edible plants and fruit. Pine nuts proved to be a favorite food source, and the yearly expedition to gather them was a major event. For cultural activities, Gosiutes participated in the Bear Dance and the Round Dance.

Early in the twentieth century, part of the tribe located on the Skull Valley Reservation in Juab and Tooele counties (Utah), while the other part moved to the Deep Creek Reservation in White Pine County, Nevada. President William Howard Taft allocated the Skull Valley region in 1912 by executive order; two years later, another such order created the Deep Creek Reservation. The tribe adopted and approved its constitution in November of 1940. By the 1990's, less than half of the tribe's members resided on the reservations.

Guale

CULTURE AREA: Southeast
LANGUAGE GROUP: Muskogean
PRIMARY LOCATION: Georgia coast

These maritime and river-oriented people were divided into northern, central, and southern groups occupying numerous permanent villages connected by language, marriage, and trade. They had a diversified subsistence base that included horticulture, hunting, gathering, and fishing.

First contact with European Americans (with a Spanish colony) occurred in 1526. Soon the Spanish drove the French from Florida and began to occupy Guale territory. By 1597, French Jesuits were active among these people; they created a Guale grammar. The Franciscans had established a mission in 1573, but by 1597 all but one missionary had been killed. In retaliation, the governor of Florida had many Guale villages and granaries destroyed, thereby bringing the Guale under Spanish control by 1601. Guale opposition to missionization continued, however, resulting in many of the Guale moving inland or to the islands of San Pedro in 1686. Facing continual conflict, the Guale fled to the Creek, who had united for the 1715 Yamasee War, among whom they lived in two missions near St. Augustine.

Haisla

CULTURE AREA: Northwest Coast
LANGUAGE GROUP: Wakashan
PRIMARY LOCATION: Gardner Canal, British Columbia coast
POPULATION SIZE: 955 (Statistics Canada, based on 1991 census)

The technology of the Haisla and their annual migration pattern reflected their dependence upon fish. Women gathered shellfish and various types of berries and fruits. The basic social units were five matrilineal exogamous clans, each with territorial rights; they formed alliances for ceremonial purposes. Haisla society was ranked into nobles, commoners, and slaves. Numerous ceremonies existed; the potlatch was important for redistribution of traditional wealth and recognition of status change.

Contact was made by Juan Zayas in 1792, and again the following year by Joseph Whidbey of the George Vancouver expedition. Hudson's Bay Company established a fur-trading post at Fort McLoughlin in 1833 near Dean Channel. Breakdown of traditional culture began to occur after the arrival of Christian missionaries in 1833. Government banning of potlatches and dancing societies brought further breakdown of Haisla culture. In 1916, the Haisla had fourteen reserves with 1,432 allotted acres. By the mid-twentieth century, many Haisla were working in the fishing and logging industries, but by the 1970's, a shift had occurred, and working in aluminum smelting had become the primary source of income.

Han

CULTURE AREA: Subarctic
LANGUAGE GROUP: Athapaskan
PRIMARY LOCATION: Yukon River, both sides of U.S./Canadian border
POPULATION SIZE: 495 (Statistics Canada, based on 1991 census)

The three autonomous, wealth-oriented, matrilineal Han clans subsisted primarily upon fishing, supplementing their diet by hunting, trapping, and a limited amount of gathering. They lived in riverine villages, in semi-subterranean dwellings, and in domed skin houses when hunting and traveling; on water they used birchbark canoes and moose-skin boats.

At the time of their first contact with European Americans and the establishment of Fort Yukon in 1847, the Han had already been influenced by European trade goods. The purchase of Alaska in 1869 by the United States brought white trapper-traders and gold miners who, through trade, diminished Han dependency upon traditional hunting and fishing subsistence by encouraging trapping and a cash economy, therefore making the Han dependent upon European American material culture. From 1919 to 1925, the Han suffered from epidemics of mumps, influenza, and measles.

Many modern Han live in the Indian village at Eagle; they are seasonally employed in road construction, trapping, government positions, and firefighting. Few traditional skills remain, though some beading, birchbark baskets, and snowshoes are manufactured, mostly for sale. The Han are now predominantly Episcopalians.

Hare

CULTURE AREA: Subarctic
LANGUAGE GROUP: Athapaskan
PRIMARY LOCATION: Northwestern Canada
POPULATION SIZE: 1,180 (Statistics Canada, based on 1991 census)

The Hare, or Kawchittine, Indians inhabited a large portion of northwestern Canada. The Hare were unique in that they depended almost entirely on the snowshoe hare for subsistence. Though a few other large animals and fish were consumed, there were not enough caribou and moose in the area they occupied to support the tribe. Because of the limited amount of game available to them, Hare Indians regularly suffered periods of starvation until as recently as 1920. Because they were required to travel great distances in search of food, their relatively small population of 700-800 people covered more than 45,000 square miles of very diversified territory.

Hare Indians hunted large game with bows and arrows as well as with spears. Trout and whitefish were captured with nets and hooks; snowshoe hare were captured in snares. Food was smoked, dried, or frozen for winter storage. The Hare used birchbark and spruce canoes for water transportation, and snowshoes for winter travel. Women dragged toboggans to transport food and family possessions. Snowshoe hare skins were woven into blankets and capes. Caribou skins were used for pants, shirts, and mittens. Families lived in tipis covered with moss for insulation.

Hare Indians placed a high value on sharing and believed in the importance of dreams. Dreams were thought to predict their future and help them make important life decisions. Medicine men were said to receive their powers from spirits, whom they called to summon game and identify the proper native medicine to use on the ill.

Though the Hare traded with local Indian tribes who visited Europeans, direct contact between Hare and non-Indians did not occur until the late 1800's. They quickly became involved in the fur trade in order to obtain western wares. "Trading chiefs" emerged within the tribe to lead expeditions to local forts. Epidemic diseases devastated the Hare several times during the nineteenth century. In 1921, they agreed to give up their lands to the Canadian government in exchange for medical and educational services. In the mid-1940's, fur prices declined, forcing many Hare into wage labor jobs in the local oil refinery. Native practices disappeared as the population became more urbanized.

It is difficult to determine population figures for the modern Hare Indians, as many have intermarried with members of other Indian groups. Many Hare descendants now consider themselves Slave (Slavey) or Bearlake Indians. There are several Hare Indians at Fort Good Hope and Colville Lake, but population figures represent several Indian tribes.

Havasupai

CULTURE AREA: Southwest
LANGUAGE GROUP: Yuman
PRIMARY LOCATION: Northern Arizona
POPULATION SIZE: 547 (1990 U.S. Census)

The Havasupai ("People of the Blue-Green Water") live in the village of Supai, located in a side canyon of the Grand Canyon of the Colorado River. They are related to the Hualapai tribe now located in Peach Springs, Arizona, and they have a long history of trading with the Hopis to the east and having their storehouses raided by the Apaches to the south. The Havasupai are noted for their basketry.

For at least six centuries they have lived in the summer at the bottom of a narrow side canyon growing corn, melons, and other crops on small farms watered by a large spring just above their village. In winter they ranged out along the south rim of the Grand Canyon hunting deer and other animals as far south as the present-day locations of Williams and Flagstaff, Arizona.

The United States government officially restricted them to a tiny reservation in Havasu Canyon in 1882, and during the 1920's white ranchers forced them off their winter hunting grounds on the surrounding plateau. The cliff-shaded canyon was an inhospitable place in the winter, lacking firewood and subject to flash floods. Three hundred people were crowded onto about 518 acres. The Bureau of Indian Affairs closed their small elementary school in 1955, forcing all students to attend boarding schools, and started a formal program of relocation the following year.

In the 1970's under the new government policy of Indian self-determination, things began to improve for the Havasupai. On January 3, 1975, Public Law 93-620 was signed by President Gerald Ford, giving back some of the plateau to the Havasupai. In the same year they took over the management of their elementary school.

As of 1995, students still needed to go to Bureau of Indian Affairs boarding schools in California or Arizona to attend high school. The village had electricity and telephone service, but by choice there was still no road to the village. Supai in 1995 was accessible only by helicopter, walking, or riding a mule or horse down an 8-mile trail. While the Havasupai still practiced a small amount of irrigation farming, the economy was based on running a campground, motel, store, and restaurant for tourists visiting the scenic waterfalls a few miles from the village.

Hidatsa

CULTURE AREA: Plains
LANGUAGE GROUPS: Siouan
PRIMARY LOCATION: North Dakota
POPULATION SIZE: 1,571 (1990 U.S. Census)

The Hidatsa were a Siouan-speaking people who lived along the middle Missouri River. Like their neighbors the Arikaras and the Mandans, the Hidatsa dwelled in villages of earthen mounds and practiced both agriculture and hunting. Their palisaded villages were near the Knife River, a branch of the Missouri in North Dakota, north of modern Bismarck.

Hidatsa mother with her child, around 1908.
(Library of Congress)

Historically, the Hidatsa had been one with the Crow before they separated in the eighteenth century. One legend has it that the split resulted from a dispute over a certain buffalo that had been killed during a hunting party. The nation at that time was governed by two factions, each with a separate chief. The wives of each of these leaders began arguing over the stomach of the dead buffalo. When one of the women killed the other, a battle began between the two factions. Several people were killed on both sides of the struggle. This resulted in the migration to the Rocky Mountains of about one-half of those remaining. These migrants became the Crow, while those left behind constituted the Hidatsa. Linguistic similarities remained after the separation.

This powerful tribe began to acquire horses in the 1730's and 1740's from nomadic Plains tribes, with whom they traded. The acquisition of these swift animals made the hunting of buffalo easier and faster. The tribe used the products of the buffalo for food, tipi covers, robes, and utensils. To aid in their hunting and to demonstrate their bravery and daring, Hidatsa warriors raided other tribes for horses and loot. War dances often preceded these raids. Occasionally the Hidatsa were raided by members of the Dakota tribe, who called the Hidatsa "Minitari."

The tribe's farming efforts yielded corn, beans, and squash. The men sometimes raised tobacco, which was considered a sacred plant. Clothing was elaborate. Made from animal skins, it was usually decorated with quills and, after the white traders arrived, with beads. The spreading eagle-feather headdress probably originated with either the Hidatsa or the neighboring Mandan.

Clans and societies were important elements of Hidatsa life. Members of these groups often had certain functions and performed particular ceremonies. The supernatural played an important role. Men often sought visions, and shamans with particularly strong visions were consulted for advice. It was believed that they were able to read the future, diagnose sickness, and perform acts of magic.

Many similarities existed between the Hidatsa and their geographical neighbors, specifically the Mandan and the Arikara. They were all semi-nomadic tribes. That is, part of the year was spent in the cultivating and harvesting of crops, while the remainder was spent on the hunt, especially for buffalo. They were also all subject to problems associated with the arrival of whites such as fewer buffalo to hunt and diseases which ravaged their populations. Smallpox epidemics occurred repeatedly through the years. In 1837, the Hidatsa were joined by about one hundred Mandan survivors of the disease. The two tribes lived together from that point.

Hitchiti

CULTURE AREA: Southeast
LANGUAGE GROUP: Muskogean
PRIMARY LOCATION: Florida, Oklahoma
POPULATION SIZE: 257 (1990 U.S. Census)

At the time of contact with Europeans in the 1540's, the Hitchitis lived on the lower Ocmulgee River in present-day Georgia. Seeing themselves as the original inhabitants of the area, the Hitchitis regarded the other tribes who came into the Creek Nation as newcomers. (Hitchiti tradition located the founding of the Creek confederacy at Ocmulgee Old Field, the site of present-day Macon, Georgia.) Culturally, the Hitchitis were similar to other Creeks, though their language was not intelligible to speakers of pure Muskogee.

Some Hitchitis moved into Florida during the eighteenth century to get away from white settlers and the dominance of the Muskogees within the Creek confederacy. They became an important component of the evolving Seminole nation. Hitchiti-speaking Seminoles were often called Micco-sukees, after a town they settled near lake Miccosukee in northern Florida. With other Seminoles and Creeks, many Hitchitis were removed to Indian Territory (modern Oklahoma) in the 1830's and 1840's. The majority of the two hundred or so Seminoles left behind in Florida were Hitchiti-speakers. In 1961, some of their descendants organized as the Miccosukee tribe of Indians of Florida and received federal recognition.

Hohokam

DATE: 600-1450
LOCATION: Central and southern Arizona, northern Mexico
CULTURES AFFECTED: Hohokam, Pima, Tohono O'odham

The Hohokam were a Classic-period southwestern culture whose heartland was centered on the Gila River and Salt River basins and whose largest site was Snaketown. Hohokam (in the Pima language, "those who have gone") shared many aspects of Classic-period southwestern culture such as maize-based horticulture, relatively dense settlements, and public, ceremonial architecture. Hohokam culture was distinctive in the presence of exotic trade goods and in its ball courts. Because of these unique characteristics, early archaeologists believed that Hohokam culture was derived from Mesoamerica. Most archaeologists now believe Hohokam origins to be indigenous to the Southwest, with roots stretching back to the hunter-gatherer societies of the Archaic period.

Although in the Classic period most Southwest societies continued to live in small, dispersed, unranked agricultural villages, new, more elaborate developments occurred in certain regions. The Hohokam represent one of these new developments, called "systems of regional integration," as their dominance grew to cover a wide region rather than remaining localized. Archaeological evidence suggests that accompanying this growth, social inequality grew among the Hohokam. Evidence pointing to inequality includes differing residential pit house dimensions and locations, public labor projects (such as platform mounds, ball courts, and extensive irrigation canals), craft specialization (especially shell jewelry), long-distance trade of exotic raw materials, and differential treatment of the dead, in that only certain burials held valuable grave goods.

Hohokam subsistence was diverse and included hunting and gathering, although maize, beans, and squash were primary staples. A complex network of irrigation canals was built near rivers. Settlement sizes ranged from communities the size of Snaketown (with about a thousand individuals) to small, dispersed farmsteads. Cremation was characteristic among the Hohokam, although other burial treatments also existed.

Although most archaeologists no longer point primarily to Mesoamerican inspirations to explain the Hohokam's rise to cultural complexity, Mesoamerican contacts may have been important in Hohokam society. Well-developed trade networks with quite distant communities existed throughout the Hohokam region. A variety of luxury goods—many from

Mexican sources—passed along well-established routes: copper bells; macaw birds and feathers; finely painted, geometric-motif pottery; stone paint palettes; onyx and argillite ornaments; serpentine; obsidian; turquoise; jet; and a variety of shell objects including conch trumpets, decorated bracelets, and beads. Participants within the Hohokam trade network may have shared a common religious and belief system originating in part with Mesoamerican societies, but it was integrated and adapted by the Hohokam as a means of legitimizing the emergence of social inequality.

Apart from prestige goods that remained mostly in the hands of Hohokam leaders, communities were largely self-sufficient. Although ball courts and luxury trade goods are common in larger Hohokam sites, their presence may reflect only superficial similarity with the Hohokam heartland, as regional cultures maintained their autonomy and distinctiveness within the broader region archaeologists have defined as sharing Hohokam culture.

For reasons still under debate, Hohokam culture went into decline; by the arrival of the Spanish, the Hohokam were gone. The modern-day Pima and Tohono O'odham (Papago) may be descendants of the Hohokam.

Hopewell

DATE: 200 B.C.E.-700 C.E.
LOCATION: Eastern United States
CULTURE AFFECTED: Hopewell

The Hopewell cultural tradition is associated with a major florescence of complex village societies in the eastern portion of North America between 200 B.C.E. and 700 C.E. The cultural system that connected societies of the Hopewell tradition is known as the Hopewell Interaction Sphere. Centered at sites in the Scioto Valley of southern Ohio, this network was marked by trade in a wide variety of exotic raw materials used in the manufacture of special craft items. These included goods such as copper from sources in Michigan and Georgia, obsidian and grizzly bear teeth from Wyoming, fine-grained stone from Minnesota and North Dakota, marine shell and shark teeth from the Gulf of Mexico, silver from Ontario, mica and quartz crystals from the southern Appalachians, and galena from Illinois and Wisconsin.

Among the most characteristic features of Hopewell sites are burial mounds and monumental earthworks. The Hopewell site near Chillicothe,

Ohio, for which the tradition is named, covered an area of 110 acres and had thirty-eight burial mounds. The largest of these was 33 feet high and 500 feet long, and it contained the burials of more than 250 individuals. One of these wore an elaborate headdress of wooden deer antlers sheathed in copper. Another was buried with a copper axe weighing 38 pounds. The central portion of this site was surrounded by a ditch and low embankment. Mound City, Ohio, has at least twenty-eight burial mounds, also within an earthwork enclosure. Elite burials here were lined with massive quantities of mica. At Newark, Ohio, the state's most extensive complex of geometric earthworks includes a circle, an octagon, and other features that have been preserved as part of a municipal golf course.

Burials in Hopewell mounds have been found to contain a wide variety of exotic artifacts. Heavy breastplates, ear spools, beads, animal cutouts, and musical instruments were made from hammered copper sheets, often decorated with embossed designs. Lumps of native copper were worked into celts, axes, adzes, and punches. Thick sheets of translucent mica were cut into the shapes of human heads and hands, bird talons, snakes, and swastikas. Obsidian and fine chert were flaked into beautiful ceremonial knives, some measuring 18 inches long. Crystals of quartz and galena were used for pendants or included in medicine bags. Among the most spectacular manufactured items, also widely traded, were carved stone platform pipes bearing appealing carvings of birds, bears, beavers, frogs, felines, and humans. Ceramic technology flourished, with a wide variety of vessel shapes decorated through plastic manipulation of the surface.

Hopewell culture frog effigy pipe found in Ross County, Ohio. (National Museum of the American Indian, Smithsonian Institution)

Sites of the Hopewell tradition have been found over a wide geographical region, ranging from the Great Lakes in the north to the lower Mississippi Valley and the central Gulf Coast. To the east, they are known from West Virginia and western Pennsylvania, while their westernmost extent is in the vicinity of Kansas City, Missouri.

Despite its apparent complexity, Hopewell culture appears to have been based on the intensive exploitation of wild resources of woodland regions, supplemented by some cultivation of sunflowers, squash, and marsh elder. Maize was probably cultivated by late Hopewell peoples, but it remained a minor part of the diet until later periods.

The Hopewell tradition does not represent a single society, but rather a broad phenomenon characterized by extensive networks for the exchange of raw materials and worked goods, the sharing of common notions about artifact manufacture and decoration, the use of mounds for burial grounds, and the emergence of social differentiation as indicated by fine craft objects and individual variation in the quality of grave goods. The apparent decline of the Hopewell tradition after 400 C.E. remains poorly understood, although it has been linked to the consequences of increased competition for farmland as maize became a more important component of the diet. These consequences included a higher frequency of intercommunity conflicts, which may have led to the disruption of existing networks for the exchange of raw materials and ideas.

Huchnom

CULTURE AREA: California
LANGUAGE GROUP: Yuki
PRIMARY LOCATION: South Eel River, northwestern California

Huchnom culture was a synthesis of Pomoan and Yuki traits and beliefs. The Huchnom village was the basic socioeconomic and political unit, usually with its own resources and territorial concerns. The Huchnom fished, hunted, trapped, and gathered acorns, seeds, and roots. Their material culture was also similar to the Yuki and Coastal Yuki, as were many of their rituals and ceremonies. They lived in thirty permanent riverine villages. The Huchnom participated with the Pomo and Cahto in rites of intensification as well as in the exchange of differential trade goods, and they served as intermediaries between the Yuki and Pomoan. They cremated their dead.

As with neighboring groups, the Huchnom were greatly affected in the 1850's when lumbermen, miners, and settlers entered their lands. Most Huchnom were forcibly removed by soldiers to the Round Valley Reservation in 1869, where they were known as Redwoods. Their population in 1850 was estimated to be twenty-one hundred, but by 1910 there were only fifteen remaining. By the early 1970's the tribe was no longer considered a distinct group.

Hupa

CULTURE AREA: California
LANGUAGE GROUP: Athapaskan
PRIMARY LOCATION: Northwestern California
POPULATION SIZE: 2,451 (1990 U.S. Census)

L ittle is known of Hupa prehistory, but their language indicates that they came from the north about thirteen hundred years ago. Living along the Trinity River in twelve villages, in an area of dense vegetation, their primary subsistence orientation was toward acorns and fish, particularly salmon, which they caught during spring and fall migratory runs with a specialized fishing technology. Hupa religious life was centered on two world-renewal and wealth-display ceremonies, the Jumping Dance and White Deerskin Dance, rituals to ward off famine and natural disaster and to ensure an abundance of resources. The autumn Acorn Feast and spring First Salmon ceremonies were also important.

Woodworking and basketweaving were important status skills. Traditional forms of wealth such as dentalium shell money, scarlet-feathered woodpecker scalp capes, obsidian blades, and albino deerskins were used for a number of purposes. These included the paying of a bride price, resolving conflicts, and paying a shaman's fee. Social control was achieved through consensus, threat of witchcraft or sorcery, and complex dietary and behavioral taboos.

First European American contact was with fur trappers in the 1840's. Contact became sustained in the 1850's when Chinese and white gold miners prospected the Hoopa Valley, some taking up permanent residence. An estimated aboriginal population of eighteen hundred was reduced to half by 1870, mostly from introduced diseases. Fort Gaston was established in 1858, and by 1864 Congress had authorized nearly the entire Hupa territory for a reservation (87,000 acres). Gradually, the Hupa took to agriculture and lumbering. Though they knew of the 1870 Ghost Dance, they never participated in the messianic movement as did their neighbors the Karok and Yurok. A government boarding school and hospital were established on the reservation.

By the 1990's, much Hupa income was from employment in numerous mills, owned mostly by whites. The wage economy adopted after World War II virtually ended all stock raising and farming. The Hupa enjoy a relatively high standard of living, and they maintain their ethnic identity through native language and self-management of internal affairs.

Huron

CULTURE AREA: Northeast
LANGUAGE GROUP: Iroquoian
PRIMARY LOCATION: Oklahoma, Quebec
POPULATION SIZE: 1,947 in U.S. (1990 U.S. Census); 1,450 in Canada (Statistics Canada, based on 1991 census)

The Hurons were a confederacy of four highly organized matrilineal and matrilocal tribes, the Attignaouantan (Bear People), Attigneenongnahac (Cord People), Arendahronon (Rock People), and Tohontaernrat (Deer People). Their historic homeland, Huronia, was in south central Ontario near Lake Simcoe, east of Lake Huron. In the early 1600's, they probably numbered about thirty thousand. The Hurons were horticultural, with women producing the staple crops: corn, beans, squash, and sunflowers. These were supplemented by game hunting, fishing, and berry picking, as well as by trade with other tribes for less common food commodities and other products. The Hurons traveled widely in the 1600's to pursue trade. They had successfully kept tribes to their west and north from trading directly with the French in New France (Quebec) so that they enjoyed a "middle-man" role in the burgeoning fur trade of the seventeenth century. All of this came to a crashing halt between 1649 and 1651 when Iroquois tribes ven-

Contemporary drawing of Hurons during the 1840's. (Library of Congress)

267

tured northwest into Huronia and completely dispersed the four Huron tribes along with neighboring tribes. The Hurons had already been plagued with disease and had their culture disrupted by French Jesuit missionaries, who introduced a foreign belief system.

The few Huron people who were not captured by the Iroquois tribes and absorbed as adoptees into those communities moved, with fellow refugees of the Tobacco Nation, north and west of Lake Huron. One group of these refugees subsequently occupied areas around Michilmackinac (Mackinac, Michigan), Green Bay (Wisconsin), the Ohio Valley, Detroit, Sandusky (Ohio), eastern Kansas, and eventually, Oklahoma. The group that eventually settled in Oklahoma took the name Wyandot (Wyandotte). The name originated as "Wendat," their name for themselves in the (nearly extinct) Huron language, meaning "islanders" or "peninsula dwellers." The word "Huron" was French and derogatorily referred to these people as "boarlike" or "unkempt."

The other group of refugees (those not eventually finding a home in Oklahoma) traveled with Jesuit missionaries to the St. Lawrence Valley in the seventeenth century, establishing a village called Lorette, near present-day Quebec City. Like their Oklahoma relatives, the Lorette Hurons are somewhat assimilated into the surrounding culture but still maintain some traditional cultural practices and beliefs.

Illinois

CULTURE AREA: Northeast
LANGUAGE GROUP: Algonquian
PRIMARY LOCATION: Oklahoma
POPULATION SIZE: 1,365 (1990 U.S. Census)

When they first encountered Europeans in the 1670's, the Illinois Indians occupied an area roughly equivalent to the present state of Illinois, though there is evidence that they had previously lived in present-day Michigan. They were among the largest tribes in the region, with an estimated population of thirteen thousand in the 1650's. The size of the tribe may explain its division into at least six subtribes: the Cahokia, Kaskaskia, Michigamea, Moingwena, Peoria, and Tamaroa. Though each of the subtribes had its own chief, all spoke the same language and acknowledged a single chief for the whole tribe.

The traditional economy of the tribe followed a yearly cycle of agriculture, hunting, and gathering. Crops were planted around summer villages;

then whole villages would embark on hunting expeditions before returning for the harvest. In winter, smaller groups would scatter to winter villages where hunting continued on a reduced scale.

The Illinois were often involved in warfare with other tribes, a pattern that continued after European contact. Several major wars were fought with the Iroquois in the seventeenth century, at times causing the Illinois to move west of the Mississippi River. The Sioux were also frequent enemies.

The decisive event in the Illinois's history came in 1673 when they established contact with the French. They subsequently became an independent ally of the French and heavily involved in the fur trade. The Illinois were involved in almost constant warfare with pro-British and pro-Spanish tribes, while disease, especially smallpox and malaria, periodically ravaged the tribe. French success in converting the Illinois to Christianity curtailed what had been a widespread practice of polygamy, with a depressing effect on the tribe's birthrate. By 1700 the number of Illinois had fallen to six thousand.

In the eighteenth and early nineteenth centuries, the tribe experienced significant fragmentation as subtribes often became divided in attitudes toward European powers or other tribes. The attempt to cultivate good relations with the new United States continued to expose the Illinois to attacks from pro-British Indians. All of these factors further weakened the Illinois until by 1800 the tribe's population had fallen to an estimated five hundred. By this time they had ceased to be a significant force in the region.

In 1832 the Illinois signed a treaty with the United States in which they gave up all their lands in Illinois except a small area around Kaskaskia (which was shortly abandoned). After several stops west of the Mississippi, the Illinois were assigned a reservation in the Indian Territory in 1867 in what is now northeastern Oklahoma. There the tribe came to be known as the Peorias and intermarried frequently with other tribes, especially the Sauk, Fox, and Kickapoo. Tribal numbers continued to decline before bottoming out in 1910, when only 130 Peorias were counted. The tribe was terminated by Congress in 1959 but was subsequently restored in 1978.

Ingalik

CULTURE AREA: Subarctic
LANGUAGE GROUP: Athapaskan
PRIMARY LOCATION: Yukon and lower Innoko rivers, Alaska
POPULATION SIZE: 600-650 (estimate)

The Ingalik were divided into two groups, the Yukon and Kuskokwim; both intermarried with contiguous Eskimo. Their dependence upon fish was reflected in rank, technology, and wealth. The Ingalik had permanent winter villages of semi-subterranean houses, and temporary spring and summer camps for exploiting a diversified food source by fishing, hunting, trapping, and limited gathering. The potlatch was one of seven major ceremonies involving redistribution of food, change of status, and promoting of group integration.

Russian fur traders and explorers established contact with the Ingalik in 1832, introducing the Russian Orthodox faith and, unfortunately, epidemics of smallpox. Some village populations were reduced by half. The Episcopalians, in 1887, and the Roman Catholics, in 1888, established churches and boarding schools. By 1900, the traditional Ingalik culture had met its demise through intermarriage with non-Ingalik peoples.

Little of the traditional culture now remains, except for some baskets of hide and birchbark and some woodworking. Employment is mostly with local resources, particularly as fishing and hunting guides. Some regional government work is available, and seasonal work is provided by utility companies. In the early 1990's, the Ingalik population was estimated to be between 600 and 650.

Inuit

CULTURE AREA: Arctic

LANGUAGE GROUP: Eskimo-Aleut

PRIMARY LOCATION: West Alaska, North Alaska, Arctic Canada (including Labrador), Greenland

POPULATION SIZE: 44,392 in Alaska (1990 U.S. Census); estimated 25,000 in Canada; estimated 46,000 in Greenland

The Inuit are one of the two major branches of the Eskimo family, the other being the Yupik of southwestern Alaska, southern Alaska, St. Lawrence Island, and Siberia. Inuit are distinguished from Yupik on the basis of both culture and language. The Inuit are distributed over the northern tier of the North American continent from Alaska to Greenland and have developed a lifestyle which allows for efficient adaptation to a cold and harsh habitat.

While the term "Inuit" (meaning "people") is an appropriate designation for all the northern Eskimo groups, there are more specific self-designations for different Inuit subgroups: "Iñupiat" in North Alaska, "Inuvialuit" in the western Canadian Arctic, "Inummaariit" in the eastern Canadian Arctic, and "Kalaallit" for Greenland.

Environment. With a few exceptions, most Inuit groups inhabit Arctic tundra north of the treeline. The climate is harsh and characterized by pronounced seasonality in temperature and light conditions. Those areas north of the Arctic Circle experience varying periods of continuous sunlight in midsummer and continuous darkness in midwinter. For example, in the community of Barrow, located at the northernmost tip of Alaska, the sun does not

Inuit woman with her child, in 1928.
(Library of Congress)

rise above the horizon for two months from November to January, while there is continuous sunlight from May through July. Because of extreme cold, high winds, and perennially frozen soil (permafrost), trees are unable to thrive in the Arctic. Even in summer, very little sunlight hits the Arctic, resulting in a low level of biological productivity for Arctic tundra, lakes, streams, and oceans. Because of this low level of productivity, most Inuit were forced to be at least seasonally nomadic in their subsistence efforts.

Physical Characteristics. Like the Aleut and Yupik, the Inuit display physical characteristics which indicate their relatively recent Eurasian origins. Eskimo-Aleut populations are more closely related genetically to Siberian groups such as the Chukchee and Koryak than to North American Indians living to the south. Many experts believe that the physical and linguistic evidence suggests that these groups represent a separate and more recent migration into the New World.

Archaeology and History. The Inuit are the direct descendants of Thule whale hunters who moved from Alaska into Arctic Canada and Greenland around the end of the first millennium c.e., a time coinciding with the Medieval Warming Period. The Thule are believed to have replaced the earlier Dorset populations, which had lived in these regions since about 3,000 years before the present. The linguistic and cultural uniformity of modern Inuit groups is the direct result of this rapid spread of Thule culture. As the Thule population spread throughout Greenland and northern Canada, different groups adapted to slightly different ecological conditions. During the Little Ice Age (1600-1850 C.E.), the climate once again cooled, resulting in changes in subsistence routines throughout most of the Eskimo region. This period led to the development of historic Inuit culture.

Contacts with Europeans probably first occurred sometime after the establishment of the Norse colonies in Greenland around 985 C.E. From the late sixteenth century onward, numerous naval expeditions set out from Europe in search of the Northwest Passage. These resulted in repeated, if fleeting, contacts with Inuit groups throughout the North. The intensification of whaling in the late nineteenth century had a more substantial impact upon Inuit groups throughout the Arctic. Not only did whalers initiate an active trade in southern manufactured goods, but they also introduced infectious diseases that took a substantial toll in lives in some areas. With the collapse of whaling at the beginning of the twentieth century, many Inuit took up trapping as a way to support themselves and obtain valued southern commodities offered by independent traders or large trading companies like the Hudson's Bay Company and the Alaska Commercial Company.

Economy and Subsistence. At contact, the Inuit were highly specialized hunters and fishers, utilizing a subsistence routine based upon the seasonal exploitation of both marine and land resources. For many groups, a summer "land" phase involved hunting and fishing in small, scattered family groups on the tundra, while a winter "maritime" phase involved exploitation of various marine mammals (whales, walrus, seals) either along the coast or on the frozen ocean, often in larger social groupings. Regional variation in subsistence routines was contingent upon ice conditions and the availability of game. In North Alaska, for example, walrus and bowhead whale hunting constituted an important part of subsistence efforts, while in certain regions of the Central Arctic, seals were the primary animal resource. In the interior regions of Alaska and Canada, Inuit groups were heavily dependent upon caribou herds.

Religion and Ritual. The religious practices of the Inuit, like those of all Eskimo groups, were largely oriented toward regulating human relationships with the animal spirit world. Shamanism was highly developed, and illness was usually explained with reference to violations of taboos. It was generally believed throughout the region that animals were not caught by hunters but gave themselves up to the individuals who followed the necessary rituals, maintained their equipment properly, and kept a respectful attitude toward the animals they hunted. Helping spirits and amulets were often important for hunting success. In most regions, ceremonies were followed to appease and thank the spirit of a recently caught animal. In the Central Arctic, it was common for a recently caught seal to be given a drink of fresh water. Considerably more elaborate procedures were followed in North Alaskan whaling communities to greet and thank the whale for giving itself up to a community, culminating at the end of whaling season with the Nalukatok (blanket toss) celebration.

Cold Adaptation. The primary method of adapting to the cold throughout the region was cultural. The preparation of tailored fur parkas, mitts, and boots was an essential survival strategy, especially in those areas with extreme subzero winter temperatures. The snowhouse of the Central Arctic Inuit and the semi-subterranean communal house of the West Greenlanders and North Alaskans were efficient in insulating their human inhabitants from the cold. Cold tolerance was also aided by a highly thermogenic diet based on fat and protein. Such diets were effective in raising the basal metabolic rate of the Inuit so they could withstand long periods of cold exposure. Some evidence also suggests that hereditary factors may be involved, since Inuits are reported to have a very efficient warming response (cold-induced vasodilation) in the extremities. Inuits are also documented to have fewer sweat glands on the body, a phenomenon which aids in keeping clothes dry and warm.

Modern Social and Political Status. The Inuit of Alaska, Canada, and Greenland now live in centralized villages and towns that are supported by schools, medical facilities, government offices, retail stores, and other social amenities. Many Inuit continue to be highly involved in subsistence hunting and fishing, often sharing harvested food with a large network of kinsmen. Hunting and fishing are now accomplished with the help of rifles, snowmobiles, all-terrain vehicles, and boats with inboard and outboard motors. In many communities, wage employment and social assistance are the primary means of support. Aside from the government sector, resource extraction industries employ many Inuit, often on a rotational basis. The Inuit arts and crafts industry has also been an important source of income for many communities.

A number of regional, national, and international Inuit organizations represent the interests of Inuit to various government agencies. The Inuit Circumpolar Conference, for example, was established in 1977 to bring together the Inuit and Yupik of the circumpolar North to address important social, political, economic, and environmental issues. Land claims settlements in Alaska and Canada have resulted in the creation of regional and village corporations which are active in northern investment and business development. Many of these corporations have a cultural resource component that sponsors archaeological and oral history research. In 1979, a Home

Rule government was established in Greenland, effectively releasing the Greenlanders from Danish colonialism. Although living standards and health conditions have improved dramatically for most Inuits, social problems such as suicide, alcohol and drug abuse, unemployment, and underemployment remain significant.

Richard G. Condon and Pamela R. Stern

Bibliography

Balikci, Asen. *The Netsilik Eskimos*. Garden City, N.Y.: Natural History Press, 1970.

Burch, Ernest S. *The Inupiaq Eskimo Nations of Northwest Alaska*. Fairbanks: University of Alaska Press, 1998.

Burch, Ernest S., and Werner Forman. *The Eskimos*. Norman: University of Oklahoma Press, 1988.

Chance, Norman A. *The Iñupiat and Arctic Alaska*. Fort Worth, Tex.: Holt, Rinehart and Winston, 1990.

Condon, Richard. *Inuit Youth: Growth and Change in the Canadian Arctic*. New Brunswick, N.J.: Rutgers University Press, 1987.

Damas, David, ed. *Arctic*. In *Handbook of North American Indians*, edited by William Sturtevant. Washington, D.C.: Smithsonian Institution Press, 1984.

Eber, Dorothy. *When the Whalers Were Up North: Inuit Memories from the Eastern Arctic*. Norman: University of Oklahoma Press, 1996.

Jacobs, Martina, and James Richardson, eds. *Arctic Life: Challenge to Survive*. Pittsburgh: Carnegie Museum of Natural History, 1983.

Langdon, Steve. *The Native People of Alaska*. 3d ed. Anchorage, Alaska: Greatland Graphics, 1993.

Lowry, Shannon, ed. *Natives of the Far North: Alaska's Vanishing Culture in the Eye of Edward Sheriff Curtis*. Mechanicsburg, Pa.: Stackpole Books, 1994.

McMillan, Alan D. *Native Peoples and Cultures of Canada: An Anthropological Overview*. 2d ed. Vancouver: Douglas & McIntyre, 1995.

Morrison, R. Bruce, and C. Roderick Wilson, eds. *Native Peoples: The Canadian Experience*. Toronto: McClelland & Stewart, 1995.

Notzke, Claudia. *Aboriginal Peoples and Natural Resources in Canada*. North York, Ont., Canada: Captus University Publications, 1994.

Iowa

CULTURE AREA: Plains
LANGUAGE GROUP: Siouan
PRIMARY LOCATION: Oklahoma, Nebraska/Kansas
POPULATION SIZE: 1,615 (1990 U.S. Census)

Sharing a common origin in the upper Great Lakes region with the linguistically related Winnebago, Oto, and Missouri tribes, the Iowas moved south and west from the Great Lakes at some point, probably in the early seventeenth century. Following the Mississippi River south from what is now Wisconsin, they settled at the confluence of the Iowa and Mississippi rivers, also migrating west at various times over the next centuries. The Iowas occupied parts of northern Missouri and southern Minnesota as well as much of what is now Iowa.

Reflecting their adaptation from a woodland to a plains environment, the Iowa economy was based on both female-oriented cultivation of crops such as corn, beans, and squash, and male-oriented hunting. The latter brought in deer, buffalo, beaver, raccoon, and otter meat. Iowa farming was known to be productive; a Frenchman who was setting up a trading post in their territory around 1700 persuaded them to move their village nearby because they were "industrious and accustomed to cultivate the earth." The Iowas were also known for their crafting and trade of catlinite pipes or calumets.

Their blending of Woodland and Plains cultures is evident in traditional Iowa choice of housing styles. At various times, they used four different types: oval or square bark houses (similar to eastern longhouses or wigwams), wattle-and-daub houses (southeastern in origin), the earthlodge, and the skin tipi (more common to the plains).

The Iowas had a complex clan system and were patrilineal (one belonged to the father's clan). Strict rules of marrying outside the clan were maintained. Clans were also the basis of political and religious officeholding, as chiefs and religious leaders were elected hereditarily in each clan. The main religious ceremony of the Iowas was the Medicine Dance, similar to those of Algonquian tribes around the Great Lakes. Mourning and burial practices were highly developed, and in the pre-reservation era especially, scaffold burial was practiced.

Although the name "Iowa" came from the French "*Aiaouez*" ("Ioway") and originally indicated "sleepy ones," the name for the Iowa people in their own Chiwere language, which they shared with the Winnebagos, Otos, and Missouris, was *"Pahoja,"* meaning "gray snow," "snow-covered," or "dusty ones." The reason for the name is unclear.

The seventeenth and eighteenth centuries brought increased warfare to the Iowa people; their primary enemies were the Dakota Sioux. Early in this period, they also warred with the Sauk and Mesquakie (Fox), but they later made peace and became closely associated with these people. By 1836, the Iowas had ceded all rights to their lands in Iowa and Missouri and settled along with the Sauk and Mesquakie people on a reservation of 400 square miles along the present Kansas-Nebraska state line. The reservation was reduced several times in the 1850's.

By the 1870's, the federal government attempted to move the Iowas to Indian Territory (now Oklahoma). A reservation was established for them there and some moved voluntarily, but others insisted on staying on the original reservation. Many of them had successfully blended into the surrounding farm economy. By 1890, both reservations had been allotted (divided into individual family plots), and the "surplus" land had been sold to non-Indians. When given the chance in the 1930's, both the Oklahoma and the Kansas-Nebraska Iowas set up tribal charters and constitutions, maintaining their political identity as a tribe. Culturally, both groups have outwardly blended with the surrounding non-Indian culture, although they are attempting to recover as much of their cultural heritage as possible.

Iroquois Confederacy

TRIBES AFFECTED: Cayuga, Mohawk, Onondaga, Oneida, Seneca, Tuscarora

CULTURE AREA: Northeast

LANGUAGE GROUP: Iroquoian

PRIMARY LOCATION: From the Ottawa River, Canada, south to Cumberland, Tennessee; from Maine west to Lake Michigan

POPULATION SIZE: 49,038 in U.S. (1990 U.S. Census); estimated 35,000 in Canada

The word "Iroquois" refers to all the tribes that speak dialects of the Iroquoian language group, including the Saint Lawrence, Mohawk, Cayuga, Onondaga, Oneida, Seneca, Tuscarora, Huron, Erie, Honniasonts or Mingues, and Susquehannock groups. Cherokee is also an Iroquoian language, but it is as different from the northern dialects of Iroquoian as German is from English. The Iroquois Confederacy, or Haudenosaunee

(People of the Longhouse), included the Mohawk, Oneida, Onondaga, Cayuga, Seneca, and, after 1722, the Tuscarora. The Longhouse People practiced extensive horticulture (centered on corn, beans, and squash) as well as fishing and hunting. They lived in fortified villages. They were little affected by European contact until after 1760, when the fall of New France in the French and Indian War opened the floodgates to English and American settlers; encroachment on Iroquois land began in earnest.

Three basic understandings were central to Iroquois life. First, all actions of individuals were based on personal decisions, and group action required consensus. Second, everybody shared; generosity and charity were paramount. Third, no one was separate from the web of life. Humankind was not outside nature, and the earth and the woodlands could be neither owned nor exploited.

European depiction of the sachem Atotarho (right), one of the founders of the Iroquois confederacy in the sixteenth century. (Library of Congress)

The Founding of the Confederacy. These central precepts were incorporated into the famous League of the Iroquois, or Iroquois Confederacy. Modern members of the original five tribes of the confederacy, to which was added the Tuscarora band in 1722, still celebrate in ritual and ceremony the founding of the league.

A Huron prophet, the Peacemaker (Deganawida), had a vision of a white pine which reached through the sky to communicate with the Master of Life.

277

An eagle perched atop the white pine was present to keep the peace and watch for intruders. This icon is now at the center of understanding of the Iroquois Confederacy, just as the tree of life is at the center of their cosmology. The tree's roots were the original Five Nations, Seneca (The Great Hill People), Cayuga (People at the Mucky Land), Onondaga (People on the Hills), Oneida (People of the Standing Stone), and Kenienghagas (Keepers of the Flint). "Mohawk," as the Kenienghagas are also known, is an Algonquian term meaning "cannibal." The soil around the tree was three principles: *skenno*, health of body and sanity of mind and peace between individuals and groups; *gaiiwiyo*, righteousness in conduct, thought, and deed, and equity in human rights; and *gashedenza*, faith and knowledge that spiritual power (*orenda*) is connected to governing and the maintenance of self-defense.

The league was probably founded between 1400 and 1600 (some scholars say between 1550 and 1600) in response to constant warfare among the tribes in the Northeast. Its purpose was to unify and pacify the infighting Iroquois and gain strength in numbers to resist the implacable opposition of both the Iroquois-speaking Huron tribe and the Algonquian-speaking people of the area.

The Haudenosaunee created a carefully constructed "constitution" that was transmitted from generation to generation orally from variously colored symbolic cues or mnemonics woven into belts of shells called wampum. (That "wampum" came to be translated as "money" or as valuable in commodity exchanges is an example of the different mindsets of Europeans and American Indians.) Originally, wampum belts passed on ritual, ceremonial, and mythological knowledge as well as political and social instructions.

Iroquois are known as great orators. Oral communication of the symbols on the wampum belts allowed speakers to become definers. The Great Law of Peace, with its social requirements and legal relationships, can take many hours, even days, to communicate.

At the onset the Onondaga were given the responsibility of keeping the central fire and sacred wampum belts. The Faithkeeper (central religious leader), always an Onondaga, calls a yearly council for the purposes of rehearing the constitution and laws and resolving differences. The council retains tribal relationships. Clan system relationships from ancient times define roles within the council. The traditional clan system was matrilineal; the oldest sensible woman of each clan of each tribe was designated in council with other tribal clan women to select a proportion of the fifty chiefs who made up the council. Chiefs served for life, but the clan mothers could remove chiefs from office for immoral or unethical behavior. Since clan mothers usually selected chiefs from their own lineage, each member of the council was answerable to the women of his maternal family. The power wielded by women had its roots in the early subsistence patterns of the five tribes, since they were dependent on agriculture.

The Confederacy in the Seventeenth Century. The Great Peace was spread by warfare. Warfare was visited on any tribe who did not accept the wampum belts of peace. In one week in March, 1649, as French Jesuit priests attested, the Five Nations essentially wiped out the Huron. Nine months later, the Petun people of western Michigan suffered the same fate. The Erie tribe, who outnumbered the Iroquois in population, were the next to fall. Those who were not killed were adopted; the Erie tribe ceased to exist. By 1700 the Five Nations, numbering fewer than thirty thousand people, were the political masters of an area from the Ottawa River in Canada south to the Cumberland in Tennessee and from Maine west to Lake Michigan. This hegemony remained in force for another 150 years.

The Five Nations of the Iroquois wrote a crucial chapter in American history. In the year 1609 Samuel de Champlain, a French fur trader and explorer, accompanied a war party of Huron and Algonquin on an expedition to the lake that now bears his name. Met by a war party of Mohawk who had never before encountered a musket, Champlain single-handedly killed three Mohawks with his firearms, scaring the others away in bewilderment and fear. This humiliation made the Mohawk doggedly hate the French from that time on. Within a few years, Five Nation Iroquois were purchasing guns from Dutch and English traders. The Hudson and Mohawk river valleys were opened to the English; the French were locked out. The subsequent British dominance in the New World was made easier by the political and military power of the Iroquois Confederacy and their hatred of the French. The opening of the frontier moved with the Iroquois and their conquering ways, not with the English or French. The Iroquois stood at a pivotal point and controlled the keys to the interior of the continent.

Following the year 1690, the Iroquois Confederacy developed a level of unity and cooperation that allowed them to capitalize on their pivotal position. They learned to play the various European traders one against the other in ways most beneficial to the Iroquois, and they followed a policy of independent neutrality with diplomatic artistry.

Colonial delegates from the Americas traveled to Albany to learn from the Iroquois. The longhouse sachems urged the colonists to form assemblies and meet to discuss common interests. In 1749 Benjamin Franklin asked, if Iroquois savages could govern themselves with such skill, how much better could the civilized English colonists do? In 1754 the first great intercolonial conference was held at Albany, and Iroquois delegates were in attendance.

Iroquois power in the eighteenth century reached the highest point of any Indian nation in North America. Yet the great orator chiefs who held the respect of all who negotiated with them had no personal wealth to display in the manner of the Europeans. "The chiefs are generally the poorest among them," wrote a Dutch pastor in Albany in 1640, "for instead of their receiving from the common people, they are obliged to give."

Origins, Warfare, and Religious Life. The Iroquois are a prime example of a group whose culture has a well-established pedigree. Archaeological evidence suggests a long period of occupancy in New York State in a cultural continuum of a thousand to fifteen hundred years. A subsistence model culture called Owasco preceded the Iroquois, and its influences are reflected in Iroquois legends and in the design of Iroquois personal clay pipes. The Iroquois carried the highly distinctive Owasco clay pipe designs to another step with more skillful carving and more elaboration in bowl shape. Owasco was preceded by the mound-building cultures of the Hopewell era (Hopewell burial attitudes were reflected in later Huron attitudes toward the dead). By 1400 C.E., proto-Iroquois villages existed, and by 1600 the culture was distinctive to the level that the people referred to themselves as Haudenosaunee.

The Iroquoian speakers of the Eastern Woodlands seemed always to be in a state of war. Before the establishment of the League of Five Nations, war was a ritual, a means of advancing individual or group prestige. Wars were fought primarily for revenge, and such warfare had degenerated into unavoidable ongoing feuds by the time of the emergence of the principles of the Peacemaker (perhaps around 1570). After the establishment of the confederacy, which ended intertribal blood feuds and instead established a spiritual reason for warrior societies, wars became conquests to expand hunting grounds and dominate neighbors—to "make women of them" if they did not accept participation in the confederacy.

The foundation of the Iroquois confederacy was the fireplace, composed of a mother and her children. Each hearth was a part of a larger *owachira*, a related or extended family traced through the mother. Two or more owachiras made a clan, and eight clans made a tribe.

Religious life was highly organized and included a priesthood of three men and three women who supervised the keeping of the faith. Even though the Iroquois are most noted for their strongly defined and impressive governing organization in which politics dovetailed with complex matrilineal associations, the Five Nations are also well known for their elaborate religious practices. Their cosmology was well defined, and their mythology was more detailed then the origin stories in the Bible. Anthropomorphic deities and complex ceremonies as well as a highly developed theology using impersonal spiritual power have not, even to this day, entirely disappeared. As with all the religious practices indigenous to North America, curing was a central part of the religious life day to day. The Iroquois also had a profound sense of the psychology of the soul and used dreams to communicate with the spirits. The mythological base of the league organization and curing societies formed a stable and traditional charter which has resulted in continuity among the Iroquois to this day despite the overwhelming influx of the Europeans.

The American Revolution to the Present. Iroquois power and strength as a confederacy grew until the American Revolution, when the tribes were divided in their allegiances to the British and the Americans. The westernmost tribes of the league were assaulted, burned out, and chased into Canada by General Sullivan's campaign of 1777. George Washington ordered the invasion of Iroquois land in order to seize land with which to pay both his troops and the Dutch bankers who were financing the revolution at that time. The effects of the American Revolution ended the military power of the Iroquois Confederacy.

The Iroquois, despite conflict and contact with European influences from the earliest times, have retained their social being and many of their cultural practices, including kinship and ceremonial ties. Midwinter ceremonies are still practiced, along with green corn and harvest thanksgiving ceremonies. Condolence songs are still sung when the maple sap flows. The firm base of the People of the Longhouse persists to this day and is still a viable model for the future.

Glenn J. Schiffman

Bibliography

Fenton, William N. *The Great Law and the Longhouse: A Political History of the Iroquois Confederacy*. Norman: University of Oklahoma Press, 1998.

Gramly, Richard M. *Two Early Historic Iroquoian Sites in Western New York*. Buffalo, N.Y.: Persimmon Press, 1996.

Henry, Thomas R. *Wilderness Messiah: The Story of Hiawatha and the Iroquois*. New York: Bonanza Books, 1955.

Josephy, Alvin M., Jr., ed. *The American Heritage Book of Indians*. New York: Simon & Schuster, 1961.

_____ . *The Indian Heritage of America*. New York: Alfred A. Knopf, 1968.

Mintz, Max M. *Seeds of Empire: The American Revolutionary Conquest of the Iroquois*. New York: New York University Press, 1999.

Shimony, Annemarie A. *Conservatism Among the Iroquois at the Six Nations Reserve*. Syracuse, N.Y.: Syracuse University Press, 1994.

Spencer, Robert F., Jess D. Jennings, et al. *The Native Americans.* 2d ed. New York: Harper & Row, 1977.

Taylor, Colin F., ed. *The Native Americans: The Indigenous People of North America.* New York: Smithmark, 1991.

Juaneño

CULTURE AREA: California
LANGUAGE GROUP: Takic
PRIMARY LOCATION: San Juan and San Mateo river drainages, California
POPULATION SIZE: 1,565 (1990 U.S. Census)

The Juaneño were river-oriented bands or tribelets living in sedentary, self-sufficient, autonomous villages of conical subterranean houses thatched with bark or tules. They exercised control over territorial rights and resources, living northwest of the Luiseño. Their subsistence was based on hunting, trapping, gathering, collecting, and fishing, with acorns and seeds constituting more than half of their food.

The first European contact with the Juaneño was by the Gaspar de Portolá expedition in 1769. In 1776, the San Juan Capistrano Mission was established among the Juaneño. In 1834, the missions were secularized, causing revolts against Mexican rancheros by Indians who were treated like serfs. Indian groups became dispersed and, despite continuing strife, many individuals became wage-earners. When Anglo-Americans entered California, even more Indians lost control of their land. Reservations at La Jolla, Pala, Potrero, and Yapiche were established in 1875.

By the 1960's, many Juaneño had been graduated from college and begun to work as professionals and in skilled labor. Numerous religions are currently practiced, and only a few elders speak the tribe's language or follow traditional beliefs.

Kalapuya

CULTURE AREA: Northwest Coast
LANGUAGE GROUP: Kalapuyan
PRIMARY LOCATION: Willamette River, Oregon
POPULATION SIZE: 50 (1990 U.S. Census)

The patrilineal, socially stratified Kalapuya (or Calapooya) people comprised approximately thirteen autonomous tribes, each with dialectic differences. Subsistence was mainly from camas and other seeds, nuts, roots, and tubers, supplemented by hunting and trapping. The Kalapuya occupied multifamily dwellings in permanent villages during the winter, and temporary shelters in spring, summer, and fall. Chieftainship was probably passed on from father to son.

First contact with European Americans occurred in 1812 with Donald McKenzie of the Pacific Fur Company and continued until the 1840's with fur traders, missionaries, and settlers, who introduced various debilitating diseases, including malaria. In 1855 treaties embracing all the Kalapuya were enacted; most of the Kalapuya were resettled on the Grande Ronde Reservation, where many Kalapuya intermarried with other groups.

In 1956 the Grande Ronde Reservation was terminated by the federal government. Indians living there reorganized themselves as the Confederated Tribes of Grande Ronde in 1974; in 1975, they incorporated as a nonprofit organization.

Kalispel

CULTURE AREA: Plateau
LANGUAGE GROUP: Salishan
PRIMARY LOCATION: Idaho, Montana
POPULATION SIZE: 210 (1990 U.S. Census)

The Kalispel, also known as the Pend d'Oreille, belong to the Plateau tribes, with their land base covering part of the Columbia River basin. Their location in northern Idaho and western Montana placed them on the eastern boundaries of the Plateau tribes. As European American contact pushed the Plains Indians farther west, the Kalispel were also affected; they were pushed farther west by tribes such as the Blackfoot.

The Kalispel comprised two groups: the Upper Pend d'Oreille, or Upper Kalispel, who lived below Flathead Lake in northwestern Montana, and the Lower Pend d'Oreille, or Lower Kalispel, who occupied areas along the Clark Fork River and Pend Oreille Lake in northern Idaho. The Kalispel had contact with other tribes throughout the area, including the Spokane, Kutenai, and Flathead. Their economy depended on gathering roots and berries and on fishing. Unlike tribes such as the Nez Perce, whose culture greatly changed with use of horses and firearms (they began to hunt buf-

Early twentieth century Kalispel girl
(Library of Congress)

falo), the Kalispel continued to rely on traditional food sources and live a traditional Plateau lifestyle.

Initial Kalispel contact with European Americans began with fur traders. In the early 1820's, Alexander Ross of the Hudson's Bay Company managed the Flathead House (near present-day Missoula, Montana) and traded with the Kalispel, Flathead, Kutenai, and Nez Perce. Further contact with European Americans occurred with the arrival of Jesuit missionaries. Similar to the Flathead, who welcomed the arrival of the "Black Robes," the Kalispel (both Upper and Lower) gave a kind reception to the Jesuits. According to legend, by the time a missionary arrived at the Lower Kalispel camp in 1842, the people already were well-versed in Christianity, having sent one of their members the previous year to the Flathead tribe to learn the faith. Many of the Upper Kalispel were later baptized. In 1844, St. Ignatius Mission was established among the Kalispel.

Traffic across their area increased, and by 1845 settlers had begun moving into the territory. In July, 1855, Washington Territorial Governor and Territorial Superintendent of Indian Affairs Isaac I. Stevens met with the Flathead, Kalispel, and Kutenai on the Hell Gate River to negotiate a treaty. In the final Hell Gate Treaty, the tribes ceded 25,000 acres to the federal government, and the Flathead chief, Victor, became head of the combined tribes. The three tribes were to be removed to the Jocko or Flathead Reservation, which covered 1,280,000 acres, near Flathead Lake. Two problems ensued. First, of the Kalispel tribe, only the Upper Kalispel signed the treaty; the Lower Kalispel were unable to travel to the negotiations because of the Yakima War. Later, most would not move to the Flathead Reservation. Second, the Flathead tribe split over the issue of removal, and many of its members remained in the Bitterroot Valley for almost forty years before accepting removal.

For the Upper Kalispel who conceded their claims and consented to removal, life during the first years on the Flathead Reservation was very poor and very difficult. In more recent times, the situation has improved; the reservation now derives income from tourist activities, timber, grazing leases, and a hydropower lease. The tribes have also been successful with several claims filed with the Indian Claims Commission. Under the Indian Reorganization Act, the tribes organized in 1935 and later became known as the Confederated Salish and Kootenai Tribes of the Flathead Reservation.

The Lower Kalispel who refused to move to the Flathead Reservation continued to live in the area surrounding Lake Pend Oreille and the Pend Oreille River. White settlement in the area persisted. Finally, in 1914, the remaining members of the Lower Kalispel were granted a reservation of almost 5,000 acres on the Pend Oreille River. The tribe organized in 1939 and is known as the Kalispel Indian Community, Kalispel Reservation. Their numbers are very small, and the economy is limited. Income is derived from grazing leases and some industry. The tribe has been successful in its claims with the Indian Claims Commission for lost territory.

Kamia

CULTURE AREA: California
LANGUAGE GROUP: Yuman
PRIMARY LOCATION: Coastal area of the west Baja and California border
POPULATION: 1,640 (1990 U.S. Census)

The Kamia include the Tipai and Ipai. The Ipai spoke a northern dialect and the Tipai a southern dialect—both being autonomous, semi-nomadic bands with thirty exogamous, localized patrilineal clans. Though bands controlled communal land, springs were always available to anyone.

The Kamia were greatly influenced from 1769 to 1821 by Spanish Franciscan and Dominican missionaries. Initially, the Tipai-Ipai resisted conversion and missionization. By 1779, however, many had adapted to mission life. In 1834, Mexico secularized all Spanish missions, with half the land going to Indians. This policy failed, however, as the Indians were treated as serfs. In 1875, the first Tipai-Ipai reservation was established. Many Indians continued to labor in mines and on ranches, and to relocate to urban settings.

By 1968, the Tipai-Ipai had twelve reservations, sharing the Pala Reservation with Takic speakers. Despite religious factionalism, Roman Catholicism is the dominant faith. Some aspects of traditional life are still followed.

Kansa

CULTURE AREA: Plains
LANGUAGE GROUP: Siouan
PRIMARY LOCATION: Oklahoma
POPULATION SIZE: 1,073 (1990 U.S. Census)

The Kansa, or Kaw, tribe, along with the Osage, Quapaw, Omaha, and Ponca, form the Dhegiha branch of the Siouan language family. The Kansa language was most similar to the Osage tongue. A relatively small tribe, the Kansa people numbered about 1,500 in 1700; by 1905 they were reduced to around 200 people, of whom only about 90 were full-bloods. Their population has rebounded considerably since then.

Tribal Name and Origin. In the sixteenth century, the Kansas were living in western Missouri and eastern Kansas, at the confluence of the Missouri and Kaw (Kansas) rivers. The origin of the name Kansa is not clear, but it was probably first used by the Spanish and then by the French, as they came in contact with this group. When Juan de Oñate traveled northeast from what is now New Mexico in 1601, he encountered a group which he called the *Escanseques*, meaning "those who stir up trouble." Indeed, the Kansa Nation developed a reputation for belligerence in subsequent centuries. Yet the word *Escanjaques* was spoken by these Indians themselves as they made a sign of peace with their hands on their breasts. In the late seventeenth century, Father Jacques Marquette and other French explorers were using the spellings "Kansa(s)" and "Kanse(s)." There is also a tradition that this root word designates "wind people" or "people of the south wind," stressing their geographic location in the sixteenth century and after in a region known for powerful winds.

The Kansa people called themselves Hutanga, meaning "by the edge of the shore," relating to their possible origins well before the sixteenth century near the Atlantic Ocean. Kansa legends support this history. From that origin well east of the Mississippi some time before 1600, the Kansa people moved west along with others of the Dhegiha linguistic group. A major separation of these Dhegiha relatives occurred at the mouth of the Ohio River, with the Quapaws (meaning "the downstream people") journeying down the Mississippi River and the Omahas ("those going against the wind or current") ascending the river. The remaining groups (Kansa, Ponca, and Osage) followed the Mississippi to the mouth of the Missouri near present-day St. Louis. The Osages remained in the lower Missouri Valley in and around the river valley which bears their name, while the Poncas traveled farther north along the Missouri. The Kansas settled around the confluence of the Kansas (or Kaw) and Missouri rivers. They were in the lower Kansas Valley when the Spanish and French made their first contacts with them.

Contact with Europeans and Americans. Spanish contact was slight, but French relations with the Kansa tribe were significant, lasting more than a century. By the late seventeenth century, French traders had established a fairly regularized trading relationship with the Kansas, bringing them into the fur trade. Hence, they were exposed regularly to French trade goods as well as French people and culture for some time before the Kansas and Missouri valley areas became American territory. Up to the 1850's, French fur trading families maintained a presence in Kansa territory to pursue the lucrative trade with this industrious tribe. French missionaries also attempted to leave their mark on these people starting in the 1720's at Forts Bourgmont and Cavagnial, established by the French in the early 1700's to pursue the fur trade with the Kansa and Osage tribes.

By the 1820's, there was a significant métis (French for "mixed-blood") community living in the lower Kansas (Kaw) Valley, a product of intermarriage between the Kansas and the French. This group spoke French as well as the Kansa language and practiced Roman Catholicism. They were accepted by neither Kansa society nor the emerging Anglo-American community encroaching on Kansa territory by that time. The U.S. government arranged differential land grants to the two groups in an 1825 treaty, the outcome of which was the pitting of the "half-bloods" and "full-bloods" against each other. Another outcome of this 1825 treaty was that the Kansa tribe ceded all of their lands in Missouri in exchange for the land grants (2 million acres) in eastern Kansas.

By 1846, another treaty ceded all those 2 million acres and sent both groups of Kansa descendants to a 265,000-acre reservation on the Neosho River farther southwest in Kansas. With very little success, Baptist, Methodist, and Presbyterian missionaries attempted to Christianize the Kansa people at a mission on the Neosho and later in Indian Territory (now Oklahoma), where the Kansa people moved in 1873. From that point on, the metis and full-blood Kansas were undifferentiated by the U.S. government. The Kansa reservation in Oklahoma was allotted in severalty (parceled out to individual families) in 1902, and consequently the tribe was no longer recognized by the U.S. government as a legal entity. By the late twentieth century, however, there was a movement to revive cultural awareness and preserve the Kansa tribal heritage.

Traditional Culture. The Kansa Nation was divided culturally into sixteen clans. Each clan included several extended families, some reckoned matrilineally, some patrilineally. Villages chose leaders who represented them in tribal-level council meetings, and war "chiefs" were chosen on an ad hoc basis. Kansa villages consisted of anywhere from 80 to 130 earthlodges, each holding an extended family and arranged according to clans.

The Kansas were traditionally matrilocal, in that a married couple would live with the wife's family and the oldest woman of an extended family was the head of each household. Women owned the round or oval wood-framed earthlodges, which were anywhere from 30 to 60 feet in diameter, depending on the size of the family. Women also controlled crop lands, as they were the farmers. Cultivating corn, beans, pumpkins, and other crops, women also gathered prairie potatoes and made much of the clothing. Men hunted a variety of game, but as time went on, buffalo became the primary concern, not only for their plentiful meat but also for hides used in making clothing and for trade with the French (and later the Americans). When French forts were in operation along the Missouri River, these Europeans traded with the Kansa people not only for buffalo hides and beaver furs but also for agricultural produce. The Kansas were industrious and successful hunters and farmers. Many of their descendants still farm in eastern Oklahoma

Gretchen L. Green

Bibliography

Bushnell, David I. *Villages of the Algonquian, Siouan, and Caddoan Tribes West of the Mississippi*. Bulletin 83. Washington, D.C.: Bureau of American Ethnology, 1927.

Hoffhaus, Charles E. *Chez les Canses*. Kansas City, Mo.: Lowell Press, 1984.

Miner, Craig, and William E. Unrau. *The End of Indian Kansas, A Study of Cultural Revolution, 1854-1871*. Lawrence: Regents Press of Kansas, 1978.

Unrau, William E. *The Kansa Indians: A History of the Wind People, 1673-1873*. Norman: University of Oklahoma Press, 1971.

_____. *The Kaw People*. Phoenix, Ariz.: Indian Tribal Series, 1975.

_____. *Mixed-bloods and Tribal Dissolution: Charles Curtis and the Quest for Indian Identity*. Lawrence: University Press of Kansas, 1989.

Karankawa

CULTURE AREA: Southeast

LANGUAGE GROUP: Karankawa

PRIMARY LOCATION: East coast of Mexico north of Tamaulipas, south Texas coast

Over the centuries the Karankawa people developed a lifeway measured by the land and the gulf upon which they depended. They lived amid riches in terms of game and fish, and they cultivated foodstuffs. They moved in dugouts or skiffs on seasonal rotation from the river valleys to the bay inlets along the coast, ranging from West Galveston Bay on the north to the Laguna Madre south of the Rio Grande. The Karankawa never exceeded ten thousand people.

Over thousands of years they nurtured a knowledge of the animals, the plants, the earth, and the sea, upon all of which their existence depended. Karankawa knowledge was passed carefully from one generation to the next. The Karankawa fished the bays and inlets from their dugout canoes, exploiting redfish, snapper, flounder, and green sea turtle; they gathered sea bird eggs and shellfish. They hunted buffalo and deer as well as smaller game, and they cultivated blackberry bushes, arrowroot, and potatoes and collected pecans, acorns, and prickly pear.

The Karankawa were spiritually centered people. People paused no matter what they were doing as the sun disappeared behind the horizon. They stood observing the sunset as a system of beauty of which they were a part. Formal celebrations were held at the time of the full moon, and they involved the use of "black drink" or yaupon tea. Music was made with song and instruments—gourd rattles, carved wooden rasps, and cedar flutes. Their sense of being included the marshes, bays, salt flats, brush, and dunes as they established patterns of sustainable behavior in the ecosystem. Karankawa people understood the changes that form the design of the coastal land and the borders of the gulf.

The site of their villages was always close to the shore or bluff. They bathed every day in the salt water, and they used shark's oil as protection against mosquitoes. The people were tall, and most were in excellent physical condition. They lived in structures made of woven mats of cane, tanned skins, and hides that covered a structurally sound framework of willow and oak resting on foundations of oyster shell. These structures sheltered the Karankawa from the winds and the rains of fall and winter.

In the late seventeenth and early eighteenth centuries, the Karankawa maneuvered diplomatically between the French and the Spanish. The mission Espiritu Santa de Zuniga was founded in 1722 specifically to influence the Karankawa, but this effort failed within a few years. Some Karankawa people did seek the protection of other missions in the late eighteenth century. Early in the nineteenth century, the Karankawa began to face the Anglo-Americans who moved into the region. Pressure increased until they migrated from Texas south of the Rio Grande into the state of Tamaulipas, Mexico, where they sought sanctuary.

Karok

CULTURE AREA: California
LANGUAGE GROUP: Karok
PRIMARY LOCATION: Northwestern California
POPULATION SIZE: 2,978 (1990 U.S. Census)

The Karok Indians occupied the northwestern corner of California. They subsisted by fishing, hunting, and gathering; tobacco was the only plant cultivated. The Karok used nets, harpoons, and clubs to catch salmon and other fish. Tribesmen used dogs, decoys, bows and arrows, and snares to hunt large animals such as deer and elk. Surplus meat was dried on scaffolds for winter use. Acorns, bulbs, seeds, and nuts were gathered and ground into flour.

Rectangular, semi-subterranean, single-family homes were constructed with cedar planks; they had small low doorways and stone porches. Men wore buckskin breechclouts or went naked; women wore deerskin skirts. Both wore fur capes and snowshoes during the winter.

Karok woman preparing food in a traditional mush basket. (Library of Congress)

The Karok placed great importance on acquiring and retaining wealth. Riches were in the form of shells, obsidian blades, and woodpecker scalps. The wealthiest person in the group also held the most respect and prestige. Dances were performed to ensure good fishing and hunting, as well as to cure sick children. These ceremonies included displays of wealth and religious rites performed by priests. Everyday life was filled with taboos, and rituals were performed regularly to fend off illness and bad luck. Shamans were usually women, who used herbal medicines or orally sucked out the "pain" that was causing the illness.

In the early 1800's, Hudson's Bay Company traders were the first white people to make contact with the Karok. In the 1850's, gold miners flooded into Karok territory and violent clashes ensued. Whites burned most of the Indian towns, and the Karok fled to the mountains.

In the late nineteenth century, mining prospects died out and many whites left. A number of half-white children were left behind. In the 1870's, many Karoks participated in the Ghost Dance religion. Ghost Dancers believed that the dances and rituals they performed would bring back dead Indians and a more traditional way of life. No reservations were set aside for Karok Indians, but several moved to Scott Valley, a Shasta reservation.

Kaska

CULTURE AREA: Subarctic
LANGUAGE GROUP: Athapaskan
PRIMARY LOCATION: North-central British Columbia, southern Yukon Territory
POPULATION SIZE: 705 (Statistics Canada, based on 1991 census)

The Kaska were territorially divided into two bands, the Upper Laird and the Dease River. They had matriarchal moieties (Wolf and Crow). The household was the main socioeconomic unit, relying mostly upon fishing, supplemented with hunting, trapping, and late-summer gathering. Trade goods were transported, according to season and terrain, by toboggans, snowshoes, dugouts, bark canoes, and mooseskin boats.

European American contact with the Kaska was established in the 1820's by the Hudson's Bay Company, primarily for fur trading—which, with the introduction of disease, brought numerous cultural changes. In 1873, gold miners first encroached upon Kaska territory. In 1897-1898, the route to the Klondike crossed their land. Roman Catholic and Protestant missionaries also brought about significant cultural changes, and by 1945 all Kaska were nominally Roman Catholic. The greatest sustained change came in 1942 with construction of the Alaskan Highway. The Kaska now have essentially a cash economy, supported by seasonal employment with fishing and guiding services that cater to hunting parties.

Kawaiisu

CULTURE AREA: Great Basin
LANGUAGE GROUP: Kawaiisu
PRIMARY LOCATION: Sierra Nevada, Piute, and Tehachapi mountains, California

As hunters and gatherers, the Kawaiisu were omnivorous in their diet, though deer meat was a favored food. They collected and stored a wide variety of roots, tubers, nuts, berries, and seeds. Acorns were stored in granaries; before eating, the tannic acid was removed by leaching. Most animals were hunted or trapped, and fishing, though minimal, supplemented their diet.

In 1776, Francisco Garcé became the first European to record contact with the Kawaiisu; John Frémont traversed their region in 1844. By the early 1850's, farmers, trappers, and stockmen occupied Kawaiisu territory, along with prospectors—all of whose activities led to ongoing conflict. In 1863, after reports of an intertribal grouping of Indians, a contingent of soldiers under Captain Moses McLaughlin killed thirty-five unarmed Indians. The introduction of disease also reduced the Kawaiisu population, from an estimated 500 to about 150 by 1910. Anthropologists believe that, by 1960, all aspects of tribal life were gone. In the 1990 U.S. Census, only two people identified themselves as Kawaiisu.

Kichai

CULTURE AREA: Plains
LANGUAGE GROUP: Caddoan
PRIMARY LOCATION: Oklahoma

The Kichai (also spelled Kitsei), a branch of the Caddoan family, lived in what is now Texas, Oklahoma, and Kansas. The Caddo tribes had inhabited the southern Great Plains for thousands of years. "Caddo" is a shortened form of *Kadohadacho* ("real chiefs"). The Caddo, the most culturally advanced peoples of the southern Plains, lived in round thatched houses in permanent villages. They were skilled agriculturalists as well as expert hunters, and they were known for their beautiful pottery and weaving. *Kitsash*, the name the Kichai had for themselves, means "going in wet sand"; the Pawnee called them "water turtles." Their first recorded contact with whites was in 1701, when they encountered the French in eastern Louisiana. They remained friendly with the French from that time. Throughout the eighteenth and early nineteenth centuries, their population decreased as they fell victim to new diseases carried by the Spanish, French, and British and as they fought with European and Mexican invaders. In 1855, they were assigned by the United States to a small reservation on the Brazos River. Three years later, they were pushed aside and killed in large numbers by Texans who wanted their land. The Kichai fled north to Oklahoma and merged with the Wichita; they were absorbed by that tribe and lost their own identity. The last speaker of the Kichai language died in the 1930's.

Kickapoo

CULTURE AREA: Northeast
LANGUAGE GROUP: Algonquian
PRIMARY LOCATION: Kansas, Mexico, Oklahoma
POPULATION SIZE: 3,577 in U.S. (1990 U.S. Census); estimated 400-500 in Mexico

Kickapoo comes from the Indian *Kiwegapaw*, meaning "He stands about," or "He moves about, standing now here, now there."

The Kickapoo lived originally in eastern Michigan with the Sauk and Fox, with whom they were most closely related culturally, ethnically, and linguistically, out of the twenty-some Algonquian tribes living in this geographic area. The Kickapoo first appear in historical accounts in the late 1660's, at which time their population was about three thousand.

The Kickapoo lived in fixed villages during the spring and summer, when their economy was primarily agricultural. They grew crops of corn, beans, and squash and gathered roots and berries. During the autumn and winter they were nomadic, hunting animals, especially buffalo, across the Mississippi River. The Kickapoo lived in oval-shaped houses with frameworks made from green saplings and covered with bark or cattail mats. Each house was built with a smoke hole in the roof, and the door always faced east. The principal Kickapoo crafts were woodworking and pottery. They were known for their wood cradleboards, ladles, and bowls.

The Kickapoo were organized into clans, or *gens*. Marriage was always outside one's gen, and children belonged to the gen of their father. The

Kickapoo had a rich mythology, centering on their belief in a cosmic substance that pervaded nature and was given special reverence. Their supreme being was Kicihiata, who lived in the sky and created earth and everything on it. Other spirits existed in earthly objects, as well as throughout the universe. Dogs were given particular significance and were sacrificed to the spirits. Their cultural hero was Wisaka, and their great cosmic myth focused on the death of Wisaka's younger brother. To him were credited all of life's good things and the hope of life in the spirit world after death, which was presided over by the younger brother. The dead were buried in village graveyards with their feet pointed west, toward the land of the dead. Priests conducted the religious life of the Kickapoo. The most important ceremony and feast was a week-long event in spring that centered on opening and restoring sacred bundles.

Although originating in eastern Michigan, the Kickapoo had been driven by the Iroquois and Sioux west into Wisconsin by the mid-1600's, where they had their first contacts with whites, the French. Unlike other Algonquian tribes, the Kickapoo were extremely conservative and independent in their attitudes toward the French and later toward the British and Americans. Their history is one of resistance to any attempts by whites to acculturate them politically, economically, or religiously.

After being driven out of their native home by the Iroquois and Sioux, the Kickapoo formed a powerful confederacy with the Fox and Mascouten tribes and waged effective warfare against the French, Iroquois, and Sioux. Around 1716, the Kickapoo turned on the Illinois Confederacy to their south, and by 1765 they occupied Illinois lands. Through the late 1700's and early 1800's, their history was characterized by a series of shifting alliances with the French, British, Spanish, Americans, and other Indian tribes.

The inexorable European American movement westward resulted in government pressure on the Kickapoo to leave their lands and move farther west, to Kansas and Missouri, which they did by 1834. Over the next thirty years, difficulties with squatters and questionable appropriation of their land by government treaties resulted in a small band of disaffected Kickapoo migrating to Mexico in 1838, where they were joined by another band in 1863, becoming known as the Mexican Kickapoo. Because of their depredations against Texans in cross-border raids, however, the U.S. government attempted to persuade these Kickapoo through warfare and negotiation to return to the United States. A number did, settling in Kansas and Oklahoma. The Kickapoo in Missouri eventually settled in Kansas. The modern Kickapoo reside on reservations in Kansas, Oklahoma, and Mexico.

The Kickapoo gave up their warlike ways and became successful farmers. All along, however, the chiefs and headmen worked hard to resist the cultural, social, and religious influences of the white culture. The pride and spirit of being a Kickapoo were instilled in the tribe. A course of conciliation with whites only when it was necessary to do so in order to survive was adopted. The Kickapoo have been remarkably successful in adhering to their old ways. As a result, the Kickapoo have retained their proud and fierce independence. Among modern Indian tribes, the Kickapoo culture is perhaps the purest of all Indian cultures.

Laurence Miller

Kiowa

CULTURE AREA: Plains
LANGUAGE GROUP: Kiowa-Tanoan (Uto-Aztecan)
PRIMARY LOCATION: Oklahoma
POPULATION SIZE: 9,421 (1990 U.S. Census)

The Kiowas, whose language is related to the Rio Grande Pueblo Indians, originally lived in western Montana. The earliest Kiowa villages in this area date to the early 1600's. The Kiowas (Kiowa means "main people") moved a century later to the Yellowstone River region in eastern Montana and eventually settled in the Black Hills of South Dakota. Here they traded with the Mandans, learned how to use horses, and began hunting buffalo. They also became noted for their military exploits and organized their tribe into military societies. As nomadic hunters they followed buffalo herds, lived in tipis, worshiped a sun god (Taimay), and performed the Sun Dance. Unlike other Plains tribes, however, Kiowas did not allow violence or self-torture during performance of the eight-day Sun Dance ceremony. Kiowa warriors fasted, prayed, exchanged sacred medicine bundles, and did penance but did not mutilate their bodies with knives or spears as did the Mandans.

Kiowas frequently fought wars against Caddos, Utes, Apaches, Arapahos, Cheyennes, and other Plains tribes. Among the Kiowa, membership in the warrior society called the "Principal Dogs," or "Ten Bravest," was highly sought after and esteemed. Only ten warriors who had repeatedly demonstrated the greatest bravery in battle could belong. The leader of the Principal Dogs wore a long sash over his shoulder when going into battle. When the fighting began he got off his horse, anchored his sash to the ground with his spear, and stood at that spot, shouting encouragement to his comrades. He could not leave his post until another Principal Dog pulled his sash from the ground.

Kiowa leader Kicking Bird led a peace faction during the 1860's and 1870's.
(National Archives)

In the 1780's the Sioux drove the Kiowas from the Black Hills, and they moved farther south into Nebraska, Kansas, and northern Oklahoma. The American explorers Meriwether Lewis and William Clark reported meeting Kiowas along the North Platte River in 1805. Comanche Indians living in the areas originally fought off the Kiowas, but the two eventually formed an alliance that lasted into the twentieth century. In their new homeland, the Kiowas continued to hunt buffalo and raid their enemies, chiefly the Apaches and Cheyennes, taking horses and territory. Peace accords were reached in the 1830's when new enemies appeared: American pioneers and traders on the Santa Fe and Butterfield trails. In the "Kiowa Wars" of the 1830's and 1840's, Plains Indians fought together against whites moving through the region on wagon trains or cattle drives. The Great Plains were not yet the destination of these migrants, because many saw the region as too empty, hot, and dry to support any type of agriculture, and called it the Great American Desert. They simply moved through the Plains heading for California and Oregon, which had more hospitable climates.

These views changed after the Civil War, however, when the Plains were considered ready for settlement because of the introduction of railroads. This postwar movement of white settlers into the center of Indian country led to another series of wars in the 1870's. The Kiowas debated how to deal with this new intrusion. Kicking Bird and Little Mountain, two principal chiefs, wanted peace, but Satank (Sitting Bear) and Satanta (White Bear), leader of the Principal Dogs, called for war. Satanta led several raids into Texas, and the Red River War of 1874-1875 began. The war faction killed Kicking Bird when he continued to oppose violent conflict. Satanta became chief but was captured by George Armstrong Custer's cavalry forces and sentenced to prison. In 1878 he took his own life, jumping from a prison hospital window in Huntsville, Texas. Other Kiowa leaders suffered similar violent deaths, Satank was shot while trying to escape from the Fort Sill,

Oklahoma, prison, and Sky Walker, the Kiowa religious leader, died in a Florida prison. Most of these Kiowa warriors were buried at Fort Sill in a cemetery referred to as the "Indian Arlington."

By 1878 most of the Kiowas had submitted to living on a reservation in southeastern Oklahoma. The modern tribe has its headquarters in Caddo County and survives by raising cattle, farming, and leasing oil rights to their land. Kiowa artworks are on display at the Southern Plains Indian Museum and Craft Center in Anadarko. Perhaps the most famous living Kiowa is N. Scott Momaday, a novelist and professor of comparative literature, who won a Pulitzer Prize in 1969 for his novel *House Made of Dawn* (1968), a sensitive portrayal of a Native American in conflict between traditional ways of life and modern culture.

Leslie V. Tischauser

Klamath

CULTURE AREA: Northwest Coast
LANGUAGE GROUP: Lutuamian
PRIMARY LOCATION: Oregon
POPULATION SIZE: 3,097 (1990 U.S. Census)

Approximately ten thousand years ago, the ancestors of the Klamath and the Modoc moved into an area encircled by the Great Basin to the east, the Cascades to the west, the central Plateau to the north, and the present-day California border. Because of these natural boundaries, the Klamath remained isolated from European Americans longer than many neighboring tribes. Klamath culture remained intact into the 1800's, and when trapper Peter Skene Ogden met the Klamath in 1826, he noted that they owned one horse. Early Klamath population figures are estimated at about a thousand.

Because their food came principally from the water, the Klamath did not require or use the horse as other tribes did for hunting, although by the mid-nineteenth century the Klamath used the horse and gun to raid other tribes. Traditionally Klamath culture followed a seasonal cycle; spring, summer, and fall were devoted to gathering roots and berries and securing a year's catch of fish. One of the staples of the Klamath diet was a pond lily seed, the wokas, which was gathered in the marshes in August. Another staple was fish, including suckers, salmon, and trout, caught in the spring runs. Fishing persisted into the winter, although the winter catch was limited.

By late fall, the Klamath began building their winter settlement, which generally already had some permanent buildings. Because the climate could be harsh (with up to several feet of snow), the Klamath built semi-subterranean earthlodges, sometimes up to 4 feet deep. They lived in these for the winter and relied on whatever provisions they had stored.

The clothing of the Klamath differed from that of their neighbors on the Columbia Plateau. Men and women wore skirts made of fibers and wore basketry caps. Buckskin was not worn until the nineteenth century. The Klamath also practiced tattooing, flattening the heads of infants, and the wearing of a dentalium through the nose. The tribe with which they had the most contact before the nineteenth century was the Modoc, who spoke a similar language. The Klamath were more influenced by Pacific Northwest culture than were the Modoc, who were closer to their southern neighbors.

By the mid-nineteenth century, the horse and gun were integrated into Klamath society. Contact with European Americans increased as whites crossed Klamath country on their way to the gold fields in Northern California; some settled in the region. The Klamath tried to sustain peaceful relations with the white settlers, and there were several instances where the Klamath punished their own for committing offenses against whites. The land that the Klamath occupied, however, was wanted for white settlement. In 1864 the Klamath signed a treaty with the federal government; in exchange for their land, they were awarded a reservation of 1,104,847 acres, the Klamath Agency, located in present-day south-central Oregon. The government planned to transform the Klamath into self-sufficient farmers once they were removed to the reservation.

By the twentieth century, their economy included ranching and some business; many incomes were supplemented by or derived from timber revenues. A small number practiced farming. In the early twentieth century, several claims were filed and won regarding boundary disputes. Tribal government consisted of a general council. In the early 1950's a movement for termination gained support. (The tribe had earlier rejected the 1934 Indian Reorganization Act.) By 1954, termination was finalized, and each Klamath enrolled in the tribe was allotted $43,500 in exchange for the sale of reservation land to the federal government. Termination meant the end of tribal status. For many Klamath, termination introduced more problems, as there were no plans for their future. Many were the victims of enterprising and unscrupulous entrepreneurs. After years of effort, tribal status was regained in 1991.

Klikitat

CULTURE AREAS: Northwest Coast, Plateau
LANGUAGE GROUP: Sahaptian
PRIMARY LOCATION: Washington State

Before contact with European Americans, the Cayuse had pushed the Klikitats west into south-central Washington, the area with which they have come to be traditionally associated. After the migration west, the Klikitats divided into two groups. The Western Klikitats continued past the Cascade Mountains into southwestern Washington and integrated with the Cowlitzes. The Eastern Klikitats lived on the north side of the Columbia River, along its tributaries, including the Klikitat, Lewis, and White Salmon rivers, in south-central Washington.

The Klikitats followed the nomadic lifestyle common to the Mid-Columbia Indians, and their subsistence patterns were a cycle of rich salmon fishing in the spring followed by the gathering of roots and berries in the summer and fall. The hunting of game supplemented their diet. The narrows at The Dalles on the Columbia River was one of the prized fishing locations. Even before contact, fishing rights were passed down from father to son, with the most powerful families claiming the locations where the salmon could be obtained most easily.

Because The Dalles was known for its plentiful catches, the area surrounding it became a popular trading post. Summer berry picking in the foothills of Mount Adams followed, and the Klikitats gathered huckleberries, which were either eaten raw, boiled, dried, or smoked. Roots were another staple, and the Klikitats dug for the camas root with a digging stick as well as digging wild carrots, onions, celery, and parsley. All the food sources—fish, berries, and roots—were preserved for the upcoming winter months. In addition to preserving the food, the women made beautiful baskets and became known for their skill.

Contact with European Americans began in the early 1800's with the Lewis and Clark expedition, followed by fur traders. Because of their location on the Columbia River, the Klikitats undoubtedly interacted with the fur traders considerably, which might explain their subsequent reputation as traders. In 1825 the Hudson's Bay Company established Fort Vancouver on the Columbia River. Company officials asked some of the Klikitats to move to the fort and act as hunters for members living at the fort. By the 1840's, Klikitats had moved into the Willamette Valley, which had been occupied by the Kalapuyas. As more and more settlers moved into the area, pressure mounted for the Klikitats to leave. Not all of their relations with the American settlers were unfriendly, as some of the Klikitats served the Americans in the Rogue Wars of the 1850's.

In 1855, Washington territorial governor Isaac Stevens held the Walla Walla Council with many of the Plateau tribes. The Klikitats were subsumed under the leadership of Kamiakin, the appointed Yakima chief. The Klikitats had always interacted closely with the Yakimas, as was noted by Lieutenant George Gibbs, who participated in a railroad survey in the Columbia Basin. Kamiakin represented fourteen signatory tribes, including the Klikitats, and the Yakima Treaty that he signed (although he claimed that he did not sign the treaty with the intention of relinquishing land) allowed for the creation of the Yakima Reservation, with a land base of 1,250,000 acres. Dissatisfied with the treaty, many Klikitats joined Kamiakin in the Yakima War of 1855 and the Cascade War of 1856. Part of the Klikitat discontent stemmed from the loss of their identity, although one of the first chiefs on the Yakima Reservation was White Swan, a Klikitat.

After 1856, many of the Klikitats moved to the Yakima Reservation and took part in such federal policies as the General Allotment Act of 1887. In 1935, the Confederated Tribes of the Yakima Reservation organized. The government consists of a general council and a Yakima tribal council. A few Klikitats still live near traditional fishing locations on the Klikitat and White Salmon rivers and continue to fish at some twenty sites along the Klikitat River.

Koyukon

CULTURE AREA: Subarctic
LANGUAGE GROUP: Athapaskan
PRIMARY LOCATION: Central Alaska

The Koyukon tribe is a subgroup of the Athapaskan family, living in small villages along the Yukon and Kuyokuk rivers in central Alaska. Actual population figures are sketchy, because census figures are notoriously inaccurate in these remote areas, but there are probably three or four hundred people who consider themselves Koyukons. The Athapaskans probably migrated from Siberia over the land bridge that existed on what is now the Bering Strait sometime during the last Ice Age, between ten thousand and twenty-five thousand years ago, and may have been the first humans to arrive in North America.

Koyukons were not known by white Americans until the 1890's, when the Klondike gold rush brought many prospectors into the area. Even then, the natives lived in widely separated tiny villages, and there was little intercourse between the two groups. The native culture was largely untouched, and the land was never taken from the Koyukons until the 1980's, when much of it became the Yukon Flats National Monument. Nearing the end of the twentieth century, the villages had few white residents, most of whom were teachers and other government workers.

Koyukons generally live in log cabins heated by wood stoves. Except in the schools, electricity is rare; it is provided by local generators, which are extremely unreliable because of the intensely cold winters. Telephone service is by satellite. There are no roads to any Koyukon village. English is the working language for most young Koyukons, though some of the older people still speak the native language, and tribal ceremonies are still held in that language.

The villages have a very loose style of government, with an elected chief whose main function is to act as a liaison with the federal and state governments. Children are taught in one-room schoolhouses, with high school available only in Fairbanks or Fort Yukon, neither of which has a significant Koyukon population.

Kutchin

CULTURE AREAS: Arctic, Subarctic
LANGUAGE GROUP: Athapaskan
PRIMARY LOCATION: Northeastern Alaska, northwestern Yukon
POPULATION SIZE: 1,995 in Canada (Statistics Canada, based on 1991 census); estimated 600 in Alaska

The Kutchin are the largest subgroup of the northern Athapaskan family of tribes. They live mostly in small villages along the major rivers of Alaska and the Yukon, although many have migrated to the cities, principally Fairbanks, in search of a more viable lifestyle.

The largest concentration of Kutchin is in the Alaskan village of Fort Yukon. The rest are scattered around Alaska and the Yukon. Their numbers are impossible to determine accurately, as few fill out the census forms they are sent. Fort Yukon is the only village with a road system, and this system does not extend outside the village. Transportation among the villages is primarily by boat in the summer and dogsled in the winter, although there are airstrips in the villages, and small planes make daily landings, bringing mail and supplies ordered from Fairbanks.

The Kutchin language and lifestyle appear to be losing ground to white culture, though this may change as the movement toward Indian pride in heritage spreads. Fort Yukon has several stores and a reliable electricity supply. Elsewhere, people live in log cabins, trade mostly by barter, and eat a diet largely composed of moose and salmon.

The Kutchins' first major encounters with white people occurred during the Alaskan gold rush of the 1890's, but except in Fort Yukon, which has a significant white population, the effects have been minimal. In the smaller villages, the native culture still survives alongside the white, Christian culture that has been imported.

Kutenai

CULTURE AREA: Plateau
LANGUAGE GROUP: Kutenai
PRIMARY LOCATION: Washington State, British Columbia
POPULATION SIZE: 643 in U.S. (1990 U.S. Census); 565 in Canada (Statistics Canada, based on 1991 census)

The Kutenai (also spelled "Kootenai" and "Kootenay") lived in southeastern British Columbia and northern Montana and Idaho. Their distinct language places them in a linguistic family of their own. In prehistoric times, they lived east of the Rocky Mountains, but they were driven westward by traditional enemies, the Blackfoot. The tribe was from early times divided into two groups speaking different dialects: the Upper Kutenai, of the upper Kootenay (Kutenai) and Columbia rivers, and the Lower Kutenai, of the Lower Kootenay River. They were a nomadic people, traveling widely in search of buffalo. Known to be unusually tall, they were skilled in canoe building and in raising horses.

Because they constantly moved about, there was no central government or chief; rather, each band had its own leader and council of elders. They worshiped the sun and expected their dead to some day meet the living at Pend Oreille Lake. The Kutenai, because of their isolated location, were among the last of the American Indian tribes to be contacted by whites. In fact, the Lower Kutenai were so isolated that they were still using stone tools in the late nineteenth century. Even into the twentieth century, they led relatively peaceful and unhampered lives. By the end of the twentieth century, the Kutenai were no longer nomadic, but lived in wood frame houses and relied mostly on wage labor for their living.

Kwakiutl

CULTURE AREA: Northwest Coast
LANGUAGE GROUP: Wakashan
PRIMARY LOCATION: British Columbia
POPULATION SIZE: 4,120 (Statistics Canada, based on 1991 census)

The Kwakiutl Indians inhabited much of the northwestern coast of British Columbia. The tribe was divided into three groups geographically and had a religion that was centered on guardian spirits. They were famous for potlatch festivals in which status was obtained by extravagant gift giving. Kwakiutl villages were composed of wooden multifamily dwellings, and the main occupation of their inhabitants was fishing. Most modern Kwakiutl are found in various reserves (reservations) throughout British Columbia.

Tribal History. The Kwakiutl Indians, whose name means "beach on the other side of the river," occupied part of Vancouver Island and the British Columbia coast between Bute Inlet and Douglas Channel. They formed three groups called the Haisla, the Heiltsuk, and the Kwakiutl proper (Southern Kwakiutl), and they spoke variants of the Wakashan Indian language. Their known history has large gaps in it; however, it is well known that their primary occupation was fishing and that they depended upon the sea for most needs. Like the other tribes of the region, the Kwakiutl were excellent craftsmen with wood, making beautiful totem poles, elaborate ceremonial masks, and highly advanced canoes. After 1780, the year of the first visits by British and American traders, the Kwakiutl obtained steel tools and became even more adept craftsmen.

Traditional Lifeways. The Kwakiutl were organized into a number of autonomous bands whose social organization included chiefs, nobles, commoners, and slaves, interrelated by complex rules. The minimal social unit in a band was an extended family, or *numaym*, wherein descent was patrilineal; the matrilineal Haisla were the exception. Haisla matrilineal descent was patterned after that of the neighboring Tsimshian, who influenced them greatly. Rights, property, dances, and religious position were parceled out to Kwakiutl according to their lines of descent.

The Kwakiutl religion was based on guardian spirits whose aid could be obtained by appropriate prayer and fasting by either men or women. The different guardian spirits divided numaym members into secret societies (such as Cannibals, Warriors, and Grizzlies), each of which had special dances and ceremonies. The most famous of the Kwakiutl ceremonies was the potlatch. These ceremonies of gift giving were common to many tribes of the Northwest Coast region. The Kwakiutl were noted for the elaborate nature of their potlatches, in which the giver might practically beggar himself through the bestowing of gifts. The potlatches were celebrated to commemorate marriages, important births and deaths, the naming of heirs, and the initiation of members into secret societies. At death, Kwakiutl were either cremated or buried. Burial was in caves, in trees, or (in the case of the very rich) in canoes.

Kwakiutl villages were orderly collections of plank houses made from the red cedar tree, whose wood is straight and easy to work with simple tools. The highly decorated Kwakiutl houses looked and were shaped somewhat like barns. Most houses in a village were each occupied by all the members of a given numaym; however, some village houses were used only for religious ceremonies. The Kwakiutl, who were great fishermen, fished and traveled in large, well-designed dugout sailing canoes, also made from red cedar logs. They also used the canoes in warfare with various neighboring tribes.

The Kwakiutl tribal economy was based mostly on fishing for salmon and, to a lesser extent, cod, halibut, herring, and hunting seals. Fishing was carried out with harpoons, nets, weirs, and many other kinds of sophisticated equipment. The Kwakiutl also hunted some deer and moose with bows and arrows. The vegetable foods of the Kwakiutl included seaweed, roots, and berries gathered by the women of the tribe. The Kwakiutl made fine clothing from bark, animal skins, wool, and dog hair.

Modern Life. Nineteenth century Christian missionaries attempted to convert the Kwakiutl, who held on to their tribal beliefs strongly. To speed Kwakiutl absorption into mainstream Canadian life, the government outlawed potlatches in the early twentieth century. The modern Kwakiutl live on various reserves throughout British Columbia. Many modern Kwakiutl have retained their language and customs, especially in giving elegant funeral potlatches. Modern Kwakiutl are often fishermen.

Sanford S. Singer

Lake

CULTURE AREA: Plateau
LANGUAGE GROUP: Salishan
PRIMARY LOCATION: Colville Reservation, Washington State

The Lake, also called Senijextee, were a branch of the Salishan family. They lived along the Columbia, Kettle, and Kootenay rivers in Washington and in the Arrow Lakes area of British Columbia, Canada, which gave them their name. Their dialect was very similar to that of another Salishan tribe, the Okanagan. Evidence suggests they migrated to Washington from Montana and Idaho in prehistoric times. The Lake lived in villages of varying size, in bands or groups of families. They dressed in wool blankets and fur robes. Because they relied on hunting and fishing—salmon was a chief staple of their diet—as well as on gathering roots and berries, they were forced to move throughout the year to find food in different seasons. This prevented the villages from growing and developing as political or social centers.

The Lake do not seem to have relied on agriculture. They were skilled in building canoes, but the rapids of the rivers along which they lived were so treacherous that most traveling was done on foot. The introduction of new diseases from Europe and changing economic conditions brought about a great decline in the numbers of surviving Lake. During the twentieth century, most of the remaining Lake Indians in the United States lived on the Colville Reservation in Washington, to which the Lake had been assigned in 1872. By the 1970's, there were no identified Lake in Canada.

Lenni Lenape

CULTURE AREA: Northeast
LANGUAGE GROUP: Algonquian
PRIMARY LOCATION: Oklahoma
POPULATION SIZE: 9,321 in U.S. ("Delaware," 1990 U.S. Census); 590 in Canada (Statistics Canada, based on 1991 census)

The Lenni Lenape were the first tribe encountered by the European explorers who landed in the area of what is now northern Delaware, New Jersey, and southeastern New York.

The name "Lenape" has been ascribed various meanings: "a male of our kind," "our men," "men of the same nation," "common," "ordinary," or "real" people. "Lenni Lenape" is redundant, as if to say, "the common, ordinary people." They are sometimes referred to as the Delawares, which is not an Indian word at all; the early English settlers, who had difficulty pronouncing Indian names, were responsible for this term. In August of 1610, Sir Samuel Argall, captain of the ship *Discovery*, sailed into the bay, which he later named De la Warre Bay in honor of Sir Thomas West, third Lord De la Warre, who was governor of the Virginia colony. The Indians who lived along the shore of the bay and the banks of the river that fed into it were called the De la Warres, later shortened to Delawares.

Subtribes. Before the arrival of the Europeans, the Lenape lived in small villages containing only twenty-five or thirty people. Scholars are not sure of the total Lenape population before the coming of the Europeans; the usual estimates range from eight to twelve thousand people.

The early Dutch, Swedish, and English explorers soon realized that the Lenape could not simply be lumped together as one unified group. There were separate groups or bands scattered along the major waterways. One main division was the Minsi ("men of the stony country"), which included the Esophus, Tappan, Haverstraw, Canarsee, and Hackensack, among others, who lived in the area of what is now northern New Jersey, Manhattan Island, and the lower Hudson River valley. The Unami ("fishermen"), which included the Raritan, Navesink, and Mantaes, lived in central New Jersey and along the Atlantic coast. The Unalachtigo ("people living near the ocean") were found along the coast in present-day Delaware and southern New Jersey. Along the upper Delaware River valley lived the Minisinks and other small, unnamed Indian bands. These groups differed greatly in their language, religious beliefs, and culture; in fact, the Unami dialect of the Delaware language was so different from the Minsi that they could barely understand each other.

Political Organization. The individual tribes did not form a single Indian nation because the Lenape villages functioned as separate political units. Each village was governed by at least two chiefs, a council, and the residents of the village. One chief, who either inherited or was elected to the position, held authority in times of peace, and his power was limited by the council and the village at large. His main function was to preside over meetings and ceremonies, direct hunting drives, and mediate disputes. The chief was usually no wealthier than his neighbors, as the Lenape practiced a communal way of life in which all members of the tribe shared equally. The second chief was a war chief, who was appointed because of his skills in war. With a war's end, the peace chief resumed his limited authority. This system of government gave all members of the tribe considerable personal liberty and great equality of wealth.

Methods of Subsistence. The early Lenapes were primarily hunters and fishermen, pursuing bear, elk, deer, beaver, and muskrat. Their weapons consisted of spears made of wood or bone with a stone point. Fish were caught with nets, lines, or spears. Later, as their life became more sedentary, they began to produce articles of clay pottery. The women of the tribe engaged in agriculture and food gathering as villages became more permanent. Corn was the primary crop, which was ground into corn meal. They also grew squash, beans, and tobacco, and learned how to preserve food for future use. Meat was dried and cured, and ground corn and beans were placed in earthen pits and covered with bark or leaves. Fish was either dried in the sun or smoked. Many of the Lenape agricultural practices and food preservation methods were later adopted by European colonists.

Village Life. The largest and most permanent villages were usually located along major rivers or other large bodies of water. They were moved from time to time when the soil was depleted, as the Lenape were unaware of methods of crop rotation. For shelter they built simple, circular structures constructed of curved saplings lashed together with hickory twigs or hemp and covered with strips of bark. A hole was left in the center of the structure to allow smoke from the inside fire to exit. In the northern parts of New Jersey, they built longhouses in which several families would live.

The Lenape wore simple clothing made from deer, elk, beaver, bear, fox, and raccoon skins. Children wore little or no clothing in summer. Both men and women wore jewelry fashioned from shark's teeth, bear claws, or shells, and for warfare and festive occasions they painted their bodies with paints made from minerals, berries, roots, and bark.

On land they traveled on foot, and for water transportation they built dugout canoes fashioned from felled trees. A fire was started in the middle of the log, and the charred pieces were slowly removed with stone axes.

European Contact. Beginning with the arrival of the explorer Giovanni da Verrazano in 1524, the Lenape had increasing contact with the Europeans. With the arrival of the Dutch and English, competition for trading with the settlers among tribes became fierce. The Lenape highly valued the articles brought from Europe, especially textiles, guns, metal tools, and jewelry.

Unfortunately, an unanticipated consequence of contact and trade with the Europeans was the introduction of two deadly commodities: alcohol and disease. The Lenapes had never known any form of alcoholic beverage, and they quickly developed a craving for beer, rum, and brandy. Alcohol was frequently abused, and many European traders took advantage of the

Indians' weakness regarding alcohol, offering them strong drink during trading encounters and then cheating them out of their money.

The Europeans also unwittingly transmitted diseases for which the Lenape had no natural immunity: smallpox, typhus, influenza, venereal diseases, and malaria. These sicknesses were so severe among the natives that they sometimes wiped out whole communities. During the colonial period, there were also epidemics of measles, chicken pox, and scarlet fever which dramatically reduced their numbers.

Social Life. The average Lenape family had from four to six children, but infant mortality was very high. Newborn children were wrapped in animal skins, which were fastened to a cradleboard by three braided strips; one went over the baby's forehead, one went over the arms, and one secured the legs. While the mother was working in the fields, the cradleboard and the baby were hung on the branch of a tree. At an early age, boys were instructed in the techniques of hunting, war, and woodcraft, while girls were trained in planting and cultivating crops as well as housekeeping duties.

Because their life expectancy was not very long, boys were considered ready for marriage at seventeen or eighteen, once they had proved that they possessed the necessary hunting skills to provide for a family. Girls were eligible for marriage once they became sexually mature, at around thirteen or fourteen years of age. Marriages were usually arranged by parents, with some consent of the couple allowed. There was little ceremony involved. In some cases, a man would simply ask a woman if she wanted to live with him, and if she agreed the tribe considered them to be married.

Death was considered to be caused by evil spirits. Burial rites were simple, the body being placed in a shallow pit lined with bark. Food, clothing, tobacco pipes, and clay pots were often placed with the corpse for use by the deceased in the next life.

Religious Beliefs. Like most Native Americans, the Lenape were a deeply religious people. Unlike the European settlers, whose Christian beliefs taught them that God favored them over other creatures, the Lenape believed that they were an integral part of the natural world. They also firmly believed in an afterlife. The soul, they thought, left the body at the time of death but remained nearby for several days, consuming the food left at the grave site. Then it departed to the land of the spirits, a pleasant place where one met one's deceased relatives and had plenty of food and good hunting.

The Lenape worshiped many gods, with a supreme being, Manito, at the head. Manito created the earth and everything on it. Lesser gods served as his agents; in addition, almost all plants and animals were considered to contain supernatural spirits. Communication with the gods was through prayers and offerings. Lenape tribes also had shamans who specialized in curing illnesses or foretelling the future. Since illness was attributed to evil spirits entering the body, it was the job of the shamans to scare the spirits away. A shaman was considered a special member of the tribe, and his secrets were passed on only to a legal descendant or a close and trusted friend. There is some evidence that a special house was constructed in some villages for the exorcism of disease.

In the early years of contact with Europeans, Lenape religion was relatively unaffected. The settlers considered the Indians to be godless, and some religious groups, most notably the Moravians, attempted to learn the Lenape language and convert them to Christianity. A few did convert, but they often quickly went back to their native beliefs; Christian sermons did not make sense within their worldview, and Christian practices simply did not fit into their way of life. Perhaps the only lasting effect of Christianity upon Lenape religion was the emergence of an annual ceremony celebrating the harvest. A "big house," a bark-covered structure about 40 feet long and 25 feet wide was constructed exclusively for this purpose. For twelve nights in mid-October, sacred fires were maintained at each entrance, and the interior was decorated with twelve posts with faces carved on them to represent the twelve gods who occupied the heavens. A cooking fire burned in the center, and deer meat was hung from a pole or tree, before which prayers were said to aid the hunters. Other prayers gave thanks for a bountiful harvest.

Relocation. The Lenape were the dominant tribe in the East until about 1720. As the white settlers continued to arrive, the Indians were gradually crowded out. The settlers had cleared many of the forests for farming, thus driving away the deer, bear, and wild turkeys. They dammed the rivers to power their mills, disrupting the annual spawning runs of fish. With these drastic changes, the traditional Lenape way of life was destroyed. Those who remained began to sell their remaining lands to the eager colonists and move across the Delaware to the west, never to return.

The Unalachtigo were the first to depart, around 1725, relocating to northern New York State. They were followed by the Minsi around 1742, who settled for a time in southeastern Pennsylvania and later in Ohio and Indiana. Some crossed Lake Erie into Canada, while others went to the area around the Kansas and Missouri rivers. In 1867, many Lenapes moved into the Indian Territory in what is now Oklahoma and were incorporated into the Cherokee tribe. A few went to Green Bay, Wisconsin, where they remained for many years.

Raymond Frey

Bibliography

Adams, Richard C., Deborah Nichols, and James Rementer. *Legends of the Delaware Indians and Picture Writing*. Syracuse, N.Y.: Syracuse University Press, 1997.

Adams, Richard C. *Delaware Indians: A Brief History*. Saugerties, N.Y.: Hope Farm Press, 1995.

Cross, Dorothy. *New Jersey's Indians*. Trenton: New Jersey State Museum, 1976. A very readable account of Lenape life; sections on Lenape culture are especially informative.

Dowd, Gregory Evans. *The Indians of New Jersey*. Trenton: New Jersey Historical Commission, 1992. A brief but well-researched history of the Lenape, including a useful bibliography of sources for further study.

Hitakonanulaxk. *The Grandfathers Speak: Native American Folk Tales of the Lenape People*. New York: Interlink Books, 1994.

Kraft, Herbert C. *The Lenape: Archaeology, History, and Ethnography*. Newark: New Jersey Historical Society, 1986. An excellent study of archaeological investigations of the Lenape, written by the foremost scholar of New Jersey Indians.

_____. *The Lenape Indians of New Jersey*. South Orange, N.J.: Seton Hall Museum, 1987. The story of the Lenape, intended for younger readers.

Philhower, Charles A. "The Aboriginal Inhabitants of New Jersey." In *New Jersey: A History*. New York: American Historical Society, 1930. A classic account of the Lenape, with an excellent discussion of their westward movements.

Lillooet

CULTURE AREA: Plateau
LANGUAGE GROUP: Salishan
PRIMARY LOCATION: Southwestern British Columbia
POPULATION SIZE: 2,570 (Statistics Canada, based on 1991 census)

The Lillooet, a branch of the Salishan family, lived in the vicinity of the Lillooet and Fraser rivers in southwestern British Columbia. They were divided into the Upper and Lower Lillooet, and each division was composed of several named bands. The name means "wild onion" and was at first applied only to the Lower Lillooet. The Upper Lillooet called themselves Stla'tlium, the meaning of which is unknown.

The Lillooet lived in small villages, each representing one clan. Their primary source of food was fish, especially salmon, which they caught with spears, nets, and traps. They also hunted bear, beaver, rabbit, raccoon, squirrel, and mountain goat. Men were the primary hunters, while women worked to preserve the meat and to gather berries and food from the wild. They made good use of the animals they hunted, using the skins for clothing, quills for ornamentation, and wool and hair for weaving cloth. Their homes were often made of logs or wood planks, and housed four to eight families. Other villages had circular earthlodges with warming earth berms for winter and mat houses for summer. In the front of a house there was likely to be a totem pole, featuring the clan's totem. Lillooets had sustained contact with white traders from about 1809, when explorer Simon Fraser and his party first traveled through their land. The Lillooet traded heavily with whites as well as with their tribal neighbors.

After gold was discovered in the area in 1858, they encountered many white miners, maintaining mostly friendly relations with them. They fought at times with their neighbors, especially the Thompsons. In 1863, a great epidemic of smallpox hit the area and killed many people; the Lillooet lost many members to the disease. Shortly afterward, they were afflicted by a famine that further reduced their numbers. Near the end of the twentieth century many still lived on traditional territory, on several small reserves, and were making their living by wood cutting and other forms of wage labor.

Luiseño

CULTURE AREA: California
LANGUAGE GROUP: Takic
PRIMARY LOCATION: Southern California (southern Los Angeles to Newport Beach and inland)
POPULATION SIZE: 2,694 (1990 U.S. Census)

Modern Luiseño shaman calling for rain.
(National Museum of the American Indian, Smithsonian Institution)

The Luiseño are among the Takic-speaking tribal groups of the Uto-Aztecan language family in Southern California. Like a number of other California groups (including the Gabrielino, Fernandeño, and Juaneño) the name by which they are known refers to the Spanish mission established in their territory; in their case, it was the San Luis Rey mission.

The Luiseño developed in a different cultural direction from those of their northern neighbors, the Gabrielino and Fernandeño, from about 1400 C.E. One of the most notable additions to the material culture of the Luiseño was pottery, clearly an influence of more southern tribal groups. The Luiseño were a conservative group who generally pursued an isolationist policy in relations with their neighbors. According to Lowell John Bean and Florence Shipek, four major aspects of the Luiseño culture are known: an extensive social class structure that extended into carefully observed property ownership and closely guarded borders, often carefully marked; a ruling family, interrelated among ruling families of the other villages; the use of hallucinogenic plants in religious ceremony; and the use of sand paintings and other religious rituals involved with recognition of Chingichngish, seen by the Luiseño as a vengeful, godlike figure.

Acorns and other seeds were the major food source for the Luiseño, who ground and cooked them in the form of mush. Like other Southern California tribes, the Luiseño also created baskets. The men wore ear and nose ornaments.

Among the Luiseño there was a hereditary chief, who had an assistant; the chief conducted negotiations in peace and war and economic matters. He was advised by a council of religious leaders who were involved in the cult of Chingichngish.

There is no Luiseño reservation, and most modern Luiseño live in southern Los Angeles and Orange counties, California.

Lumbee

CULTURE AREA: Southeast
LANGUAGE GROUP: Siouan (?)
PRIMARY LOCATION: North Carolina
POPULATION SIZE: 48,444 (1990 U.S. Census)

The origins of the Lumbee Indians are obscure. When they first attracted the serious attention of their white neighbors in the early 1900's, they were already English-speaking small farmers living largely in Robeson

County, North Carolina. At one time, it was believed that they descended from Croatan Indians who had absorbed the survivors of Sir Walter Raleigh's "lost colony." Some Lumbees have claimed descent from the Cherokees and Tuscaroras. Most likely, however, they are descendants of Siouan-speaking Cheraw Indians who inhabited southeastern North Carolina in the seventeenth and eighteenth centuries. General use of the name Lumbee (from the Lumber River) dates only from 1953; previously, the Lumbees were referred to as Croatans, Indians of Robeson County, or, derisively, as "Scuffletonians."

Lumbee history has been a struggle to preserve an Indian identity. In 1835, North Carolina classified them as "free people of color." (Many white Carolinians believed them as much African as Indian in background.) When the state attempted to draft Lumbees as laborers during the Civil War, armed resistance led by Henry Berry Lowry resulted. After the war, North Carolina began to recognize the Lumbees as Indians, establishing schools and a college for them. Under the Jim Crow system of racial segregation, North Carolina Indians occupied a third category distinct from whites and blacks.

Lumbee assertion of Indian identity continued into the twentieth century. In 1958, the Lumbees gained national attention when they forcibly broke up a Ku Klux Klan rally. In 1968 the Lumbee Regional Development Association was organized, serving as a tribal government as well as an economic development agency. Rural poverty remained a major tribal problem, prompting many to move to cities, especially Baltimore. Lumbees also became increasingly active in pan-Indian activities. Federal recognition became a goal. (The Lumbees had no treaty relationship with the United States government.) While an act of Congress did take formal notice of the Lumbees as an Indian tribe, a 1987 petition for full federal recognition was not successful.

Lummi

CULTURE AREA: Northwest Coast
LANGUAGE GROUP: Salishan
PRIMARY LOCATION: Washington State
POPULATION SIZE: 2,956 (1990 U.S. Census)

In their homeland of the San Juan Islands and adjacent mainland in northern Puget Sound, the Lummi people traditionally spoke a dialect of

Coast Salish which was also spoken by the Songish people of southern Vancouver Island. Their economy was based on sockeye salmon, caught in nets from canoes, and herring, codfish, dog salmon, humpback salmon, and silver salmon caught with traps, weirs, hooks, dip nets, and spears. Ducks were also caught in underwater nets, and clams and crabs were gathered along the shorelines. In addition, the Lummis occasionally hunted and trapped beaver, otter, muskrat, and bear. Camas bulbs and other roots were dug and cooked in rock-lined pits to add variety to the diet. Plentiful berries also added to the variety of foods.

Cedar was used for many purposes, such as building the large extended family longhouses in which Lummi people lived in their permanent coastline villages. Cedar was also used to make huge dugout canoes, the bark used for clothing, baskets, and other uses. The Lummis traded and intermarried with tribes as far north as the Fraser River and as far south as the White River. Warfare occasionally disrupted peaceful relations, making palisades in front of their villages necessary. In 1827, a Hudson's Bay Company post invaded the region, and by the 1850's, settlers were also intruding on the Lummi homeland. Disease, unscrupulous trading, and alcoholism, as well as the cession of most of Lummi territory to the United States government, took their toll on this proud nation. Nevertheless, the Lummi population was higher in 1980 than it had been in the 1790's. The Lummi Reservation near Bellingham, Washington, was home to about 2,500 Lummi people in the late twentieth century. The Lummis have experienced a cultural renaissance by reviving many traditional cultural and spiritual celebrations. They have also embarked on a pioneering self-government project, giving them independence from the U.S. Bureau of Indian Affairs. In the 1980's, the tribal government set up an ambitious aquaculture project to preserve salmon, oysters, trout, and other marine species.

Mahican

CULTURE AREA: Northeast
LANGUAGE GROUP: Algonquian
PRIMARY LOCATION: Hudson River valley (New York State), Wisconsin, Saskatchewan, Oklahoma
POPULATION SIZE: 2,069 ("Stockbridge," 1990 U.S. Census)

The Mahican were Algonquian-speaking people closely related to the Delaware or Lenni Lenape and very strongly influenced by the Mohawk. They lived on both sides of the Hudson River and in northern New York nearly to Lake Champlain. When the Iroquois Confederacy became an allied military force after 1650, and Dutch and English settlers began moving into the lower Hudson River valley, the Mahican were pushed first east of the Hudson and then onto settlements in western Massachusetts near present-day Stockbridge.

Mahican, translated as "People of the Wolf," are easily confused with the Mohegan, also of Delaware lineage, who lived in the Connecticut and lower Hudson River area. (It is not certain which tribe James Fenimore Cooper was referring to in his 1826 novel *The Last of the Mohicans*.)

White encroachment and the Iroquois alliance forced many Mahican in the early 1800's to migrate south into Pennsylvania and then down the Ohio River. Some migrants continued with other Delaware tribes into Oklahoma, while others went north through the straits of Mackinaw into Canada.

Mahican who stayed behind became associated with the Stockbridge Indians. Educated in white mission schools, many assimilated into white culture. During the revolutionary war, Stockbridge Indian men in high percentages joined the American army, influenced in part by the Iroquois alliance with the British.

History's most famous Mahican was John W. Quinney (Quinequan, 1797-1855). He was instrumental in purchasing Menominee land in Wisconsin to secure the survival of the remnants of the Mahican. Quinney also created a constitution for his people and resisted American citizenship for his tribe, that they might better preserve their heritage. He served as grand sachem from 1852 until his death.

A beaded coat on display in the Milwaukee Museum shows craftsmanship and design patterns closely related to northeast Algonquian-speaking Narragansett people. There is no visible Iroquois influence. The Mahicans had three clans: Bear, Wolf, and Turtle. The office of sachem was hereditary. The sachem was assisted by councillors called Hero, Owl, and Runner, indicating lineage to the Delaware. Mahican lived in longhouses and were matrilineal. Their lifestyle was identical to the way of life of Eastern Woodland natives.

Bibliography

Dyer, Louisa A. *The House of Peace*. New York: Longmans, Green, 1955.

Frazier, Patrick. *The Mohicans of Stockbridge*. Lincoln: University of Nebraska Press, 1992.

LePoer, Barbara Leitch. *A Concise Dictionary of Indian Tribes of North America*. Edited by Kendall T. LePoer. Algonac, Mich.: Reference Publications, 1979.

Skinner, Alanson. "Mahican Ethnology." *Bulletin of the Public Museum of the City of Milwaukee* 2, no. 1 (1912): 87-116.

Maidu

CULTURE AREA: California
LANGUAGE GROUP: Maiduan
PRIMARY LOCATION: Northern California
POPULATION SIZE: 2,271 (1990 U.S. Census)

Maidu Indians occupied a large portion of northeastern California. They hunted, gathered, and fished for subsistence. Women and children gathered acorns, grass seed, roots, nuts, and berries. Surplus foodstuffs were dried, ground into flour, and stored in baskets. The Maidu used nets to catch salmon and other fish. Surplus fish were dried whole and ground into a powder that was eaten dry. They hunted deer, bear, elk, rabbit, and geese with bows and arrows, spears, and hunting dogs. Extra meat was dried for winter usage. Fishing and hunting lands were owned by the entire tribe.

Because of the warm climate, the Maidu wore very little clothing. Men might wear deerskin breechclouts or nothing at all; women wore apron skirts decorated with tassels made from the same material. Fur robes and snowshoes were worn in winter. Maidu lived in dome-shaped, semi-subterranean, earth-covered dwellings that housed two to three families. During the summer, flat-roofed shade shelters were constructed with oak branches.

The Maidu believed that mysterious powers and spirits surrounded their world, and superstitions abounded. They depended on their shamans' mysterious powers and ability to speak to the spirit world. Tribal shamans oversaw political meetings, directed ceremonies, and cured the ill.

European explorers originally came through Maidu territory in the first half of the nineteenth century. A few Hudson's Bay Company trappers later worked in the area. Gold miners came in the mid-1850's and hired local Indians at low wages. As soon as white settlers permanently moved onto Maidu lands, food became scarce and the Indians raided local farms for livestock. Violent skirmishes between Maidu and settlers resulted.

In 1863, soldiers forced 461 Indians onto Round Valley Reservation. During the two-week journey, thirty-two Maidu died. Through the twentieth century, Maidu Indians experienced very high unemployment and poor education, housing, health, and sanitary conditions. At the same time, there was renewed interest in traditional values and increased pride in Maidu heritage.

Makah

CULTURE AREA: Northwest Coast
LANGUAGE GROUP: Chinookan
PRIMARY LOCATION: Washington State
POPULATION SIZE: 1,597 (1990 U.S. Census)

Living on the northwestern tip of the Olympic Peninsula of present-day Washington State, the Makah were one of twenty-eight tribes of Native Americans living along 1,400 miles of coast from Northern California to southeastern Alaska who collectively formed the Northwest Coast Native American culture area. The Makah were bordered on the west by the Pacific Ocean, to the north by the Strait of Juan de Fuca, to the east by the Klallam tribe, and on the south by the Quileute/Hoh. Although Makah origins are unclear, anthropologists believe ancestors of the Makah were living in the same area ten thousand years ago.

About the time of the arrival of Christopher Columbus, the Makah were part of a thriving culture and society. At this time, a Makah village at Ozette was covered in an enormous mudslide. In 1966, Washington State University anthropologists began excavating the site. This natural disaster perfectly preserved thousands of artifacts including several wooden longhouses, harpoons, whale lances, and various wooden artworks such as totem carvings. This find is now preserved at Neah Bay, Washington, at the Makah Cultural and Research Center. Dale Croes and Eric Blinman have written about a more recent find at the Hoko River, believed to be a twenty-five-hundred-year-old fishing camp.

When Europeans arrived after 1775 and docked at Makah settlements, they found a people who were willing trade partners and had an abundance of goods to trade. The Makah had little to no agriculture, but they were probably among the wealthiest tribes in North America. There was such an abundance of food in the Pacific Northwest that the Makah needed to hunt, fish, and gather only from May through September. This provided them with plenty to eat and enough surplus to trade for externally produced goods, both with other tribes and with European merchants.

The region's climate, which is moderate and wet, yielded food in abundance. Salmon, trout, cod, halibut, herring, whales, sea lions, sea otters, clams, mussels, sea urchins, seaweed, berries, bird eggs, deer, elk, bear, wolves, mountain goats, and beavers were some, but not all, of the available resources.

Perhaps the greatest excitement in the Makah cyclical calendar of events involved the whale hunt. When a whale was seen near the coast, the men would jump into cedar or redwood dugout canoes and chase it. On the bow, the chief harpooner (a position passed down from father to son), who held a musselshell-bladed 18-foot harpoon with attached buoys, stood ready to throw. Once the whale tired and died, the canoes would pull the mammal back to shore, where the village would make use of every part of the catch (meat, oil, and bones).

Although anthropologists have generally considered agriculture a prerequisite for a sophisticated civilization, the complexity of the Makah culture emerges when one examines a few of the Makah rituals, beliefs, and ways of life. The Makah believed that the salmon were gods who lived

Circa 1895 photograph of a Makah fishing village on Tatoosh Island, showing the contrast between a traditional plank house and adopted European American styles.
(National Archives)

during the winter in houses under the sea but who sacrificed themselves each year to humans. An elaborate ceremony surrounded the year's first catch of salmon, and the Makah were careful to throw the salmon bones back into the water to ensure a return of the fish the following year.

The Makah had a strict social division based on wealth and rank. A combination of material ownership and birth determined one's position in the village. Sometimes, though not often, a lower-class person could wield great influence, perhaps as a shaman (man or woman) who was believed to possess great magical powers.

Several families lived within the long wooden houses, which always faced the sea; the highest in rank would receive the premium sleeping and storage space near the back wall of the house. The wealthiest Makah would periodically host potlatches, extended feasts intended to impress neighbors and reinforce the host's status in the society. Often, many guests were invited and gifts were given liberally. At these potlatches, private and exclusive songs might be performed which would signify and reinforce the rank of the performer and his or her family.

The Makah represent the wealth, trade, and social structuring present among Northwest Coast Indians before the arrival of the Europeans and exemplify the efforts of Native American groups to preserve the heritage of their ancestors.

Maliseet

CULTURE AREA: Northeast
LANGUAGE GROUP: Maleseet-Passamaquoddy
PRIMARY LOCATION: New Brunswick, Quebec, Maine
POPULATION SIZE: 1,705 in Canada (Statistics Canada, based on 1991 census); 900 in U.S. (1990 U.S. Census)

The Maliseet (also spelled Malecite) include both the Passamaquoddy and the Natick peoples. The Passamaquoddy settlement patterns were maritime, whereas the Natick were oriented along inland waterways with an emphasis on land-mammal hunting. Both had extended family organization. Chieftainship was patrilineal. Birchbark was utilized for implements, housing, canoes, and other utilitarian products. Hunting and trapping of moose and deer and other animals was supplemented by saltwater and freshwater fishing. Periodic boat excursions were made to neighboring islands for shellfish, lobsters, clams, and seals.

In 1604, Samuel de Champlain visited and described the inhabitants at the mouth of the Saint John River. Relations with the French were friendly; they were less so with the British, who issued land grants to non-Indians. Many Maliseet moved to the Kingsclear and Tobique reservations. Other reservations were established as population increased. By the 1900's, assimilation had increased, and more Indians were living off-reservation. The 1960's and 1970's saw a revitalization of traditional knowledge and language, a reduction of factionalism, nonprofit tribal corporations, and an increase in college graduates.

Manahoac

CULTURE AREA: Southeast
LANGUAGE GROUP: Algonquian
PRIMARY LOCATION: Potomac and North Anna rivers, Maryland/Virginia

Little is recorded about the river-oriented Manahoac tribe, who had a diversified subsistence base that included horticulture, hunting, trapping, fishing, and gathering of nuts, seeds, roots, and tubers. They wintered in permanent villages that were part of the Manahoac Confederacy, and there may have been seven tribes. They warred with the Iroquois and Powhatan and maintained an allegiance with the Monacan. Eventually the Manahoac were forced from their territory by the Susquehanna in the mid-seventeenth century.

John Smith was probably the first European American to observe the Manahoac. Thomas Jefferson, in 1801, said that he had found some of the Manahoac living on the Rappahannock River, but he probably had observed the Hassinunga, a tribe of the Manahoac Confederacy. Disease, combined with continual warfare, brought the Manahoac to ethnographic extinction; by the late colonial period, the Manahoac were no longer a distinct tribe.

Mandan

CULTURE AREA: Plains
LANGUAGE GROUP: Siouan
PRIMARY LOCATION: North Dakota
POPULATION SIZE: 1,207 (1990 U.S. Census)

The Mandan, a branch of the Siouan-speaking people, migrated from their original homes along the Ohio River to the northern Great Plains in the early 1400's. Since then they lived in the region around the Big Bend of the Missouri River.

Traditional Culture. Mandans were called the "Prairie People" by other Indians. They lived in permanent villages and grew corn, beans, squash, and tobacco. Once a year hunting parties went into the prairies in search of buffalo, which, until the introduction of horses in the 1750's, were killed by warriors on foot driving the buffalo off high cliffs. After learning how to use horses, Mandan warriors went out more frequently on these hunts, but killing methods did not change. Huge graveyards of buffalo bones have been found at the bottom of killing cliffs in North Dakota and eastern Montana. The Mandan depended on the buffalo for food, clothing, and shelter.

Mandan religious beliefs centered on a sun god and the yearly Sun Dance. Warriors performed the dance twice, before and then after the buffalo hunt. The eight-day ceremony included self-torture and mutilation. The event's chief sponsor, the Okipa (or Okeepa) maker, gave away large quantities of his wealth and was required to suffer more extreme tortures than anyone else. The ceremony began with a fast. Then volunteers were brought into a sacred lodge and hung from leather thongs inserted into their arms and chests. The warriors who withstood the most pain without crying out were considered the bravest. After the torture they ran around the lodge with buffalo skulls tied on ropes attached under the skin of their legs. Most men did this only once in their lives as part of an initiation ceremony, but others—holy men and great warriors—underwent this test of endurance many times. Warriors gained power (Hopini) from this torture, and the more often it was endured the mightier they became. Young warriors often fasted and suffered until they had visions of a guardian spirit (manitou), who would become a personal god and guardian. This spirit could be called upon for strength and protection until the day the warrior died.

Power also was gained through being kind to old people, participating in religious rituals (including frequent fasts), learning the ancient language of the gods, being generous, and inviting an older man to have sexual relations with one's wife. The older man's power would be passed on to the wife, who would then pass it on to her husband. (This misunderstood practice caused much confusion among white merchants and fur traders, who accused Mandans of being totally immoral.)

Mandan villages each had a sacred bundle, containing items such as a buffalo skin and pipe that belonged to Good Furred Robe (an important god), a fox skin headdress, some white sage, a pair of moccasins, a clay pot, the heads of several blackbirds and a duck, and various food items grown in village gardens. This bundle was brought out only on certain important religious occasions and was handed down intact from one generation to the next. Individual warriors kept their own bundles, also brought out only on holy days, which contained items considered sacred by them. These bundles were normally transferred to the eldest son upon the death of the father. **Post-contact Life.** Mandans first made contact with whites, mainly French fur trappers, in the mid-1700's. It was not until 1837, when the American Fur Company established a trading post along the Missouri River at Fort Clark, that a permanent relationship developed. Only a few months after the building of Fort Clark, a serious smallpox epidemic broke out. This disease, brought in by white merchants, killed thousands of Mandan people. The population, estimated at nine thousand in 1750, fell to less than two hundred after the devastation. The smell of dead bodies became so noxious that Fort Clark had to be abandoned temporarily. Two years later, many of the remaining Mandan villagers were slaughtered during a Sioux attack. After the killing, Sioux warriors burned the entire Mandan camp to the ground.

In 1874 a government census found 241 Mandans living in North Dakota. Most were moved to a reservation, where they lived on land allotments provided by the General Allotment Act (Dawes Severalty Act) of 1887 and tried to survive on corn and beans. Few full-blood Mandans can still be found, as there has been considerable intermarriage with Sioux and Chippewa (Ojibwa) residents of the Fort Berthold Reservation.

Leslie V. Tischauser

Massachusett

CULTURE AREA: Northeast
LANGUAGE GROUP: Algonquian
PRIMARY LOCATION: Massachusetts

The word "Massachusett" meant "at the great hill." The Massachusett tribe (from whom the state gets its name) inhabited a coastal region centered on Massachusetts Bay. To the north, across the Charles River, was the Pawtucket tribe. To the south were the Wampanoag, with the boundary near modern Marshfield. Like other Algonquian-speaking peoples of southern New England, the Massachusett were horticulturists subsisting principally on the corn, beans, and squash raised by the women. Men hunted game to provide meat, and both sexes joined in collecting the rich harvest of fish and shellfish provided by the area's rivers and estuaries.

Captain John Smith reported that in 1614 the Massachusett occupied thirty villages. The villages had several hundred inhabitants who lived in bark-covered wigwams. Each wigwam typically housed two or more nuclear families. A sachem ruled over each village, advised by a small council made up of men who had earned the rank of *pniese* through success in warfare and other deeds. A chief sachem held a tenuous but traditionally defined authority over the entire nation.

The Massachusett were traditionally considered to number three thousand warriors, implying an overall population of twelve thousand to fifteen thousand, but even before European settlement Old World diseases to which the Indians had no immunity began their ravages. From 1617 to 1619 an epidemic of European origin struck, killing more than half the Massachusett. A 1633 outbreak of smallpox destroyed many of the survivors. By 1674, there remained only a tenth of the original number (three hundred warriors). By that date, much of the remnant population, largely Christian converts, lived in several villages of so-called "praying Indians." Natick, near Boston, was the largest and most enduring of these. During King Philip's War of 1675-1676, these villages were dispersed, as both pagan Indians and suspicious Englishmen attacked the Christian Massachusett. Many of the survivors took refuge with other Indians in the region, and by the nineteenth century the Massachusett had ceased to exist as a separate people.

Mattaponi

CULTURE AREA: Northeast
LANGUAGE GROUP: Algonquian
PRIMARY LOCATION: Virginia
POPULATION SIZE: 490 (1990 U.S. Census)

The Mattaponi, a small tribe of the Algonquian family, lived on the river of the same name in Virginia. Along with other tribes, they were members of the Powhatan Confederacy. In 1608, the British explorer John Smith visited their village and found about one hundred members. He included the tribe, which he spelled *Mattapanient*, on his map of the area. In 1781, Thomas Jefferson visited the Mattaponi, recording the visit in his *Notes on Virginia* (1825). They were closely related to the Pamunkey, another Powhatan tribe. By 1900, the Mattaponi and Pamunkey were living side by side on reservations, intermarrying freely but maintaining continuity as tribes, as they had for more than three hundred years.

In the twentieth century, a small number of people—probably all of mixed blood—still claimed the name Mattaponi. They worked at hunting, trapping, and fishing, although state game laws now forbade several traditional methods. The state of Virginia funded a shad hatchery on the Mattaponi Reservation, which was run by the Indians. Women still made honeysuckle-stem baskets in the late twentieth century, and the tribe was run by an elected chief and his council of elders. Most Mattaponi were Baptists and attended the Mattaponi Indian Baptist Church, established in 1931. The reservation school was closed by the state in 1966, causing some concern at the time that traditional ways would not be passed to the next generation.

Mattole

CULTURE AREA: California
LANGUAGE GROUP: Athapaskan
PRIMARY LOCATION: West of Trinity River to Pacific Ocean
POPULATION SIZE: 62 (1990 U.S. Census)

Though linguistically and territorially contiguous, the groups referred to collectively as Mattole—consisting of the Nongatl, Lassik, Sinkyone, and Wailaki—were autonomous. They maintained trade of differential resources. Where possible, villages were on a river. Vertical-slab, conical houses were built. The Mattole's main food was acorns and other nuts and seeds, supplemented by hunting, trapping, fishing, and gathering of numerous roots and tubers. The Sinkyone exploited sea mammals. Anadromous fish were important for winter food and trade.

By 1853, these groups had interacted with European Americans. They were assigned to reservations in the Round Valley and to the Smith River reservations. Armed conflict continued between the Indians and settlers, lumbermen, miners, and government agents, which, along with introduced disease, reduced the indigenous populations. This conflict was exacerbated by the settlers' forbidding the Indians to practice controlled burning and by a general misuse of the land and resources by non-Indians. Many modern Mattole people live and work off the reservations, and some are involved with traditional lifestyle and religious revitalization.

Maya

CULTURE AREA: Mesoamerica
LANGUAGE GROUP: Mayan
PRIMARY LOCATION: Central America, Southern Mexico

Mayas inhabited southern Mexico and most of Central America. The heart of their territory was centered in the present Mexican state of Chiapas and the Yucatán peninsula, and the countries of Belize, Honduras, and Guatemala.

Origins. The origin of the Maya is unknown, although some believe their roots were in the Petén region of Guatemala, where old and relatively crude ceremonial centers have been discovered. Others locate their roots more northerly, in the Olmec region of Mexico, because of traces of Olmec culture seen in the Maya dot-and-bar calendar system and in ceremonial centers with their early round mud pyramids.

One reason that so much mystery surrounds such a relatively advanced civilization as the Maya is that Bishop Diego de Landa, in his fervor to convert these indigenous people, seen as savage pagans, publicly burned almost all hieroglyphic records of Maya history and religion in 1552. Hundreds of idols, inscribed stelae, and altar stones were also destroyed. Ironically, however, Landa is credited with providing the single best source of information about the Maya: His book on the Maya included not only details of their life but also some explanation of their calendar, which contained two main cycles, one of 260 days and the other of 365 days.

The only three Maya hieroglyphic texts known to have survived are named after the places where they are preserved. These are the Codex Dresdensis in Dresden, Germany; the Codex Peresianus in Paris, France; and the Codex Cortesianus in Madrid, Spain. In addition to these, a number of stelae also exist; however, not all Maya hieroglyphics have been deciphered. A few later textual records, or books, also exist. The *Popol Vuh* was written by the Quiche Mayas in historical times using letters of Spanish script. It deals primarily with the story of creation. The *Books of Chilam Balam* are mythological histories of the Maya, and the *Annals of the Cakchiquels* presents a genealogical history of the Cakchiquels and relates the events of the Spanish conquest. In all these works, religion and myth are intertwined with factual history.

History. Scholars who study Maya history have divided it into three major periods. The Formative period (1800 B.C.E.-100 B.C.E.) was characterized by the gradual development of complex ceremonial centers, monumental architecture, hieroglyphic writing, calendrics, social stratification, trade networks, and city states. The Classic period (200 C.E.-900 C.E.) saw the maturation of the above, resulting in large, powerful ceremonial centers, ritual and solar calendrical systems, large agricultural bureaucracies, and often violent competition between ceremonial centers. This period is sometimes referred to as the "Old Empire." The Post-Classic period (1000 C.E.-conquest) was a time of renaissance in the northern, or Yucatán, region under Toltec influence. Religious compulsion was largely replaced by military concerns, resulting in secular government gaining ascendance over religious leadership. This period is sometimes referred to as the "New Empire."

In reality, the Maya never formed an empire, since there was no dominant capital city or single ruler. Rather, there was a loose federation of city-centers bound together by similarities of culture and religion under the control of religious leaders. These priest-rulers, who maintained power by virtue of their superior education and knowledge of the supernatural, shared common interests and concerns. Under their leadership Maya civilization witnessed extraordinary achievements in fine arts, architecture, engineering, astronomy, mathematics, and hieroglyphic writing. Two accomplishments deserving special mention were the development of the mathematical concept of zero and a calendar which was more accurate than the Gregorian calendar introduced in Europe in 1582. These accomplishments enabled Mayas to record the dates of important events accurately on Katun stones, or stelae, every twenty years.

Building was a constant part of Maya life. Ceremonial centers were built, rebuilt, and enlarged. These centers typically included one or more pyramids with a temple on top, a paved courtyard or plaza, and a number of low stone buildings. Often there was a ball court where a game was played utilizing a small hard rubber ball, leather hip pads, and stone rings on the walls. The marketplace was set up, especially on important ceremonial days, near the temple-pyramid. These ceremonial centers were ruled by a largely hereditary class of priest-aristocrats who had almost a total monopoly on education, wealth, and power. The great Maya centers of Tikal, Uaxactun, Palenque, and Copan experienced long dynasties of priest-rulers. Copan, one of the longest-lived dynasties, had sixteen rulers. One, Smoke Imix, ruled for sixty-seven years.

Around 800 C.E., Maya civilization in the southern lowlands began to decline; it had virtually collapsed by 900. Maya civilization continued to flourish in Yucatán. Possible explanations for the demise in the southern area include natural causes, such as disease, soil exhaustion, or change of climate, as well as social causes, such as continued warfare or the loss of control by the priest-aristocracy. Whatever the reasons, the result was the end of the classic indigenous cultures in Mesoamerica.

The conquest of the Maya by the Spanish began around 1524 and ended with the defeat of five thousand Itzás at Lake Petén Itzá in 1697 by Martín de Ursua. During these years some fierce battles took place, but the Maya were unsuccessful in defending their land against the invaders from Spain. Meanwhile, Spanish soldiers under the command of Francisco de Montejo subdued the Maya in Yucatán, where they were aided by a prophecy which had foretold the coming of white men with beards. Because of the efforts of missionaries such as Fray Andres de Avendano y Layola, who learned their history, culture, and language, the Maya were converted to Christianity, thus fulfilling another of their prophecies: "All moons, all years, all days, all winds take their course and pass away."

Religion. Religion was at the heart of Maya life. Religious ceremonies controlled the activities of the seasons and the growth of crops. Religion was also the driving force in the development of science and art. The Maya universe contained an array of divinities who controlled every aspect of nature. Each day of the week was regarded as a god whose behavior could be divined through the use of an intricate calendar system. Mathematics and astronomy were important to the divinations and astrology that were basic elements of their religious beliefs. At birth, children were taken to priests who predicted the future of the baby with the aid of astrological charts and sacred books. They also identified the specific god to whom the child would owe lifelong devotion based on the exact time and date of birth. A perpetual round of sacrificial ceremonies, prayers, fasting, and incense burning was required to please the gods. The elevated status and power of priests was thus ensured. The gods also required human blood. Accordingly, human sacrifices were offered, as was self-mutilation. Priests and other pious individuals pierced their tongues, earlobes, and genitals in order to draw blood and thereby please the gods.

According to the *Chilam Balam*, one of their sacred books, the earth was flat with four sides, each with its own color: white for north, yellow for south, red for east, and black for west. The color of the center was green. Four gods upheld the sky, and on each side there was a sacred ceiba, or wild cottonwood tree. In the center stood a giant green ceiba with its roots in the underworld and its branches in the upperworld. Surrounding the earth were thirteen heavens and nine hells. The heavens were ordered in six ascending and six descending steps, with the seventh at the top. Similarly, the nine hells were arranged in four descending and four ascending steps, with the fifth at the bottom. This structure of the universe is reflected in the form of the stepped pyramids crowned with temples. They served as the link between heaven and earth, with the priests as mediators.

In another sacred book, the *Popol Vuh*, the story of creation is recorded. The gods inhabited a dark world when they decided to create humankind. First they created men from mud, but they were soft and pliable, without mind or soul. The gods destroyed these men. Men were created a second time from wood, but they were stiff and inflexible without mind or soul, unable to remember their creator. Most of these were destroyed by a flood of fiery rain, while those who survived were changed into monkeys. The gods created men a third time. Four men were formed from the dough of white and yellow corn. They possessed intelligence and wisdom, but these powers were limited so they would be less than gods. Next, four women were created to be wives for the men. After the humans multiplied in the world of darkness the gods created the Morning Star, Icoquih, which precedes the sun. Then the sun arose and humankind rejoiced. Maya tradition locates the birthplace of the gods and man in the Usamacinta Valley in the region near Palenque.

Although the Mayas recognized and served a multitude of gods, not all were of equal rank. Belief in the Feathered Serpent god was shared with other indigenous people of Mesoamerica. This god, commonly known as Quetzalcóatl by the Aztecs, was called Kukulcan by the Mayas, among whom it became one of the most important deities.

Art and Architecture. Mayas have been called the Greeks of the New World not only because of their level of civilization but also because of the development of their art and architecture. Both art and architecture were ancillary to religion. Artists painted murals in bright colors recording selected aspects of Maya life. These paintings, as well as stone carvings and vase decorations, often show priests as they receive offerings, give orders, or pass judgments. Artists also worked in stucco and formed large plaster masks of rulers which symbolized the institution of kingship. Mosaic jade masks and small busts were also made of important individuals.

Works of art which are particularly noteworthy are the sarcophagus lid for the ruler Pacal, which was found in a hidden chamber at Palenque, and the large carved jaguar throne found in a sealed chamber at Chichén Itzá. The lid was carved in bas-relief on a single 12-foot slab of limestone. It depicts the cosmos at the time of Pacal's death, including his image and a large cosmic tree decorated with jewels, mirrors, bloodletting bowls, dragons, bones, and a celestial bird on top. The gaping jaws of the underworld await at the bottom in the form of two huge skeletal dragons joined at the chin. At Chichén Itzá the throne carved in the form of a jaguar was discovered in the Temple of Kukulcan. It was painted bright red, with eyes of jade and fangs of flint. The spots on its coat were made of inlaid jade disks.

Certain symbols or images appear repeatedly in Maya art and architecture. These include the jaguar, earth-dragon or crocodile, screech owl, bat, rattlesnake, snail, and butterfly. These and other animal forms served as guardian spirits and were found in the sacred calendar. Not all art was dedicated to religious purposes, however; common people and daily activities were also represented, especially on pottery and clay figures.

Professional musicians also flourished. A wide array of musical instruments was used, including wooden drums, hollow tortoise-shell drums, reed flutes, bone whistles, clay whistles, long wooden trumpets, conch shell trumpets, and rattles. Music was utilized for battles, celebrations, and funeral processions.

Maya architecture was among the most impressive in the New World. The use of cut stones made their structures strong and durable, able to survive the passage of centuries. They were often monumental in scale. They built pyramids topped with temples which soared more than 200 feet in the air, a ball court the size of a football field, a 320-foot-long building on the top of a hill, a stone arch 20 feet high, a four-story stone tower, and a building with scores of stone columns which supported a vaulted stone roof. They also built celestial observatories, water reservoirs, and irrigation systems.

Common architectural features include majestic temples topped with stone combs, the use of corbeled roof vaults or the "false arch," carvings on the facades and lintels of stone structures, steep-sided pyramids crowned with temples, and paved courtyards. It was customary to cover older structures such as pyramids or courtyards with new ones. At the end of the Classic Period, some architectural changes occurred in Yucatán. Pyramids were smaller, stone combs on the top of temples were smaller, and ornamental figures on facades became more abstract designs.

Although the traditional culture of the Maya gradually disappeared, there are still an estimated 3.2 million people who speak the Mayan language.

Philip E. Lampe

Bibliography

Coe, Michael D. *The Maya*. 6th ed. New York: Thames and Hudson, 1999.

Craine, Eugene R., and Reginald Reindorp, eds. and trans. *The Codex Perez and the Book of Chilam Balam of Mani*. Norman: University of Oklahoma Press, 1979. Collection of documents, including almanacs, prophecies, horoscopes, computations of time, herbal remedies, methods of bleeding, land documents, and history of the Itzas and Xius. Contains drawings and photocopies of documents.

Culbert, T. Patrick. *Maya Civilization*. Washington, D.C.: Smithsonian Institution Press, 1993.

Everton, Macduff, et al. *The Modern Maya: A Culture in Transition*. Albuquerque: University of New Mexico Press, 1991.

Henderson, John S. *The World of the Ancient Maya*. 2d ed. Ithaca, N.Y.: Cornell University Press, 1997. Examines the Maya cultural tradition from earliest settlements through the period of the Spanish conquest in the sixteenth century. Contains many useful maps, drawings, and photographs.

Hunter, C. Bruce. *A Guide to Ancient Maya Ruins*. Norman: University of Oklahoma Press, 1974. Excellent source for discussion and description of selected major archaeological sites. Contains maps and site plans as well as drawings, illustrations, and photographs.

Landa, Diego de. *Yucatan Before and After the Conquest*. Translated by William Gates. 1937. Reprint. New York: Dover, 1978. Begins with a historical explanation of the manuscript by Landa, which is the source of much of the information available on Maya history and culture. Includes documents, maps, drawings, and photographs.

Miller, Mary Ellen, and Karl A. Taube. *An Illustrated Dictionary of the Gods and Symbols of Ancient Mexico and the Maya*. New York: Thames and Hudson, 1997.

Roberts, Timothy R. *Gods of the Maya, Aztecs, and Incas*. New York: Metro Books, 1996.

Schmidt, Peter J., Mercedes de la Garza, Enrique Nalda, and Grassi Palazzo. *The Maya*. New York: Rizzoli, 1998.

Sharer, Robert J., and Sylvanus G. Morley. *The Ancient Maya*. 5th ed. Stanford, Calif.: Stanford University Press, 1994.

Stuart, Gene S., and George E. Stuart. *Lost Kingdoms of the Maya*. Washington, D.C.: National Geographic Society, 1993.

Taube, Karl A. *Aztec and Maya Myths*. 2d ed. Austin: University of Texas Press, 1995.

Thompson, John Eric S. *Maya History and Religion*. Norman: University of Oklahoma Press, 1970. Broad coverage of Maya life with an emphasis on religion. Contains photographs, drawings, and maps. Includes a useful bibliography of earlier sources and references.

Time-Life Books. *The Magnificent Maya*. Alexandria, Va.: Time-Life Books, 1993.

Menominee

CULTURE AREA: Northeast
LANGUAGE GROUP: Algonquian
PRIMARY LOCATION: Great Lakes region
POPULATION SIZE: 7,543 (1990 U.S. Census)

The Menominees belong to the large family of indigenous people called the Algonquians. They occupied the Great Lakes region since before recorded history. They were travelers and traders, visiting distant clans in their birchbark canoes. Today there is a Menominee reservation on the Wolf River in northeastern Wisconsin.

Culture. Menominee culture resulted from environmental experience, clan and tribal oral histories, and information gathered via the tribe's network of water and land trails. Intertribal marriage gained acceptance to maintain extended family units, while diminishing the chances for inbreeding among the original clans. The earliest French explorers and trappers reported the Menominees to be "gentle of spirit," although they boasted of their warlike exploits and supernatural adventures. A rigidly defined social system required strict adherence to gender roles and various customs. There were some positions, such as war chief, that could be achieved only by men, but most were open to women. Menominees have traditionally been a matriarchy. The Menominees prized individual rights for all people, including children. This belief precluded punishment for disobeying social rules.

The numeral 4 was considered to be sacred by the tribe; its sacredness may be surmised as having come from the four directions—crucial for navigation on water. Prayers are repeated four times, sometimes to each of the four directions. The Signing of the Cross taught by the French Roman Catholic missionaries, with four points on the body, may have coincidentally created a powerful inducement for religious conversion. Early priests had no initial trouble converting Menominees to Roman Catholicism. The Menominees did not believe in one omnipotent being, but in several levels of gods, encompassing humor and even violence. Menominees who sought to improve their spiritual luck prayed to many different deities and performed many rituals. Tribal members belonged to many societies in a poly-religious blend of science, superstition, and stoicism.

There were once witches and sorcerers among the people, but they were not thought to be evil. Magic as well as medicine was thought to be neutral, but there were inevitably some who wished harm to others. These people would "witch" the target with incantations and a bundle made of herbs and minerals that was referred to as a "witch bag." These animal-hide pouches were reputed to be fed the released human energy occurring upon death and other misery. The Serpent Cult, a secret society which celebrated the commission of evil, was once a potent force within some clans.

Geography. The Menominees trace their beginnings to a village near the mouth of the Menominee River. During the early colonial era, the French documented the tribal range, which was bordered by the Milwaukee River to the south, the Mississippi River to the west, and Lakes Superior, Huron, and Michigan to the north and east. This territory encompassed ten million acres. The predominant geography is small lakes, interconnected with rivers, and large stands of timber. There was surface copper that was considered a source of tribal wealth.

The tribe made four types of snowshoes, each named after a clan, to deal with the heavy snowfalls of the region, but the Menominees were primarily a water people. A significant part of their diet was derived from shallow waters. Living near waterways eased transportation problems and allowed a sense of community. It was proximity to navigable waterways that brought the tribe to European attention as early as 1634.

Tribal History. The birthplace of the tribe can be traced through its oral history. The present city of Menominee, Michigan, was once known as Mini' Kani, the source of the Menominees. According to their legends, the Great Mystery permitted a Giant White Bear with a copper-colored tail to emerge from an underground den as the first man and establish the village. This village established by the White Bear became home to the Bear Clan. Each clan and village had its own chief, but all were subordinate to the Bear Clan. There were several original clans, including the Beaver, the Wolf, and the Eagle. The Menominees spread to other rivers that drain into Lake Michigan. There were reputed to be more than thirty major Menominee villages on the shores of Lakes Michigan, Huron, and Superior, with another center of population near Detroit.

Rivers provided an abundance of sturgeon and wild rice to eat. The dependence on wild rice, in fact, provided the name for the tribe.The Algonquian word for wild rice was *manomin*; hence an eater of wild rice became *Manominee*, now generally spelled Menominee. Rivers provided freshwater mussels, fowl, and other game besides the staple of wild rice. Only war could bring famine.

A trail network maintained by Potawatomis and protected by Menominees existed from present-day Detroit to St. Louis, and from the north around Lake Superior south to Chicago. Both white and Indian groups used the same trade routes and sites for their cities.

European Contact. Menominee involvement in world politics began in 1608. Their list of allies began with the French, the first white people they had seen; then the English, who bought their allegiance with gifts of firearms and alcohol; and finally, the Americans, who were glad to get their military help. Since the first treaty with the Americans, there have been Menominees who served in all U.S. wars.

Menominees inadvertently became enemies of the Iroquois, hence the English, after French interference. In 1608 near the north shore of Lake Superior, the governor general of New France, Samuel de Champlain, and two other white companions, accompanied by an exploratory force of Algonquian people, encountered an Iroquois party. The battle was decided by the French use of matchlock rifles. This united the Iroquois tribes in a war that spread to involve the entire Great Lakes region. Constant fear of attack on the waterways, which were primary trade routes, spread to involve the entire St. Lawrence drainage system. This interrupted the fledgling fur-trading industry. By 1611 the Iroquois, who were well armed, spread war to all waterways except Lakes Superior and Michigan. Menominees provided refuge to fellow Algonquians, a fact which created a population explosion that had dire consequences through the eighteenth century.

The first official meeting between France, represented by Jean Nicolet, and Menominees took place at Mini' Kani in 1634, with a signed pledge of peace. With the hope of profits from the fur trade, the French planned for the exploitation of their New France territory. The Menominees formed an instant market for costly goods. The price for a matchlock rifle from the French was a stack of furs piled alongside the weapon. The low price paid for pelts placed the Great Lakes ecosystem in distress while keeping the growing number of inhabitants virtually unarmed. Thus, France interceded and protected the tribe from the better-armed Iroquois.

There was no further Menominee involvement with the French until 1661, when Me'dort des Grosilliers and Pierre Esprit Radisson entered the main village of Mini' Kani and were amazed at the amount of fish and game in the region. Another Frenchman, Father Jerome Lalemont, explored Lake Superior and found nearly pure lead mines, fist-sized copper nodules, and veins of turquoise and amethyst.

Sometime after this contact of 1661 there occurred a great war, noted by Claude Allouez in 1670. He stated that he found the tribe almost exterminated. When Jacques Marquette visited in 1673 and recorded the use of wild rice by the tribe, however, he made no mention of recent war. It is probable that the Sturgeon War occurred in the spring of 1669 or 1670. This large battle took place in a village on the Menominee River after the erection of a dam prevented the sturgeon from moving upriver. The combatants may possibly have been Chippewa, yet they could have been another band of Menominees. Whoever was involved, the reason as remembered by tribal elders was stress on the environment from the swelling population. It was 1682 before a coalition of Algonquians, including many Menominees, decisively thwarted the English and Iroquois in two separate actions at Chicago and near the Illinois River near Utica, Illinois.

The Nineteenth and Twentieth Centuries. The English sought the friendship of the Menominees after the French departure. With gifts, the English were able to maintain an alliance against the Americans. Although not friends with the English, Menominees kept their agreements. In the War of 1812, the tribe victoriously fought the Americans at Prairie du Chien, Wisconsin, and on the island of Mackinac, Michigan.

During the Civil War the tribe responded with many volunteers. At the Battle of Petersburg, Company K, consisting of Wisconsin infantry volunteers, suffered eleven Menominee wounded, nine killed in action, seven dead in prison camp, and two released from prison camp because of illness (they later died). The company was on duty at Washington, D.C., during the trial and execution of the conspirators in the Abraham Lincoln assassination.

After a treaty with the Americans in 1856, the tribe lived on 235,000 acres. The fur trade had finally collapsed, and they were forced to log their beloved forest. The Bureau of Indian Affairs (BIA) built a sawmill in 1908 and managed the resources. The tribe sued the bureau for mismanagement in 1934 and finally won its suit in 1951.

A 1952 report from BIA Commissioner Dillon Myer issued instructions to tribes for a step-by-step withdrawal of the BIA from their affairs. In 1954, President Dwight Eisenhower signed the Menominee Termination Act, effective on May 1, 1961. A 1965 survey reported that there were 2,526 Menominee County residents, 57 percent of whom were under nineteen years of age. Social problems and economic instability were epidemic. The Menominee Restoration Act of December, 1973, returned the tribe to federally recognized status.

Beginning in the late 1980's, the tribe created a new school district, including a community college. Indian gaming in the 1990's provided enough revenue for social programs and investment. In 1992, the reservation comprised 222,552 acres and had a population of 3,182 American Indians. The median age was 21.4 years old; 48.7 percent were high school graduates, and 74 percent of persons sixteen to nineteen years old were enrolled in school.

Thomas F. Weso

Bibliography

Hosmer, Brian C. *American Indians in the Marketplace: Persistence and Innovation Among the Menominees and Metlakatlans, 1870-1920*. Lawrence: University Press of Kansas, 1999.

Ourada, Patricia K. *The Menominee Indians: A History*. Norman: University of Oklahoma Press, 1979. A comprehensive history of the tribe, particularly concerned with the pre-1900's.

Peroff, Nicholas C. *Menominee Drums: Tribal Termination and Restoration, 1954-1974*. Norman: University of Oklahoma Press, 1982. A documentation of the political and socioeconomic strife precipitated by termination of federal recognition as a tribe. Gives a personal perspective to the push to gain federal restoration of identity.

Rentmeester, Jeanne. *Tomah: A Chief of the Menominee Nation*. Howard, Wis.: J. & S. Rentmeester, 1997.

Skinner, Alanson. *Social Life and Ceremonial Bundles of the Menomini Indians*. Vol. 13. New York: American Museum of Natural History, 1913. A source for the cultural history and folktales of the Menominee Indians.

Smith, Huron H. *Ethnobotany of the Menomini Indians*. Westport, Conn.: Greenwood Press, 1970. Originally published in 1923 as the *Bulletin of the Public Museum of the City of Milwaukee*, a dated and somewhat biased account of the edible and medicinal plants found among the tribal territory.

Spindler, George, and Louise Spindler. *Dreamers with Power: The Menominee*. Prospect Heights, Ill.: Waveland Press, 1971. A view of the culture of the tribe with particular care given to the religious and belief system.

Methow

CULTURE AREA: Plateau
LANGUAGE GROUP: Salishan
PRIMARY LOCATION: Colville Reservation, Washington State

The Methow, a branch of the Salishan family, lived along the Methow River and Chelan Lake in eastern Washington. A detached band, the Chilowhist, spent the winters on the Okanogan River. The Methow were related to another group called the Moses Columbia band. The name they called themselves is not known. "Methow" (pronounced Met how) was given them by whites, after their location. Evidence suggests they migrated to Washington from Montana and Idaho in prehistoric times. The Methow lived in villages of varying size. Because they relied on hunting and fishing—salmon was a chief staple of their diet—as well as on gathering roots and berries, they were forced to move throughout the year to find food in different seasons. This prevented the villages from growing and developing as political or social centers.

The Methow do not seem to have relied on agriculture. They were skilled with horses and used them in their travels after food. Generally, Salishan tribes enjoyed relatively peaceful lives and were involved in no protracted struggles with their neighbors. In the late nineteenth century, the Methow were pushed out by whites who wanted their land. They were resettled on the Colville Reservation in Washington in 1872. By the end of the twentieth century, the Methow lived very much like their non-Indian neighbors and made their living by raising cattle, farming, and logging.

Miami

CULTURE AREA: Northeast
LANGUAGE GROUP: Algonquian
PRIMARY LOCATION: Oklahoma, Indiana
POPULATION SIZE: 4,477 (1990 U.S. Census)

The Miami occupied the Green Bay, Wisconsin, region in the seventeenth century but later migrated to the southern end of Lake Michigan. The name "Miami" is most probably derived from the Ojibwa word *oumamik*, "people of the peninsula."

The tribe had a fairly sophisticated political structure, based largely on the clan system. Each Miami belonged to his or her father's clan. Clan chiefs in each village made up a council that ruled the community. Village councils sent delegates to band councils, which in turn sent chiefs to a tribal council.

The Midewiwin, or Grand Medicine Society, was a hallmark of tribal life. It consisted of priests noted for their special curing powers. Other Miami shamans used roots and herbs to combat disease. According to most accounts, the sun was the principal deity for the Miami and was called the "Master of Life."

Miami villages consisted of pole-frame houses covered by rush mats. Each village usually had a large council house for council meetings and ceremonies. The tribe was famed for its superior strains of corn; the Miami also grew melons, squash, beans, and pumpkins. Buffalo were hunted once a year.

Originally, the Miami consisted of six separate bands: Atchatchakan-gouen, Kilatika, Mengakonkia, Pepicokia, Wea, and Piankashaw. The first three united into the Miami proper, and the Pepicokia were absorbed by the Wea and Piankashaw. The Wea and the Piankashaw were separate entities from the Miami, and they were politically independent by 1818, the year they set up separate tribal councils.

During the eighteenth century, the Miami in Michigan migrated to the headwaters of the Maumee in Ohio. Similarly, the Wea and Piankashaw moved to the Wabash region of Indiana. In the late eighteenth century, the tribe fought a valiant battle to save their lands from the tide of white settlement.

In the late eighteenth Battle of Miami, Chief Little Turtle led the Miami to a decisive victory over U.S. troops, but the Miami themselves were badly defeated only three years later.
(Library of Congress)

The Miami war chief Michikinikwa, known to the white people as Little Turtle, led a coalition of Miami, Shawnee, Potawatomi, and others against United States troops. Little Turtle's warriors gained a major victory over General Arthur St. Clair on November 4, 1791. The Americans lost 647 dead and 217 wounded in the battle, one of the worst defeats the United States Army ever suffered at the hands of the Indians.

The Indian triumph was short-lived. Little Turtle and Shawnee leader Blue Jacket were decisively defeated at the Battle of Fallen Timbers in 1794.

337

By the Treaty of Greenville in 1795, the Indians ceded most of Ohio and a slice of Indiana to the United States.

Between 1832 and 1840, the Miami moved to Kansas, where they were given reservations. Following a separate course, the Wea and Piankashaw joined the Peoria. Both the Peoria and the Miami settled in Indian Territory (now Oklahoma) in 1867. Most of their descendants live in Ottawa County, Oklahoma. A few members of the Miami tribe managed to avoid removal to the south and stayed in their original homelands. Their descendants, mostly of mixed ancestry, live around Peru, Indiana.

Micmac

CULTURE AREA: Northeast
LANGUAGE GROUP: Algonquian
PRIMARY LOCATION: Maritime Provinces, Quebec
POPULATION SIZE: 14,625 in Canada (Statistics Canada, based on 1991 census); 2,765 in U.S. (1990 U.S. Census)

The Micmac, a branch of the Algonquian family, lived a migratory life in Nova Scotia, northern New Brunswick, and Prince Edward Island. Their name, from their own language, means "allies." The Micmac were divided into several clans, each with its own chief and identifying symbol. These symbols were tattooed onto members' bodies, painted on canoes and snowshoes, and used as ornaments on clothing and jewelry.

During the winter, the Micmac lived inland in small groups in the forest; they hunted moose, caribou, and porcupine. In warmer weather, they moved in groups of two hundred or more to the seashore and fished, hunted seals, and gathered shellfish. They made cone-shaped wigwams and canoes from birchbark, wooden bowls and bows, and stone or bone weapons and tools. They also made beautiful baskets and porcupine-quill embroidery. They had a rich tradition of impressive rituals—for marriage, death, installation of chiefs, and passage to adulthood. They also enjoyed games, including an indigenous form of football.

The Micmac welcomed white visitors—traders and missionaries—from the first. They accepted Christianity from the Jesuits and traded and intermarried with the French colonists. They were strong allies of the French, and they fought with the French and English to eradicate the Beothuk Indians of Newfoundland in the late eighteenth century. This close association with whites, however, was in many ways costly to the Micmac. A third of their population was killed by typhus in 1746. They lost their traditional religious beliefs; they adopted agriculture as a means of livelihood perhaps more reliable than hunting; they stopped practicing their traditional crafts; and they intermarried so freely that it is doubtful whether any pure-blooded Micmac were left by the mid-twentieth century. By 1970, many men were employed in "high steel," and government scholarships enabled Micmac men and women to learn skilled trades. At the end of the century, the Micmac were poor but generally no poorer than other people in the Maritime Provinces.

Mimbres

DATE: 1000-1150
LOCATION: Central Arizona
CULTURES AFFECTED: Western Pueblo tribes

The Mimbres culture, especially Classic Mimbres, represents a localized florescence of Mogollon culture in the Mimbres Valley of the central highlands of Arizona between 1000 and 1150 C.E. During this time there was a rapid growth in local population size together with the establishment of several large pueblos that each housed several hundred people. Mimbres is best known for its beautiful black-on-white ceramic bowls, decorated with designs of people and animals. Unfortunately, unscrupulous collectors and looters have practically obliterated existing Mimbres sites in their attempts to recover prehistoric art objects. These activities have silenced the archaeological record with respect to many questions about Mimbres culture.

Most of the known pueblos in the Mimbres Valley, such as the Swarts and Mattocks ruins, are quite large, with 60 to 125 rooms. These were constructed of mud and stone masonry walls that were coated with mud plaster on the interior. Rooms were rectangular and were roofed with wooden beams. They usually contained storage bins, wall niches, fireplaces, and benches. Burials were often made under the floors of pueblo rooms that had been abandoned as living quarters. In some instances, however, graves were covered with stone or clay, and the rooms presumably continued to be used. Grave offerings consisted of tools, precious stones, jewelry, and decorated pottery vessels. The Swarts site was organized into two large house blocks of about sixty rooms each, some built on two levels. Its population is estimated to have been 175 people or thirty-five families during the Mimbres phase.

The Mimbres people were agricultural, with a subsistence system based on the rainfall cultivation of maize, beans, squash, sunflowers, cotton, and other domesticated plants. Wild foods continued to be an important part of the diet. Hunting in upland regions and fishing in rivers supplemented the diet with animal protein, while nuts and seeds were collected during periods of seasonal abundance. Evidence for Mimbres ceremonialism is found on painted vessels from burials. Practices included the use of prayer sticks, elaborate tablita-style headdresses and masks, and shrines. Costumes and ornaments were made with turquoise and exotic feathers, such as those from parrots and macaws.

The most distinctive pottery type of Classic Mimbres is called Mimbres black-on-white. Jar and bowl forms are known. These were decorated with both geometric and highly stylized naturalistic designs. The former include arrangements of hatched and solid triangles, scrolls, zigzags, and frets in black and white. The latter, especially as executed on the interior surfaces of open, hemispherical bowls, are among the most striking of indigenous American art traditions. The center of the bowl was utilized as a visual focal point, in which were painted representational designs. These include depictions of humans and animals in a wide variety of attitudes. Representations of deer, sheep, birds, fish, rabbits, frogs, and even insects were utilized.

A large number of the paintings on Mimbres vessels portray scenes from both daily and ceremonial life. There are depictions of hunting, fishing, and gathering wood. There are also representations of childbirth, dances, game playing, and even human sacrifice. Interestingly, the majority of these painted bowls have been "killed" through the ceremonial puncturing of the vessel bottom. This may have been done in order to release a spiritual essence of the artifact prior to its deposition as a burial offering.

Mississippian

DATE: 900-1540
PRIMARY LOCATION: Midwestern and southeastern North America
CULTURES AFFECTED: Caddo, Cherokee, Chickasaw, Choctaw, Creek, Natchez, Pawnee

The Mississippian tradition was a widespread cultural phenomenon that affected peoples of the vast Missouri-Mississippi drainage and neighboring regions of the Midwest and southeastern United States between 900 C.E. and the arrival of the first Spanish expedition by Hernando de Soto in

1539-1540. Also known as the "temple mound" period, the Mississippian tradition was characterized by the presence of sedentary, village societies with marked social ranking whose agricultural economies were characterized by a strong reliance on the cultivation of maize and whose technology included shell-tempered pottery. Large Mississippian settlements, such as Cahokia, Etowah, and Moundville, were dominated by the presence of massive, pyramidal mounds of earth that served as the bases for temples and residences of powerful individuals. The term "Mississippian" has been applied to a wide variety of sites and complexes, and the culture was by no means uniform.

The Mississippian people were accomplished at a variety of crafts. Among them was the manufacture of elaborate ceramic vessels, often bearing symbolic decorations. A distinctive class of vessels are those sculpted to look like trophy heads taken in warfare. Ground stone objects included elaborate pipes and ceremonial axes. From a number of sites, most notably the Spiro Mound in eastern Oklahoma, come beautiful shell gorgets, carved with representations of warriors, snakes, and esoteric symbols. Cold-hammer metallurgy was used to manufacture copper sheet-metal portraits and representations of warriors.

The religious life of the Mississippians included the observation of celestial events, such as the summer and winter solstices, and occasional human sacrifice. Toward the end of the period, a phenomenon called the "Southern Cult" is manifest in the production and trade of ceremonial objects decorated with symbols such as hands with eyes, crosses, and snakes as well as depictions of individuals dressed in bird costumes holding severed human heads. Some archaeologists have suggested that these are related to ceremonial traditions from Mesoamerica.

The Mississippian tradition came to an end as a result of a variety of stresses. The most significant of these was the introduction of European diseases and the subsequent devastation of native populations by fatal epidemics in the sixteenth century. Problems such as malnutrition and internecine warfare were present long before the arrival of the Spanish, however, resulting in the decline and abandonment of large sites such as Cahokia generations before European contact. The legacy of complex Mississippian societies continued into the historic period among tribes such as the Creeks.

Missouri

CULTURE AREA: Plains
LANGUAGE GROUP: Siouan
PRIMARY LOCATION: Oklahoma
POPULATION SIZE: 1,840 ("Otoe-Missouria," 1990 U.S. Census)

The Missouri occupied villages on the Missouri River near present-day northwest Saline County, Missouri. They were related linguistically to the Winnebagos, Otos, and Iowas. Their semisedentary lifestyle combined hunting and gathering with horticultural activities. When not hunting large game such as deer and buffalo, they inhabited settlements—especially in the spring and fall—to tend to agricultural duties, woodworking, and pottery. While once a strong tribe, they were gradually weakened with their westward movement because of divisions and wars.

Oral traditions trace the origins of the Missouri to the area of the Great Lakes near Green Bay, Wisconsin. Before the period of European contact in this area, there lived a group of Indians called the Hotonga, or "fish eaters." The Hotonga divided at Green Bay, and the group that remained there became known as the Winnebago. The ones who left went to the confluence of the Mississippi and Iowa rivers. Here a further division took place: The Iowa remained there, and those who continued on to the confluence of the Missouri and Grand rivers became the Missouri. A final split produced the Oto, who traveled farther up the Missouri River. The Missouri, after a war with the Osage, separated again; a part went to live with the Iowa, and another group followed the Oto.

The Missouri were first known to have been in contact with French fur traders in 1673, when they were contacted by Jacques Marquette. Thereafter, they made treaties, traded, and intermarried with the French from Detroit to St. Louis until the 1820's, the time of Missouri statehood. They made a peace treaty with the United States on June 24, 1817. Between the time of contact and statehood, the Missouri suffered devastating tribal attacks by the Sauk and Fox as well as a series of epidemics. The remaining Missouri had combined with the Oto by 1829, forming the Oto-Missouri tribe. All of their lands, except for the reservation at Big Blue River, Nebraska, were ceded to the government by 1855. The descendants of this group continue to exist on reservation land in Oklahoma.